Junges Kartellrecht

Volume 2

2. Tagung Junges Kartellrecht

Wien 2024

Ranjana Andrea Achleitner | Eva Fischer
Lena Hornkohl | Bernadette Zelger [eds.]

Questioning the Role of Competition Law in the 21st Century

Nomos

HART

The Deutsche Nationalbibliothek lists this publication in the Deutsche Nationalbibliografie; detailed bibliographic data are available on the Internet at http://dnb.d-nb.de

ISBN 978-3-7560-3054-5 (Print)
978-3-7489-5364-7 (ePDF)

British Library Cataloguing-in-Publication Data
A catalogue record for this book is available from the British Library.

ISBN 978-1-5099-9679-7 HB (Hart)

Online Version
Nomos eLibrary

1st Edition 2025

Table of Content

Introduction 7

Biographies of editors and authors 19

Part I: Goals of Competition Law

Silvia Retamales Morales
Public interest as a goal of competition law and policy? A comparative revision 29

Christiane Wakonig
What is Fairness?
Reflections on the Concept of Fairness in European and Austrian Competition Law 57

Luca Graf and Giulia Sonderegger
Exploring the Application of Article 102 TFEU to Abuses in Seasonal Agricultural Labour Markets 81

Part II: Tools of Competition Law

Selcukhan Unekbas
Competitiveness and Antitrust Law: Between Feasibility and Desirability 117

Annika Stöhr
Section 19a GWB as a measure of counter-power against "Undertakings with Paramount Significance for Competition across Markets" 145

Elaine Dunne
Rethinking Remedy Design in EU Competition Law Enforcement 171

Part III: Competition Law, Crisis and Geoeconomics

Nicole Deneka
State aid and international crises: balance between market's intervention and integrity? 203

Sophie Bohnert
Geopolitics and Competition Law: An Odd Couple or a Match Made in Heaven? 227

Pierfrancesco Mattiolo
Competition law as *'a continuation of policy with other means'*? The application of the Foreign Subsidies Regulation to concentrations 263

Part IV: EU Competition Law Beyond the EU

Richard Bunworth
Competition Copycats: The Brussels Effect and the Diffusion of the EU's Social Values 301

Tamta Margvelashvili
EU Accession Reboot: Integrating Competition Enforcement Trends for Digital Platforms into Eastern Partnership Talks 335

Introduction

Recent developments in digital markets, along with the evolving geopolitical landscape surrounding the EU, have given renewed impetus to the process of regulating markets in the 21st century, notably through initiatives like the DMA, the Data Act, and the AI Act. These changes have prompted competition law scholars to reconsider what role competition law should play in preserving or shaping the functioning of competitive markets and the economy. The increasing integration of public interest values, fairness, labour rights, and strategic goals into the regulatory landscape has sparked debates about whether our current competition laws are still fit for purpose or in need of revision. Many new regulatory instruments, particularly in the digital domain, have moved away from traditional principles of competition law, with the DMA, for example, omitting efficiency defences and questioning the more economic approach. This shift reflects a broader transformation, where competition law is not only being viewed as an economic tool but as a critical component in achieving broader societal and geopolitical objectives. As these regulatory changes unfold, especially amidst ongoing global crises, the landscape of competition law is being fundamentally reshaped to balance market integrity with strategic goals, creating significant challenges and opportunities for the future of EU competition policy. Recent discussion has focused much on digital markets and new (regulatory) instruments such as the DMA, the AI Act, the Data Act. However, competition law as such also undergoes significant modification, also considering the ongoing geopolitical crisis. Furthermore, the role of competition law in the EU's geopolitical strategy is gaining prominence, as competition law is seen as a tool that can advance the EU's global position. The EU's more economic approach to competition law, which focuses primarily on economic efficiency, is now being critiqued for its insufficiency in addressing broader strategic and societal challenges. Proposals for a recalibrated competition policy, one that integrates industrial, trade, and geopolitical considerations, are gaining traction. This integrated approach could allow the EU to better respond to contemporary challenges, including technological competition, economic inequality, and sustainability. The ongoing geopolitical shifts demand that EU competition law be adapted to align more closely with these strategic goals.

This second volume of the Young Competition Law Scholars Conference's edited collection maps out the new role traditional competition law plays in new markets and in times of crisis. It therefore examines the transformative landscape of competition law, focusing on the interplay between traditional economic objectives and emerging societal values. It also sheds light on competition law in times of geopolitical divergence and crisis. Therefore, the book encounters change in the field of competition law (enforcement), diving deep into the question what goals competition law should be following (Part I). For such goals to be effectively implemented (current) enforcement tools are analysed (Part II). Authors then delve deep into enforcement mechanism outside of traditional competition law and ask for the geopolitical dimension of changes in enforcement strategies (Part III). The book then asks for the effects of such changes in the field of competition law outside of its territorial scope of application (Part IV).

Competition law, traditionally focused on economic efficiency and consumer welfare, is now being critiqued for its narrow approach. In this vein, *Remortales* in "Public Interest as a Goal of Competition Law and Policy? A Comparative Revision" argues for a broader understanding of competition law that incorporates non-economic public interest values, such as job preservation and regional economic development. She challenges the prevailing view that competition law, particularly following the influence of Chicago School economic theory, should be focused exclusively on promoting consumer welfare, thus excluding non-economic public interest values. The author argues that competition law must be understood in the context of the social realities of different jurisdictions, as markets are embedded within specific societal structures. Consequently, competition law can and should include non-economic public interest values relevant to a given country's unique circumstances. For this, the author revises the notion of competition law as a neutral, economically-driven tool and contends that historical contexts of U.S. and European Union competition laws demonstrate that such laws have always been shaped by societal values and aims. By reviewing these legal frameworks, the paper contends that it is inaccurate to regard competition law as immune to public interest considerations, and that non-economic objectives, such as job preservation and regional economic development, should be incorporated where applicable. Under this premise, a key case examined is South Africa's Competition Act, which explicitly integrates public interest values into its competition law framework. The paper scrutinizes the procedural and substantive reasoning of the Competition Tribunal and the Competition Court of Appeal during merger reviews, emphasizing that public interest concerns, such as employment and small business impact, should be considered alongside traditional competition assessments. However, these concerns must be clearly defined and should not be invoked in a general or open-ended manner. The South African legal framework provides specific guidelines to help authorities balance economic efficiency with public interest considerations in merger cases. In practice, this has not led to the prohibition of mergers that do not restrict market competition, but instead has resulted in conditional approvals designed to mitigate public interest risks. Building on the South African experience, the paper proposes a model for incorporating public interest concerns into competition law assessments. This model suggests that competition authorities first assess the competitive effects of a proposed action before considering its potential public interest implications. Moreover, the model advocates for clear legal frameworks that define specific public interest goals, reducing uncertainty and enhancing predictability for market participants. The author also stresses the importance of a proportionality exercise in which the benefits of maintaining market competition are weighed against the potential benefits of public interest goals, with prohibitive measures only being justified by substantial public interest impacts.

Similarly, *Wakonig's* work on "What is Fairness? Reflections on the Concept of Fairness in European Competition Law, Taking Into Account Provisions of Austrian Competition Law" highlights the need for a more inclusive approach, addressing not only market efficiency but also fairness in the distribution of benefits across society. This aligns with calls for a reimagined competition framework that integrates social responsibility alongside traditional economic goals. The author discusses whether fairness is required for a well-functioning or for a competitive market. Accordingly, fairness has been established as an objective in recent European legislative and policy acts, as well as in the activities of national competition authorities. Although the concept of fairness is explicitly mentioned within the context of EU competition law, it is still unclear what it encompasses exactly. Moreover, it remains unclear what lessons can be learnt from the European fairness discourse for the Member States' competition law and its impact at the national level, and vice versa. Against this backdrop the concept of fairness within Austrian legislation and its specific provisions is analysed in order to add new perspectives to the current European discourse. Therefore, *Wakonig* reviews how fairness is currently understood in academia and jurisprudence. Subsequently, the relevance of fairness and its implementation within the Austrian Federal Cartel Act, the Federal Act Against Unfair Competition and the Federal Fair Competitive Conditions Act are discussed. Lastly, it is evaluated what new insights can be deduced from this discussion, relevant to the European discourse.

Without using the term fairness, labour markets also call upon competition law in order to solve questions of questionable working conditions. The increasing complexity of these labour markets, particularly in sectors like agriculture, underscores the need for a more inclusive competition law that protects vulnerable workers. The work by *Graf* and *Sonderegger* brings attention to Article 102 TFEU, questioning whether competition law should also extend to the protection of migrant workers in seasonal agricultural markets. By considering worker welfare in addition to consumer welfare, competition law can expand its protective role in the labour market. Their paper on "Exploring the Application of Article 102 TFEU to Abuses in Seasonal Agricultural Labour Markets" examines whether competition law is bound to prioritize products while neglecting the welfare of the workers who create those products, just as Upton Sinclair's book "The Jungle" inadvertently led to food safety reforms rather than improvements in workers' conditions. Against the timely background of the increasing momentum of competition law enforcement in labour markets, it considers this topic relevant, as despite stringent EU labour protections, these workers remain highly vulnerable to power imbalances, often resulting from their disadvantaged backgrounds and lack of awareness of their rights. The methodology employed within this article is strictly legal, based on existing case law. It excludes the broader normative and policy questions related to the proper role of competition law in these markets. The analysis begins with the key conditions for the application of Article 102 TFEU, thereby discussing the realities of migrant labour. It then explores whether the concept of abuse, typically focused on product markets and consumer welfare, can effectively support labour laws and other regulations in addressing worker exploitation while directly fostering worker welfare.

Not fairness, but competitiveness is also one way of enlarging the scope of application of competition law provisions. In *Ünekbas* view, the dynamic nature of competitiveness in the EU has prompted calls for modernizing EU antitrust law to foster long-term economic growth and innovation. In "Dynamic Competition Law – Between Feasibility and Desirability" the author advocates for incorporating competitiveness into EU antitrust law, arguing that competition law should not only prevent anti-competitive behaviour but should also stimulate innovation and market evolution, particularly in the context of the digital economy. This contribution examines the evolving role of antitrust law in the European Union (EU), with a particular focus on its relationship to the concept of competitiveness. Antitrust law serves as a mechanism to preserve a competitive internal market, ensuring that firms capable of succeeding in this integrated environment can benefit from it. While free movement rules and harmonization measures allow firms to scale across the EU, antitrust law ensures that market success is based on dynamic efficiency, which includes fostering innovation and the ability of firms to challenge established players. However, the practical application of dynamic efficiency remains a challenge for antitrust law, as the meaning of "efficiency" itself is contested. The concept of competitiveness has been central to EU economic policy since the early stages of European integration. The EU has long recognized the need to create competitive European firms that can withstand global competition. Contemporary views on competitiveness link macroeconomic objectives with the performance of individual firms and markets. Firms that produce innovative and attractive products not only improve their own competitiveness but contribute to the broader economic competitiveness of their countries, enhancing terms of trade, attracting investment, and boosting welfare. Modern economic thinking emphasizes that competitiveness is a dynamic, future-oriented process, which stands in contrast to outdated views that prioritize the preservation of static industries. This evolving understanding of competitiveness suggests that antitrust law should adapt to a changing market landscape. Rather than focusing solely on preventing anti-competitive behaviour, antitrust law can promote long-term economic growth by fostering a competitive environment conducive to innovation and market evolution.

To meet current challenges of digital markets, the German legislator has rather recently incorporated section 19a of the German Competition Act (GWB). Dominant tech giants present new challenges that require nuanced approaches to market power regulation, while Sec. 19a GWB aims to curb anti-competitive practices in digital ecosystems. *Stöhr* discusses this legislative initiative as a key tool for addressing anti-competitive conduct in digital ecosystems in the contribution "Paramount Significance for Competition Across Markets: First Case Practice and Theories of Harm". The Federal Cartel Office's (FCO) initial application of this provision highlights both successes and limitations in regulating market power in the digital age. The author points the finger to where improvements in enforcement and clarity of legal standards are needed. First, she examines Section 19a of the German Competition Act (GWB) as a crucial modernization measure aimed at enhancing abuse control in digital markets. Specifically, Section 19a targets firms deemed to have "paramount significance for competition across markets" (UPSCAM), with a particular focus on digital ecosystems. The research evaluates the Federal Cartel Office's (FCO) initial applications of this provision and its economic consequences, offering both legal and economic perspectives on its implementation. Unlike conventional antitrust measures, Section 19a allows for pre-emptive action against firms that could undermine competition across multiple markets, particularly those operating in digital ecosystems dominated by a small number of large firms. This provision empowers the FCO to take targeted actions to curb anti-competitive behaviours and practices before they significantly distort market competition. A key focus of the paper is the analysis of the FCO's first cases under Section 19a, involving major tech companies such as Alphabet, Amazon, Apple, Meta, and Microsoft. The study scrutinizes how the FCO designates these companies as UPSCAMs and assesses the economic reasoning behind their decisions. It also examines the procedural steps taken in these cases, including the firms' responses and the resulting interventions by the FCO. The paper discusses how the FCO has used behavioural and structural remedies to address anti-competitive conduct, highlighting both successes and challenges in these initial proceedings. The author further delves into the economic implications of Section 19a's application. It notes that while some early interventions, such as those involving Alphabet and Meta, have been relatively successful, these cases often represent "low-hanging fruit"—issues with clear and widely accepted resolutions. The real test for Section 19a will come with more complex cases, where firms may resist cooperation or where there is insufficient consensus regarding the practices in question. Moreover, the paper raises concerns about the enforcement and sanctioning mechanisms of Section 19a, pointing out that the absence of direct sanctions for non-compliance could undermine the provision's effectiveness, especially when firms challenge the FCO's decisions. Finally, the author discusses policy implications and suggests potential improvements to Section 19a. It calls for clearer guidelines on how the FCO should assess firms' significance across markets and more robust enforcement mechanisms to ensure compliance with the law. The paper contrasts Section 19a with the Digital Markets Act (DMA) and suggests that, while Section 19a offers greater flexibility, it may require stronger sanctions and more explicit rules to enhance its impact on promoting competition in digital markets.

As the EU faces new challenges in the digital and global markets, the design of remedies in competition law enforcement is increasingly important as it determines the effectiveness of its legislative initiatives. Remedies therefore play a critical role in ensuring the effectiveness of competition law in maintaining a competitive market environment. In "Re-thinking Remedy Design in Competition Law Enforcement" *Dunne* explores the complexities of remedy design within EU competition law enforcement, focusing on how the European Commission addresses anti-competitive practices to maintain market integrity and protect consumer welfare. The primary research question examines the efficacy of existing remedies under Regulation 1/2003 and the balance between legal principles such as proportionality, legal certainty, and legitimate expectations. By analysing current remedial practices and the jurisprudence of the Court of Justice of the European Union (CJEU), the author investigates the practical challenges and limitations of current enforcement strategies. Therefore, she examines the legal framework governing remedy design, followed by a critical analysis of constitutional constraints, and a review of existing remedial practices and reform proposals. The author suggests that the Commission should leverage its broad discretion more assertively to address anti-competitive practices in emerging sectors, proposing reforms that align with the dynamic nature of modern economies.

Another area of law employed in handling current international crisis is state aid law. The growing intersection of competition law and geopolitics is particularly evident in discussions about the EU's response to international crises, including the COVID-19 pandemic and Russia's aggression against Ukraine. In state aid law, temporary frameworks have been introduced that allow for greater flexibility during emergencies. While such frameworks are essential for member states to adapt to crises, there are concerns about potential distortions to market competition. In "The Role of State Aid in Times of International Crises" *Deneka* reflects on challenges of European integration, alongside significant international crises such as the 2007–2009 financial crisis, the COVID-19 pandemic, and Russia's aggression against Ukraine. The author lays out how the European Union has repeatedly introduced temporary crisis frameworks within state aid law to address the emerging challenges in response to these crises. The discussion around these special regulations is twofold: proponents argue that greater flexibility in state aid law is essential to adapt to rapidly changing social and economic conditions, ensuring that member states can respond effectively to crises. On the other hand, critics caution that the introduction of such temporary measures could lead to significant distortions of competition and inefficient allocation of public resources, potentially undermining the principles of the internal market. The author seeks to determine the aim of these regulations during international crises by analysing relevant frameworks.

A broader stand is taken by *Bohnert*, who explores the intersection of competition policy and geopolitics within the European Union (EU). In "Geopolitics and Competition Law: An Odd Couple or a Match Made in Heaven?" the author argues that competition law should play a more prominent role in advancing the EU's geopolitical objectives and addressing its competitiveness challenges. The author critiques the EU's current "more economic approach" to competition law, which prioritizes economic efficiency and consumer welfare, suggesting that this framework is politically motivated and insufficient to meet the EU's broader strategic goals. Drawing a parallel between competition in markets and geopolitical competition, asserting that, much like firms vying for market share, geopolitical actors compete for trade, investment, technological leadership, and military dominance, the author highlights the interconnectedness of competition, trade, and industrial policies, asserting that EU competition law should not be pursued in isolation, but rather should be integrated with these other policy areas to strengthen the EU's global position. If EU competition law and trade law are complementary, then both aim to promote market integration, albeit through different mechanisms, with competition law focusing on private actors and trade law addressing state barriers. The author states that the EU's existing focus on consumer welfare, embedded in the "more economic approach," inhibits the closer alignment of competition, industrial, and trade policies. This isolationist approach, characterized by policy silos, limits the EU's ability to respond to contemporary geopolitical challenges, including economic inequality, technological competition, and sustainability. The author therefore first suggests that the adoption of a more integrated policy approach—considering not only economic efficiency but also broader public interest and geopolitical objectives—could better position the EU in the face of global competition. And proposes second that EU competition law should be recalibrated to allow for a more integrated approach, one that takes into account trade, industrial policy, and geopolitical considerations. This could involve reassessing how the EU addresses strategic sectors, foreign subsidies, and "killer acquisitions," while also exploring mechanisms to promote European champions in critical industries. Here, an example is drawn from the United States, which has also begun to recognize the links between trade, competition, and industrial policy, and suggests that the EU could benefit from a similar reassessment of its policies.

One clear example of a legislative measure in times of crises is the Foreign Subsidy Regulation (FSR), which examines foreign investments in the EU. *Mattiolo*'s work on the FSR explores how competition law might be increasingly used to address not only economic concerns but also geopolitical and strategic objectives, blurring the line between economic and political considerations. While 'purely political' considerations are the norm in investment screening and 'purely economic' considerations guide merger reviews, the FSR may allow for both, as the author explains in "Competition Law as 'a Continuation of Policy with Other Means'? The Application of the Foreign Subsidies Regulation to Concentrations, Between Legal Certainty and (Geo)political Considerations". The contribution analyses the FSR, particularly its module on concentrations, to understand the Commission's ability to screen operations orchestrated by foreign entities – and its political discretion in the enforcement. It juxtaposes FSR provisions with those of Regulation (EC) 139/2004 (the Merger Regulation, or EUMR) to explore their interactions and assess if and how they can be used to integrate economic and geopolitical considerations into merger control. Then, the author considers the interactions between the FSR and FDI Screening, which is administered by MSs and only loosely coordinated at the EU level. The overlapping between these two tools reveals how the FSR could be used to scrutinize the investments of companies linked to foreign government at the EU level, pending the 'Europeanisation' of FDI Screening. This provocative statement is tested by briefly considering the current FDI regime, its limits and the calls for its reform, especially the recent EU Economic Security Package. The fact that one acquisition may be investigated separately under all three instruments creates some concerns for investors: the changing fortunes of the Chinese company CNRC, which acquired a share of the Italian Pirelli in 2015, provide an example of the complexity and expansion of State powers, so the case is briefly examined. This exercise may reveal whether EU competition law is expanding to defend new interests not previously addressed in the Commission's enforcement — or, depending on one's perspective, it may unveil how purely 'legal' considerations are receding to make room for political ones.

The implications of this new role of Competition Law are reaching beyond the EU internal market with the so-called Brussels effects and with accession talks that – in facing crisis on the EU borders – can arguably be fostered with Competition Law mechanisms. *Bunworth* examines the growing global influence of the European Union (EU) through the "Brussels Effect," a phenomenon where EU regulations, particularly in competition law, are adopted by non-EU countries. As the EU's legal model gains traction, especially amid declining global influence of the U.S.'s more market-driven and less interventionist approach, many jurisdictions are choosing EU-style frameworks. *Bunworth* argues that the Brussels Effect allows the EU not only to shape international competition law but also to embed its social values—enshrined in the EU Treaties—into global legal norms. While previous literature has focused on the EU's role in areas like environmental regulation, this work highlights competition law as a key arena of EU regulatory influence. The paper proposes that the EU should actively leverage this influence to promote fairness, public interest, and broader social objectives alongside market efficiency. It outlines the EU's foundational social values, analyzes the regulatory competition between the EU and the U.S., and explains why the EU's approach has proven more influential globally. The benefits of the Brussels Effect for non-EU and developing countries are explored, and the paper concludes by addressing critiques and examining how EU norms might continue to shape the evolution of global competition policy.

The growing intersection between competition law and geopolitics has also influenced the EU's approach to EU accession talks, especially with Eastern Partnership countries like Georgia, Ukraine, and Moldova. These countries are increasingly prioritizing competition law as a key element of their EU integration process. The need for digital market regulation and the harmonization of competition enforcement in the digital era presents new challenges in the context of EU enlargement. Including digital market enforcement in accession talks is not only vital for enhancing the economic competitiveness of these countries but also aligns with the EU's broader commitment to shaping global regulatory standards in the digital age. In "EU Accession Reboot: Integrating Competition Enforcement Trends for Digital Platforms into Eastern Partnership Talks" *Margvelashvili* argues that the accession journey marks a critical juncture for the Eastern Partnership (EaP). The trio of Georgia, Ukraine, and Moldova is actively paving their paths to unlock heightened economic prosperity. For almost eight years, the Association Agreements have underpinned multifaceted cooperation and integration between the EU and EaP countries, requiring those countries to form a strong legal framework for competition enforcement. However, in an age of rapid digital transformation, the sole focus on traditional competition enforcement policies may no longer suffice. It is worth asking how the notion of "comprehensive competition laws" has evolved over the past eight years. Is it adequate for EU accession if the EaP countries prioritize traditional market dynamics in their competition laws? Against this backdrop, *Margvelashvili* argues that the EU should rethink its approach and incorporate digital market competition enforcement as a pillar of accession talks. Digital markets transcend geographical boundaries, necessitating a harmonized approach to competition enforcement across the EU and its neighbouring regions. Including digital market competition enforcement in accession talks will enhance the economic competitiveness of these countries and reflect the EU's commitment to shaping global regulatory standards in the digital realm.

We look back on two exciting days in Vienna, where young antitrust law scholars from all across the World gathered for lively discussion under the auspices of the 'Young Competition Law Scholars Conference'. The discussions of more than 100 participants significantly contributed to each paper, the result of which can be found in this conference volume. We would like to thank our sponsors, without whom neither the conference nor this volume would not have been possible namely the University of Vienna, Johannes Kepler University Linz, Land Oberösterreich, Helmuth M. Merlin Stiftung, Wolf Theiss, Schönherr, Schalast, Binder Grösswang, Haslinger Nagele, Barnet Egermann Illgasch and Nomos Verlagsgesellschaft. We would also like to special thank the University of Vienna for its organisational and monetary support as well as the academic setting, as well as the University of Vienna, Linz, Innsbruck and Munich. We thank our helpers on site: Jil M. Abt, Sophie Haiden and Barbara Justen for their extra-mandatory and enthusiastic assistance and Nils Imgarten, Lars Maritzen, Corinna Potocnik-Manzouri, Christoph Raab, Thomas Thiede and Sathita Wimonkunarak for moderating the panels. Avin Nazemann and Luca Giehl have rendered outstanding services in the editing of this book. We would also like to thank Marco Ganzhorn from Nomos Verlag for his prompt and impeccable supervision of this second volume of this series!

We are looking forward to meet again at the European University Institute (IT) in October 2025!

Vienna/Linz/Innsbruck/Munich in April 2025

Ranjana Andrea Achleitner (University of Linz)/Eva Fischer (LMU Munich)/Lena Hornkohl (University of Vienna/University of Heidelberg)/Bernadette Zelger (University of Innsbruck)

Biographies of editors and authors

Editors

Ranjana Andrea Achleitner is Assistant Professor at the Institute of European Law at Johannes Kepler University Linz, where she is pursuing her post-doctoral qualification (Habilitation). She holds a PhD in Law from Johannes Kepler University Linz, with a dissertation on geo-blocking in the Digital Single Market that received multiple awards. She also holds a Master in Law from the University of Vienna and Johannes Kepler University Linz, as well as a Master in Political Science from the University of Vienna. She worked at the Linz Institute of Technology Law Lab and gained professional experience at law firms in Vienna and Cologne, as well as at the Austrian Mission to the OECD in Paris. In November 2023, she participated as an academic guest in research meetings at the Information Law Institute, New York University, School of Law.

Eva Fischer is a PhD candidate and academic assistant at LMU Munich at the Chair of Civil Law, European and International Business Law (Prof. Dr. Thomas Ackermann, LL.M. (Cantab.)). During her doctorial studies, she visited the Vienna University of Economics and Business, Oxford University and the European University Institute. She holds a Law Degree and a Bachelor's in History both from LMU Munich. Prior to joining the LMU as a researcher she worked with an international law firm. Her work is published in leading German and International Journals and she teaches widely in Competition Law, Torts, IP Law and Civil Law at LMU.

Lena Hornkohl is an Assistant Professor (Tenure Track) for European Law at the University of Vienna and a Postdoctoral Candidate (Habilitandin) at the University of Heidelberg. She holds a Ph.D from the University of Heidelberg, an LL.M. in European Law and Economic Analysis from the College of Europe, is a fully qualified lawyer in Germany, and studied law in Heidelberg and Uppsala. She worked as a Postdoctoral Researcher at the Max Planck-Institute for Procedural Law in Luxembourg, as a lawyer at an international law firm in Brussels, as a research fellow at the University of Heidelberg, and as a legal clerk at the Higher Regional Court Karlsruhe.

Bernadette Zelger is an Assistant Professor and graduate from the University of Innsbruck (Dr. iur., Mag. iur.), King's College London (Postgraduate Diploma in EU Competition Law) and Queen Mary University of London (LL.M. in Competition Law) as well as a qualified lawyer in Austria (Bar exam 2014, inactive). Before having joined the Department of European and Public International Law, University of Innsbruck (2020), Bernadette worked as a Research Assistant for Prof. Ioannis Kokkoris, Professor for Law and Economics at the Centre for Commercial Law Studies, Queen Mary University of London, United Kingdom and as an Assistant Professor at the Department of Commercial Law, University of Innsbruck. Bernadette holds/held various esteemed Fellowships, including research stays abroad, such as, inter alia, a DOC-Fellowship of the Austrian Academy of Sciences, a Fellowship of the Max Planck Institute for Innovation und Competition and an Emile Noël Fellowship at NYU School of Law, Jean Monnet Center for International and Regional Economic Law & Justice, New York. She has published extensively in peer-reviewed national and international journals and been a regular speaker at national and international conferences. Moreover, Bernadette's academic work has been awarded prestigious national (e.g. Franz-Gschnitzer Förderpreis) and international (2024 Antitrust Writing Awards) prizes.

Bernadette's research focus lies with EU and International Economic Law (in particular Competition Law, Internal Market Law, EU State Aid Law, Economic Constitutional Law). Her most recent work focuses on the role of EU (constitutional) law in a federal, multilevel political system as well as the role of courts and negative integration in this regard.Furthermore, Bernadette gained practical experience as a lawyer for a period of 5 years in full service law firms headquartered in Vienna (Schoenherr Attorneys at Law, WOLF THEISS Attorneys at Law), the European Commission, DG COMP, E1 (Unit for Antitrust – Pharma and Health Services) in Brussels, Belgium, and as Legal Counsel (Unternehmensjuristin) at the Legal Department of a Bank (BTV, headquarter in Innsbruck).

Authors

Sophie Bohnert holds a Bachelor of Laws and a Master of Laws in Business Law from the Vienna University of Economics and Business/Maastricht University. She also holds a Bachelor of Science in Business, Economics and Social Sciences with a major in Business Administration from the Vienna University of Economics and Business. During her studies she worked as a Tutor at the Institute for Company Law and as an eLearning Assistant at the Institute for International and European Law at the Vienna University of Economics and Business. In 2024, she graduated from the College of Europe with a Master's degree in European Legal Studies, specializing in European law and economic analysis. In the same year, she was awarded a doctoral degree from the Vienna University of Economics and Business. Her doctoral thesis provided a comparative legal analysis of the phenomenon of common ownership under US antitrust law and EU competition law. During her doctoral studies, she worked as a Teaching and Research Assistant at the Institute for International and European Law of the Vienna University of Economics and Business.

Richard Bunworth is a PhD candidate at the Sutherland School of Law, University College Dublin. He received a Sutherland Doctoral Scholarship at the commencement of his PhD and was subsequently awarded a prestigious Government of Ireland Postgraduate Scholarship. He was also awarded the highly competitive Laura Bassi Scholarship in 2021 in relation to his research. He is also a lecturer in intellectual property law at Trinity College Dublin. He studied law as an undergraduate at Trinity College, Dublin. Following completion of his undergraduate degree, Richard read for the Bachelor of Civil Laws degree at the University of Oxford. In addition, Richard obtained a Master of Arts in EU Competition Law from King's College London, having completed a thesis on innovation competition. Richard is a solicitor, qualified to practice in Ireland and the UK, having worked in the finance department of one of Ireland's foremost corporate law firms. Prior to that, he held a role as a researcher at a commercial litigation firm in London. He acted as a consultant to the Irish Competition and Consumer Protection in 2022, advising the Competition and Merger Enforcement division. Subsequently, he was appointed as a non-governmental advisor to the Irish CCPC and was the youngest ever appointee to the role. Richard has published articles in a number of international peer-reviewed journals, including the European Competition Law Review, the International Review of Intellectual Property and Competition Law, and the International Sports Law Journal. Richard's primary research interests lie in EU competition law, with a particular emphasis on the consumer welfare standard and the application of public interest factors in competition law. In addition, Richard has published in the area of sports law and maintains a keen interest in the interaction of sports and competition law.

Nicole Deneka is currently a PhD candidate in the discipline of Legal Sciences at the Doctoral School of the University of the Commission of National Education in Krakow, Poland where she commenced her research in October 2023. Her doctoral research focuses on EU state aid law in times of international crises. She earned her Master's Degree in Law from Jagiellonian University in 2023, with a thesis on state aid in research, development, and innovation, which received second prize in the national competition organized by UOKiK (Polish Office of Competition and Consumer Protection). Her thesis explored the complexity of public aid law systems for research and innovation activities, emphasizing the influence of non-binding legal acts and EU policies on the development of regulations in this field. During her studies, she also earned certificates from East China University of Political Science and Law and Kobe University, focusing on China-Poland Bilateral Investment Treaties and Japanese Administrative Law, respectively. Nicole has garnered substantial professional experience, primarily in the field of indirect taxes. She has also interned at the Ministry of Finance in the Tax Analyses Department. She has been recognized for her academic achievements with multiple scholarships, including the Scholarship of the Minister of Education and Science of Poland for significant scientific achievements. Nicole has actively participated in moot courts and national competitions, securing top positions, and has contributed to several publications.

Elaine Dunne completed her state exams in 2017. After that, she undertook a Bachelor of Civil Law (BCL) degree at the Sutherland School of Law, University College Dublin. Elaine graduated with a BCL in 2022 and from there completed the Law Society of Ireland Examinations – Final Examinations First Part (FE1 Exams). Elaine entered into a training contract with DLA Piper Ireland LLP in 2023 and was admitted to the Professional Practice Course (PPC) at the Law Society of Ireland, which she completed in May 2024. Elaine is currently working as a trainee solicitor with the corporate team of DLA Piper's Dublin office. Elaine will qualify as a solicitor in April 2026.

Luca Nicola Graf graduated with a bachelor's and master's degree from the University of Zurich in 2018 and 2020, respectively, and an LL.M. in competition law from King's College London in 2020. He has worked as a research assistant at the University of Portsmouth, the University of Nottingham, and as a trainee at DG COMP. He is currently working as a research assistant at the Chair of Prof. Heinemann at the University of Zurich and writing his PhD Dissertation on the topic of environmental degradation as a theory of harm under Art. 102 TFEU.

Giulia Aurélie Sonderegger, graduated with a bachelor's and master's degree from the University of Zurich in 2018 and 2020, respectively, and an LL.M. in competition law from the Queen Mary University of London in 2019. During her studies, she completed three internships: two at law firms in Zurich in 2015 and 2017 and one at the Organization for Economic Co-Operation and Development (OECD) in 2020. She then received a Ph.D. for her dissertation on "Killer Acquisitions in Digital Markets: An Analysis of the EU Merger Control Regime" from the University of Zurich in 2024. During her doctoral studies, she worked as a research assistant at the Chair of Prof. Heinemann. Besides that, she also worked part-time in financial crime compliance at Credit Suisse. She published several articles in the field of competition law and recently completed her traineeship at White & Case in Brussels.

Tamta Margvelashvili, studied law at Ivane Javakhishvili Tbilisi State University, where she is currently pursuing her Ph.D. She holds an LL.M. in International and European Business Law from KU Leuven, Belgium. She also completed an exchange semester at Friedrich Schiller University of Jena, Germany. Since September 2022 till October 2023, Tamta served a research fellow at the Institute for German and European Economic Law, Competition Law, and Regulatory Law of the Free University of Berlin, under the DAAD one-year grant doctoral program. Her research focuses on competition law enforcement for sectoral regulators in Georgia under EU influence. Tamta's professional career includes her current role as Director of Competition, Capital & Financial Markets Practice at "Nodia, Urumashvili and Partners" LLC, a leading full-service law firm in Georgia. She is actively engaged in law-drafting, presents at national and international conferences, and serves as an independent expert in banking and finance, competition, corporate and M&A, data protection, and ADR. In addition to her practical work, Tamta is also an associate professor at Georgian National University and an invited lecturer at Ilia Chavchavadze State University in Tbilisi. She has received a number of scholarships, grants, and participated in exchange programs in the EU and beyond, graduating with distinctions. Her academic contributions include several articles and book chapters in national and international publications.

Pierfrancesco Mattiolo is a Graduate Teaching and Research Assistant and PhD Candidate in European and International Economic Law at the University of Antwerp, Belgium. His primary research interests encompass competition law and policy, international trade law and policy, and economic diplomacy. He is currently conducting doctoral research on the EU Foreign Subsidies Regulation and its interaction with international trade and industrial policy. He is one of the editors of the CELIS Blog, an emerging space for academic discussion on economic security issues, and a fellow of the Young Academic Network of the Foundation for European Progressive Studies (FEPS YAN – 9th Cycle). As a researcher, he has been invited to give seminars at other academic institutions (University of Bologna, Zhongnan University of Economics and Law) and for stakeholders (IndustriALL Europe). Before starting his PhD, he gained professional experience as a policy assistant trainee at the Permanent Representation of Italy to the EU in Brussels. Here, he closely followed various FTA negotiations and legislative processes, including the International Procurement Instrument. His professional journey also includes prior work with the School of Policies, an organisation founded by former Italian PM Enrico Letta and affiliated with AREL, one of the main policy think tanks in Rome. In addition to his academic and professional pursuits, Pierfrancesco actively collaborates with the Italy-ASEAN Association and China Files, a leading Italian news agency specialising in Asian affairs, writing on EU-Asia economic relations and regulatory affairs. He holds a Master's Degree in Law from the University of Trento, attained with a thesis on the EU CarbonBorder Adjustment Mechanism and its compatibility with international trade and climate law, written under the supervision of Professor Giuseppe Nesi. During his studies, he spent one semester at KU Leuven.

Silvia Retamales M. has been recently appointed as a Judge of the Chilean Competition Tribunal. She is a lawyer from the Universidad de Chile and holds an LLM in Competition, Innovation, and Information from New York University (2022). Additionally, she holds a Diploma in Competition Law and Policy from the Universidad de Chile (2015–16). From 2022 to June 2024, she served as the Director of the Competition and Regulation Team at Ferrada Nehme. She has also worked as an external advisor and fellow at the International Energy Agency, OECD, in Paris (2022), a research associate at the Center for Civil Justice at New York University (2021), and a clerk at the Chilean Competition Tribunal from June 2016 to December 2020. She is a professor at the Law School of the University of Chile, where she has taught undergraduate lectures such as Microeconomics, Law and Economics, Market Regulation, and Competition Litigation Seminar, as well as postgraduate lectures in the Diploma in Competition Law and Policy, organized by the Centre for Regulation and Competition of the Law Faculty of the Universidad de Chile (RegCom). She was also the co-coach of the University of Chile team that won the Competition Law Moot Court organized by BFE+ and the Faculty of Law of the Universidad del Pacífico in 2023. Her research interests focus on competition, economic, private, and procedural law. In 2020, she was awarded as a Hauser Global Scholar, a full merit-based scholarship granted by the University of New York to the 10 best students from countries all over the world.

Annika Stöhr, received her PhD in 2022 with a thesis on "Economic Evaluation and Reform Implications of German Competition Policy". Her dissertation focused on merger control. In particular, she dealt with non-economic effects and so-called public interests that (should) potentially influence competition regulation. Her research generally operates at the intersection of competition economics, competition law and competition policy, under the premise that innovation and dynamism are both facilitators and goals of functioning competition (regulation). Her current work deals with the regulation of large digital ecosystems, e.g. through Section 19a GWB and the DMA and DSA, as well as with the regulation of algorithmic recommender systems in particular. Her research benefits from more than two years of professional experience at the German Federal Ministry of Economic Affairs and Climate Action. Since April 2023 she is working as a postdoctoral researcher at the Chair of Economic Theory at Ilmenau University of Technology.

Selçukhan Ünekbas, is a PhD Researcher at the European University Institute (EUI), Florence, Italy and a Research Fellow at the Haas School of Business, University of California, Berkeley. Under the supervision of Professor Nicolas Petit, his research focuses on European competitiveness and antitrust enforcement. Selçukhan has been trained as a jurist in Turkey, Belgium, and Italy. His research received funding from the European Commission, the American Bar Association, the Turkish Ministry of Treasury and Finance, the Italian Ministry of Foreign Affairs, and the Finnish Prime

Minister's Office. Selçukhan was the 2024 International Scholar-in-Residence of the Antitrust Law Section of the American Bar Association, which he completed as a Visiting Researcher at Georgetown University Law Center, Washington, D.C. His publications have appeared or are forthcoming in leading journals, including the Antitrust Law Journal, Journal of European Competition Law & Practice, European Journal of Legal Studies, the Journal of World Investment & Trade, and the Yearbook of Antitrust and Regulatory Studies. He taught antitrust law, internal market law, and innovation policy at the EUI, Istanbul Bilgi University, and the Free University of Brussels (VUB). Selçukhan worked as an associate at an international law firm before joining academia. He is a native Turkish speaker and is fluent in English, with a working knowledge of Italian.

Christiane Wakonig is a case handler at the Austrian Federal Competition Authority, where she works on merger cases, abuse of dominance cases as well as cartel cases and co-organizes the annual Austrian Cartel Law Moot Court. During her studies she was a participant of the Willem C Vis International Commercial Arbitration Moot Court, where her team was ranked under the top 10 percent out of 357 teams from 80 countries, with their written submissions achieving various honourable mentions. Furthermore, she worked as student assistant at the Department of Civil Law of the University of Vienna (Prof. Palten) and at the Department of Commercial and Business Law of the University of Vienna (Prof. Schumacher). Her current research interests include Law Against Unfair Competition and Antitrust.

Part I:
Goals of Competition Law

Public interest as a goal of competition law and policy? A comparative revision

Silvia Retamales Morales[*]

A. Introduction

There has been a general understanding among antitrust scholars and authorities that the competition law aims to promote consumer welfare. Although it is hard to provide an exact definition of what consumer welfare standard means, in this article, we will define it as "*the ability of consumers to benefit from lower prices and higher output.*"[1] Moreover, some scholars have proposed that other economic notions, such as promoting the competitive process[2] and greater economic efficiency in the form of total welfare[3], are also competition law objectives. As noted, the critical element in this traditional understanding of competition law, either conservative or more progressive, is that other non-economic public interest goals, such as fairness, the promotion of small businesses, equity, gender, and employment, should not be included in the competition law assessment.

Accordingly, judges "*must not weigh against consumer welfare any other goal, such as the supposed social benefit of preserving small business against superior efficiency.*"[4] Promoters of this competition law understanding, especially in the United States of America ("US"), have argued that balancing the public policy goals belongs to Congress, not the antitrust enforcers[5].

---

* *Lawyer, Universidad de Chile. LLM New York University. Universidad de Chile Law School Lecturer. Judge of Chilean Competition Tribunal.*

1 *Lianos,* Polycentric Competition Law, 71 Current Legal Problems (2018), 161, 163.

2 *Wu,* The 'Protection of the Competitive Process' Standard, Columbia Public Law Research Paper (2018), No. 14–612, https://ssrn.com/abstract=3276896 (accessed 30 January 2025).

3 "[W]e believe that it is total welfare rather than consumer welfare that should drive antitrust analysis", *Blair/Sokol,* Welfare Standards in U.S. and E.U. Antitrust Enforcement, 81 Fordham Law Review (2013), 2497, 2499.

4 *Bork*, The Antitrust Paradox: A Policy at War with Itself, Free Press 1993, xi.

5 Organisation for Economic Co-operation and Development OECD, *Horizontal Agreements in the Environmental Context: Key findings, summary and notes*", (OECD

Judges "*are supposed to enforce the law, not make political judgments*"[6] since they are "*poorly situated to make assessments about the 'right' price or quality for anything.*"[7]

As a result, the antitrust analysis should focus on the effects on price. Non-price benefits are not accepted as pro-competitive justifications for conduct that likely will increase prices or restrict output.[8] Behind this tradition is the claim that the consumer welfare standard (or other economic concepts such as market efficiency) provides a measurement mechanism[9] for rigorous economic analysis. It gives certainty and a degree of legal neutrality. In other words, following this notion, a narrow technical-economic core of competition law must be protected, justifying the exclusion of different non-economic social values from this law.

This article will argue that the view of competition law as a law immune from other public interest values needs to be revised. As each country has its own legal tradition, history, geographic market, and economy, national competition law and policy could reflect these realities (and have done it-at least- in its origins in some jurisdictions). Thus, it might be possible that balancing non-economic public interest values into the competition framework would be essential for a jurisdiction, precisely, to respond to a particular social context. The last conclusion is more pronounced in developing countries, for which the consumer welfare standard may not be sufficient to address issues such as "*highly concentrated markets, high barriers to entry and expansion, pervasive state or parastatal ownership and privileged privatized business, an extensive informal economy.*"[10] Therefore,

---

Roundtables on Competition Policy Papers, No. 120), 11, https://doi.org/10.1787/c788a7fb-en (accessed 30 January 2025).

6 *Carlton/Picker, Antitrust and Regulation* (National Bureau of Economic Research, Working Paper No. 12902, 2007), 12, https://www.nber.org/system/files/chapters/c12565/revisions/c12565.rev0.pdf (accessed 30 January 2025).

7 *Carlton/Picker* (n 6) 12.

8 Particularly in the US system, "[c]ourts do not consider non-economic factors to be procompetitive justifications for the purpose of antitrust analysis. The belief that antitrust analysis should be limited to economic factors has held strong in over one hundred years of Sherman Act jurisprudence". *Koga*, Teamwork or Collusion? Changing Antitrust Law to Permit Corporate Action on Climate Change, 95 Washington Law Review (2020), 1989, 2011.

9 *Hovenkamp*, The Slogans and Goals of Antitrust Law, New York University Journal of Legislation and Public Policy (2023), 705, 779.

10 *Fox*, Competition, Development and Regional Integration: In Search of a Competition Law Fit for Developing Countries, in Drexl/Bakhoum/Fox/Gal/Gerber (eds.),

"*developing countries need to develop a perspective of their own,*"[11] and including public interest values may be critical.

The concept of public interest can be ambiguous and may vary significantly across different jurisdictions, so it is important to establish a clear definition for this paper. However, providing a definitive list of specific objectives that can be classified as serving the public interest would be incomplete. Consequently, in this paper, the term "public interest" will be used to distinguish between competition law objectives that are fundamentally economic, such as consumer welfare standard or total welfare, and those that are not purely economic.[12] The latter may include considerations such as protecting disadvantaged populations, inequality, fairness, and supporting small and medium-sized enterprises, among others.

This paper will follow the next structure. First, it will review how competition law from the beginning, at least in the US and the European Union ("EU"), has included some public interest values as goals to respond to a social context (B). Then, it will examine the case of South Africa, where the legislator has chosen to incorporate public interest considerations into the competition law statute and assessment (C). Next, following the South African experience, this article will show how public interest values may be considered in the competition law framework without affecting legal certainty and the technical richness of the traditional competition law assessment (D). Then, it will offer some conclusions (E).

Finally, an important warning must be made. This paper will not assume that competition law and policy is the unique way to solve public problems. It merely seeks to show how they have been, are, and can be part of the toolkit available for policymakers and legislators, particularly in developing countries, as an instrument to promote economic growth and integration.

Competition Policy and Regional Integration in Developing Countries, Edward Elgar 2012, 1, 12.

11 *Fox* (n 10) 23.

12 Organisation for Economic Co-operation and Development OECD, *Public Interest Considerations in Merger Control* (OECD Roundtables on Competition Policy Papers, No. 187), 8, https://doi.org/10.1787/21950340-en (accessed 30 January 2025).

B. Competition Law: The roots

A historical review of two crucial jurisdictions in terms of competition law — the US and EU[13] — reveals that competition law initially aimed to achieve various relevant goals. These goals included reducing concentration, balancing market power, promoting diversity, and facilitating market access. The study of this historical context also shows that competition law (or antitrust law) and policy are closely connected to a specific country's social and political circumstances. In both the US and the EU, competition law was initially developed in response to issues that hindered the country or continent from realizing and pursuing important public values at a specific point in time. As a result, these public values were incorporated as objectives of the competition law and policy.

Specifically, as we will review next, the first federal antitrust law was passed in the US to sanction and combat economic concentration and market dysfunction. It sought to create an environment in which every citizen could undertake. Meanwhile, in the EU, one idea that inspired competition law was to create a common market within Europe.

I. The Federal US

In the case of the US federal tradition, the Sherman Act was adopted in 1890 as a response to concerns about market concentration and the power of large corporations. At the time, the US markets were dominated by trusts and collaborations among competitors, allowing them to combine their resources to create large enterprises.[14] Through these collaborations, companies could raise prices, control supply, and reduce the prices they pay for raw materials.[15] These actions impacted various economic sectors, leading to widespread dissatisfaction in the political arena as they affected the lives of customers, employees, suppliers, and competitors.[16]

---

13 The selection of these two jurisdictions is explained due to their relevance in the international antitrust and competition law debates. Many countries, especially developing ones, use the EU and the US experiences as examples for their regulation.

14 *Collins*, Trusts and the Origins of Antitrust Legislation, 81 Fordham Law Review (2013), 2279, 2315.

15 *Collins* (n 14) 2334.

16 *Collins* (n 14) 2335.

As a result of this social context, Congress passed the Sherman Act, a federal law against the trust ("antitrust law"). The legislative history of the Sherman Act strongly suggested that the distrust of the perceived power of the giant trusts was the main reason that gave birth to the statute.[17] Above all, members of Congress "*reflected the concern of the people with the perceived power and greed of the trusts, with the exploitation of those who dealt with the trusts, and with the demise of the small industrial proprietor*".[18] Accordingly, the Sherman Act was motivated by at least three goals[19]: (i) the distribution of political economic power, (ii) the prevention of unjust wealth transfers from consumers and small suppliers to large entities, and (iii) the preservation of open markets. Therefore, "*it is undeniable that a multitude of political, social, and economic concerns animated lawmakers*"[20]. Moreover, in the early years, the US Supreme Court applied the Sherman Act, reflecting this legislative history and the goal to "*protect competition for the benefit of-all -consumers, entrepreneurs, and 'the public good"*.[21]

A few years later, in 1914, the Clayton Act was passed. It condemned several exclusionary conducts. This law looked to prevent "*big businesses fencing out competitors from access to markets*".[22] Economic opportunity's freedom is the fundamental idea in the Clayton Act Legislative History[23]. Later, in 1950, Congress approved the Celler-Kefauver Amendment of Clayton's Act Section 7 to prohibit all mergers that substantially lessen competition, not just the operation among direct competitors. The committee reports, and legislative debates show that Congressmen strongly believe in the adverse effects of market concentration. Indeed, there were arguments that "*concentration narrowed the opportunity to have one's own business, depressed local initiative, and civic responsibility, and diminished the scope of entrepreneurship by forcing small businesses to become ever more subject to the dictates of large concerns*".[24]

17 *Fox*, The Modernization of Antitrust: A New Equilibrium, 66 Cornell Law Review (1981), 1140, 1147.

18 *Fox* (n 17) 1148.

19 *Khan/Vaheesan*, Market Power and Inequality: The Antitrust Counterrevolution and Its Discontents, 11 Harvard Law & Policy Review (2017), 235, 279.

20 *Khan/Vaheesan* (n 19) 279.

21 *Fox* (n 17) 1148.

22 *Fox/Sullivan*, Antitrust – Retrospective and Prospective: Where Are We Coming From? Where Are We Going?, 62 New York University Law Review (1987), 936, 940.

23 *Fox* (n 17) 1149.

24 *Bok*, Section 7 of the Clayton Act and the Merging of Law and Economics, 74 Harvard Law Review (1960), 226, 236.

Further, regarding the application by the Supreme Court of the Clayton and Sherman Act during the following years, the 1960s and early 1970s, it defined competition as a process that required multiple players[25]. Nevertheless, the Supreme Court recognized that antitrust law does not have the protection of a specific company as a goal. In this context, the decision in the case "*Brown Shoe*"[26] is significant. In that case, the Supreme Court clearly stated that despite "*competition, not competitors, which the Act Protects*", they must respect Congress's decision to protect decentralization.[27]

Consequently, during this period (1940s to early 1970s), antitrust was conceived as a form of social regulation[28] that protected small companies from giant corporations to ensure everyone's freedom to engage in business. Access to the market and the protection of the competition process "*were essential in order to ensure that markets could be considered fair and providing equal opportunities to all*".[29] Some scholars have described this period as the time when an emerging view of structuralism accompanied antitrust enforcement[30]. Accordingly, "*market structure (i.e., the number, market share, and characteristics of market participants), and concentration in particular (i.e., the domination of a market by a few large firms), should be [was] the focus of antitrust intervention*"[31].

Therefore, a historical review of the origins of federal US antitrust law shows that the consumer welfare standard did not play a fundamental role in the discussion. The idea of consumer welfare and purely economic goals as the primary aim of antitrust law emerged later, particularly with the rise of the Chicago School in the late 1970s.

---

25 *Fox* (n 17) 1151.

26 (1962) Brown Shoe Co INC v United States 370 US 294.

27 "*Their expansion is not rendered unlawful by the mere fact that small independent stores may be adversely affected. It is competition, not competitors, which the Act protects. But we cannot fail to recognize Congress´s desire to promote competition through the protection of viable, small, locally owned business. Congress appreciated that occasional higher costs and prices might result from the maintenance of fragmented industries and markets. It resolved these competing considerations in favor of decentralization. We must give effect to that decision*" (1962) Brown Shoe Co INC v United States 370 US 294, 344.

28 *Lianos*, Competition Law as a Form of Social Regulation, 65 The Antitrust Bulletin (2020), 3, 14.

29 *Lianos* (n 28) 14.

30 *Francis/Sprigman*, Antitrust: Principles, Cases, and Materials, 2nd edition 2024, 21.

31 *Francis/Sprigman* (n 30) 21.

This movement originated as a response to the antitrust enforcement of the 1960s and early 1970s. The Chicago school emphasized that this enforcement had prevented companies from taking actions that would benefit consumers. According to them, enforcement aimed at non-economic goals harmed consumers, and instead, competition law should focus solely on consumer welfare and market efficiency. This movement greatly influenced the antitrust law decisions and agencies' work, especially after President Ronald Reagan's[32] elections and his agenda to reduce the government's role in business.[33] As a result, "*'the public good' has been excised as the generalized goal of antitrust. In its place is a goal called "consumer welfare"*.[34] The Chicago ideas impacted the way antitrust law was perceived. They moved away from the conception of antitrust as a tool of social regulation. They proposed an "*instrument aiming to promote economic efficiency, making heavy use of the toolkit of neoclassical economics in interpreting the law*".[35]

While some criticisms from the Chicago School may be valid, especially those pointing out that including public values beyond consumer welfare in the competition law analysis could create problems of certainty and may lead to issues of political bias in the assessment, the reality is that "*Chicagoans assert an ahistorical view of antitrust*".[36] To enact the different antitrust statutes, Congress considered values beyond efficiency that support the dispersal of power, economic opportunity, and competition, all of which deserve equal consideration.[37]

Furthermore, the fact that the Chicago School's ideas do not align with the historical perspective of the law is relevant since it fails to consider the contextual basis of competition law. While seeking a technical economic framework that allows for a more straightforward application of competition law and policy is desirable, this analytical approach will face challenges from the social environment and the constantly evolving markets.[38] The history of the US federal antitrust law has demonstrated that it serves consumer welfare and other public interest values, including economic

32 In office between 1981–1989.

33 *Kovacic*, The Antitrust Paradox Revisited: Robert Bork and the Transformation of Modern Antitrust Policy, 36 Wayne Law Review (1990), 1413, 1413.

34 *Fox/Sullivan* (n 22) 946.

35 *Lianos* (n 28) 16.

36 *Fox*, The Battle for the Soul of Antitrust, 75 California Law Review (1987), 917, 918.

37 *Fox* (n 17) 1154.

38 For example, nowadays, the eruption of new platforms and multisite markets has challenged traditional competition law analysis, forcing the revisiting of the consumer welfare approach and competition law enforcement.

diversity, market deconcentration, and competition process. From its inception, this law has served as a tool for regulators and legislators to tackle social challenges.

II. The EU

Regarding communitarian European competition law, the 1951 adoption by Belgium, France, Italy, the Federal Republic of Germany, Luxembourg, and the Netherlands of the Treaty establishing the European Coal and Steel Community (ECSC) can be highlighted as a starting point.[39] The ECSC aimed to establish a common market for coal and steel and to contribute to economic expansion, employment, and better living standards.[40] To achieve this goal, the ECSC banned, among other things, unfair competitive practices and discriminatory and other practices capable of distorting competition.[41] Within the reasons that might explain the adoption of the ECSC likely will be[42], the prohibition of discriminatory practices for guaranteeing equal access to coal and steel, and the consideration of free competition in the markets as desirable for the European economy, especially after the US success.

A few years later, a second Treaty relevant to communitarian European competition law was adopted. In 1957, Belgium, France, Italy, Luxembourg, the Netherlands, and West Germany signed the Treaty of Rome to establish the European Economic Community (ECC) and work towards integration and economic growth.[43] The ECC aimed to create a common market based on the free movement of goods, people, services, and capital. Further, the ECC has been amended several times since 1957. The relevant amendments are the Maastricht Treaty of 1992 and the Treaty of Lisbon of 2009, renamed the ECC the "Treaty on the Functioning of the European Union" (TFUE).

39 *Motta*, Competition Policy: Theory and Practice, Cambridge University Press 7th edition 2007, 13.
40 Treaty Establishing the European Coal and Steel Community, ECSC Treaty (Paris, 1951). Article 2. See https://eur-lex.europa.eu/legal-content/EN/TXT/?uri=legissum:xy0022 (accessed 30 January 2025).
41 Treaty Establishing the European Coal and Steel Community, ECSC Treaty (Paris, 1951). Article 2.
42 *Motta* (n 39) 13.
43 Treaty establishing the European Economic Community EEC (Rome, 1957) https://eur-lex.europa.eu/EN/legal-content/summary/treaty-of-rome-eec.html (accessed 30 January 2025).

The ECC established rules crucial for the development of competition law in Europe. Remarkably, the Treaty prohibited vertical and horizontal agreements that might prevent, restrict, or distort competition within the internal market and any abuse by one or more undertakings of a dominant position. Firstly, these rules were designed to sanction anticompetitive conduct. However, they were also conceived as pillars for fostering the development of a European common market. Above all, the EU competition law "*has been understood primarily as part of a program designed to achieve the specific goal of unifying the European Market*".[44]

This single market's goal resulted in European competition law and policy mainly focused on eliminating discrimination based on national grounds.[45] Accordingly, during the 1960s and 1970s, enforcement was more centered on investigating and sanctioning vertical restraints than horizontal ones[46] since vertical agreements involved a higher risk of restricting or distorting the flow of goods across national borders.[47] This concern led the Commission to challenge various agreements manufacturers and distributors use to protect domestic markets.[48] Also, during this period, the Commission aimed to support small and medium-sized enterprises (SMEs) facing international competition by encouraging collaboration among such companies.[49]

Although the revision of the ECC and the European Commission's decisions at that time made it difficult to indicate a precise and unique goal of competition law. Clearly, the idea of competition itself was not an objective, nor was consumer welfare. Instead, history shows that in its origins, communitarian European competition law pursued the market integration of the countries that signed the ECC. While some authors have viewed this goal purely as an economic one[50], it's essential to note that regardless of the macroeconomic nature of this objective, its inclusion in the law

44 *Gerber*, The Transformation of European Community Competition Law, 35. Harvard International Law Journal (1994), 97, 98.

45 *Motta* (n 39) 14.

46 *Jebsen/Stevens*, Assumptions, Goals and Dominant Undertakings: The Regulation of Competition Under Article 86 of the European Union, 64 Antitrust Law Journal (1996), 443, 458; Ezrachi, 'EU Competition Law Goals and the Digital Economy' (Oxford Legal Studies Research Paper No. 17/2018, 2018), https://ssrn.com/abstract=3191766 (accessed 30 January 2025).

47 *Gerber* (n 44) 112.

48 Case 30/78, EU:C:1980- *Distillers Co Ltd v Commission.*

49 *Gerber* (n 44) 113.

50 *Lianos* (n 28) 3–86.

demonstrates that the EU considered competition law as a tool to address a significant social concern of that time. The ECC likely "*was intended as a way to promote economic progress and the welfare of European citizens, the latter being one of the objectives of the EC[C] as stated by Article* 2".[51] Thus, communitarian European competition law has not been neutral to the social context in which it is created and applied; instead, it enables the pursuit of specific public policy goals. This is, of course, in addition to the technical nature and certainty that it must embody.

Afterward, during the 1970s and mid-1980s, the EU economy experienced a recession.[52] During this time, competition law continued to aim to promote the common market. However, the social contexts pressured the Commission to consider the economic situation when enforcing the law. This allowed competition law to address pressing needs, such as promoting job creation, as a goal of competition law intervention.[53]

Finally, during the 1990s, a movement arguing the necessity of a "modernization" of EU law arose. Reform proposals were set out in 1998, and the modernization program started in 1999.[54] This plan impacted the institutional design and the procedural and substantive EU competition law approach. Particularly regarding the objective sought by competition law, a shift from the protection of freedom to trade to the promotion of the competition process and consumer welfare occurred.[55] This new focus led to a more economical approach. Nevertheless, it is still possible to appreciate some "social" goals included in the competition law framework. For example, the EU jurisprudence limited the freedom of action of dominant undertakings since they have a "*special responsibility*" to not harm the competitive process[56]; the crisis cartels defense; or the favorable consideration of state aid given to SMEs in the form of subsidies loans and other assistance.[57]

51 *Motta* (n 39) 14.
52 Factors of the starting of OPEC affected the European economy.
53 *Gerber* (n 44) 119.
54 *Whish/Bailey*, Competition Law, Oxford University Press 7th edition 2012, 53.
55 *Fox/Gerard*, EU Competition Law: Cases, Texts and Context, Edward Elgar 2017, 13.
56 *Lianos* (n 28) 17.
57 *Motta* (n 39) 16.

III. Summary: Competition law has not been neutral to social context

The historical revision of EU and US federal competition law conducted above reveals that regulators have used competition law to pursue certain public interest values relevant to specific social contexts. Yet, arguing that competition law has been—and needs to be—"neutral" and cannot include non-economic public interest objectives is inaccurate[58]. On the contrary, revising these two jurisdictions has shown that competition law does *"not exist in a vacuum: it is an expression of the current values and aims of the society"*[59].

Further, antitrust law was mainly relevant to the maturity and development of the US and EU markets. In both jurisdictions, competition law evolved to take a more economic view, focusing on the impact on consumers—whether it was beneficial or harmful. Nonetheless, this does not contradict the fundamental role that competition law has played in the US and EU's market development, as it filled gaps that other public policies could not address (for example, to prevent market concentration). This was achieved by incorporating public interest objectives into competition law. Consequently, there is no reason to deprive today's economies of the opportunity to follow the path of maturity that markets in the US and Europe have already navigated. Institutions would need a transformation in these economies, and regulators might utilize all available tools to boost the economy, including competition law.

Therefore, a competition law solely based on theoretical and static principles and exclusively focused on the narrow consumer welfare approach limits the competition law's potential and fails to recognize the broader impact of this law in promoting public interest values. Precisely, some countries actively consider public interest values when applying competition law. Next, we will review the South Africa's case, where public interest values are explicitly included in competition law. This review aims to understand how to balance traditional efficiency with non-economic values in assessing competition law.

58 "It is a flawed and outdated approach." *Mkatshwa/Tshabalala /Phalatse*, Prioritising Gendered Public Interest Considerations in OECD, Gender Inclusive Competition Policy (OECD, 2021), 2.

59 *Whish/Bailey* (n 54) 20.

C. The South African example

I. The Reconstruction and Development Program ("RDP")

In 1994, after winning the election, the new South African government faced the challenge of transforming the country and developing a new national organization after years of apartheid discrimination and inequality. In response, the government settled the RDP, a policy instrument to guide the transformation strategy. This program was detailed in the "White Paper on Reconstruction and Development".[60]

The RDP aimed to mobilize all the country's resources toward the eradication of the apartheid's effect. It sought to build a "*democratic, non-racial and non-sexist future*"[61] for South Africa. To achieve its goals, it implemented several reforms in various sectors. These reforms led to the development of new public policies related to the fiscal sector, the functioning of the state, and the economy. Among these reforms, the RDP included competition law.[62] The government expressed its intention to review competition law to align it with new objectives and use it to transform the South African economy.

Specifically, the government planned to introduce strict antitrust regulations to create a more competitive and dynamic business environment. They aimed to establish a new institutional framework to address the historical concentration of economic power, collusive practices, and abuses of dominance.[63] According to the RDP, the primary objective of the new policy was to reduce excessive economic concentration, eliminate collusive and abusive dominance practices, and ensure the efficient participation of small and medium-sized enterprises in the economy.[64]

Finally, the new South African Competition Act ("CA")was passed in 1998.[65] The Act's preamble highlighted the ideas that inspired this new

60 South African Government, *White Paper on Reconstruction and Development* (White Paper, vol. 353 no.16085, 1994), https://www.gov.za/sites/default/files/gcis_document/201409/160850.pdf (accessed 30 January 2025).
61 South African Government (n 60) 7.
62 South African Government (n 60) 25.
63 South African Government (n 60) 25.
64 South African Government (n 60) 25.
65 The South African Competition Act has been amended several times since then. To review it visit: https://www.comptrib.co.za/legislation-and-forms/competition-act (accessed 30 January 2025).

competition law regulation. Among others, it was set as motivations (the highlight is ours):

> *"That* ***apartheid*** *and other discriminatory laws and practices of the past resulted in* ***excessive concentrations of ownership and control*** *within the national economy, inadequate restraints against anti-competitive trade practices,* ***and unjust restrictions on full and free participation in the economy by all South Africans.***
>
> *That the economy* ***must be open to greater ownership by a greater number of South Africans.*** *That credible competition law, and effective structures to administer that law, are necessary for an efficient functioning economy.*
>
> *That an* ***efficient, competitive economic environment, balancing the interests of workers, owners and consumers and focused on development, will benefit all South Africans".***

Furthermore, these public interest values were clearly reflected in the goals of competition law. According to Chapter 1, section 2 of the CA, its purposes include a mix of traditional economic objectives and non-economic ones (the highlight is ours):

> *(a) to promote the* ***efficiency, adaptability and development*** *of the economy;*
> *(b) to provide consumers with competitive prices and product choices;*
> *(c) to* ***promote employment and advance the social and economic welfare of South Africans;***
> *(d) to* ***expand opportunities for South African participation*** *in world markets and recognise the role of foreign competition in the Republic;*
> *(e) to ensure that* ***small and medium-sized enterprises have an equitable opportunity*** *to participate in the economy;*
> *(f) to promote a* ***greater spread of ownership****, in particular to increase* ***the ownership stakes of historically disadvantaged persons****; and*
> *(g) to detect and address conditions in the market for any particular goods or services, or any behaviour within such a market, that tends to impede, restrict or distort competition in connection with the supply or acquisition of those goods or services within the Republic.*

It is evident that South African regulators explicitly state the historical context and the economic impact of apartheid on a segment of the population as justification for its new competition law framework. Therefore, in the process of rebuilding and transforming the nation and its economy, competition law was viewed as a tool to help achieve these objectives.[66] Accordingly, The South African government developed a new competition law with goals beyond consumer welfare and purely economic factors. Concretely, the Competition Act includes a public interest clause establishing non-economic goals.

Since these objectives have influenced the competition law assessment conducted by the South African enforcers – the South African Competition Commission, the Competition Tribunal, and the Competition Court of Appeal – some questions have arisen. Specifically regarding how non-economic factors are considered in their competition law analyses, which analytical methods are used, and if this integration has any limitations. To answer these questions and understand how the South African model can guide us in incorporating public interest issues into competition law, we will now examine a pivotal case in the history of South African competition law: the merger between Walmart Stores, Inc. ("Walmart") and Massmart Holdings Limited ("Massmart").

II. Walmart/Massmart merger case

On September 27th, 2010, the international retailer Walmart sought to acquire 51 % of the South African retailer Massmart, a company focused on wholesale and retail selling groceries, liquor, and general merchandise.[67] It had the leading share in liquor and general merchandise sales in South African markets and was second in wholesale food.[68] Massmart was also present in other sub-Saharan countries.[69] With this merger, Walmart sought to expand its presence in emerging and attractive markets.

This transaction was reported to the South African Competition Commission ("South African Commission") because, under Chapter 3 Section 12 of the Competition Act (CA), parties involved in intermediate and large

66 *Roberts*, The role for competition policy in economic development: the South African experience, 21 Development Southern Africa (2004), 227, 227, 230–231.

67 *Walmart Stores Inc and Massmart Holdings Limited* (Case No 73/LM/Dec10) [2011] South African Competition Tribunal, [7].

68 *First/Fox*, Philadelphia National Bank, Globalization, and the Public Interest, 80 Antitrust Law Journal (2015), 307, 330.

69 *First/Fox* (n 68) 330.

mergers are required to notify the authorities. A merger is classified as intermediate or large based on the thresholds specified in a general notice made by the Minister of Economic Development in consultation with the Competition Commission. These thresholds consider the turnover and assets of the merging parties. In the case of the Walmart-Massmart operation, it represented a large transaction.[70]

Following its notification, a merger in South Africa will be approved after competition authorities (South African Commission or Competition Tribunal) have carried out a two-step analysis: First, these authorities will evaluate whether the transaction is likely to substantially restrict or prevent competition. Second, they will determine whether the transaction can be justified on public interest grounds (Chapter 3, 12A of the CA). To evaluate this last justification, the competition authorities must consider the impact that the merger will have on (Chapter 3, Section 12A (3) of the CA):

> "*(a) a particular industrial sector or region;*
> *(b) employment;*
> *(c) the ability of small and medium businesses, or firms controlled or owned by historically disadvantaged persons, to effectively enter into, participate in or expand within the market;*
> *(d) the ability of national industries to compete in international markets; and*
> *(e) the promotion of a greater spread of ownership, in particular to increase the levels of ownership by historically disadvantaged persons and workers in firms in the market.*"

Besides, the merger review process may involve various authorities. The South African Commission is responsible for the initial review of all mergers that need to be notified. In the case of large transactions, like the Walmart-Massmart merger, the South African Competition Tribunal also plays a role. After the South African Commission evaluates the transaction, it must refer the merger notice to the Competition Tribunal along with a recommendation for approval or rejection. The Competition Tribunal then conducts its review process to decide whether to approve or reject

---

70 A merger with a value at or above the higher threshold, that is, the combined annual turnover or assets of both the acquiring and transferred / target firms are valued at or above R6.6 billion, and the annual turnover or asset value of the transferred / target firm is at least R190 million.

the merger. Parties are entitled to appeal Competition Tribunal decisions directly to the South African Competition Court of Appeal.

The South African system also allows third parties to participate in merger proceedings. For instance, the Competition Act permits government ministers to participate in proceedings before the South African Commission, Competition Tribunal, or the Competition Court of Appeal to represent public interest grounds (Chapter 3, 18 (1) of CA). Additionally, the merger parties must provide a copy of the merger notice to any registered trade union that represents a substantial number of its employees, or the employees concerned, or representatives of the employees concerned (Chapter 3, 13A (2) of CA).

Within this framework, the South African Commission concluded its merger investigation on February 2nd, 2011. In the initial phase, it found that the transaction was unlikely to substantially prevent or lessen competition.[71] Then, the South African Commission conducted the merger's public interest exam. It reviewed pre-merger retrenchments at Massmart, the effect of the merger on (i) suppliers, (ii) employment, and (iii) the future terms of employment of Massmart employees, and the right to association and acceptance of unionized labor.[72] In addition, the merger faced opposition from three unions, a trade union federation, and three government ministries: the Minister of the Economic Development Department, the Minister of the Department of Trade and Industry, and the Minister of the Department of Agriculture, Forestry and Fisheries.[73] Despite this opposition, the South African Commission did not identify public interest risks in the transaction and recommended that the Competition Tribunal approve the merger without imposing any conditions.

During the process before the Competition Tribunal, the Ministry of Economy and Development voiced its opposition to the merger on the grounds that Walmart's distribution chain heavily relied on importing products that could potentially replace locally produced goods. The Ministry argued that Walmart had buying power, allowing it to buy products

71 *Walmart Stores Inc and Massmart Holdings Limited* (Case No 73/LM/Dec10) [2011] South African Competition Tribunal, [22].

72 *Walmart Stores Inc and Massmart Holdings Limited* (Case No 73/LM/Dec10) [2011] South African Competition Tribunal, [22].

73 *Walmart Stores Inc and Massmart Holdings Limited* (Case No 73/LM/Dec10) [2011] South African Competition Tribunal, [18].

overseas.[74] This approach could have a significant and detrimental impact on local trade. Additionally, trade union associations expressed concerns about the merger's potential effects on employment. They cited an apparent Walmart's international practice of low wages and the risk of job losses. To emphasize their concerns, they adopted the slogan "the high cost of low prices."[75]

Walmart and Massmart defended the transaction by highlighting its benefits for consumers, including lower prices and the creation of new jobs. Additionally, Massmart argued that the deal would enable them to acquire new skills and technologies. Walmart's expertise in business would strengthen Massmart's distribution chain, improve the variety of products available to consumers, and enhance the quality of service.

In its first step of revision (competition law assessment), the Competition Tribunal quickly concluded that the transaction was unlikely to create a risk for the competition in the market. However, when addressing public interest concerns, the Tribunal conducted a more profound examination, focusing on:

(1) Downsizing: The issue of downsizing was raised by some trade unions, prompting the Competition Tribunal to review the Walmart-Massmart plans concerning Massmart's employees. The Tribunal did not find any internal documents from the merging parties that indicated a strategy for downsizing. On the contrary, the parties intended to expand, and likely it will create new jobs. However, the Competition Tribunal noted that there was no clear evidence regarding the locations of this expansion. Ultimately, since the merging parties offered a commitment to future layoffs, the Competition Tribunal approved it anyway.[76]
(2) Reinstatement of retrenched employees: Trade unions have raised concerns regarding the 503 employees laid off by Massmart, likely due to the merger. Although the Competition Tribunal found no direct link between the reduction and the merger, it reasonably considered the

74 *Walmart Stores Inc and Massmart Holdings Limited* (Case No 73/LM/Dec10) [2011] South African Competition Tribunal, [73].
75 *First/Fox* (n 69) 332.
76 *Walmart Stores Inc and Massmart Holdings Limited* (Case No 73/LM/Dec10) [2011] South African Competition Tribunal, [39–44].

merging parties' offer to provide preferential employment opportunities to the 503 former employees.[77]

(3) Collective bargaining: The labor union presented evidence of Walmart's negative stance on collective bargaining in the U.S., especially regarding salaries. The union argued that salaries will likely be lower than the industry average after mergers. The Competition Tribunal approved a commitment regarding collective bargaining power, but this only aims to protect existing labor rights, which may be specific to the merger. The Tribunal emphasized that creating additional rights not currently enjoyed by unions was beyond the scope of this process.[78]

(4) Procurement and local suppliers[79]: The government argued that after the merger, Massmart would use Walmart's experience and logistics to expand its product range and import goods from overseas, offering lower prices than competitors. This would represent a significant shift in the industry, moving purchasing decisions away from South African manufacturers toward foreign producers, particularly those from Asia. This issue sparked relevant discussions, and various parties submitted reports from experts to the Tribunal.

The Competition Tribunal concluded that while it is difficult to assess the actual impact, the merger could change Massmart's procurement strategy, leading to an increase in overseas purchases. This shift would have the potential to transform the entire industry. However, the Tribunal noted that local suppliers will likely try to compete with these imports. The Tribunal also emphasized that this change probably will result in lower prices for consumers, and therefore, it should not impose restrictions against this objective. Finally, based on the assumption that there will be some transition from local procurement to imports after the merger, the Competition Tribunal approved the parties' commitment to support local suppliers.

77 *Walmart Stores Inc and Massmart Holdings Limited* (Case No 73/LM/Dec10) [2011] South African Competition Tribunal, [45–58].

78 *Walmart Stores Inc and Massmart Holdings Limited* (Case No 73/LM/Dec10) [2011] South African Competition Tribunal, [59–71].

79 *Walmart Stores Inc and Massmart Holdings Limited* (Case No 73/LM/Dec10) [2011] South African Competition Tribunal, [72–121].

Consequently, the Tribunal approved the transaction under certain conditions to mitigate some public interest concerns. Specifically, the merging parties agreed to the following commitments[80]:

(1) The merged entity must ensure that there are no retrenchments based on the merged entity´s operational requirements in South Africa for two years from the effective date of the transaction.
(2) When employment opportunities become available within the merged entity, the 503 previously laid-off employees will be given preference for reemployment.
(3) The merged entity must honor existing labor agreements and must continue to honor the current practice of the Massmart group with the largest representative union within the merged entity for at least three years from the transaction's effective date.
(4) The merged entity must establish a program aimed exclusively at the development of local South African suppliers, including SMMEs, funded in a fixed amount (about US 7 million) to be contributed by the merged entity and expended within three years from the effective date. In addition, a training program to train local South African suppliers on how to do business with the merged entity and Walmart had to be established.

The initial resolution was appealed by one of the trade unions (South African Commercial, Catering and Allied Workers Union, SACCAWU)[81]. Finally, in March 2012, the Competition Court of Appeals granted approval for the merger. Nonetheless, they modified condition (4) to require the parties to conduct a study of the measure's effectiveness and submit it for review within 3 months of the merger's approval and implementation.

III. Highlights from the Walmart/Massmart merger case

It is essential to remark several procedural aspects, key findings, and the reasoning employed by the Competition Tribunal and the Competition Court of Appeals during the merger review process. These elements help

80 *Walmart Stores Inc and Massmart Holdings Limited* (Case No 73/LM/Dec10) [2011] South African Competition Tribunal, order.

81 The government sought another legal strategy challenging the process before the Competition Tribunal.

clarify how South African competition law authorities defined the assessments they needed to conduct.

Regarding the procedural aspects, both merging parties and opponents made significant efforts to support their claims and fulfill the burden of proof. The evidence provided by the parties extended beyond traditional competition law concerns, such as the relevant market, product substitution, and the merger's economic efficiency. They also submitted economic reports[82] on the merger's effects related to public interest, focusing on employment, post-merger wages, and the potential impact of imports on small and medium-sized enterprises. Furthermore, during the proceedings before the Competition Tribunal, several witnesses[83] and economic experts presented oral testimony on behalf of the parties. The Competition Tribunal and the Competition Court of Appeal considered this type of evidence in their reasoning. This evidentiary aspect is significant as it demonstrates that parties must substantiate their arguments during the trial or authority's investigation. Simply referencing potential risks or benefits based on public interest grounds is insufficient.

Further, regarding the court's reasoning. The Competition Tribunal and the Competition Court of Appeal upheld the interpretation that the public interest analysis should not be conducted in a general manner. They noted that public interest considerations are not open-ended and that the CA provides specific factors to guide this assessment (Chapter 3, Section 12A (3))[84]. Therefore, the inclusion of public interest must be focused on the goals explicitly indicated by the legislator in the Competition Act.

Additionally, the Competition Tribunal stated that public interest considerations must be specific to the merger at hand. They remarked, "[*U]nless the merger is the cause of the public interest concerns, we have no remit to do anything about them. Our job in merger control is not to make the world*

82 Merging parties submitted an economic report made by Mr. Simon Baker from RBB Economics, while the Ministries submitted an economic report written by Mr. Jame Hodge from Genesis Analytics.

83 *Walmart Stores Inc and Massmart Holdings Limited* (Case No 73/LM/Dec10) [2011] South African Competition Tribunal, [19–20].

84 *Walmart Stores Inc and Massmart Holdings Limited* (Case No 73/LM/Dec10) [2011] South African Competition Tribunal, [29–30]. *Walmart Stores Inc and Massmart Holdings Limited* (Case No 110/CAC/Jul11; 111/CAC/Jun11)) [2012] South African Competition Court of Appeal, [97].

a better place, only to prevent it becoming worse as a result of a specific transaction."[85]

The Competition Tribunal acknowledges that it must consider public interest factors in its analysis. However, it notes that this power has been used cautiously. The Competition Tribunal states that since the introduction of the Competition Act, "*in no case has an adverse public interest condemned an otherwise unproblematic merger, nor has a problematic merger from a competition perspective been rescued on public interest grounds*".[86] The Tribunal highlighted that when public interest concerns arose, they were addressed by granting conditional approval for the merger, dependent on measures to mitigate specific risks.[87]

Furthermore, the Competition Court of Appeal stated that the various interests involved in assessing the merger – economic factors and public interest concerns – must be balanced through a 'proportionality exercise'. As a result, the Court concluded, "*unless the effect upon public grounds, as set out in s 12 A (3) is shown to be substantial, the court cannot employ the public interest test to disallow the merger.*"[88]

Ultimately, we saw that public interest concerns did not result in the prohibition of the merger, which had already passed the initial test of not restricting or preventing market competition. Instead, the South African competition authorities decided to impose measures on the merging parties to mitigate the risks to the public interest.

D. Considering Public interest in the competition law framework

I. Learning from the South African experience

The Walmart-Massmart case serves as a powerful example of how to analyze competition law through a public interest lens. It offers invaluable insights, especially regarding mergers and preliminary assessments. Building on its lessons, we will outline a model for conducting a preliminary

85 *Walmart Stores Inc and Massmart Holdings Limited* (Case No 73/LM/Dec10) [2011] South African Competition Tribunal, [32].

86 *Walmart Stores Inc and Massmart Holdings Limited* (Case No 73/LM/Dec10) [2011] South African Competition Tribunal, [34].

87 *Walmart Stores Inc and Massmart Holdings Limited* (Case No 73/LM/Dec10) [2011] South African Competition Tribunal, [34].

88 *Walmart Stores Inc and Massmart Holdings Limited* (Case No 110/CAC/Jul11; 111/CAC/Jun11) [2012] South African Competition Court of Appeal, [114].

competition law assessment for relevant actions proposed by companies in the market. This model will encompass both economic goals, such as the consumer welfare standard and competitive processes, as well as non-economic objectives, like job promotion.

Primarily, we will start with an outline of three important lessons learned from the South African experience.

The first lesson emphasizes the importance of having a clearly defined assessment structure established in advance. This approach aims to minimize uncertainty by creating legal provisions that offer companies and competition law authorities a clear framework. The law is likely more successful in seeking non-economic goals if "*the legal rules and frameworks for analysis are clear*".[89]

The second lesson is the necessity of undoubtedly identifying the public interest goals that the competition law seeks to achieve and determining how these goals will be integrated into the revision process. In other words, to effectively enforce regulations, competition authorities need to have specific public interest goals in mind that will guide their analysis.[90] It is advisable to avoid vague references to a general public interest clause without limitations. Instead, a detailed list like Chapter 3, Section 12A (3) of the CA should be provided.[91] Utilizing concrete and previously defined terms in competition law is crucial for enabling market participants to anticipate better the factors that competition authorities will consider during their assessments. This practice reduces the likelihood of unexpected decisions and highlights the importance of clarity and predictability in competition law enforcement.

Finally, a third important lesson is that any assessment should include a "proportionality exercise."[92] In this process, authorities must weigh the risks and efficiencies of competition law against public interest concerns and benefits. Only a significant impact on public interest should justify

---

89 *Fox*, Equality, Discrimination, and Competition Law: Lessons from and for South Africa and Indonesia, 41:2 Harvard International Law Journal (2000), 579, 594.

90 *Fox* (n 89) 594.

91 "The limited scope of the PICS [Public interest considerations] seeks to set a clear distinction between industrial policy considerations that are caught by the Act and those that are not." *Mkatshwa/Tshabalala/Phalatse* (n 58) 19.

92 *Walmart Stores Inc and Massmart Holdings Limited* (Case No 110/CAC/Jul11; 111/CAC/Jun11) 1) [2012] South African Competition Court of Appeal, [100] and *Mkatshwa/Tshabalala/Phalatse* (n 58) 20.

prohibiting an action that might otherwise be neutral or even beneficial for the markets.[93]

II. Vision against the inclusion of public interest consideration in competition law

Further, before explaining the model in depth, it is necessary to briefly review three typical arguments against including public interest considerations in competition law. This review will help us enhance the model's effectiveness.

Firstly, critics argue that the definition of a public interest objective can be too broad, making it difficult for authorities to determine its specific content. Furthermore, this concept may evolve over time[94], leading to legal uncertainty and populism.[95] As a result, *"[t]heir inclusion therefore creates risks of legal uncertainty and unpredictability in the enforcement of competition law."*[96] To address this criticism, any model that includes non-economic goals should clearly define these objectives in advance within the legal framework. Additionally, agencies can issue guidelines to provide clarity and facilitate a deeper understanding of these considerations.[97] Moreover, "*the boundaries of competition law enforcement should also be clear and limiting principles to state intervention developed in order to avoid the dominance of politics over the marketplace.*"[98]

Secondly, there is a concern, particularly in the context of South Africa, that "*giving priority to the specified public interest categories can serve to undermine the primary competitive analysis in mergers, thus harming the*

93 *Mkatshwa/Tshabalala/Phalatse* (n 58) 20.

94 Organisation for Economic Co-operation and Development OECD (n 12) 4.

95 To Carl Shapiro, three camps are now engaged in a debate over the Future of Antitrust; one of them is the "Populist": "They favor deconcentrating the economy to reduce that power and thereby open up opportunities for small businesses, benefit workers, and lessen racial and economic inequities. They favor simple, bright-line rules and are highly skeptical of the role of economics and expertise in antitrust. They see the consumer welfare standard, which is deeply embedded in antitrust case law, as fundamentally flawed". *Shapiro*, Antitrust: What Went Wrong and How to Fix It, 35 Antitrust No. 3 (2021), 33, 34.

96 Organisation for Economic Co-operation and Development OECD (n 12) 6.

97 Organisation for Economic Co-operation and Development OECD (n 12) 6.

98 *Lianos* (n 28) 84.

broad 'public interest' that competition policy aims to promote."[99] To mitigate this risk, it is crucial for authorities to focus their analysis on substantial and relevant public interest considerations.[100]

Thirdly, some argue that competition authorities may not be best equipped to evaluate public interest issues[101], suggesting that other legal bodies may be more suited to handle such matters.[102] To address this concern, when competition authorities incorporate public interest considerations into their assessments, they should coordinate their actions with other regulatory and administrative bodies within the country.

The criticisms and potential solutions outlined above will be essential in shaping the model proposed in this paper. The model described next is based on several key principles: (i) the necessity of having a clear understanding of the public interest; (ii) changes to traditional competition assessments should only occur when there are substantial public interest considerations; (iii) it is essential to ensure predictable outcomes for market participants; and (iv) mandatory collaboration is required between the competition authority and other state agencies.

III. Model for a preliminary competition law assessment including non-economic considerations

This paper proposes the following model for a preliminary assessment of relevant[103] acts intended by parties in the market:

---

99 *Balkin/Mbikiwa*, South Africa: 'Have The Competition Authorities Correctly Applied The Public Interest Test In The Competition Act?', (Mondaq, 2014), https://www.mondaq.com/southafrica/antitrust-eu-competition-/292878/have-the-competition-authorities-correctly-applied-the-public-interest-test-in-the-competition-act (accessed 30 January 2025).

100 *Balkin/Mbikiwa*, (n 99).

101 ICN, *Merger Working Group: Analytical Framework Sub-group, The Analytical framework for merger control*, (Office of Fair Trading, London, Final paper for ICN annual conference, 2002), 14.

102 "[A]ntitrust law and antitrust institutions are ill suited to directly address concerns associated with the political power of large corporations or other public policy goals such as income inequality or job creation." *Shapiro*, Antitrust in a time of populism, 61 International Journal of Industrial Organization (2018), 714, 714.

103 By relevant, we refer to acts or contracts that likely will overcome each national threshold (turnover or assess).

The first step should be **competition law application in its traditional form.**[104] Authorities can utilize existing tools to assess whether the intended action poses any risk to competition in the market. This screening aims to determine if the act will likely impact consumer welfare, the competitive process, or other economic objectives that competition law aims to achieve. There are two possible outcomes from this analysis:

(1) The act likely will not substantially restrict or prevent competition in the market. If this condition is met, authorities should move on to the second part of the test, which involves assessing whether the act poses any risk to the public interest.
(2) The act does significantly restrict or prevent competition in the market. In this case, it is important to analyze whether that restriction can be justified by a public interest objective.

Regarding situation (1), if an intended action does not significantly restrict or prevent competition in the market – similar to the Walmart-Massmart merger case – authorities should evaluate whether it poses any risks to public interest objectives. For instance, they would consider its impact on job creation or local suppliers. One possible outcome of this assessment is that the action may not raise any public interest concerns either. If this is the case, the intended action by the parties should be approved without any conditions.

When risks to the public interest are identified, as seen in the Walmart-Massmart merger case, it would be prudent to approve the action on the condition that parties must implement effective measures to mitigate these risks. This approach allows the parties involved in the act or action to proceed, enabling them to reap benefits while minimizing any negative impacts on public interest goals.

The South African case illustrates that it is more effective to implement tailored measures that reduce risks to public interest objectives instead of completely prohibiting an act that could benefit the market. This strategy seems to strike an optimal balance between the traditional objectives of competition law and the public interest.

In situation (2), we face a more complex challenge. If an action significantly restricts or hinders competition in the market, the competition authority is likely to block it, prioritizing objectives such as consumer welfare and the competitive process. However, in a framework that considers public

104 Organisation for Economic Co-operation and Development OECD (n 12) 116.

interest concerns in competition law revision, the authority must grapple with the difficult task of approving an action based solely on public interest grounds.

To address this issue, an action should only be justified and approved on public interest grounds if it represents a unique solution to a specific public interest concern. If there is a less restrictive alternative that achieves the same public interest benefits without harming competition, or if the action is not tailored specifically for the public interest issue at hand, then it should not be permitted. In such cases, authorities should explore other, less restrictive options to achieve the public interest goals. In other words, sacrificing competition in the market is unjustifiable when other viable alternatives exist to pursue public interest objectives. Also, this is a way that allows authorities to define whether the public interest consideration is substantial (see *supra*.D.II). Thus, if there are other tools to aim it, the public interest consideration will be unsubstantial for this model.

Finally, it is essential to consider whether the authority conducts an examination under hypothesis (1) or (2), they face the significant challenge of assessing and measuring the potential harm or benefits to the public interest resulting from a specific action. To simplify this assessment, as illustrated by the Walmart-Massmart case, it is crucial to establish clear rules regarding the burden of proof for the parties involved. Companies wishing to undertake the act or action under review must provide competition authorities with evidence and econometric tools to facilitate a more precise and accurate evaluation and estimation of public interest concerns.[105]

Additionally, in any analysis, competition authorities should give special consideration to sector regulators. Collaborating with other administrative authorities is crucial for maintaining a balanced system in which regulations and authority decisions are effective. This is particularly important because public interest concerns often span various areas. Regulators are typically better positioned and possess more information than competition authorities to make decisions regarding public policy in these domains.

105 "The determination of the appropriate remedy is heavily guided by the evidence presented by the intervenors rising concerns" *Mkatshwa/Tshabalala/Phalatse* (n 58) 21.

E. Final remarks

Competition law is not a legal framework that can be separated from its social context. Contrary to the classical perspective derived from Chicago School ideas, this article contends that competition law pursues objectives beyond mere consumer welfare or competitive processes. The origins of competition law in both the United States and the European Community illustrate that these legal systems have incorporated non-economic objectives and public interest values as part of their competition law goals.

The article argues that "*antitrust law does not exist as a Platonic ideal out there for us to find. Rather it is for us to design.*"[106] This capacity to create context-based competition law is essential for countries aiming to achieve both economic and non-economic goals, ultimately impacting their development and enabling economic growth. The experiences of developing countries have demonstrated various approaches instead of relying on a single model.[107]

The article also explores how non-economic or public interest factors can be integrated into competition law regulations, using South African legislation as a model. In South Africa, the inclusion of public interest considerations in competition law was not solely a response to the legacy of Apartheid and its effects on the economy and society; it also served as a powerful instrument for the country's reconstruction and transformation through competition law.

Additionally, this paper reviews a pivotal case in South African competition law: the Walmart-Massmart merger case. This case illustrates how competition law and public interest considerations have been factored into regulatory decisions regarding mergers. The South African experience suggests a framework for the initial assessment of competition law, where authorities must carefully balance both economic and non-economic objectives in their regulations.

Based on the South African experience, the paper proposes a clear approach to integrating public interest values into competition law. It presents a model for evaluating any intended actions by companies, encompassing both traditional competition law objectives and public interest concerns.

---

106 *Ezrachi/Stucke*, The Fight Over Antitrust's Soul, 9 Journal of European Competition Law & Practice (2017), 1, 2.

107 *Roberts* (n 66) 231.

According to this model, the process should begin with a traditional review of competition law to determine if the intended action will significantly prevent or restrict competition in the market. Only after addressing this question should authorities proceed to the second part of the review: examining whether the action harms any public interest value or if there is a justification for the act based on public interest grounds.

Additionally, the article emphasized that for any model assessing actions in the context of competition law and public interest, it is essential for the law to clearly specify in advance which specific public interest goals should guide competition law and the authorities in their evaluations. Competition policy is frequently viewed as a tool to achieve goals like pluralism and fairness.[108] However, caution is essential. In South Africa, the Competition Tribunal and the Competition Court of Appeal have approached public interest consideration with great care. They design tailored measures in collaboration with sector regulators, but only when the potential risks to market competition are justified by a unique public interest benefit gained from the merger.

This caution underscores the complexity of the issues and the challenges involved in achieving socio-political values through competition policy. It is also important to remember that competition law alone does not solve all public interest issues facing a nation. Rather, a country should have a diverse toolkit available to foster its economy, with competition law being a part of that broader strategy. As it has been remarked in the last OECD Global Forum of competition (2024), "*there are tasks that competition law can and cannot do well (...) competition law can do something significant about keeping markets open, thus enhancing mobility and helping people and firms without power. Competition law can directly help promote equality of opportunity, empowering people and giving them a better chance.*"[109]

108 *Organisation for Economic Co-operation and Development OECD, Secretariat,* The Objectives of Competition Law and Policy and The Optimal Design of a Competition Agency, 5 OECD Journal of Competition Law and Policy (2003), 7, 9.

109 Fox. *Competition and Inequality, Background Note* (OECD, Paris, Global Forum on Competition, Session 1, 2004), 13 https://one.oecd.org/document/DAF/COMP/GF(2024)5/en/pdf (accessed 30 January 2025).

What is Fairness?

Reflections on the Concept of Fairness in European and Austrian Competition Law

Christiane Wakonig[*]

A. Introduction

In the ongoing discourse regarding the purpose of competition law and the consideration of non-economic factors therein, one factor particularly stands out: fairness.

The notion of "fair" competition law has been increasingly invoked in debates about European competition policy.[1] There, *Margrethe Vestager* during the time she served as Commissioner for Competition repeatedly recurred to the importance of fairness as a basis for and motivation of EU competition law,[2] and revived the term fairness *"by consistently referring to it in her public statements"*.[3] This resulted in discussions about how

* Christiane Wakonig works as a Case Handler at the Austrian Federal Competition Authority. The views expressed in this paper are strictly personal.

1 Cf *Dunne,* Fairness and the Challenge of Making Markets Work Better, 84 The Modern Law Review (2020), 230; cf *Kokott/Dittert* Das Konzept der Fairness im europäischen Wettbewerbsrecht, in Kokott/Pohlmann/Polley (eds.), Europäisches, Deutsches und Internationales Kartellrecht Festschrift für Dirk Schroeder, Verlag Dr. Otto Schmidt KG 1st edn. 2018, 407.

2 Cf for instance *Vestager*, 'Fairness and competition' (Speech at the Global Competition Law Centre Annual Conference) (25.1.2018), https://wayback.archive-it.org/12090/20191129212136/https:/ec.europa.eu/commission/commissioners/2014-2019/vestager/announcements/fairness-and-competition_en (accessed 30 January 2025).

3 *Laitenberger*, 'Fairness in EU competition law enforcement' (Speech at the British Chamber of Commerce EU & Belgium) (20.6.2018), https://competition-policy.ec.europa.eu/about/news/competition-speeches-archive-1995-2020-2020-01-01_en (accessed 30 January 2025); see also *Gerard*, Fairness in EU Competition Policy: Significance and Implications, 9 Journal of European Competition Law and Practice (2018), 211, who credits Vestager *"for spurring a renewed interest for fairness in today's policy discourses"*.

"*Vestager's 'fairness' mantra rattles through EU competition law*".[4] It has even been proposed to name a new school, the '*Vestager School*' after her.[5] Similarly, also academia increasingly advocated to consider non-economic factors within competition law.[6] Those discussions especially evolved around the question whether to consider fairness within competition law,[7] leading to extensive debates about the term in competition law academia[8] and prompting scholars to state that fairness "*in antitrust has been a relentless bone of contention.*"[9] Moreover, national competition authorities include the term "fairness" in their logo or announce that their activities will be guided by fairness.[10] Alongside these discussions, fairness has been established as an objective in recent European legislative and policy acts. Those acts contain the term fairness not only in their text but also in their title.[11]

4 *Crofts/Newman/Panichi*, 'Margrethe Vestager and EU Competition Law' MLex Insight (Podcast) (23 March 2017), https://mlexmarketinsight.com/news-hub/podcasts/podcast-margrethe-vestager-and-eu-competition-law (accessed 30 January 2025).

5 *Volmar/Helmdach*, Protecting consumers and their data through competition law? Rethinking abuse of dominance in light of the Federal Cartel Office's Facebook Investigation, 14 European Competition Journal (2018), 195, 204.

6 For an overview over the ongoing discourse, see for example *Scharf*, Datenmissbrauch im Kartellrecht, LexisNexis ARD ORAC 1st edn. 2018, 190 et seqq.

7 Cf *Kokott/Dittert* (n 1), 407 who reflect that there is to be a more pressing need to discuss fairness-problems publicly and to solve them adequately or *Lamadrid de Pablo*, Competition Law as Fairness, 8 Journal of European Competition Law & Practice (2017), 147 who detects that "*Recently, a popular view has emerged calling for greater competition law enforcement to pursue different objectives.*" or *Dunne* (n 1), 233 who refers to the equivalent debate – the hipster anti-trust movement – occurring "*across the Atlantic*".

8 For example, the Global Competition Law Centre (GCLC) focused on the significance and implications of fairness in competition law and policy in its 13th annual conference in Brussels on 25 January 2018.

9 *Marco Collino*, The Antitrust F Word: Fairness Considerations in Competition Law, 5 Journal of Business Law (2019), 332.

10 See e.g. prominently the logo of the German Bundeskartellamt "Offene Märkte – **Fairer** Wettbewerb" (eng. „open
markets – **fair** competition") and the motto of the Austrian Ferderal Competition Authority "...weil es uns um **fairness** geht" (eng. "**fairness** matters") (emphases added).

11 Cf Regulation (EU) 2022/1925 of the European Parliament and of the European Council of 14 September 2022 on contestable and **fair** markets in the digital sector and amending Directives (EU) 2019/1937 and (EU) 2020/1828 (Digital Markets Act) [2022] OJ L 265, Regulation (EU) 2019/1150 of the European Parliament and of the European Council on promoting **fairness** and transparency for business users of online intermediation services, L 186/57 [2019] OJ L 186 (P2B Regulation) and Directive (EU) 2019/633 of the European Parliament and of the European Council of 17 April 2019 on **unfair** trading practices in business-to-business relationships in

However, while the concept of fairness has – according to some – "*always been a value underpinning EU competition law and its enforcement*"[12] and even is explicitly mentioned within the context of EU competition law,[13] it is still unclear what this concept encompasses exactly or what "fairness" as a legal term explicitly means.[14] Therefore, and in the absence of a definition, fairness has been deemed "*not an operational concept* [that] *needs to be translated into more specific rules, standards and tests underpinned by the law, the jurisprudence, economic analysis and the painstaking establishment of the facts of each case.*"[15] Applying the concept of fairness in practice, therefore, proves difficult and could have negative repercussions concerning legal certainty.[16]

Against the backdrop of these considerations and the discussions on the concept of fairness in European competition law, this paper aims to add new perspectives to the current discourse and to provide a more precise explication of the concept of fairness in European competition law. Therefore, the paper first discusses how fairness is currently understood in European competition law, academia and jurisprudence by identifying and categorizing the various points of view. It then analyses the Austrian legislation and its specific provisions in terms of how they incorporate fairness and how Austrian competition law relates to the identified categories. Thereafter, it will be discussed how these fairness considerations help to gain a more concrete understanding of the concept of fairness in general. For this reason, special focus will be placed on the Austrian Federal Cartel Act,[17] the Austrian Federal Act Against Unfair Competition[18] and the Austrian Federal Fair Competitive Conditions Act.[19]

---

the agricultural and food supply chain [2019] OJ L 111 (UTP Directive) (emphases added).

12 *Laitenberger* (n 3).

13 Art 102 TFEU describes an abusive practice as one which directly or indirectly imposes **unfair** purchase or selling prices or other **unfair** trading practices (emphases added).

14 Cf *Dunne* (n 1), 231; cf *Kokott/Dittert* (n 1), 407; cf *Lamadrid de Pablo* (n 7), 147.

15 *Gerard* (n 3), 211.

16 Cf *Kokott/Dittert* (n 1), 407 et seq.

17 In German: Bundesgesetz gegen Kartelle und Wettbewerbsbeschränkungen.

18 In German: Bundesgesetz gegen den unlauteren Wettbewerb.

19 In German: Bundesgesetz zur Verbesserung der Nahversorgung und der Wettbewerbsbedingungen.

B. The Notion of "Fairness" in European Competition Law, Academia and Jurisprudence

When interpreting the term "fairness" both European primary and secondary law must be considered. While EU primary competition law mentions the term "fairness" infrequently,[20] secondary legislative acts, such as the ECN+ Directive[21], the Digital Markets Act[22], the UTP Directive[23] or the P2B Regulation[24] mention fairness at various points. However, neither EU primary nor secondary law contain an authoritative definition of what exactly fairness means or what it encompasses. The CJEU – with regards to a definition of the term "fairness" – refrains from articulating a coherent vision as well, however, generally favoring a more conservative understanding, i.e. in alignment with the more economic approach.[25]

Although there have been attempts trying to define the concept of fairness, a considerable amount of uncertainty remains, leaving the concept of fairness relatively vague.[26] It has been argued that any definition of fairness

20 The English version of the Treaty on the Functioning of the European Union (TFEU) references "fair competition" as overarching objective. Art 101 (3) TFEU calls for – among other things – "a fair share of the resulting benefits" for the consumers as requirement for an individual exemption. Pursuant to Art 102 (a) TFEU an abuse of a dominant position may consist in directly or indirectly imposing unfair purchase or selling prices or other unfair trading conditions.

21 Directive (EU) 2019/1 of the European Parliament and of the European Council of 11 December 2018 to empower the competition authorities of the Member States to be more effective enforcers and to ensure the proper functioning of the internal market [2019] OJ L 11 (ECN+ Directive).

22 Regulation (EU) 2022/1925 of the European Parliament and of the European Council of 14 September 2022 on contestable and fair markets in the digital sector and amending Directives (EU) 2019/1937 and (EU) 2020/1828 (Digital Markets Act) [2022] OJ L 265; in this context see also *Hoffmann*, Fairness in the Digital Markets Act, 8 European Papers (2023), who, in his paper, puts the notion of fairness in the Digital Markets Act into context.

23 Directive (EU) 2019/633 of the European Parliament and of the European Council of 17 April 2019 on unfair trading practices in business-to-business relationships in the agricultural and food supply chain [2019] OJ L 111 (UTP Directive).

24 Regulation (EU) 2019/1150 of the European Parliament and of the European Council on promoting fairness and transparency for business users of online intermediation services, L 186/57 [2019] OJ L 186 (P2B Regulation).

25 Cf *Dunne* (n 1), 246.

26 Cf *Kokott/Dittert* (n 1), 407; cf *Scheuerer*, The Fairness Principle in Competition-Related Economic Law, 72 GRUR International (2023), 919; cf *Schweitzer*, The Art to Make Gatekeeper Positions Contestable and the Challenge to Know What is Fair: A Discussion of the Digital Markets Act Proposal, 29 ZEuP (2021), 504, 513 who for

must presuppose a means to balance diverging interests.[27] Nonetheless, it seems that fairness "*is typically presented as an inherently subjective goal that is prone to different, ideological interpretations*".[28] It has also been noted that the decisions made by the European Commission are not based on a "fairness reasoning", but rather based on an "*assessment against the specific legal rules that have fairness as their rationale*".[29]

Competition law scholars therefore "*have displayed some discomfort towards the inherently multifaceted nature and seemingly limitless reach of fairness as an enforcement principle*"[30]. While it seems that "*a fairness-deprived antitrust policy* [...] *is not sufficient to control the nefarious consequences of unrestrained market power*", there is also a "*risk of unpredictability attached to fairness considerations which must be addressed to ensure legal certainty and to avoid the misuse of antitrust*".[31] Hence, it has been argued that fairness is rather a "*guiding principle* [and] *not an instrument that competition enforcers can use off the shelf to go about their work in detail*."[32]

Despite this, there are generally two aspects of competition law where the concept of fairness can be considered: the substantive aspect and the procedural aspect. While there is a wide consensus that ensuring fairness in competition proceedings is fundamental and well established (in any field of the law), the question of how the concept of fairness can be considered within the substantive assessment of competition law cases remains disputed.[33]

---

example aptly stated that "*Fairness can mean different things in different settings.*" Also in line with this is *Dunne* (n 1), 234 who describes it "*as an inherently malleable concept, meaning different things to different people*".

27 Cf *Kokott/Dittert* (n 1), 407.

28 *Lamadrid de Pablo* (n 7), 147 where he contrasts the concept of fairness to efficiency and writes that efficiency is attributed an "*aura of mathematical objectivity*" and is "*presented as a measurable benchmark to assess the economic effects of a given practice.*".

29 *Laitenberger* (n 3).

30 *Gerard* (n 3), 211.

31 *Marco Collino* (n 9), 331.

32 *Laitenberger* (n 3).

33 Cf *Kokott/Dittert* (n 1), 407; cf *Marco Collino* (n 9), 329.

I. The Procedural Aspect of the Concept of Fairness

It is well established that courts and national competition authorities, when applying competition rules, need to consider basic rules of fairness (i.e. fundamental rules of procedure).[34] Correspondent to this, procedural fairness has been characterized as being not specific to competition-related economic law. Hence, general principles of procedural fairness ("fair trial") are applied in competition law.[35] Nonetheless, several aspects of procedural fairness that are specific to competition law can be found in administrative as well as in judicial proceedings. This aspect, however, lies outside the scope of this paper. Aspects of procedural fairness that are specific to competition law will therefore only be briefly discussed in the following.

In the course of administrative proceedings, the procedural aspect becomes apparent at multiple points. For example, during procedures in Arts 101 and 102 TFEU investigations. During such, the parties are, amongst others, entitled to access the European Commission's case file[36] where the European Commission grants access to the files that have been obtained, produced and/or assembled during the course of the investigation. The parties can furthermore seek assistance from the Hearing Officer "*for* [an] *independent review* [of] *any issues regarding the effective exercise of their procedural rights which have not been resolved in prior contacts with DG Competition*".[37] The Hearing Officer – in accordance with the general mission of the Hearing Officer – safeguards "*the effective exercise of procedural rights throughout competition* [i.e. antitrust as well as merger] *proceedings*

34 Cf *Kokott/Dittert* (n 1), 408.

35 Cf *Scheuerer* (n 26), 920.

36 Cf European Commission Notice on the rules for access to the European Commission file in cases pursuant to Articles 81 and 82 of the EC Treaty, Articles 53, 54 and 57 of the EEA Agreement and European Council Regulation (EC) No 139/2004 [2005] OJ C 325.

37 *Wils*, The Role of the Hearing Officer in Competition Proceedings before the European Commission, 35 World Competition (2012), 10. On its website, the European Commission provides an overview of the proceedings as well as the parties procedural rights, cf European Commission, 'Procedures in Article 101 Investigations', https://competition-policy.ec.europa.eu/antitrust-and-cartels/procedures/article-101-investigations_en (accessed 30 January 2025) or European Commission, 'Procedures in Article 102 Investigations', https://competition-policy.ec.europa.eu/antitrust-and-cartels/procedures/article-102-investigations_en (accessed 30 January 2025).

[only] *before the Commission.*"[38] The Hearing Officer has "*depending on the procedural right and the situation concerned* [...] *decisional powers, may make a recommendation, or may report on the matter to the Competition Commissioner and to the College of Members of the Commission.*"[39] During proceedings around merger review cases, the parties procedural rights are, for example, granted during State-of-Play-Meetings[40] or in response to a Statement of Objections, when consulting the European Commission's case file. Just like in antitrust proceedings, the parties to merger proceedings can also approach the Hearing Officer.[41] In addition to the Hearing Officer, also the Union Courts safeguard adherence to these aspects.[42] Furthermore, the European Commission publishes Horizontal and Non-Horizontal Merger Guidelines ensuring that comparable cases are treated the same way (procedurally and on substance).

During judicial proceedings the following aspects of procedural fairness – understood as fundamental rules of procedure – in relation to competition law were identified: For example, the CJEU considered as an infringement of fundamental rules of procedure in cartel cases an excessive duration of the proceedings[43] or a denial of the right to access to the file.[44] Furthermore, the CJEU ruled that there are certain limits when it comes to the European Commission's investigative powers when entering premises

38 Decision 2011/695/EZ of the President of the European Commission of 13 October 2011 on the function and terms of reference of the Hearing Officer in competition proceedings, [2011] OJ L 257/29. See further *Wils* (n 37), who describes in detail the role of the Hearing Officer in antitrust and merger proceedings before the European Commission. In his paper, *Wils* (n 37) also describes that the Hearing Officer is not competent to address complaints relating to the (effective) exercise of procedural rights in proceedings before national competition authorities.

39 *Wils* (n 37), 10. The Hearing Officer can – apart from reviewing issues that the parties refer to him – also act on his own initiative, see further *Wils* (n 37), 27 et seqq.

40 European Commission, 'Competition: Merger control procedures', https://competition-policy.ec.europa.eu/document/download/8543e71c-4f88-4b37-92c5-a3ec0a0f56f1_en?filename=merger_control_procedures_en.pdf (accessed 30 January 2025).

41 European Commission, 'Competition: Merger control procedures', https://competition-policy.ec.europa.eu/document/download/8543e71c-4f88-4b37-92c5-a3ec0a0f56f1_en?filename=merger_control_procedures_en.pdf (accessed 30 January 2025).

42 Cf *Laitenberger* (n 3).

43 Cf for example Case C-40/12P, EU:C:2013:787 – *Gascogne Sack Deutschland v European Commission*, para. 97–102.

44 Cf for example Case C-109/10 P, EU:C:2011:686 – *Solvay v European Commission*, paras. 51 et seqq.

of undertakings[45] and that the European Commission has an obligation to record conducted interviews in full.[46]

II. The Substantive Aspect of the Concept of Fairness

There is an ongoing debate about how fairness can be applied in EU substantive competition law.[47] Accordingly, the concept of fairness has been approached from different angles. A review of the current literature on the topic reveals that the discussions about the substantive aspect of the concept of fairness can be categorized as follows: **1.** Fairness as an Implicit Property of Competition Law, **2.** Fairness Through Competitive Process or as an Outcome of Competition **3.** the Right to a Fair Competition.

1. Fairness as an Implicit Property of Competition Law

Generally, there seems to be a tendency to interpret the existence of competition law in itself as an expression of fairness, thereby questioning the relevance of further fairness considerations beyond that. According to some authors, the substantive aspect of fairness in competition law lies in its objective.[48] Accordingly, the goal of competition law is to safeguard a fair competitive business practice between two or more businesses, businesses and consumers and between businesses and their contractual partners. By ensuring a level playing field, the existence of competition rules in themselves are an expression of fairness. On this level playing field, every market participant has to abide by the rules; those who do not will face punishment.[49] The answer to the question as to what business practices exactly are not in accordance with these rules and therefore (un)fair proves to be

45 Cf for example Case C-583/13P, EU:C:2015:404 – *Deutsche Bahn v European Commission*, para. 23.

46 Cf for example Case C-413/14P, EU:C:2017:632 – *Intel v European Commission*, paras. 90–91, in conjunction with para. 84. This concerns any (formal and/or informal) interview.

47 Cf *Zimmer/Nittenwilm*, For whose sake, and by which means? Fairness Concepts in European Law A reflection on the occasion of recent European legislation, especially the passage of the Digital Markets Act, 30 ZEuP (2022), 820, 822.

48 Cf *Kokott/Dittert* (n 1), 410.

49 Cf *Kokott/Dittert* (n 1), 410; this suggestion of a 'level-playing-field' is rejected by Dunne, see below under 2.

somewhat more difficult.[50] Specific business practices such as price fixing cartels or other business practices that are per-se prohibited are unfair in any event. Those per-se prohibitions, however, remain the exception and should not be interpreted extensively.[51] A similar approach is followed when a distinction between fairness through antitrust and fairness in antitrust is made.[52] Fairness through antitrust ascertains – through legislation – effective competition, thus resulting in fair conditions within the market. Accordingly, fairness can be best ensured, when antitrust law is enforced effectively. Fairness in antitrust on the other hand, comprises aligning antitrust legislation with the concept of fairness. According to this approach, considering fairness when interpreting legislative acts is not disputed when the norms in question themselves mention fairness.[53] This view remains cautious, however, when considering fairness beyond that. According to another view, fairness is understood as something that "*competition law should not – and does not need to – be diverted to pursue* [...] *because it is already about fairness.*"[54] This means that "*the very notion of merit-based competition carries implicit in it a sense of fairness, understood as equality of opportunity*" and that "[f]*airness, in other words, is not an abstract standalone goal liable to divert or distort a correct enforcement of the law, but rather its natural outcome.*"[55]

2. Fairness Through Competitive Process or as an Outcome of Competition

Another distinction is made when differentiating between understanding fairness as either characterizing a process or an outcome.[56] Where EU competition law is concerned, it has been argued that there is a clear focus on the process dimension. Rivalry in the market should be decided based on the competition on the merits.[57] This view seems to be confirmed by

50 Cf *Dunne* (n 1), 235.
51 Cf *Kokott/Dittert* (n 1), 411; cf Case C-67/13P, EU:C:2014:2204 – *Groupement des cartes bancaires v European Commission*, para. 58.
52 *Heinemann*, Fairness, 6 NZKart (2018), 389.
53 For example, when Art 101 (3) refers to a „**fair** share of the resulting benefit" or Art 102 (a) TFEU refers to "**unfair** [...] prices or other trading conditions" mentioned in Art 102 (a) TFEU (emphases added).
54 *Lamadrid de Pablo* (n 7), 148.
55 *Lamadrid de Pablo* (n 7), 148.
56 Cf *Schweitzer* (n 26), 512.
57 Cf *Schweitzer* (n 26), 512.

the case law of the European courts that focuses more and more on context of an incrimination.[58] When it comes to protection of the competitive process,[59] a situation is considered not fair when a market participant's success is not based on a better performance (i.e. based on the principle of merit) but rather on competitive distortions. Conversely, it is considered fair when a market participant attains a dominant position (while not violating competition law), even if that means that other competitors are forced out of the market.[60]

On the other hand, it has been argued that – while accepting that fairness connotes at its most basic rules of 'fair play'– a fair competitive process goes beyond that and fairness "*evidently goes beyond the pursuit of equality of opportunity*",[61] thereby rejecting the idea of reducing fairness to a 'level-playing-field'. In this sense fairness "*is more fundamental and all-encompassing*".[62] Other authors link the concept of fairness with distributive justice.[63] In this context *consumers "are the most prominent such party in antitrust analysis, partly because of the 'obviousness' of a society committed to democracy protecting everyone—as everyone consumes."*[64]

3. The Right to a Fair Competition

Another view deals with the question whether there exists a right (of consumers and/or competitors to a cartelist) to a fair competition. With regards to this question, a two-step analysis is carried out that, in a first step, identifies consumers' interests and, in a second step, asks whether these interests could be protected. In this sense, a consumers' right to a fair competition could either stem from a right of consumers to property (more specifically a right to a certain amount of wealth that when being transferred from consumers to producers could be characterized as robbery) or

58 Cf *Kokott/Dittert* (n 1), 411 et seq.

59 Cf *Kokott/Dittert* (n 1), 410ff, *Schweitzer* (n 26), 512; Bundeskartellamt 28.10.2010, B2–47250-Fa-52/10, 98 et seqq.

60 Cf Case C-413/14P, ECLI:EU:C:2017:632 – *Intel Corp. v European Commission*, paras. 133 et seqq.

61 *Dunne* (n 1), 239.

62 *Dunne* (n 1), 239.

63 Cf *Ayal*, Fairness in Antitrust: Protecting the Strong from the Weak, Bloomsbury Publishing 1st edn. 2016, 28; *Zimmer/Nittenwilm* (n 47), 824 interpret this as fairness being related the result of competition.

64 *Ayal* (n 63), 28.

from a right of consumers to contractual freedom.[65] Different from that is the right of competitors. According to some, their protection appears to stem from the fact that it can serve as a tool to achieve other objects, such as consumer welfare.[66] The profit of a competitor "*is not protected as a vested right, as losing money or even going bankrupt are viewed as potential and legitimate consequences of competition.*"[67] It is, however argued, that what should be protected "*is not competitor's right to a specific result, but a right to the process.*"[68]

III. Fairness as a Legal Principle

The following paragraphs demonstrate how fairness can – following another view and in contrast to the former approaches – also be understood as a legal principle, going beyond its procedural and substantive manifestations. Detailing some of this views most relevant points, it is discribed how this legal principle can be viewed as integrating competition related economic law with societal values.[69] Generally, legal principles are understood to refer to legal norms that are "*not, not explicitly or not completely codified within a legal order, but nonetheless exist within and influence the interpretation of this legal order.*"[70] In the paragraphs below, it will therefore be first discussed how fairness fulfills the necessary criteria for a legal principle. This will be done by examining whether a fairness legal principle is theoretically convincing, generalizable and fairness-specific, both substantively and as an unwritten meta principle. Based on these interpretations, it will then be discussed how fairness can serve as incorporating societal norms into legal norms. Finally, it will be discussed how fairness, viewed as a legal principle, constitutes a "*bridge between* [competition related economic] *law and society*".[71] As such, the "Fairness Principle" has been defined to "*normatively*

65 Cf *Ayal* (n 63), 85 et seqq, 101 et seqq.
66 Cf *Zimmer/Nittenwilm* (n 47), 826.
67 *Ayal* (n 64), 117.
68 *Ayal* (n 63), 117.
69 Competition-related economic law further encompasses, according to *Scheuerer* (n 26), 920, unfair competition law, intellectual property law, trade secrecy law, contract law, data law and to a certain extent anti-discrimination law.
70 *Scheuerer* (n 26), 920.
71 *Scheuerer* (n 26), 927.

[moderate] *the interplay of state and non-state market order*[72] and to "*select [...] and enforce [...] the binding and just rules out of the sociological array of regulatory offers*".[73]

1. Fairness From a Substantive Point of View

In the first place, from a substantiative point of view, fairness can be found to be an (explicit) criterion in statutory law as well as case law within all fields of competition related economic law. It appears that all those (explicit) fairness clauses in the fields of law examined can be interpreted as them transferring societal influences into legal norms,[74] i.e. fairness norms can be "*concretized by taking recourse to extra-legal, yet inner-societal ordering mechanisms*".[75] Thereby, "fairness" displays the necessary characteristics of a (legal) principle. In antitrust law, for example, it is regarded as an appearance of fairness when the views of the market participants are considered.[76] In addition, the mode in which this "Fairness Principle" appears (i.e. taking recourse to social norms) convinces on a theoretic level. It does this by serving as a "*bridge between business ethics and economic efficiency*"[77], i.e. by defining the relevancy of societal norms in view of their social context and market impact concurrent with insights from behavioral economics, as opposed to their metaphysical moral quality.[78] Moreover, the defined principle can be generalized as all competition related economic law is influenced by societal norms.[79] Lastly, the proposed principle is also "fairness specific" in the sense that, although – similar to all general clauses incorporating non-legal factors – fairness can rather be seen as a "*special kind of general clause*".[80] First, there are general clauses that do not allow for societal norms to be considered. Second, competition-related economic law is – as opposed to other fields of law – more dynamic in the sense that it is "*more pertinently influenced and driven by societal norms*".[81] Third,

72 *Scheuerer* (n 26), 927.
73 *Scheuerer* (n 26), 932.
74 Cf *Scheuerer* (n 26), 925.
75 *Scheuerer* (n 26), 925.
76 Cf *Scheuerer* (n 26), 925.
77 *Scheuerer* (n 26), 925.
78 Cf *Scheuerer* (n 26), 925.
79 Cf *Scheuerer* (n 26), 925.
80 *Scheuerer* (n 26), 925.
81 *Scheuerer* (n 26), 925.

considering societal influences within the interpretation of fairness clauses is in line with doctrinal tradition. Last, despite the fact that societal influences also play a role in other fields of law it is "*characteristic for fairness to conduct such a reception*"[82] within competition related economic law.[83]

Applied in practice, using non-state norms (i.e. societal norms as described above) to concretize (explicit) fairness clauses in legal norms requires them to be legitimate. Depending on the approach taken, a societal norm can either be procedurally legitimate or substantively legitimate. Procedural legitimacy follows the idea that a decision – provided certain standards of how a decision is reached are met and that all relevant stakeholders are represented in the norm-setting process – can also be presumed substantively legitimate. With regards to its substantive legitimacy, a societal norm can – generally but with limitations in, for example, situations where the parties bargaining powers are distorted – be viewed as being legitimate if they are based on consent.[84] The legitimacy of a social norm can also be judged by means of their compliance with certain fundamental rights (public welfare parameter), meaning that if, for example, private companies act – as (societal-) norm setters – similar to states, they should be subjected to the same restrictions (i.e. fundamental or human rights).[85] Societal norms should then be applied in conformity with the principles of burden of proof, meaning that – when recognized and considered in a judicial proceeding – they are weighed against other arguments with their weight depending on their legitimacy.[86]

2. Fairness as an Unwritten Meta Principle

Secondly, fairness also seems to appear as an unwritten meta principle within competition related economic law. In this sense, fairness, for example, is understood to describe "*the aim of antitrust as serving society*".[87] In regard to this metaphysical character, fairness can most convincingly be interpreted as addressing the interaction between law and society.[88] Also,

82 *Scheuerer* (n 26), 925.
83 Cf *Scheuerer* (n 26), 925.
84 Cf *Scheuerer* (n 26), 930.
85 Cf *Scheuerer* (n 26), 930 et seq.
86 Cf *Scheuerer* (n 26), 931.
87 *Scheuerer* (n 26), 926.
88 Cf *Scheuerer* (n 26), 925 et seqq.

in this context, viewing fairness as a legal principle has been shown to be theoretically convincing as *"it is to a significant extent in harmony with Fairness associations in common language use, as people regularly consider fair what is in conformity with the values they are customarily used to in light of their sociological-cultural background."*[89] It is also flexible with regards to incorporating societal change and is not identical to *"purely economic paradigms"*[90] in the sense that it also recognizes the rationality of other social systems. Furthermore, it is more concrete by relating to *"factually existent, even empirically verifiable patterns of order"*.[91] Lastly, it is also generalizable and fairness-specific in the same way as described above.

As a meta principle applied in practice, the "Fairness Principle" takes into account that non-state norms exist and influence non-state actors. By way of, for example, soft law guidelines or monetary incentives, positive incentives for complying with public welfare goals are given.[92]

C. The Concept of Fairness within Austrian Competition Law

To evaluate how the concept of fairness is dealt with within Austrian competition law, three legislative acts were analyzed. The analysis especially focused on identifying clauses in which the term "fairness" has been mentioned. In addition, relevant rulings from Austrian courts were incorporated into the analysis to investigate how the concept of fairness is interpreted and applied by the courts. This paper did not focus its analysis on the various norms referring to practices that are considered unfair. While those enumerations are potentially helpful in narrowing down what can be understood as fair, conducting this analysis was deemed beyond the scope of the paper.

I. How Austrian Competition Law Incorporates Fairness

The concept of fairness can be found – to a varying extent – within the following Austrian competition law: the Federal Cartel Act (**"KartG"**), the

89 *Scheuerer* (n 26), 927.
90 *Scheuerer* (n 26), 927.
91 *Scheuerer* (n 26), 927.
92 Cf *Scheuerer* (n 26), 930.

Federal Act Against Unfair Competition ("**UWG**") and the Federal Fair Competitive Conditions Act ("**FWBG**"). These acts are connected with each other and form one unitary field of law in the sense that they all – from different angles – aim at protecting fair competition based on the merits and as a consequence influence each other.[93] While the Federal Cartel Act aims at protecting fair competition based on the merits by setting forth rules to maintain a competitive market structure, the Federal Act Against Unfair Competition aims at accomplishing this through rules of conduct for the market participants.[94] The Federal Fair Competitive Conditions Act is considered to be a supplementary law to the Federal Cartel Act. While the Federal Cartel Act addresses – among other things – dominant undertakings, the Federal Fair Competitive Conditions Act does not. Similar to the Federal Cartel Act, the other two legislative acts examined (Federal Act Against Unfair Competition, Federal Fair Competitive Conditions Act) aim at maintaining a competitive structure, furthermore, both legislative acts contain similar prohibitions. Pursuant to § 9 FWBG, the rules of the Federal Fair Competitive Conditions Act and of the Federal Act Against Unfair Competition are applied cumulatively.

In the following sections, each legislative act will be analyzed as to how the concept of fairness is incorporated.

93 Cf *Schuhmacher*, Zum Wettbewerbsverständnis im österreichischen Recht, 33 wbl (2019), 376; *Scheuerer* (n 26), 920 argues similarly when stating that the „*evaluation of a legal principle spanning several areas of law furthermore requires certainty on the teleological link between these areas, as this link is key to understanding their mutual interrelations and thus the characteristics of a potential briding principle.* [...] *"competition-related economic law" which I understand as comprising neighboring areas of economic law which in one way or another revolve around regulating competition"*. Competition-related economic law in this sense comprises amongst others antitrust law and the law against unfair competition.

94 Cf *Heidinger/Handig/Wiebe/Frauenberger/Burgstaller,* § 1 UWG, in Wiebe/Kodek (eds.), UWG Gesetz gegen den unlauteren Wettbewerb, 107 MANZ Verlag Wien 2nd edn. 2023, para. 286.

II. The Concept of Fairness in the Austrian Federal Cartel Act[95]

As part of the revision of its Federal Cartel Act, the Austrian legislator harmonized its substantive antitrust law with (then) Artt 81 and 82 TFEU.[96] However, contrary to the English version of European primary law, where the term fairness is explicitly mentioned,[97] the Federal Cartel Act does not explicitly mention the term "fair" or "fairness" anywhere in its German (i.e. authentic) version.[98] This is in line with the German translations of both Art 101 (3) and Art 102 (a) TFEU that also do not contain the term "fair".

Regarding Art 101 (3) TFEU, "fair share" is translated to "angemessene Beteiligung" in both of Art 101 (3) TFEU (German version) and § 2 (1) KartG. Interestingly, § 2 (1) KartG further specifies the "fair share"-requirement of Art 101 (3) TFEU by stating that a share is to be considered "fair" (in German: "angemessen") if it substantially contributes to an ecologically sustainable or climate neutral economy.

Regarding Art 102 (a) TFEU that speaks about "unfair purchase or selling prices or other unfair trading conditions" its German version translates the word "unfair" in line with Art 101 (3) TFEU with "unangemessen". § 5 (1) KartG,[99] however, does not use the word "unangemessen" but rather provides a specification of what should be understood by "unfair purchase or selling prices or other unfair trading conditions" by stating that these are purchase or selling prices or other conditions that deviate from those that would arise with a high probability under effective competition. It also highlights that the behavior of undertakings in comparable markets with effective competition is to be particularly taken into account.

Furthermore, despite not being explicitly mentioned, the concept of fairness becomes relevant in the context of the KartG due to the interpretation of its provisions by the courts. In connection with the abuse of a dominant

95 Bundesgesetz gegen Kartelle und andere Wettbewerbsbeschränkungen (Kartellgesetz 2005 – KartG 2005) BGBl I 2005/61.

96 Cf ErläutRV 926 BlgNR 22 GP 1.

97 I.e. Art 101 (3) TFEU, Art 102 (a) TFEU or the preamble to the TFEU.

98 I.e. especially in § 2 KartG, § 5 KartG that correspond to Art 101 (3) and Art 102 (a) TFEU, respectively.

99 § 5 (1) KartG states: „*der Forderung nach Einkaufs- oder Verkaufspreisen oder nach sonstigen Geschäftsbedingungen, die von denjenigen abweichen, die sich bei wirksamem Wettbewerb mit hoher Wahrscheinlichkeit ergeben würden, wobei insbesondere die Verhaltensweisen von Unternehmern auf vergleichbaren Märkten mit wirksamem Wettbewerb zu berücksichtigen sind*".

market position, Austrian jurisprudence – with reference to case law of the European Courts – argued that a suspension of relations, i.e. measures necessary to protect its business interests, by a dominant undertaking can be objectively justified. This is the case if those measures are fair and proportionate to the threat.[100] For example, the suspension of relations can be objectively justified, i.e. are fair and proportionate, with regards to the other parties willingness to pay, ability to pay or in case of a serious breach of contractual obligations by the other contractual party,[101] inability to deliver[102] or lack of customer satisfaction.[103]

Moreover, the notion of fairness influenced Austrian competition policy. When transposing the Damages Directive[104] the ministerial proposal for the act amending the Federal Cartel Act[105] suggested revisions following the goal in the governments accord of creating fair rules for competition.[106]

III. The Concept of Fairness in the Federal Act Against Unfair Competition[107]

The concept of fairness is most obviously dealt with by the law against unfair competition: by establishing rules of conduct for market participants, the law against unfair competition intends to create a framework where fair competition is possible.

---

100 Cf, among other decisions, OGH 15.05.2000, 16 Ok 1/00, where the Austrian Supreme Court ruled that "*Ein marktbeherrschendes Unternehmen ist immer berechtigt, die zum Schutz seiner Geschäftsinteressen erforderlichen Maßnahmen zu ergreifen. Diese Maßnahmen müssen jedoch* ***fair*** *sein* ***und*** *in einem* ***angemessenen*** *Verhältnis zu der Bedrohung stehen.*" (emphases added).

101 Cf OGH 17.7.1997, 16 Ok 22/97.

102 Cf KG 6.11.2009, 29 Kt 13, 14/08.

103 Cf OGH 19.3.2013, 4 Ob 205/12v.

104 Directive 2014/104/EU of the European Parliament and of the European Council of 26 November 2014 on certain rules governing actions for damages under national law for infringements of the competition law provisions of the Member States and of the European Union.

105 Bundesgesetz, mit dem das Kartellgesetz 2005, das Wettbewerbsgesetz und das Bundesgesetz zur Nahversorgung und der Wettbedingungen geändert werden (Kartell- und Wettbewerbsrechts-Änderungsgesetz – KaWeRÄG 2017) BGBl I 2017/56.

106 Cf ErläutRV 1522 BlgNR 25. GP, 1, where the German wording reads as follows: „***Faire*** *Spielregeln für Wettbewerb schaffen*" 248/ME XXV (emphasis added).

107 Bundesgesetz gegen den unlauteren Wettbewerb 1984 – UWG BGBl 1984/448.

At the European Level, the UCP Directive[108] is of great importance. Art 3 defines the scope of the Directive and restricts its application to unfair business-to-consumer commercial practices. Although businesses are not directly protected, the Directive still "*indirectly protects legitimate businesses from their competitors who do not play by the rules in this Directive and thus guarantees fair competition in the fields coordinated by it.*"[109] The reason for this lies within the weaker position of consumers in relation to companies from an economic as well as a legal point of view.[110]

In Austria, the legislative act containing norms against unfair competition is the Federal Act Against Unfair Competition. In contrast to the UCP Directive, the Federal Act Against Unfair Competition widens its scope beyond the protection of unfair business-to-consumer practices and prohibits unfair business practices towards other businesses as well. Since there is no definition of the protective purpose within the Federal Act Against Unfair Competition, its protective purpose has rather been established by the courts and legal scholars.

Fair competition as understood by the Federal Act Against Unfair Competition is safeguarded by provisions that prohibit unfair business practices in specific situations (§§ 7, 9 UWG), through a general clause (§ 1 UWG) and a list of business practices that are per se unfair (Annex to the Federal Act Against Unfair Competition listing commercial practices that are in all circumstances considered unfair).

IV. The Concept of Fairness in the Federal Fair Competitive Conditions Act[111]

The Federal Fair Competitive Conditions Act, formerly titled "Nahversorgungsgesetz", has been in force for quite some time, but its significance

108 Directive 2005/29/EC of the European Parliament and of the European Council of 11 May 2005 concerning unfair business-to-consumer commercial practices in the internal market and amending European Council Directive 84/450/EEC, Directives 97/7/EC and 2002/65/EC of the European Parliament and of the European Council and Regulation (EC) No 2006/2004 of the European Parliament and of the European Council ('Unfair Commercial Practices Directive') [2005] OJ L 149.

109 Unfair Commercial Practices Directive (n 108), Recital 8.

110 Cf Case C-59/12, ECLI:EU:C:2013:634 – *BKK Mobil Oil Körperschaft des öffentlichen Rechts v Zentrale zur Bekämpfung unlauteren Wettbewerbs eV.* para. 35.

111 Bundesgesetz zur Verbesserung der Nahversorgung und der Wettbewerbsbedingungen (Faire-Wettbewerbsbedingungen-Gesetz FWBG) BGBl 1977/392.

has been doubted.[112] On various occasions, there have been voices in literature demanding its abolition.[113] However, the transposition of the UTP Directive[114] in the Federal Fair Competitive Conditions Act lead, amongst others, to its increasing importance and was also of significance for the concept of fairness in this legal act. With this directive, the Federal Fair Competitive Conditions Act has, for example, been renamed and now contains the term "fair" in its title. Its norms are aimed at regulating contractual relationships that are characterized by an imbalance. The Federal Fair Competitive Conditions Act, therefore, aims at counterbalancing this imbalance by protecting the "weaker" contractual party from conduct by the "stronger" contractual party that is perceived as unfair. In this sense, the Federal Fair Competitive Conditions Act focuses primarily on regulating the behavior of businesses that fall within the scope of its application and not so much on protecting competition (or a specific market structure) as such.[115] With regards to an earlier version of the Federal Fair Competitive Conditions Act, the Austrian Supreme Court ruled that the aim is to maintain a fair competition and a certain competition standard characterized by the existence of many small and medium-sized businesses.[116] The Austrian Supreme Court furthermore ruled, also with regards to an earlier version of the Federal Fair Competitive Conditions Act, that it contains provisions that correspond to the provisions of the Federal Cartel Act. The provisions dealing with exploitation and discrimination specify in greater detail how businesses that do not have market power cannot behave. By its wording, those provisions apply to all businesses and not only to companies with market power.[117]

---

112 Cf *Wolf-Posch,* Vor § 1 FWBG, in Egger/Harsdorf-Borsch (eds.), Kartellrecht Kommentar, Linde Verlag 1st edn 2022, para. 1 where, according to her, the statement "*Totgesagte leben länger.*" applies to the FWBG as well.

113 For example *Reidlinger/Nageler*, Gleichbehandlung für Alle? Weg mit dem Nahversorgungsgesetz!, 2 ÖZK (2009), 47.

114 Directive (EU) 2019/633 of the European Parliament and of the European Council of 17 April 2019 on unfair trading practices in business-to-business relationships in the agricultural and food supply chain, O. J. 2019 L 11, 59.

115 Cf *Wolf-Posch* (n 110), Vor § 1 FWBG para. 6, where she describes the aim of the Federal Fair Competitive Conditions Act.

116 Cf OGH 21.2.2003, 4 Ob 210/02i, where in in its authentic wording the decision states *„dass das NahVersG den leistungsgerechten Wettbewerb schützt und einen bestimmten Wettbewerbsstandard erhalten will, der durch die Existenz vieler mittlerer und kleinerer Unternehmen gekennzeichnet ist.“*

117 Cf OGH 12.07.2018, 16 Ok 1/18k (16 Ok 2/18g), para. 15.1 et seqq.

The term "good commercial conduct" is of significant importance within the Federal Fair Competitive Conditions Act, as practices that deviate from it and are likely to endanger fair competition are prohibited. Within the FWBG, there is no definition as to what is to be understood by good commercial practices, leaving it open to interpretation. As tools for interpretation serve, for example, the fairness catalogue[118] by the Austrian Federal Competition Authority. This catalogue is not legally binding. However, it aims at facilitating the assessment of behavior that is contrary to good commercial practices.[119]

Furthermore, § 5d FWBG provides for a so-called point of initial contact ("Fairness-Büro"). Its intention is to resolve conflicts unbureaucratically. There, suppliers can anonymously and confidentially submit complaints about unfair trading practices.

D. Analysis of the Austrian Concept of Fairness in Light of the European Fairness Discourse

I. Procedural and Substantive Fairness Aspects

The analysis of the concept of fairness within certain provisions of Austrian competition law revealed that there are both procedural and substantive aspects to be considered. Procedural fairness, however, is not specific to competition law but rather relevant in any field of law [see B.I.]. This aligns with the European discourse on the concept of fairness [see B.].

In contrast, the substantive fairness aspects, especially within the provisions of the Austrian Federal Cartel Act revealed that the term "fairness" is rarely mentioned [see C.I.1.]. These scarce (explicit) citations of the term "fairness" could suggest that the Federal Cartel Act falls under the category that argues for fairness being an implicit property of competition law [see B.II.1.], i.e. that the existence of competition law as such is an expression of fairness. However, with § 2 (1) KartG [C.II.], the Austrian legislation adds to the substantive meaning of fairness by introducing the notion that fairness contains ecological sustainability, which can be generalized to serving the greater good of society.

118 Cf *Austrian Federal Competition* Authority, Fairnesskatalog für Unternehmen – Standpunkt für unternehmerisches Wohlverhalten (Leitfaden 2022).

119 Cf *Austrian Federal Competition Authority* (n 118), 7.

Additionally, the Federal Act Against Unfair Competition extends its provisions to practices between businesses [see C.III.] and thus introduces a new substantive component into the concept of fairness. The Federal Cartel Act and the Federal Act Against Unfair Competition both regulate fair competition, albeit from different perspectives [see C.]. Since the Federal Act Against Unfair Competition extends its scope of application to practices between businesses and also aims at protecting a fair competition based on the merits, it should be considered to take into account the provisions of the Federal Act Against Unfair Competition and their understanding of fairness to concretize the substantive concept of fairness in competition law.

II. Legal Principal

Analyzing the provisions of the Austrian Federal Cartel Act [see C.II.], the Federal Act Against Unfair Competition [see C.III.] and the Austrian Federal Fair Competitive Conditions Act [see C.VI.] revealed that the concept of fairness found within Austrian competition law displays parallels to the above-mentioned category that argues for a "Fairness Principle" [see B.III]. These parallels will be discussed in the following.

1. The Substantive Benchmark Characteristic of the Fairness Principle

Regarding the substantive benchmark characteristic of the proposed Fairness Principle [see B.III.1.], the following observations with respect to the Austrian competition law could be made:

The term "fair" in Art 102 (a) TFEU (in its English version) is seen to focus on an interpretation in economic terms,[120] which is in line with the German translation of Art 102 (a) TFEU, as well as § 5 (1) KartG. However, besides the clear economic mode in which fairness appears in these provisions, § 5 KartG leaves room for the "Fairness Principle" on a substantive level. This is because § 5 KartG states that the behavior of market participants (i.e. the societal norms of their behavior) in comparable markets must be used to judge whether a trading condition is fair or not. This is in line with the interpretation that the "Fairness Principle" takes recourse to clear observable ordering structures (i.e. societal norms) of

120 Cf *Dunne* (n 1), 246.

market participants to judge whether a behavior is fair or not, and that extra-legal factors are incorporated into law.

As mentioned [see C.II.], Austrian jurisprudence ruled that, while dominant undertakings are allowed to pursue measures to protect their own business interests, these measures must be fair and proportionate (i.e. German "fair" and "angemessen", respectively). In this context it is relevant to note that here, the Austrian courts refer to the term "fair" in conjunction with "angemessen". So far, the term "angemessen" has been used in the German version of the TFEU, as well as in § 2 (1) KartG to translate the English word "fair", thereby especially highlighting the economic understanding of this term within these clauses. From this, it can be concluded that Austrian jurisprudence, by mentioning "fair" in conjunction with "angemessen", invokes a "Fairness Principle" to judge whether a measure is in compliance with the KartG or not. Against this backdrop it could be reasoned inductively that Austrian Jurisprudence generally regards fairness as a benchmark for evaluating whether a measure is considered abusive or not in the sense of Art 102 TFEU.[121] Whether the "Fairness Principle" used in rulings of Austrian Courts is in line with the proclaimed "Fairness Principle" (i.e. recourses to societal norms as a substantive benchmark, [see B.III]), is out of the scope of this article, and needs to be examined further in the future.

Fairness most clearly displays characteristics of a principle within the Federal Fair Competitive Conditions Act, as it prohibits practices that are contrary to "good commercial conduct", without clearly defining what "good commercial conduct" is. Thereby, the Federal Fair Competitive Conditions Act incorporates extra-legal factors into the legal order. Furthermore, the special emphasis put on "good commercial conduct" in this context can be interpreted as the FWBG taking recourse to societal norms or factual existing social ordering structures, thereby displaying a fairness concept in line with the proclaimed "Fairness Principle".

121 Cf especially the recent case T-612/17, EU:T:2021:763 – *Google Shopping*, confirmed by the CJEU C-48/22P, EU:C:2024:726 – *Google Shopping*, where the principle of equal treatment is accepted as a general principle of EU law and where the Court clarified that this general principle of EU law applies in the context of Art 102 TFEU.

2. The Meta Level Character of the Fairness Principle

Regarding the meta level character of the proposed Fairness Principle [see B.III.2.], the following observations with respect to the Austrian competition law could be made:

Within Art 101 (3) TFEU "fair share" is interpreted rather in the sense of allocation of efficiency gains[122] not so much in the sense of the ongoing discussion about fairness [see B.]. In line with this, the German version of Art 101 (3) TFEU and also § 2 KartG do not contain the word "fair", even though it exists in the German language, but rather use the phrase "angemessene Beteiligung", thereby again highlighting the economic understanding. However, the sustainability clause added by the Austrian legislator in § 2 (1) KartG could be interpreted in a way that the Austrian legislator adopts the proposed "Fairness Principle".[123] It could be concluded that, by means of this paragraph, an incentive for market participants to change their behavior has been provided. This is done by not forbidding cartels whose endeavors produce an increase in ecological sustainability (i.e. serving the greater good of society).

It has also been shown that fairness played a role as a guiding principle for Austrian legislative acts [see C.II. While it can be concluded from this, that the meta level aspect of the proposed "Fairness Principle" did apply here, it is out of the scope of this article to assess if the legislative acts resulting from this are in line with the proclaimed character of this principle (i.e. serving as a bridge between law and society).

The meta level of the "Fairness Principle" can most evidently be observed in the context of the Federal Act Against Unfair Competition [see C.III.], as here, the Austrian Legislator has codified specific rules of conduct in its provisions. Furthermore, by widening the scope of the Federal Act Against Unfair Competition also to business-to-business relations, the provisions directly influence the social structure of market participants. This is in line with the proposed "Fairness Principle" being a bridge between law and society.

---

122 Cf Case C-56/64, EU:C:1966:41 – *Consten and Grundig*, para. 348.

123 See for a comprehensive discussion on the content of this provision *Tokić*, Freistellungsfähigkeit von Nachhaltigkeitsvereinbarungen nach europäischem und novelliertem österreichischen Kartellrecht, 36 wbl (2022), 301; regarding the consideration of sustainability aspects see also *Hiersche/Mertel*, § 2, in Egger/Harsdorf-Borsch (eds.), Kartellrecht Kommentar, Linde Verlag 1st edn 2022, paras. 54 et seqq.

The fact that Austrian institutions, such as the Austrian Federal Competition Authority, have established guidelines that help to concretize the unspecific concept of "good commercial conduct" within the Federal Fair Competitive Conditions Act [see C.VI.], is in line with the proposed "Fairness Principle" by serving as a bridge between law and society [see B.III.], even if those guidelines are not legally binding.

E. Conclusion

Fairness understood by Austrian competition law can most convincingly be understood to fall within the category that proclaims fairness as a legal principle. This principle does not exclusively rely on economic interpretation but is open to including non-economic goals in its analysis as well.

This is in line with recent European Jurisprudence outright accepting that there is a general principle of equal treatment applicable in the context of Art 102 TFEU.[124] The Austrian Cartel Act and its explicit recurrence to sustainability [see C.II.] especially seems to display the "*changing reality of markets and accompanying calls to include non-economic goals*".[125] The analysis seems to confirm, however, that considering "*non-economic goals, such as fairness, must not necessarily collide with economic efficiency*"[126] but that they rather help to choose "*amongst various efficient scenarios*".[127]

124 Cf the cases T-612/17, EU:T:2021:763 – *Google Shopping*, confirmed by the CJEU C-48/22P, EU:C:2024:726 – *Google Shopping*.

125 *Hornkohl*, Article 102 TFEU, Equal Treatment and Discrimination after *Google Shopping*, 13 JCLAP (2022) 99, 106.

126 *Hornkohl* (n 125), 106 et seq.

127 *Hornkohl* (n 125), 107.

Exploring the Application of Article 102 TFEU to Abuses in Seasonal Agricultural Labour Markets

Luca Graf and Giulia Sonderegger***

A. Introduction

Upton Sinclair's seminal book "The Jungle"[1] exposed the exploitation and harsh realities of migrant workers in the US meatpacking industry during the Gilded Age. Yet, it turned out that while the book "aimed at the public's heart, by accident [it] hit their stomach"[2], the resulting public outrage led to the adoption of food safety regulations as it ignored the call for improving workers' horrendous conditions.

More than a century later, millions of seasonal agricultural workers in the EU still face similar challenges despite strict EU labour rights for both migrant seasonal workers from the EU[3] and third-country nationals[4] that ought to protect them from exploitation. However, due to the dependency that migration models produce on workers in the agricultural sector, they represent one of the most vulnerable groups of workers in the Union,[5] with women being exposed to added risks.[6]

In fact, labour inspectors frequently report violations of migrant workers' rights regarding their working conditions, wages, housing and safety

* PhD Researcher in Law, University of Zurich.
** Scientific collaborator FOJ)at the Swiss Federal Office of Justice (FOJ).

1 *Sinclair*, The Jungle, Doubleday 1906.

2 *Kantor*, Upton Sinclair and the Pure Food and Drugs Act of 1906, 66 American Journal of Public Health (1976), 1202.

3 See Art. 45 TFEU.

4 See Directive (EU) 2014/36 of the European Parliament and of the Council of 26 February 2014 on the conditions of entry and stay of third-country nationals for the purpose of employment as seasonal workers, OJ L 94, 28 March 2014, 375.

5 See European Parliament, 'Migrant seasonal workers in the European agricultural sector' European Parliament (February 2021), https://www.europarl.europa.eu/thinktank/en/document/EPRS_BRI(2021)689347 (accessed 27 May 2024).

6 European Parliament, 'The vulnerability to exploitation of women migrant workers in agriculture in the EU: the need for a Human Rights and Gender based approach' European Parliament (May 2018), https://www.europarl.europa.eu/RegData/etudes/STUD/2018/604966/IPOL_STU(2018)604966_EN.pdf (accessed 10 June 2024).

standards. Short-term contracts with no or very little job security and social coverage are typically their harsh reality, making them particularly susceptible to modern slavery and trafficking. Power imbalances between employers and workers, often resulting from the latter's disadvantaged backgrounds and lack of awareness of their rights, as well as the language barriers, leave migrants regularly with no or little choice for improved working and living conditions.[7]

These prevailing power imbalances in the agricultural sector beg the question of how competition law, especially Art. 102 TFEU, could be used as a remedy to improve the current realities of such workers. Given that in the EU, the application of Art. 102 TFEU has so far focused on the product side, i.e., those abuses that are practised in relation to goods and services, and not on production factors like work,[8] several interesting aspects are raised.

Thus, this article assesses (i) the importance of Art. 102 TFEU in the context of migrant seasonal workers, (ii) how Art. 102 TFEU can be applied to labour markets, (iii) if it can frame the harm suffered by workers in a satisfactory manner and (iv) whether the focus on market power could enable competition law to complement labour law and other regulations. To this end, this article analyses migrant workers' harsh realities in light of the key concepts of Art. 102 TFEU, namely the market definition, the concept of dominance and the notion of exploitative abuse.

This article aims to evaluate whether competition law could tackle the problems occurring in labour markets at its heart or whether Art. 102 TFEU is meant to remain focused on the "stomach" of competition law by ensuring low prices for product inputs. It is important to point out that this article's assessment is strictly legal: it only explores the potential and limits according to the existing case law for applying competition law to migrant labour markets rather than discussing whether competition law should be applied from a policy perspective.[9]

---

7 *European Parliament* (n 6).

8 *Heinemann*, Kartellrecht auf Arbeitsmärkten, 07–08 Wirtschaft und Wettbewerb (2020), 371, 372.

9 It must be noted that this article does not engage in policy discussions on whether applying competition law to labour markets in the EU is the best possible instrument compared to more traditional tools. For more information in this regard, see, e.g., *Maggiolino*, The Application of Competition Law to Labour Markets: Some Unresolved Issues, 11 Journal of Antitrust Enforcement (2023), i127; *Lianos/Countouris/de Stefano*, Re-thinking the Competition Law/Labour Law Interaction: Promoting a Fairer Labour Market, 10 European Labour Law Journal (2019), 291; *Dimick*, Conflict of Laws?

B. Importance of Art. 102 TFEU in the Context of Migrant Workers

With less than 500 large corporations pulling the strings worldwide,[10] the agri-food sector is featured by highly concentrated food production, processing and retail markets. From a competition perspective, this is concerning as highly concentrated labour markets give employers great bargaining power, allowing them to suppress wages and impose horrendous working conditions. The imbalances in bargaining power are, for instance, reflected in reports from competition authorities in Spain and Italy, revealing that agricultural suppliers frequently experience retroactive changes to contract terms and often accept these changes out of fear of commercial retaliation. As a result, farmers and small operators frequently lack bargaining power, forcing them to keep production and labour costs low.[11] Given that migrants are one of the most vulnerable groups of workers—frequently not speaking the language in the respective country and often lacking knowledge of employment rights—these market conditions make them particularly susceptible to the consequences of concentration.[12]

Yet, although the application of competition law to labour markets has drawn attention from academics[13] and governments[14] across the world in

---

Tensions Between Antitrust and Labor Law; 90 The University of Chicago Law Review (2023), 379; *Broulík*, Harm to Workers in EU Competition Law: A Sufficient Condition for Intervention, 12 Amsterdam Center for Law & Economics Working Paper (2024), 1.

10 Cornwell University, 'Industrial Agriculture Could Use Information Cascades' Cornwell University (Course blog 12 November 2020), https://blogs.cornell.edu/info2040/2020/11/12/50011/ (accessed 28 May 2024).

11 See European Commission, Tackling unfair trading practices in the business-to-business food supply chain, COM(2014) final 472.

12 See European Parliament, 'Migrant seasonal workers in the European agricultural sector' European Parliament (February 2021), https://www.europarl.europa.eu/thinktank/en/document/EPRS_BRI(2021)689347 (accessed 27 May 2024).

13 See e.g., *Cengiz*, The conflict between market competition and worker solidarity: moving from consumer to a citizen welfare standard in competition law, 41 Legal Studies (2021), 73; *d'Estaintot*, Antitrust policy and EU labour markets - Lessons from the US and comparative prospects (PhD, Florence 2024). For jurisdictions outside of the EU, see also e.g., *Epstein*, The Application of Antitrust Law to Labour Markets - Then and Now, 15 New York University Journal of Law and Liberty (2022), 327; *Smith*, Labour Market Arrangements and Competition Law in Australia: Time for Change?, 57 The Australian Economic Review (2024), 432.

14 E.g., the Japan Fair Trade Commission (JFTC) issued a Report of Study Group on Human Resource and Competition Policy in 2018 and aims to fosters the application of the Antimonopoly Act to competition for human resources, see JFTC, 'Report of the Study Group on Human Resource and Competition Policy' JFTC (15 February

the past few years, the focus of the discussions has mainly revolved around questions related to Art. 101 TFEU,[15] including challenges raised by non-compete, wage-fixing and no-poach agreements. The fact that unilateral conduct on labour markets have generally been considered less problematic is not least reflected in the fact that there is no case law on the application of Art. 102 TFEU to labour markets in the EU. Hence, this article aims to address this gap by showing the importance of Art. 102 TFEU in the context of migrant workers.

C. Application Requirements of Art. 102 TFEU

Having highlighted the importance of addressing unilateral conduct in the context of the agricultural sector, this chapter analyses the application requirements of Art. 102 TFEU in light of migrant workers in the EU.

I. The Concept of Undertaking

The addressees of Art. 102 TFEU are undertakings.[16] The concept covers any entity that "is engaged in an economic activity, regardless of the legal status of the entity and the way in which it is financed".[17] An economic activity consists of offering goods or services for remuneration, whereby a functional approach is applied, which is characterised by the fact that the definition is not based on the undertaking as such but on the way in which it acts.[18] Accordingly, the definition also includes individuals who offer goods or services on the market and thus bear financial risks attached to their performance. However, it excludes employees, as they perform dependent and therefore subordinate work and consequently cannot be

---

2018), https://www.jftc.go.jp/en/cprc/reports/studygroups/index_files/180215.pdf (accessed 28 May 2024).

15 d'Estainto discusses the narrow revitalisation prospects for Art. 102 TFEU, showing why Art. 102 TFEU has a limited application to labour markets, see *d'Estainto* (n 13) 213–237.

16 See the wording of Art. 102 TFEU, according to which it covers abuses by one or more undertakings.

17 Case C-41/90, EU:C:1991:161 – *Höfner and Elser*, para. 21.

18 *Zimmer*, Art. 101 AEUV, in Immenga/Mestmaecker (eds.), Wettbewerbsrecht, vol 1, C.H. BECK 7th edn. 2025, para. 14.

considered autonomous market participants.[19] This is also confirmed by the ECJ's case law.[20]

Maggiolino further contends that if employees are considered to belong to the same economic unit as their employers, they technically cannot be considered victims of anticompetitive practices, as they constitute part of the same (dominant) undertaking.[21] In this regard, she argues for the need to recall the purpose and functional nature of the notion of undertaking: the identification of economic relationships that economic agents can limit and distort to the detriment of competition. By following this logic, one can recognise that employees represent a separate sphere of interest from their employers.[22]

While Maggiolino argues that it is necessary for competition law to recognise employees as separate undertakings from employers, this article posits an alternative perspective. It finds that the notion of undertaking has no implication for the identification of victims of coordinated or unilateral anticompetitive practices. In *Albany* the Court clearly stated that "it was beyond question that certain restrictions of competition are inherent in collective agreements between organisations representing employers and workers".[23] Yet, as Lianos et al. note, the case law developed a comprehensive exception for such instances on the basis of social policy.[24] More precisely, if the finding (or lack thereof) of inter-firm relationships had consequences beyond identifying the undertakings subject to the prohibitions under Art. 101 and 102 TFEU, the case law regarding the (non-)application of competition law to collective bargaining agreements would not have needed to rely on a special exclusion based on "social policy".[25] Instead, it could have simply relied on the absence of an inter-firm relationship, which is prone to distorting competition, in order to negate the presence of an undertaking.

Based on these observations, it can be concluded that while the case law establishes that workers are not considered undertakings, this does

19 *Zimmer* (n 18) para. 11.

20 See Case C-22/98, EU:C:1998:419 – *Becu and Others*, para. 26.

21 *Maggiolino* (n 9) i131 fn 13.

22 See *Maggiolino* (n 9) i131.

23 Case C-67/96, EU:C:1999:430 – *Albany*, para. 59.

24 See *Lianos/Countouris/de Stefano* (n 9) 298–301.

25 See Case C-67/96, EU:C:1999:430 – *Albany*, paras. 54–63. It shows how the exclusion was premised on both treaty-based textual and policy justifications. Moreover, it demonstrates the fact that the objective of collective bargaining agreements is to improve employees' working conditions.

not imply that they cannot be victims of competition law violations. In turn, although employees are not undertakings within the meaning of Art. 102 TFEU, the question remains as to whether employers as such can be considered undertakings. This leads to the second point of this analysis: employers as undertakings.

In this context, especially the *FENIN* case could pose an obstacle. According to the ECJ, demand as such does not constitute an economic activity, but it must be assessed whether the subsequent use of the purchased goods constitutes an economic activity.[26] Yet, as Heinemann explains, the *FENIN* case is not only questionable at the general level for product markets because it ignores the otherwise fundamental role that case law assigns to the protection of the competitive process itself,[27] but it is also impracticable in the context of input markets, such as labour, because it precedes production and distribution, which are unrelated to the issue of unchanged forwarding of products. Moreover, on closer inspection, *FENIN* takes place within the significantly different context of the trade of products.[28] Accordingly, this case should not be expanded to employers' demand for labour,[29] and employers ought to be viewed as undertakings.

II. The Concept of Dominance

As established above, employees can be victims of Art. 102 TFEU violations, while employers can be undertakings and therefore addressees of the same provision. Attention now turns to the next application requirement: dominance..

For Art. 102 TFEU to be applied, the undertaking in question needs to hold a degree of dominance in the relevant market. A company is viewed as dominant if it has the ability "to behave to an appreciable extent independently of its competitors, customers and ultimately of its consumers"[30],

26 Case C-205/03 P, EU:C:2006:453 – *FENIN*, para. 26.

27 See e.g., Case C-501/06 P, C-513/06 P, C-515/06 P and C-519/06 P, EU:C:2009:610 – *GlaxoSmithKline*, para. 63.

28 See Case C-205/03 P, EU:C:2006:453 – *FENIN*, paras. 25–27.

29 See *Heinemann* (n 8) 374.

30 Case 27/76, EU:C:1978:22 – *United Brands Company v European Commission*, para. 65.

which may include competing employers in the affected labour markets as well as the employees on the opposing side of the market.[31]

According to the *Continental Can* methodology, dominance is to be assessed through a two-step test: first, the relevant market must be identified; and second, dominance must be established, i.e., the undertaking's position in said market and its competitive constraints must be analysed.[32]

1. Relevant Market

a) Labour Markets

In the context of labour markets, the traditional concept of substitutability must be revised, as its focus is currently on products rather than on factors of production.The key economic question in analysing buyer power in labour markets is: which alternatives would workers consider if labour market conditions worsened, and where would they do so?

Similar to product markets, frameworks for determining how substitution affects competitive constraints on firms can be adapted to labour markets. One way to do that is to assess whether a hypothetical monopsonist could profit from a "small but significant and non-transitory decrease in wages" ("SSNDW")[33] or other worsening of terms[34], thereby assessing whether workers could switch employers in response, making such changes unprofitable for the employer. Accordingly, it could be ascertained how employees would react to a 5–10 % reduction in their salary. If such a wage reduction or a worsening of terms is profitable for the employer because a noticeable switch to other employers does not occur, the labour markets for the affected job profiles are restricted to that one company, making it a monopsonist. If, instead, a sufficient number of employees switch to other employers as a result of the wage reduction, these other employers are included in the relevant labour markets.

However, as Smith observed, while in such instances, workers would otherwise switch to another firm employing the same type of labour, this

31 *Heinemann* (n 8) 380.

32 Case 6–72, EU:C:1973:22 – *Continental Can*, para. 32.

33 *Naidu/Posner/Weyl*, Antitrust Remedies for Labor Power, 132 Harvard Law Review (2018), 536, 574.

34 See US Merger Guidelines, section 4.3.

switch might not occur if it requires significant retraining, relocation or other hurdles.[35]

In fact, Naidu et al. find that since labour markets are matching markets, i.e., are based on the preferences of both the firms and the workers, their market definition may generally be narrower than in other markets.[36] This is because given that EU national workers tend to "consider seasonal work unattractive",[37] employers frequently hire third-country nationals for seasonal work. Most agricultural work is physically demanding, repetitive and characterised by low wages and high occupational health and safety risks.[38] These types of devalued labour markets, where cost pressures have driven down wages and working conditions, correspond to what Piore coined as "secondary forms of employment" in his dual labour market hypothesis.[39] Accordingly, although some parts of the native population may still be willing to engage in this work,[40] a distinction between native and migrant workers seems to emerge from a supply-side perspective.

This supply-side perspective, where wages and working conditions have been driven down to a level where EU nationals are not willing to engage in these types of work, seems to be mirrored in the demand-side perspective of employers.[41] For example, studies of employers' hiring practices in the UK agricultural sector show a preference for migrant workers who are perceived as "more hardworking", "more reliable, flexible, and compliant", and with a better "work ethic" compared to the native workers being instead perceived as more "lazy and work-shy".[42] As Scott remarks, "[i]n a very

35 *Smith* (n 13) 435.

36 *Naidu/Posner/Weyl* (n 33) 575.

37 European Commission, Proposal for a directive of the European Parliament and of the Council on the conditions of entry and residence of third-country nationals for the purposes of seasonal employment, COM(2010) 379 final, 2–3.

38 See Eurostat, 'Health and Safety at Work in Europe (1999–2007) A Statistical Portrait' European Commission, (2010), https://ec.europa.eu/eurostat/documents/3217494/5718905/KS-31-09-290-EN.PDF.pdf/88eef9f7-c229-40de-b1cd-43126bc4a946?t=1414775047000 (accessed 31 July 2024).

39 See *Piore*, Birds of passage: Migrant labor and industrial societies, Cambridge University Press 1979, 35 et seqq.

40 *Piore* (n 39) 86 et seqq.

41 *Hunt*, Making the CAP Fit: Responding to the Exploitation of Migrant Agricultural Workers in the EU, 30 the International Journal of Comparative Labour Law and Industrial Relations (2014), 131, 135.

42 See *Scott*, Migrant-Local Hiring Queues in the UK Food Industry, 19 Population, Space and Place (2013), 459; *Findlay/McCollum*, Recruitment and employment regimes: Migrant labour channels in the UK's rural agribusiness sector, from acces-

crude sense, they are more exploitable, and more self-exploiting than domestic workers".[43] Accordingly, assuming that empirical results confirm this point on a case-by-case basis, it should be expected that secondary forms of employment in the agricultural sector could constitute separate labour markets for migrant workers. However, it should likely be questioned whether the very existence of a separate labour market for migrant workers could be considered in itself a symptom of the cellophane fallacy.

b) Geographical Scope

Geographic substitutability from workers' perspective depends on many factors, such as personal mobility and transport costs and times. As with the geographic definitions of product markets, the criterion of homogeneity of competitive conditions is decisive. Accordingly, the SSNDW test should also be used here, meaning that the geographic range of alternatives after a change in relative wages should be considered. Geographically, it may be the case that product markets need to be defined globally, while labour markets need to be defined locally, regionally, or nationally. The outcome of the assessment largely depends on the circumstances of the individual case, i.e., the geographic alternatives available to employees.

On the basis of studies conducted in the US, labour markets are expected to be more concentrated than regular product markets because they tend to be more local. This trend is particularly strong for low-skill workers, especially for those working in rural areas.[44]

In the context of migrant labour, it has been observed that migrant networks, i.e., sets of interpersonal ties that link migrant, former migrants, and non-migrants in origin and destination areas through bonds of kinship, friendship, and shared community of origin, play a fundamental role in establishing recruitment mechanisms. These networks shed light on how

sion to recession, 30 Journal of Rural Studies (2013), 10; *MacKenzie/Forde*, The rhetoric of the 'good worker' versus the realities of employers' use and the experiences of migrant workers, 23 Work, Employment and Society (2009), 142; *Dench/Hurstfield/Hill/Akroyd*, Employers' Use of Migrant Labour: Summary Report (2006), HomeOffice, London; *Rogaly*, Intensification of Workplace Regimes in British Horticulture: The Role of Migrant Workers, 14 Population, Space and Place (2008), 497.

43 *Scott* (n 42) 461.

44 *Marinescu/Posner*, Why has Antitrust Law Failed Workers?, 105 Cornell Law Review (2020), 1343, 1356–1357.

new workers join the labour market, find residential settlements and create social connections.[45]

While the concept of migrant networks is more widely used in the field of sociology and anthropology,[46] economists have also recognised how these bonds shape the likelihood of migrations by reducing the costs and increasing the expected returns from migration.[47] Personal connections with people who have experience in the destination area contribute to reducing various costs, such as travel expenses (transport, food, and lodging), job search costs (information and search efforts), opportunity costs (lost income during the search) and psychological costs (the psychological toll of leaving one's home country). Therefore, while migration at the beginning is costly, on the basis of these social bonds, every new migrant reduces the cost of subsequent migration for relatives and friends, which in turn reduces the cost for a new set of people. Eventually, once the number of connections in a migrant network reaches a critical level, migration becomes self-perpetuating since migration itself creates the social structure needed to sustain it.[48] It is interesting to note how this mechanism mirrors the market dynamics of direct network effects and tipping, which competition law already recognises for example in social networks of digital markets.[49]

This mechanism is further entrenched by the nature of migrant work, which is characterised by the temporality of the employment, the low salaries and a shortage of renting opportunities that force migrant workers to look for cheap and informal living arrangements near agricultural production areas.[50] These settlements have two main features: proximity to the

45 See *Massey*, Economic Development and International Migration in Comparative Perspective, 14 Population and Development Review (1988), 383, 396–399.

46 See *Ambrosini*, Delle reti e oltre: processi migratori, legami sociali e istituzioni, in Decimo/Sciortino (eds.), Stranieri in Italia: Reti Migranti, Il Mulino 2006, 21.

47 See e.g., *Greenwood*, An analysis of the determinants of geographic labor mobility in the United States, 51 Review of Economics and Statistics (1969), 189; *Massey/España*, The Social Process of International Migration, 237 Science (1987), 733. For a broader discussion on the relationship between sociology and economics see *Portes*, Economic Sociology of Immigration: A Conceptual Overview, in Portes (ed.), The Economic Sociology of Immigration, 1.

48 *Massey* (n 45) 397.

49 For more information on network effects and tipping in digital markets see e.g., *Sonderegger*, Killer Acquisitions in Digital Markets: An Analysis of the EU Merger Control Regime (PhD, Zürich 2023), 21–24.

50 See *Brovia/Piro*, Ghettos, camps and dormitories: Migrant workers' living conditions in enclaves of industrial agriculture in Italy, in Rye/O'Reilly (eds.), International Labour Migration to Europe's Rural Regions, Routledge 2020, 52.

areas of agricultural production and the limitation of workers' mobility.[51] They work as important nodes in migrant networks and provide workers with housing, healthcare, in some instances even social and legal services, and —most importantly— with the opportunity to find employment. This phenomenon channels migrants into communities which are completely separated from the hosting social fabric since all the services that migrants rely on are found within these secluded geographic areas. In turn, this means that the social mobility of migrants within the labour markets is de facto limited to these migrant networks and informal settlements.[52]

These findings seem to coincide with Piore's observation that, in secondary labour markets,[53] employers are generally in a position to stimulate an increase in the supply of workers through existing channels by simply spreading the word to their own workers that they are recruiting.[54] This further suggests that hiring practices should lead to narrowly defined labour markets.

c) Single Employer as an Own Labour Market

Before moving on, the question arises as to whether a labour market can consist of a single employer. In *Commercial Solvents,* it was established that raw materials as inputs may constitute their own product markets.[55] Going even further, in *Magill,* the Court accepted the distinction of a separate input market, even where the producer uses it exclusively for its own purpose.[56] Although the reasoning for raw materials cannot be translated to labour so directly, it is unclear why, depending on the actual circumstances, a distinct labour market in rural areas could not be equal to a single employer.

---

51 *Brovia/Piro* (n 50) 55.

52 See *Perrotta/Raeymaekers*, Caporalato capitalism. Labour brokerage and agrarian change in a Mediterranean society, 50 The Journal of Peasant Studies (2023), 2002, 2010; *Giampaolo/Ianni*, 'The Master Gang System in Italy, Faces of Immigration Project: Case Study Report N.1' (2020), 3, https://gcap.global/wp-content/uploads/2020/12/CSR-n.-1-ENG-11.12.2020.pdf (accessed 30 January 2025).

53 For more information, see *Piore*, The Dual Labor Market: Theory and Implications, Routledge 2nd edn. 2001.

54 See *Piore* (n 39) 98–99.

55 Case 6 and 7/73, EU:C:1974:18 – *Commerical Solvents*, para. 22.

56 See Cases C-241–242/91 P, EU:C:1995:98 – *Magill*, para. 24.

The conceptual hurdles are even lower in the case of labour markets of workers who are not classified as employees since they fit the definition of economic activity better than the justification of a potential or hypothetical market for inputs used in the case law.[57]

2. Dominance

Once the relevant market has been defined, dominance needs to be established. Various elements can be assessed to examine whether a dominant market position exists. For the purpose of this article, a few factors will be discussed in more detail below.

a) Market Shares as a Proxy for Market Position

The main proxy used for the assessment of an undertaking's market position is market shares. While in product markets they are generally calculated on the basis of sales volume, in labour markets they can be calculated on the basis of vacancies.[58] The higher the market shares, the more likely dominance is established. The presence of market shares above 50 % allows a rebuttable presumption of dominance.[59] However, market shares usually need to be complemented by the analysis of other factors, some of which will be discussed in more detail below.

b) Countervailing Worker Bargaining Power (or Lack Thereof)

In traditional cases of dominance related to supply-side market power, the case law recognises the presence of countervailing buyer power as an important competitive constraint. It relates to the ability of buyers to switch to competing suppliers.[60] Similarly, the presence of strong unions and other regulatory protections which strengthen the bargaining power of workers should be considered. However, just like the presence of said

57 See Case C-418/01, EU:C:2004:257 – *IMS Health*, paras. 43–45.
58 For a demonstration, see *Marinescu/Posner* (n 44) 1352.
59 See Case C-62/86, EU:C:1991:286 – *AKZO*, para. 60.
60 See European Commission Decision of 29 April 2014, Case AT.39985 – *Motorola*, paras. 237–268.

features should be relevant to the analysis, their abnormal absence should also be accounted for.[61] Of course, it is impossible to assess the strength of the bargaining power of migrant seasonal workers in the abstract, as the situation to be analysed is going to change drastically, depending on the Member States concerned and even the region at hand.

Nevertheless, some factors should be mentioned. One such example is the possibility under local laws to classify workers under atypical forms of work, like very short-term fixed contracts and zero-hours contracts, which are generally associated with reductions in employment terms and conditions.[62] In fact, most agricultural work is characterised by uncertainty regarding the continuity of employment, lack of control over labour processes, little regulatory protection and worker representation.[63] This, in turn, can completely prevent their ability to collectively bargain because of their lack of status as employees.

Another important factor is the migrant status. Recently arrived migrants who are not yet fluent in the arrival country's language are frequently not yet knowledgeable about their contractual and labour rights and have yet to build a trusting relationship with the local population or labour unions who could inform them about their rights. Accordingly, they find themselves in an even weaker bargaining position *vis-à-vis* their employers.[64] This is especially true for recently arrived migrants who, during the phase between arrival and request of asylum in the country, have lost access to their protective networks from the country of origin and have not yet established new protective ones in the country of destination. In this regard, Zadra's study observes how recently arrived migrants, hosted in reception centres, have been systematically and deliberately targeted by exploitative employers due to their vulnerability.[65]

---

61 *Heinemann* (n 8) 380.

62 See *Hunt* (n 41) 136.

63 *Hunt* (n 41) 137–138.

64 See *Zadra*, Times of Exploitation: Rhythms of migrant labour in Italian agriculture, XXV, 2 The Lab's Quarterly (2023), 65, 77.

65 *Zadar* (n 64) 81.

c) Unavoidable Trading Partner

The case law recognises circumstances where an undertaking can become an unavoidable trading partner, which puts the other parties "in a position of economic dependence which is characteristic of the existence of a dominant position".[66] The concept differs from the traditional analysis of dominance in its focus on the bilateral relationship between the dominant company and the other party and the (in)ability to switch to alternatives rather than a broader structural analysis of the market.

While this concept has been incorporated into national provisions, which do not require the presence of dominance, the case law of Art. 102 TFEU recognises economic dependence as a parameter of the assessment. The most consequential example can be found in *ABG/Oil*,[67] where the Commission argued that a finding of dominance could be accepted solely on the basis of a bilateral dependence of customers on suppliers.[68] Although it was based on the exceptional finding of a shortage dependence during the oil crisis, it nevertheless implies situations where independence *vis-à-vis* customers can show dominance.[69] Nevertheless, other cases accept economic dependence as a complementary factor in a finding of dominance. For example, in *British Airways*, the Commission's finding of dominance with a comparatively lower market share of 39.7 % was based *inter alia* on the economic dependence of travel agents, which "substantially depend on the income they receive from BA in consideration for their air travel agency services",[70] thus rendering BA "an obligatory business partner of travel agents".[71] Similarly, the Commission established a finding of dominance in *TACA* on the basis of "the limited ability of its

66 European Commission Decision 89/205/EEC, *Magill TV Guide, BBC and RTE*, OJ L 78/43 (21.3.1989), para. 22.

67 It must be noted that the ECJ quashed the European Commission's decision on the grounds that BP had not abused its dominant position, however, without expressing themselves on the Commission's proof of the dominant position. See Case 77/77, EU:C:1978:141 – *Benzine en Petroleum Handelsmaatschappij BV and others v European Commission.*

68 See European Commission Decision 77/327/EEC, *ABG/Oil*, OJ L 117/1 (9.5.1977).

69 *Këllezi*, Abuse below the Threshold of Dominance? Market Power, Market Dominance, and Abuse of Economic Dependence, in Mackenrodt/Gallego/Enchelmaier (eds.), Abuse of Dominant Position: New Interpretation, New Enforcement Mechanisms?, Springer 2008, 55, 74.

70 Case T-219/99, EU:T:2003:343 – *British Airways*, para. 216.

71 Case T-219/99, EU:T:2003:343 – *British Airways*, para. 217.

customers to switch to alternative suppliers, thereby making the TACA an unavoidable trading partner even for its disaffected customers".[72]

The above reasoning in the case law can be paralleled with labour markets where a shortage of job opportunities can place farm workers in a situation of economic dependence *vis-à-vis* their employers. This is especially important in cases where a single employer can be its own labour market, thus collapsing the differentiation between the structural analysis of dominance and the bilateral analysis of economic dependence.

d) Market Conduct

The case law recognises the conduct of an undertaking as a relevant factor in the assessment of dominance.[73] The inclusion stems from the fact that an undertaking's conduct itself can deter competitors' entry. Therefore, the case law generally focuses on exclusionary conduct.

Yet, in this article, it is argued that conduct which harms workers' bargaining positions should be equally relevant. The Commission more broadly affirmed in *Eurofix-Bauco* that the undertaking's conduct was "witness to its ability to act independently of, and without due regard to, either competitors or customers on the relevant markets in question" and that "[t]his behaviour and its economic consequences would not normally be seen where a company was facing real competitive pressure".[74] Accordingly, conduct that hinders workers' ability to engage in collective bargaining or that would not be observable in a market where the employer faces competitive pressure should be considered within the scope of already established case law when assessing dominance. This factor is particularly relevant to conduct affecting agricultural workers. The field of legal geography emphasises in this respect how rural areas are often a legal space relatively bereft of state actors and institutions. These less robust or even

72 European Commission Decision 99/243/EC, *TACA*, OJ L 95/1 (9.4.1999), para. 538.

73 See Case C.27/76, EU:C:1977:173 – *United Brands*, paras. 67–68; Case C-62/86, EU:C:1991:286 – *AKZO*, para. 61.

74 European Commission Decision 88/138/EEC, *Eurofix-Bauco v. Hilti*, OJ L 65 (11.3.1988), para. 71.

absent manifestations of law diminish rural societies' expectations of law and accordingly cause law to underperform.[75]

Given the combination of the above-mentioned factors of vulnerability, such as migrant workers' legal status and the absence of legal enforcement in rural areas, it is possible to observe conduct which would otherwise never occur in a competitive market. Documented examples are (i) the underdeclaration and incomplete payment of working hours and wages, (ii) repressions of protests and enforcement of accelerated productive rhythms and longer working days through blackmail and other forms of coercion and (iii) wrongful classifications as unskilled workers in contracts, even where the relevant tasks required expertise and even special licenses. Also, "pause time" is a common practice.[76] Therefore, these acts could never occur in a competitive labour market and should be used accordingly as evidence of dominance.

III. Further Requirements

Two additional requirements for the application of Art. 102 TFEU are (i) dominance to extend to a substantial part of the internal market and (ii) the ability to affect trade between Member States. In traditional competition law analyses, these requirements tend to be easily met. However, in migrant labour markets, these requirements may be harder to satisfy.

Although these requirements do not relate to the physical size of the geographical scope of the market in relation to the EU,[77] and the case law has already repeatedly held that a single facility may satisfy the test of substantiality,[78] it is clear that not every dominant employer will satisfy these two requirements. Yet, this remains an empirical question. For example, Monti observed 20 years ago that farmer cooperatives can hold national

75 *Pruitt*, The Rural Lawscape: Space Tames Law Tames Space, in Braverman/Blomley/Delaney/Kedar (eds.), The Expanding Spaces of Law: A Timely Legal Geography, Stanford University Press 2014, 195.

76 See *Zadra* (n 59) 76–78.

77 Rather the case law seems to look at the volume and pattern of production and consumption as a relevant metric. See Case C-40/73, EU:C:1975:174 – *Suiker Unie*, para. 371.

78 See Case C-179/90, EU:C:1991:464 – *Merci Convenzionali*, para. 15; Case C-163/99 EU:C:2001:189 – *Portugal v European Commission*, para. 63.

market shares of between 64–90 %[79] and would accordingly be able to hold a dominant position in a substantial portion of the internal market while affecting inter-state trade. Furthermore, NCAs would still remain free to apply stricter national law counterparts of Art. 102 TFEU in their own jurisdictions, which do not contain these two requirements.

D. Abuse of Monopsony Power

In the EU, competition law does not prohibit dominance as such, only its abuse. Art. 102 TFEU distinguishes between exploitative and exclusionary abuse. The former enables the undertaking to increase its profits by exploiting its market power, while the latter aims to exclude rivals from the market. Art. 102(a) TFEU finds that a dominant company may engage in exploitative abuse if it directly or indirectly "imposes unfair purchase or selling prices or other unfair trading conditions." By doing so, the EU recognises that dominance on the buy side can lead to unlawful, unfair pricing and non-pricing terms for counterparties and thus can violate competition law.[80] Accordingly, the theory of harm discussed below is going to be broadly based on Art. 102(a) TFEU, although it must not be forgotten that the types of possible abuses under Art. 102 TFEU is non-exhaustive, and new forms of abuse beyond the established archetypes are possible. However, before concrete theories of harm can be elaborated on, it must be understood how EU competition law, given the predominance of the consumer welfare standard, can assess competitive harm in labour markets.

I. Abuse qua Worker Welfare?

In the EU, there is currently no unequivocal legal precedent which states that the scope of competition law analysis of labour markets considers worker welfare directly. At the moment, the most explicit institutional source is the Commission's guidelines on Art. 101 TFEU. Consequently, the

79 *Monti*, The relationship between CAP and competition policy – Does EU competition law apply to agriculture?, *European Commission* (COGECA Conference speech, 13 November 2003), 5, https://ec.europa.eu/commission/presscorner/api/files/document/print/en/speech_03_537/SPEECH_03_537_EN.pdf (accessed 31 July 2024).

80 See Case 298/83, EU:C:1985:150 – *CICCE v European Commission.*

following argument is a pragmatic one which does not aim to provide a comprehensive justification of the objective of worker welfare amongst the goals of competition law and/or its relationship to consumer welfare.[81]

At the outset, it is important to understand that the case law distinguishes between "by object" and "by effect" competitive restrictions – a difference that is methodological: the former allows the establishment of a presumption of competitive harm on the basis of formal analysis, while the latter requires direct evidence of said competitive harm. In the words of the GC in *Michelin II*, "establishing the anti-competitive object and the anti-competitive effect are one and the same thing. If it is shown that the object pursued by the conduct [...] is to limit competition, that conduct will also be liable to have such an effect".[82]

With regards to labour markets, the Commission subsumes "agreements to fix wages" under buyer cartels and classifies them as restrictions of competition by object.[83] As stated in the guidelines on Art. 101 TFEU, the reason for this approach is that a "buyer cartel reveals by its nature a sufficient degree of harm to competition such that it is not necessary to assess the effects that it may have".[84] Accordingly, it views such agreements as object restrictions.

This article posits that the reason for the classification of wage-fixing and no-poach agreements as object restrictions (if they satisfy the CJEU's methodology)[85] is based on the straightforward economic insight that labour market concentration leads to worsening working conditions (e.g., lower wages) for employees,[86] rather than more complex justifications

81 For two alternative and extensive discussions of such a justification for the introduction of worker welfare as an objective of EU competition law, see *Broulík* (n 9) 18–34.

82 Case T-203/01, EU:T:2003:250 – *Michelin II*, para. 241. It must be noted that in *France Télécom,* the GC used the milder formulation "may, in some cases, be one and the same thing", yet this does not affect the broader point on the relationship between formal and effects-based analysis. See Case T-340/03, EU:T:2007:22 – France Télecom, para. 195.

83 European Commission Communication, Guidelines on the applicability of Article 101 of the Treaty on the Functioning of the European Union to horizontal co-operation agreements, OJ C 11 (14.1.2011), 1–72, para. 279.

84 *European Commission* (n 83) para. 282.

85 See Case 56/65, EU:C:1988:38 – *Société Technique Minière*, paras. 52–54.

86 For some empirical studies in the US see *Azar/Marinescu/Steinbaum*, Labor Market Concentration, NBER working paper 24147 (2017); *Benmelech/Bergman/Kim*, Strong Employers and Weak Employees: How Does Employer Concentration Affect Wages?, 57 Journal of Human Resources (2018), 200.

based on the relationship between lower labour market dynamism, employee salaries and firm productivity, which in turn may lead to worse outcomes for consumers.[87]

Based on empirical analysis,[88] EU competition law is polycentric,[89] and therefore can accommodate worker protection as a standalone goal amongst others. However, this article's argument does not require the introduction of an additional goal, just a broader interpretation of the notion of welfare that goes beyond a narrow consumer-based approach. The same instruments with which competition law pursues consumer welfare in product markets can be employed to pursue worker welfare in labour markets. It merely requires the realisation that, as posited by Cengiz, "workers and consumers are essentially the same group of people and one's welfare cannot be increased or decreased without affecting the other's".[90]

Accordingly, this suggests that worker welfare on the supply side would play a comparable role to consumer welfare on the demand side. Of course, it remains to be seen whether the CJEU will follow this approach after the first labour cases are tested in court.

This reasoning can also be extended to Art. 102 TFEU. The ECJ explicitly held in *Continental Can* that "[t]he restraint of competition which is prohibited if it is the result of behaviour falling under Article [101], cannot become permissible by the fact that such behaviour succeeds under the influence of a dominant undertaking".[91] This does not mean that unfair wages should be considered a *per se* abuse under Art. 102 TFEU because they are an object restriction under Art. 101 TFEU, but merely that the same competitive harm (e.g., lower wages) is prohibited independently of the form it takes, as long as it is the result of weakened competition.

Furthermore, the proposed interpretation of Art. 102 TFEU below is in alignment with the requirement of policy coherence established in *Albany*.[92] Policy coherence enabled the interpretation of competition law to pursue one of the goals of labour policy or, as specified in *Albany*, it "contributed directly to improving one of their working conditions, namely

87 See *Naidu/Posner/Weyl* (n 33) 558–559.

88 See *Stylianou/Iacovides*, The goals of EU competition law: a comprehensive empirical investigation, 42 Legal Studies (2022), 620.

89 See *Lianos*, Polycentric Competition Law, 71 Current Legal Problems (2018), 161.

90 *Cengiz* (n 13) 74.

91 Case 6–72, EU:C:1973:22 – *Contintetal Can*, para. 25.

92 See Case C-67/96, EU:C:1999:430 – *Albany*.

their remuneration."[93] Just like the ECJ held that the scope of Art. 101 TFEU does not extend to collective bargaining agreements in order to ensure consistency between competition and labour policy,[94] this article puts forward an expansive interpretation of competition law (or more precisely, of Art. 102 TFEU), which aligns the objectives of competition policy to labour policy, thus creating policy consistency.

II. Exploitative Abuse of Monopsony Power under Art. 102(a) TFEU

The ECJ's case law finds exploitation where a dominant company uses the opportunities arising from its position to obtain commercial advantages that it would not have obtained in the case of normal and sufficiently effective competition.[95] Given the absence of more directly applicable case law to abuses of monopsony power, one can outline a potential interpretation of "imposition of unfair wages and working conditions" by transposing the economic logic of consumer welfare to worker welfare. The logic that frames the imposition of excessively high selling prices as unfair should view excessively low wages in the same way.

An important requirement that needs to be considered is that of (normative or strict) causality between the dominant position and the abuse. Yet, as Heinemann explains, if a strong position in the demand for labour is leveraged to enforce worse working conditions or even conditions that violate labour law, the requirement of causality is satisfied even under its stricter interpretation.[96]

The case law on excessive pricing, as set out in the *United Brands* test, can provide a good starting point for establishing a legal test. The test seeks to ascertain the unfairness of prices through the relationship between the economic value of the product and the price.[97] In order to do so, the ECJ puts forward two cumulative tests: excessiveness and unfairness,[98] which will now be discussed.

93 Case C-67/96, EU:C:1999:430 – *Albany*, paras. 62–63.
94 Case C-67/96, EU:C:1999:430 – *Albany*, para. 60.
95 Case C.27/76, EU:C:1977:173 – *United Brands*, para. 249.
96 *Heinemann* (n 8) 380.
97 Case C.27/76, EU:C:1977:173 – *United Brands*, para. 250.
98 See C.27/76, EU:C:1977:173 – *United Brands*, paras. 235–268.

III. Excessive Prices and Insufficient Wages

Excessiveness measures the dominant company's profitability as it generally requires the comparison of the cost of production to the price charged. Thus, the legal test first requires an assessment of the production costs to ascertain profitability.[99]

An approach developed for the assessment of excessive prices through costs cannot be directly transposed to measure the insufficiency of wages as the latter are costs themselves. Nevertheless, one can transpose the economic reasoning behind antitrust's scrutiny of excessive prices to insufficient wages.

1. Allocative Inefficiency in Labour Markets

A company is dominant if it has "the power to behave to an appreciable extent, independently of its competitors, customers, and ultimately of its consumers"[100] and, more specifically, in the context of prices, has the ability to—at the loss of some demand—profitably raise prices. The higher the price is raised, the greater the loss of demand. After continuously raising the price, the firm reaches the "optimal monopoly price". Thus, the markup measured as the difference between the dominant company's price and their costs represents the same difference between the monopoly price and the competitive price.[101] As O'Donoghue/Padilla explain, the consumer harm resulting from allocative inefficiency is twofold: (i) a wealth transfer in the form of monopoly rents takes place from consumers to firms (Area A), and (ii) it reduces welfare by forcing out of the market consumers who are not willing to pay the marked-up price but would have been willing to pay the competitive price (Area B).[102] The welfare loss can be visualised as follows:

99 C.27/76, EU:C:1977:173 – *United Brands*, para. 252.

100 C.27/76, EU:C:1977:173 – *United Brands*, para. 65.

101 *Naidu/Posner/Weyl* (n 33) 556–557.

102 *O'Donoghue/Padilla*, The Law and Economics of Article 102 TFEU, Hart Publishing 2020, 894.

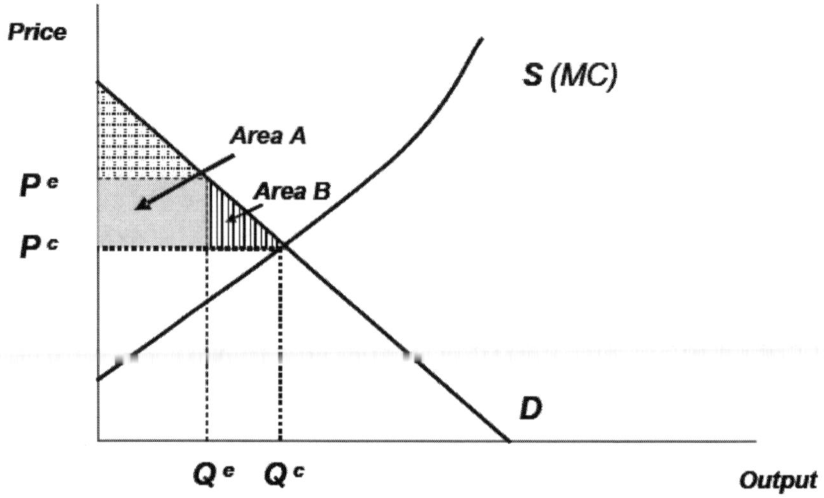

Figure Z: allocative inefficiency (excessive prices).[103]

The analysis of monopsony power in labour markets follows the same logic.[104] In Pigou's words, "[e]xploitation on the part of the employers forces workpeople to accept in payment for their services less than the value which the marginal net product of their services has to these employers".[105] The diagram below shows how this reasoning can be extended to labour markets in the same way: exploitation can be measured as the difference between the monopsony wage and the competitive wage.

The diagram must be read as follows: the X-axis represents the amount of labour, while the Y-axis is the wage rate for said labour. The employers' demand curve (DD´) and the workers' supply curve (SS´) intersect at the wage rate that would result in competitive conditions (PM). By looking further left, one can identify a wage most profitable for the employer (RM´). According to Pigou, exploitation inevitably emerges as soon as the employer manages to pay a wage that is lower than the competitive price (PM). Before delving deeper, Pigou's terminology must be differentiated from the competition law vocabulary. According to him, exploitation is

103 *O'Donoghue/Padilla* (n 102) 895.

104 For a concordant but more extensive explanation of the negative effect of employers' market power on labour markets, see Maggiolino (n 9) i133-i140.

105 *Pigou*, The Economics of Welfare, McMillan 1920, 511–512.

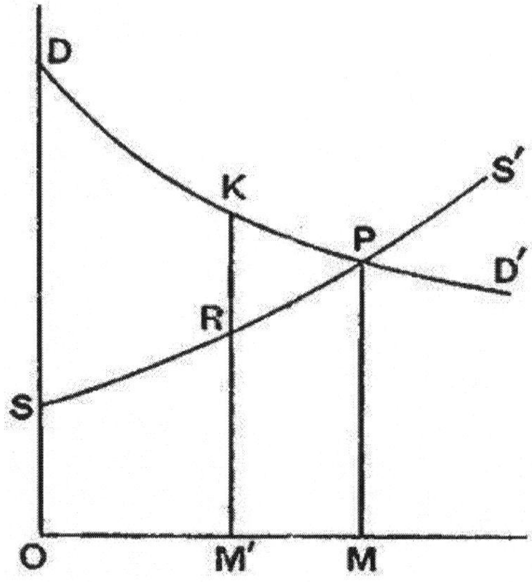

Figure X: Exploitation of monopsony power.

measured in the wage difference between RM′ and KM′, i.e., the difference in the amount of labour M′ between the wage the workers would be willing to pay K and the wage the employers are actually paying R. Instead, he refers to unfairness as a qualified part of exploitation. The latter is measured in the wage difference between the competitive PM and RM′, i.e., the difference between the marked-down wage and the wage that would have been paid under competitive conditions (which in competition law analysis would constitute the counterfactual).[106] Therefore, a comparison of the two diagrams makes apparent how the welfare loss from Pigou's concept of unfairness in wages corresponds to the deadweight loss that results from excessive prices (i.e., Figure Z's area B). This is important to understand since in a (perfectly) competitive market, undertakings equate the workers' wages to their "marginal revenue product", i.e., the amount of additional revenue the worker can generate. On this basis, the same logic espoused above follows: raising wages will allow the employer to hire more workers by also raising overall labour costs;[107] lowering wages will come at the loss of some workers. Just like in the monopoly case, the

106 *Pigou* (n 105) 512.

107 Wages are also raised for existing workers because normally employers cannot distinguish reservation wages of their workers.

monopsonist will not internalise this effect on employees and will find an "absolute wage markdown" level below the competitive "marginal revenue product".[108] Therefore, the measurement of a dominant company's absolute markdown of wages can justify a finding of "insufficiency".

To summarise, the effects on allocative efficiency between monopoly and monopsony are paralleled. Product market power (i) redistributes a bigger share of wealth from the consumers to the firm (exploitation) and (ii) creates deadweight loss from the consumers who would have been willing to pay the competitive price but not the one charged by the dominant company (inefficiency). Similarly, labour market power (i) redistributes wealth from the workers to the employer (exploitation) and (ii) creates allocative inefficiency from the workers who would have worked for the employer if they had been paid their full marginal revenue product (i.e., under competitive conditions) but not for the marked-down wage of the dominant company (inefficiency).[109] In both cases, the first step of the legal test shows a significant deviation from competitive conditions as a result of the exploitation of market power.

2. Target Earners and the Supply of Labour

In the context of Piore's secondary labour markets, two special characteristics of workers' behaviour should be considered. Yet, these considerations remain theoretical and understanding how these secondary labour markets actually operate would require empirical research that to this day is still missing.[110] In this regard, market investigations by competition authorities could help fill this gap.

Migrant workers[111] tend to be target earners, i.e., the effect of rising incomes, all other things being equal, is to increase the rate at which they return home and thus leave the labour market.[112] This is represented by a backwards-bending supply curve and affects the way that they will respond to economic pressures.[113]

108 *Naidu/Posner/Weyl* (n 33) 556–557.

109 *Naidu/Posner/Weyl* (n 33) 558.

110 *Piore* (n 39) 96.

111 It must be noted that while not all non-native agricultural workers will fit this description, many non-migrant workers in low-income jobs might.

112 *Piore* (n 39) 95.

113 *Piore* (n 39) 61.

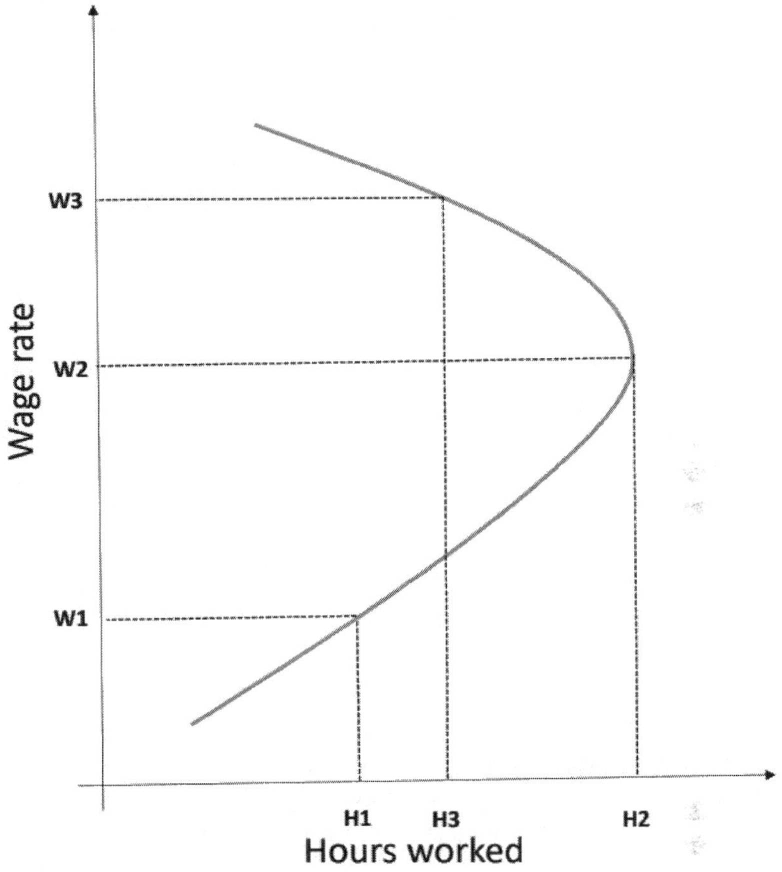

Figure Y: backwards-bending supply curve of labour

Increases in their hourly wage reduce the number of hours an individual worker is willing to supply. Yet, as Piore observes, the fact that individual workers and even the market may have a backwards bending supply curve does not necessarily apply to individual firms in said market. If a firm is small relative to the total market, it can potentially expand its own labour supply by raising wages and drawing labour from competitors. According to this logic, each firm experiencing a labour shortage will raise its wages, which means that workers will want to supply less labour, thus driving the wages even higher. Conversely, any surplus of labour will set off a downward wage spiral: as soon as firms notice the existence of unemployment, they will reduce the wages, which means that workers will remain longer in the market, thereby increasing the total supply of labour and lowering wages accordingly.[114]

A second important feature of the supply of migrant labour is its extremely elastic nature. Employers are generally able—without raising wages—to increase their supply of migrant labour by spreading the word that they are hiring amongst their existing workers. Given the disparities in income between developed and undeveloped areas, there is a near-infinite number of new sources of migrant labour to draw upon as the existing channels are exhausted.[115]

Accordingly, migrant workers' length of stay in the market is a crucial factor which determines the supply of labour. Therefore, it is conceivable that a dominant undertaking, able to set insufficient wages because of its market power, can negatively influence market outcomes by restricting job opportunities and creating unemployment, thus setting off an artificial downward pressure on wages.

IV. Unfair Wages and Working Conditions

The criterion of "unfairness" assesses the relationship between the price and the economic value of the product. The underlying idea is that competitive prices must reflect the value of the product.[116] Accordingly, it is necessary to understand the concept of value as established in the case law.

1. Unfairness and (Economic) Value

Prices can be unfair either "in themselves" or "when compared to competing products". This can be done through (i) price-cost comparisons, (ii) price comparisons across markets or competitors, geographic price comparisons or (iii) comparisons over time.[117] The case law shows two approaches to ascertaining a product's economic value.

114 *Piore* (n 39) 96.
115 *Piore* (n 39) 98–99.
116 See Case C.27/76, EU:C:1977:173 – *United Brands*, para. 250.
117 Case C.27/76, EU:C:1977:173 – *United Brands*, para. 253.

On one hand, the case law shows a supply-side analysis related to costs. This reflects the idea that unfairness may be found when radically different prices are charged for services with the same cost structure or the same prices for a comparable service.[118] On the other hand, the case law also demonstrates a different approach that comes closer to the neoclassical understanding of economic value relating to demand-side considerations.[119] More precisely, a higher willingness to pay for a product may justify its higher economic value to consumers (on the basis of a wide range of tangible and intangible factors), thus negating a finding of unfairness.[120]

In this context, the case *AKKA/LAA* is particularly interesting. In that case, the Court explicitly recognised that a finding of unfairness by way of a price comparison across different Member States must take account of factors such as "consumption habits and other economic and sociocultural factors, such as gross domestic product per capita and cultural and historical heritage".[121] Furthermore, in line with previous case law,[122] the *AKKA/LAA* judgment also shows that—if the specific circumstances of the case allow for it—a competition authority could exclusively rely on "significant and persistent" differences through benchmark comparisons. In doing so, it would fall on the dominant company to justify the difference through cost-based arguments.[123] Based on this logic, comparisons with wages in similar labour markets, adjusted for case-law-recognised economic and sociocultural parameters, could be used to find unfairness. In particular, the Purchasing Power Parity Index (PPP-Index) is explicitly recognised in the case law as one such factor in the context of excessive prices.[124] PPP is a measure of the price of specific goods in different countries, used to compare the absolute purchasing power of consumers. Hence, if the PPP-index is considered a relevant factor to better ascertain the (un)fairness of comparable prices, it should also be relevant to assess the (un)fairness of

118 See Case 226/84 EU:C:1986:421 – *British Leyland*, paras. 25–34 (charging of different prices for inspection of left-handed to right-handed vehicles, despite similar costs being involved).

119 See *O'Donoghue/Padilla* (n 102) 900.

120 See e.g., European Commission Decision of 23 July 2004, Case COMP/A.36.568/D3 – *Scandlines Sverige AB v Port of Helsingborg*, paras. 227–231.

121 Case C-177/16 EU:C:2017:689 – *AKKA/LAA*, para. 42.

122 See Case 395/87 EU:C:1989:319 – *Ministère public v Jean-Louis Tournier*, paras. 34–46; Joined Cases 110/88, 241/88, 242/88EU:C:1989:326 – *Lucazeau*, paras. 21–33.

123 See Case C-177/16 EU:C:2017:689 – *AKKA/LAA*, paras. 52–61.

124 See Case C-177/16 EU:C:2017:689 – *AKKA/LAA*, para. 51.

comparable wages. For example, the ILO has already relied on the PPP-index to compare minimum wages across countries.[125]

Yet, the Court also explicitly mentions that "other ways may be devised—and economic theorists have not failed to think up several—of selecting the rules for determining whether the price of a product is unfair".[126] The fundamental requirement for these novel approaches is to be based on "objective, appropriate, and verifiable criteria".[127] Accordingly, the next sub-chapter will seek to put forward an additional vision of unfairness based on the core of demand-side considerations: consent.

2. Unfairness, Illegality, and Consent

Under Art. 102(a) TFEU, the price plays a (if not the) central role. Yet, unfair trading conditions' decisive influence on the price/performance ratio and, thus, on the appropriateness of the price must not be underestimated.[128] Conditions that are particularly advantageous for customers may, under certain circumstances, justify excessive prices and thus escape the scope of the prohibition of abusive practices.[129] Accordingly, logic prescribes that particularly disadvantageous terms and conditions may exacerbate or even establish the inappropriateness of the price, especially if they entail a direct financial advantage for the dominant seller and thus influence his profit.

In the context of migrant agricultural workers, working conditions may play a central role in establishing an outcome which significantly deviates from a competitive market. The previously mentioned structural conditions and systemic lack of enforcement of migrant workers' employment and social rights expose migrant workers to working conditions which should not be considered fair.

The conceptual difficulty of subsuming these working conditions under a competition law framework arises from the fact that its economic analysis is usually applied to individuals who are in a comparatively much stronger

---

125 See ILOSTAT, 'Statistics on wages' ILOSTAT (2024), https://ilostat.ilo.org/topics/wages/ (accessed 17 October 2024).

126 Case C.27/76, EU:C:1977:173 – *United Brands*, para. 253.

127 Case C-177/16, EU:C:2017:689 – *AKKA/LAA*, para. 41.

128 See *Fuchs*, Art. 102 AUEV, in Immenga/Mestmäcker (eds.), Wettbewerbsrecht, vol 1, C.H. BECK 7th edn 2025, para. 239.

129 See e.g., European Commission Decision of 23 July 2004, Case COMP/A.36.568/D3 – *Scandlines Sverige AB v Port of Helsingborg*, paras. 227–231.

bargaining position relative to their employers. In fact, economic theories of labour exploitation assume that workers engage voluntarily in the labour market, i.e., they are free to engage in bilateral transactions, free to make their own choice about their supply of labour and enter and exit the labour market.[130]

It is unclear why competition law should ignore the welfare of migrant workers while exclusively focusing on that of the generally less vulnerable white-collar workers subjected to non-compete clauses and wage-fixing agreements.[131]

Subsuming unfair trading conditions as components of the excessiveness of prices, measured through the proxy of a reasonable markup, does not have to be the only way recognised in competition law. At the heart of the concept of exploitative abuse lies the pursuit of profits at the impairment of the interests of trading partners/consumers. The benchmark for abuse in the case law is "whether the dominant undertaking has made use of the opportunities arising out of its dominant position in such a way as to reap trading benefits which it would not have reaped if there had been normal and sufficiently effective competition".[132] For this reason, the instrumentalisation of market dominance is often conceived as the most direct way to exploit the dependence of trading partners, even though it is not a necessary component of the concept of exploitation.[133] Although the EU institutions have not yet developed general criteria for its assessment, this does not prevent a finding of obviously unfair contractual terms which disproportionately disadvantage the trading partner.[134]

Therefore, other methodologies should be accepted in order to assess the unfairness of wages and working conditions in those instances where workers are most vulnerable. Systemic violations of labour law, or even modern slavery provisions, on the part of the dominant undertaking, could be considered unfair.

---

130 See the CORE Econ Team 2023, The Economy 2.0: Microeconomics, Chapter 5.2. and 5.6., https://core-econ.org/the-economy/ (accessed 24 June 2024).

131 By applying the law of diminishing marginal utility to competition law enforcement's case selection, it could even be argued that, in order to maximise welfare, the most vulnerable workers should be prioritised. See *Samuelson/Nordhaus*, Economics, McCraw-Hill 19th edn. 2010, 84 et seqq.

132 Case 27/76, EU:C:1978:22 – *United Brands Company v European Commission*, para. 249.

133 See *Jung*, Art. 102 AUEV, in Grabitz/Hilf/Nettesheim (eds.), Das Recht der Europäischen Union: EUV/AUEV, C.H. BECK 83rd edn. 2024, para. 166.

134 See *Jung* (n 133) paras. 169–175.

Such an approach would be compatible with the German *Meta* case's reasoning, which considered the relevance of the GDPR for assessing competition law violations. In light of this article, it is relevant to mention that the case established that (non-)compliance with other branches of the law can be relevant for competition law's analysis. More precisely, its extremely broad consent form was deemed, based on its (non-)compliance with the GDPR as a benchmark, to constitute unfair conduct.

The GDPR prohibits the processing of consumers' personal data (unless exceptions apply) and stipulates (under Art. 7 GDPR) the necessary conditions for consumers' consent to be legally binding: it must be freely given, specific, informed, and unambiguous.

The ECJ held that "it may be necessary [...] also to examine whether that undertaking's conduct complies with rules other than those relating to competition law".[135] The GDPR was considered relevant to the competition law assessment because of the importance of its regulatory object (i.e., personal data) to the competitive dynamics of digital markets.[136] Accordingly, it stated that "excluding the rules on the protection of personal data from the legal framework to be taken into consideration by the competition authorities when examining an abuse of a dominant position would disregard the reality of this economic development and would be liable to undermine the effectiveness of competition law within the European Union".[137]

Violations of GDPR provisions are not sufficient by themselves to justify a competition law violation. They were nevertheless deemed relevant to the assessment of abuse (under the question of whether consumers could have consented to the elaboration of their personal data) since they concerned a situation where the dominant company's position is "liable to affect the freedom of choice of that user, who might be unable to refuse or withdraw consent without detriment".[138] The reasoning can be summarised as follows: (i) the GDPR rules regulate important parameters of competition and therefore can be relevant to the assessment, (ii) the GDPR's rules on the validity of consent constitute an important factor for the competition law assessment since a dominant position is liable to affect consumers' ability to consent.

---

135 Case C-252/21, EU:C:2023:537 – *Meta*, para. 48.
136 Case C-252/21, EU:C:2023:537 – *Meta*, para. 49.
137 Case C-252/21, EU:C:2023:537 – *Meta*, para. 51.
138 Case C-252/21, EU:C:2023:537 – *Meta,* para. 148.

Accordingly, violations of legal provisions aimed at protecting the bargaining position of workers and ensuring a minimum level of compensation should be considered relevant in the competition law assessment since they, too, play an important role in shaping competitive dynamics (arguably even in a clearer and more straightforward way than access to data and privacy as a competitive parameter). The question of consent is particularly interesting in this context. As mentioned above, economic theory generally presumes the consensual nature of market transactions, and the reasoning in *Meta* shows that competition law recognises that dominance has the ability to undermine said consent.[139] Therefore, labour law and other provisions aimed at protecting vulnerable workers from the superior economic position of employers should be considered in the assessment of abuse since consent cannot and should not be presumed.

Furthermore, in the context of the EU agricultural sector, Art. 39 TFEU states that one of the objectives of the Common Agricultural Policy is to "ensure a fair standard of living for the agricultural community" and that "supplies reach consumers at reasonable prices". Art. 42 TFEU clarifies that competition rules are only applicable to trade in agricultural products to the extent that "account [is] taken of the objectives set out in Article 39". As Holmes highlights, reasonable prices are not equal to low prices. Interpreting competition law on the basis of Art. 42 in connection with Art. 39 would bring the words exploitation and unfairness closer to their actual meaning. After all, the concept of fairness should not allow for wages that cannot cover basic needs[140] or impose working conditions that go as far as modern slavery or human trafficking.[141]

---

139 See Case C-252/21, EU:C:2023:537 – *Meta,* paras. 147–151.

140 For an account of the direct link between the ability of competition regimes to address abuses of power in supply chains and the enjoyment of the right to adequate food, see *de Schutter*, Addressing Concentration in Food Supply Chains, Briefing Note 03 (2010), 1.

141 See *Holmes*, Climate change, sustainability, and competition law, 8 Journal of Antitrust Enforcement (2020), 354, 385.

V. The Case for Enforcement for the Protection of the Most Vulnerable Workers

An approach which relies on the identification of eye-catching abuses[142] of market power against workers through the establishment of low boundaries in the case law makes sense from an enforcement perspective for two reasons.

First, as D'estaintot observes, the above-discussed exercises of determining whether an employer's "insufficient wage" through the same methods of excessive prices runs into several technical obstacles. For example, wage levels are influenced by multi-dimensional determinants which exacerbate the already demanding *United Brands*' case law on excessive pricing. Ultimately, the estimation of static harm to welfare provides more conjectures than certainties.[143] Maggiolino similarly notes the difficulty in identifying unfair wages exclusively by way of comparison of a reference wage to the wage charged by the dominant employer.[144] This point is also supported by Fuchs who notes how the conceptual obstacles to a fairness-based analysis of unfair conditions are not as significant as in the case of unfair prices. Abuse can be identified when blatantly unfair or disproportionate terms are imposed. Accordingly, a case-by-case analysis on the basis of the principle of proportionality can guide the identification of abuse.[145] Thus, the identification of real-world examples of unfair working conditions which deviate so significantly from what should be expected in a normal labour market instead provides a clear target for the identification of abuse. In doing so, complex counterfactual analysis and comparisons to hypothetically efficient labour market outcomes can be avoided.

Second, competition law enforcement which pursues such abuses is also welfare maximising from the perspective of the principle of diminishing marginal utility. The principle states as a person consumes more and more of a specific product, the amount of marginal utility they gain from it declines. In terms of money, one euro is valued less by a rich person compared

---

142 For one of the latest examples of agricultural workers' inhumane working conditions, see *Prandi in Foggia/Parent/Levitt*, 'Working here is hell': latest death of farm worker in 40C heat shocks Italy' The Guardian (27 August 2024), https://www.theguardian.com/global-development/article/2024/aug/27/indian-migrant-worker-death-heat-stress-italy (accessed 23 January 2025).

143 See *d'Estaintot* (n 13) 221–225.

144 See *Maggiolino* (n 9) i145.

145 *Fuchs* (n 128) para. 239.

to a poor person.[146] In welfare economics, this argument provides a basis to (i) prohibit welfare transfers from poor (e.g., workers or consumers) to rich (e.g., undertakings) since they are welfare reducing and (ii) pursue the reverse as they are welfare increasing.[147] While in antirust literature it has even been argued that the consumer welfare standard was intended by the U.S. congress as an injunction against illicit transfers of wealth from consumers to monopolists,[148] this article's argument is more moderate: as a matter of enforcement prioritisation, competition law intervention can maximise its welfare gains by striving to protect the poorest and most vulnerable workers.

To summarise, this suggests that improving the working conditions of workers in conditions of modern slavery is not only easier to identify as abuse but also generates a greater increase in welfare compared to, for example, the (nonetheless legitimate) pursuit of raising the previously depressed wages of white collars workers in tech jobs.

While economic theory has ignored this principle ever since the ordinalist revolution of the 1930s supplanted cardinalist approaches to welfare,[149] it must be remembered that it was never a conscious normative choice but rather an instrumental one, based on methodological expediency for the purpose of bypassing the problem of interpersonal utility comparisons.[150]

Economists have explained the relationship between employers' market power and low wages. It is now up to competition law to decide if and how to intervene[151] and, as has been argued above, the case law allows for such intervention beyond the narrow confines of neoclassical theory.

---

146 See *Samuelson/Nordhaus* (n 131) 84 et seqq.

147 See *Marshall*, Principles of Economics (London: Macmillan and Co. 8th edn. 1920), Book III Ch. 6 and Book V Ch. 2.

148 See e.g., *Lande*, Wealth Transfers as the Original and Primary Concern of Antitrust: The Efficiency Interpretation Challenged, 34 Hastings Law Journal (1999) 67.

149 For an account of this development see *Lianos*, The Poverty of Competition Law: The Long Story, 2 CLES Research Paper Series (2018) 1, 20–29.

150 See *Blaug*, The Fundamental Theorems of Modern Welfare Economics, Historically Contemplated, 39 History of Political Economy (2007) 185, 188.

151 In particular, it must be reminded that the choice of the economic theory which informs the competition law analysis is and must always remain a legal one, carried out by lawyers. For a more thorough explanation of this argument in the context of Swiss competition law see *Amstutz/Carron*, Art. 7 KG, in Amstutz/Reinert (eds.), Basler Kommentar, Helbing Lichtenhahn 2nd edn. 2022, para. 8.

Thus, the methodological shortcomings of neoclassical economics do not have to limit competition law enforcement when faced with real-world abuses that can be articulated in legal tests.

E. Conclusion

This article discussed whether competition law and, more precisely, Art. 102 TFEU can be applied to labour markets by using the welfare of workers as a basis for theories of harm. To do so, the most relevant application requirements of Art. 102 TFEU have been analysed.

It has been argued that the special features of labour markets (and secondary labour markets for migrant labour, more precisely) should be considered relevant by the case law on market definition and the assessment of dominance. In doing so, it is expected that comparatively smaller undertakings in labour markets could be found dominant relative to undertakings in product markets.

Lastly, this article looked at the concept of abuse, thereby establishing that on the basis of the Commission's latest sources, worker welfare can function as consumer welfare in product markets to provide the basis for theories of harm. Based on these findings, a labour theory of harm has been proposed which (i) fits within the case law of exploitative abuses and extends the reasoning of the ECJ in the *Meta* case from privacy regulation to labour law and (ii) transposes the economic reasoning that underlies excessive prices as abuse to labour markets and takes particular consideration on the effect of monopsony power on wages in secondary labour markets.

Part II:
Tools of Competition Law

Competitiveness and Antitrust Law: Between Feasibility and Desirability

*Selcukhan Unekbas**

A. Introduction

The competitiveness of European industry is on the agenda again. A recent report by the European Commission ("EC") writes:

> *"Current concern over the competitiveness of industry arises from a widely-held but vague general feeling that the [Union] is in danger of 'losing the race'. Several factors have combined to bring about this unease: the decline of a number of traditional industries which, in the past, provided the main-stay of economic prosperity; [...] the emergence of newly industrializing and certain developing countries as direct competitors for a wide range of markets; [...] and the recognition of the importance of the new technologies to 'post-industrial' society and the awareness that other countries [...] are further advanced than the [Union] in the commercial application and development of these technologies."*

Similarly, another inquiry by the European Parliament ("EP") regrets the EU's "failure to grow as vigorously, in productivity terms, as countries in its peer group, particularly the United States. [...] Some of this is attributable to slower adoption of new technologies, primarily IT. [...] The EU also trails the US and, increasingly, China in patents in frontier technologies."

These examples, and many others, converge on a common theme: declining European competitiveness resulting from failures to embrace technological change, productivity slowdown, and the rise of rivalling economies.[1] At this point, the reader is asked to forgive us for playing a little trick. For the quotes provided above only partially reflect the truth. In fact,

* PhD Researcher in Law, European University Institute (EUI), Florence, Italy; Research Fellow at the Haas School of Business, University of California, Berkeley.

1 In 2019, the EU altered its stance toward China by declaring it "an economic competitor and [...] a systemic rival". See, *European Commission,* 'EU-China – A strategic outlook' Join(2019) 5 final.

whereas the EP's statements were published in 2024[2], the EC quote is more than four decades old.[3] It seems that the EU's competitiveness problem is a persistent one indeed.

Some figures can illustrate the discussion. Although positive, average productivity growth in the EU has been weaker than other major economies.[4] Rapid growth by catching-up with the technological frontier lasted only for the 1960s and 70s, and once imitation opportunities were exhausted, Europe started stagnating.[5] Today, the EU creates fewer than half the number of successful startups as China, and only 12 % as the US.[6] In terms of material welfare, the picture is similar. One study concludes that if EU countries were US states, they would belong to the poorest group. If trends continue, the wealth gap between the average European and American in 2035 could be as big as between the average European and Indian today.[7] These facts show that "the EU's representation among the world's largest economies [has been] sharply decreasing in favor of rising Asian economies", not to mention its "lagging behind the US".[8]

There are no easy answers to a perennial question like the EU's competitiveness problem.[9] Addressing it would likely involve the EU's entire legal and policy apparatus. But what about antitrust law and policy? Not only is antitrust law responsible for ensuring that the internal market remains undivided, but it also enables effective competition, therefore bolstering the

2 European Parliament, 'Coordination for EU competitiveness' (2024) EP EGOV Paper No. 747.838 https://www.europarl.europa.eu/RegData/etudes/STUD/2024/747838/IPOL_STU(2024)747838_EN.pdf (accessed 3 March 2025).

3 *European Commission*, 'The Competitiveness of European Community Industry' (1982) Document No. III/387/82 http://aei.pitt.edu/5542/1/5542.pdf (accessed 3 March 2025).

4 *European Commission*, "Long-term competitiveness of the EU: looking beyond 2030" COM(2023)168 final.

5 *Alesina/Giavazzi*, The Future of Europe: Reform or Decline, MIT Press 2006.

6 *European Commission* (n 4) 8.

7 *Erixon/Guinea/du Roy*, 'Comparing Economic Growth Between EU and US States' (2023) ECIPE Policy Brief No. 07/2023 https://ecipe.org/wp-content/uploads/2023/06/ECI_23_PolicyBrief_07-2023_LY02.pdf (accessed 3 March 2025).

8 *Letta*, 'Much More Than A Market: Empowering the Single Market to deliver a sustainable future and prosperity for all EU citizens' (2024) https://www.consilium.europa.eu/media/ny3j24sm/much-more-than-a-market-report-by-enrico-letta.pdf (accessed 3 March 2025).

9 *Editorial Comments*, The EU's integrated policy approach towards competitiveness, 61 Common Market Law Review (2024), 1; *Thurik/Stam/Audretsch*, The rise of the entrepreneurial economy and the future of dynamic capitalism, 33 Technovation (2013), 302.

EU's economic power. As noted by Craig, antitrust law has "always been of real significance for attainment of the overall economic objectives of the EU".[10] But is that claim true for competitiveness? Or to put the question in another way, could we envisage the goal of EU antitrust law as supporting competitiveness?

The idea of competitiveness has undergone transformation in European integration and antitrust law (**Part B**). But the antitrust-competitiveness nexus remains underexplored. This contribution argues that, unlike earlier views, a modern understanding of competitiveness could form a legitimate goal for EU antitrust law (**Part C**).

B. Competitiveness, European Integration, and Antitrust Law

I. Competitiveness in European Integration

Competitiveness has long occupied the central stage in European integration. Although the European project's ultimate goal was political, this was never an isolated target. Rather, the accompanying aim was to enable Europe to carve a space of "relative economic autonomy" for itself.[11] As early as 1970, the EC acknowledged that "the unity of Europe" and "the maintenance of economic growth" go hand in hand with "a reasonable degree of independence [from] major world powers".[12] It specifically singled out the importance of creating "transnational European firms" that can face up to competition from abroad, including "the big American corporations". The desire for competitiveness was based on "a fear of falling behind", which remains "as old as European integration itself".[13] Both official and academic accounts attest to this.

---

10 *Craig*, The Lisbon Treaty, Revised Edition: Law, Politics, and Treaty Reform, Oxford University Press 2013.

11 *Lavery/Schmid*, European Integration and the New Global Disorder, 59 Journal of Common Market Studies (2021), 1322.

12 . *European Commission* (n 3), 18.

13 *Seidl/Schmitz*, Moving on to not fall behind? Technological sovereignty and the "geo-dirigiste" turn in EU industrial policy, 31 Journal of European Public Policy (2023), 2147.

1. Official investigations

Official investigations of European competitiveness began with the Spaak Report.[14] The Report was the result of the 1956 Intergovernmental Conference held in Messina. It is important for two main reasons. First, the report emphasized Europe's continuous economic recovery and development. Second, it identified the mechanism to achieve that aim. Accordingly, the common market was "established in the name of greater productivity", "rational distribution of activities", and an "optimum rate of economic expansion".[15] The grounding of integration on economic performance was palpable.

Between the Treaty of Rome and the Single European Act, the European institutions regularly revisited the issue of competitiveness.[16] An important piece was the "Cost of Non-Europe" studies, more widely known as the "Cecchini Report" or "the European Challenge 1992".[17] The Cecchini Report was the foundation for the Single European Act.[18] It placed the continent's competitiveness problem center-stage. Accordingly, the issue was to be resolved by completing the single market and establishing "a new and pervasive competitive climate...[o]ne in which the players of the European economy can exploit new opportunities and better use available resources".[19] The report specifically underlined economies of scale and efficient allocation of resources, thereby following a price-based competitiveness strategy.

Competitiveness was central to the Lisbon Strategy as well. The Lisbon Strategy aspired to transform the EU into "the most competitive and dy-

---

14 *Spaak*, Intergovernmental Committee on European Integration: The Brussels Report on the General Common Market, EEC 1956.

15 *Spaak* (n 14), part II.

16 For example, the "Davignon plan", an interventionist industrial policy, was set up to boost European competitiveness during the 1970s; *Alter/Steinberg*, The Theory and Reality of the European Coal and Steel Community, in Meunier/McNamara (eds.), The State of the European Union – Making History: European Integration and Institutional Change at Fifty, Oxford University Press 2007, 89.

17 *Cecchini/Catinat,/Jacquemin*, The European Challenge 1992: The Benefits of a Single Market, Wilwood House 1988.

18 *Sandholtz /Zysman*, 1992: Recasting the European Bargain, 42 World Politics (1989), 95.

19 *Cecchini et al.* (n 17), 73.

namic knowledge-based economy in the world".[20] The reasons behind this drive were familiar. China's accession to the multilateral trading system and the information technology revolution required the EU to remain competitive within the context of globalized markets and accelerating technological change.[21] However, what distinguished the Lisbon Strategy was the means. Earlier reports mainly underscored scale economies, emanating from integrated markets, as the driver of competitiveness. In addition, the Lisbon Strategy acknowledged the EU's "structural productivity problem, rooted in systemic inadequacies of its innovation system, calling for an innovation-based economic model".[22] This signified increasing attention on non-price competitiveness.

Nonetheless, the Lisbon Strategy proved disappointing.[23] Hence, subsequent inquiries continued to ponder the competitiveness problem. For instance, a 2014 EP study titled "Cecchini Revisited" found significant deficiencies in competitiveness due to the fragmentation of the internal market, logging annual losses of EUR 58 billion as a result.[24] A more recent example took place where this dissertation is being written. At the European University Institute, an executive board member of the European Central Bank has warned of a "competitiveness crisis", citing EU economic performance lagging significantly behind rivals like the US and China.[25] And reports by Enrico Letta and, especially, Mario Draghi took the policy world by force, drawing attention to the stickiness of European competitiveness deficiencies and proposing dramatic reforms.[26]

The recurring nature of the competitiveness problem is striking. Virtually every decade since the Treaty of Paris has witnessed an official competi-

20 Council of the European Union, 'Presidency Conclusions – Lisbon European Council' (2000).

21 *Bongardt/Torres*, Lisbon Strategy, in Jones/Menon/Weatherill (eds.), The Oxford Handbook of the European Union, Oxford University Press 2012, 469.

22 *Bongardt/Torres* (n 21), 502 Page isn't in accordance with starting page 469; *Sapir et al.*, An Agenda for a Growing Europe: The Sapir Report, Oxford University Press 2004.

23 *Kok et al.*, Facing the Challenge: The Lisbon strategy for growth and employment, EU Publications Office 2004.

24 *Pataki*, The Cost of Non-Europe in the Single Market – "Cecchini Revisited"' European Parliamentary Research Service Paper No. PE 510.981 (2014).

25 *Schnabel*, From laggard to leader? Closing the euro area's technology gap (Inaugural Lecture of the EMU Lab, Florence, February 2024).

26 *European Commission*, 'The Future of European Competitiveness' (September 2024) https://commission.europa.eu/document/download/97e481fd-2dc3-412d-be4c-f152a8232961_en accessed [...].

tiveness inquiry. These explored similar topics, identified analogous reasons why European competitiveness was lagging, and proposed solutions that were broadly aligned. The continued issuance of inquiries implies chronic dissatisfaction with the EU's economic performance. In short, competitiveness has been an evergreen issue for the EU. And success has been elusive.

2. Academic investigations

The discussion of European competitiveness in academic literature has deep roots and remains lively.[27] Scholars on both sides of the Atlantic with diverse views and ideologies have been commenting on European competitiveness for decades.

Academics viewed competitiveness as a natural aim of European integration long before the project took root. In a 1939 essay, Friedrich Hayek explored the economic benefits of federalism.[28] Although not speaking of a 'European Union', Hayek predicted many features of contemporary EU law, including free movement and mutual recognition. He later argued that a federal Europe should be less protectionist and enjoy borderless trade to cultivate greater competitiveness.[29] Around the same time, Ernst Jünger, a German philosopher, argued that post-World War II, Europe would need new institutions to bolster the strength and unity of the continent. He described the "plight of Europe, sandwiched between two superpowers" and hoped that "the Union of Europe might prove a third force able to compete with the United States and Russia".[30]

The academic literature on European competitiveness zeroes in on Europe's position against the US. Many works demonstrate that Europe simultaneously envied and dreaded US economic performance. On one hand, European integration was inspired by the success of US economic union.[31]

---

27 *Egan*, The evolution of single markets in Europe and the United States, in Koutrakos/Snell (eds.), Research Handbook on the Law of the EU's Internal Market, Elgar 2017, 500.

28 *Hayek*, The Economic Conditions of Interstate Federalism in Lewis (ed.), Essays on Liberalism and the Economy, Routledge 2022, 100.

29 *Morgan*, Hayek, Habermas, and European Integration, 2 Critical Review (2003), 1.

30 *Honsberger*, A Difference of Degrees: Ernst Jünger, the National Socialists, and a New Europe, Boston College 2006.

31 *Lippmann*, Western Unity and the Common Market, Little, Brown & Co. 1962; On the similarities between US and EU economic laws, see *Waller*, Understanding and Appreciating EC Competition Law, 61 Antitrust Law Journal (1992), 55.

On the other hand, the primary beneficiary of European integration were American multinationals.[32] This gave rise to a fear of American industrial hegemony over Europe. Perhaps the book that best illustrates this tension is *The American Challenge*.[33] Criticizing the "economic colonization" of Europe by American industry, the book explores how European competitiveness must be rebuilt through better organization and technological development. For instance, a passage reads[34]:

> *"The path of [Europe's] counterattack [against the United States] is clearly marked: creation of large industrial units capable of competing with the American giants, both by their size and their management; [and] carrying out 'major operations' of advanced technology...".*

In the following decades, the European economy registered surpluses in trade with the US.[35] But except for few scholars like Wilhelm Röpke, who repeatedly argued that anxiety over US competition was misguided, the sentiment of European regression continued.[36]

Academic debate on European competitiveness revolves around a technology gap. The concept refers to Europe's relative weakness in developing, producing, and benefitting from technology. Following the Second World War, American firms quickly dominated technology-intensive industries like aviation, computers, and electronics in Europe.[37] This sentiment remained "very strong" throughout the 1980s and 90s.[38] For example, a study sponsored by the EC highlighted that "Europe is losing ground precisely where it matters for the future [...] to Japanese and American competitors".[39] Europe's technological lag continues to feature in contem-

---

32 *Hellmann*, The Challenge to U.S. Dominance of the International Corporations, Dunellen 1971.

33 *Servan-Schreiber*, The American Challenge, Penguin 1969.

34 *Servan-Schreiber* (n 33), 125.

35 *Klein*, The Single Market in Europe: An American Appraisal, in Dewatripont/Ginsburgh (eds.), European Economic Integration – A Challenge in a Changing World, Elsevier 1994, 1.

36 *Röpke*, International Order and Economic Integration, D. Reidel 1959.

37 As one commentator described it, the dominance of US firms was so strong that it would not be permitted under US antitrust laws. See, *Krause*, European Economic Integration and the United States, Brookings 1968.

38 *Woods*, Western Europe: Technology and the Future, Atlantic Papers No. 63 (1987).

39 *de Woot*, High Technology Europe: Strategic Issues for Global Competitiveness, Basil Blackwell 1990.

porary discussions.[40] This implies a recognition of European weakness in non-price competitiveness.

Another recurring theme in the literature is the relationship between competitiveness and the division of economic activities between private and public sectors. Contemporary economies are mixed. The public sector participates in the economy in many ways. For example, public goods, such as national defense and the justice system, and welfare state functions, such as education and universal healthcare, are often provided by States. Furthermore, many States, including European ones, have a tradition of supplying certain economic goods. These typically include infrastructure like utilities, communications, and transport. In this context, the question is whether economies with larger public sectors are more competitive, and what lessons this can hold for Europe.

This is a long-standing discussion in European integration.[41] The literature features two streams of thought. One view essentially relies on the efficiency of markets, defending that markets allocate resources to efficient firms. They argue that only those firms capable of withstanding competition should remain in the market. Empirical evidence shows that private firms are generally more efficient than public ones.[42] Since efficiency is associated with competitiveness, this argument suggests that the division of activity in the economy should bias the private sector. This conclusion is especially salient in public supply of economic services like utilities. As one scholar noted, "the success of European integration hinges upon the [Union's] ability to break down monopoly-protecting regulations within each country".[43] The other view defends public participation in the economy. As opposed to private initiative, the public sector is generally not subject to market accountability.[44] But this does not mean that public

40 *Berend*, Changing Europe's Economic History, in Segers/Van Heke (eds.), The Cambridge History of the European Union: European Integration Inside-Out, Cambridge University Press 2023, 565.

41 *Amato*, Antitrust and the Bounds of Power: The Dilemma of Liberal Democracy in the History of the Market, Hart 1997.

42 *Szarzec/Dombi/Matuszak*, State-owned enterprises and economic growth: Evidence from the post-Lehman period, 99 Journal of Economic Modelling (2021), 105490.

43 *de Jong*, Stagnation and Competition in the European Economy, in Fauljaber/Tamburini (eds.), European Economic Integration: The Role of Technology, Kluwer 1991, 83.

44 *Maduro*, Ensuring Market and State Accountability: The Private-Public Distinction in the EU Internal Market, in Andriychuk (ed.), Antitrust and the Bounds of Power – 25 Years On, Bloomsbury 2024, 33.

participation in the economy is universally detrimental to competitiveness. The public sector fulfils important objectives and social functions. The positive externalities stemming from these activities can be significant.[45] In this light, supporting competitiveness likely requires a delicate balance between reaping the efficiency of markets whilst safeguarding the benefits of public services as much as possible. After all, the Treaties describe the goal for the European economy with two simultaneous adjectives: "highly competitive" *and* "social".

II. Competitiveness in Antitrust Law

Antitrust literature rarely devotes attention to competitiveness, and when it does, it is usually hostile. This generally stems from a suspicion of competitiveness. Consequently, the few works that study competitiveness and antitrust do so only indirectly.

1. Hostility toward competitiveness

Antitrust literature takes a siloed approach toward competitiveness. The argument goes something like this. Antitrust is microeconomic policy. Thus, it minimally interacts with competitiveness, which is viewed as a macroeconomic phenomenon. This leads antitrust to define competitiveness in microeconomic terms, such as how effective a market is in producing the beneficial results of competition. In this exercise, market structure is commonly used as a proxy to determine the competitiveness of markets. For example, market characteristics approximating perfect competition (*e.g,* many sellers with little pricing power) or simply the absence of monopoly are often taken as indicators of competitiveness. In this vein, dominant firms may signify that a market is uncompetitive.[46] By contrast, some suggest that monopolistic markets can be competitive provided that entry

45 *Mosley/Schmid*, Public services and competitiveness, in Hughes (ed.), European Competitiveness, Cambridge University Press 1993, 200.

46 A seminal judgment of the ECJ reads: "The concept of abuse is an objective concept relating to the behaviour of an undertaking in a dominant position which is such as to influence the structure of a market where, *as a result of the very presence of the undertaking in question, the degree of competition is weakened...*". The judgment remains good law. See, Case C-85/76, EU:C:1979:36 – *Hoffmann-La Roche.*

is easy.[47] Other sources, including court judgments, adopt a middle-ground approach and pursue "workably competitive" markets.[48]

When it comes to the relationship between antitrust and international competitiveness, the traditional view is not very positive. Besides the disinterest stemming from the "micro/macro division", it is common to see antitrust as detrimental to competitiveness.[49] For example, scholars commonly argue that antitrust is excessively trigger-friendly, and aggressive enforcement against poorly understood conduct chills initiative and harms competitiveness.[50] There is also the industrial policy debate, which is more pronounced in Europe. In general, EU law scholars portray competitiveness as a function of industrial policy. And it follows from such characterization that antitrust law needs to be relaxed, perhaps for certain industries, to allow firms to grow and compete internationally.[51] It is rare to see discussions beyond such caricaturizing. This inhospitality tradition creates an undertheorized nexus between antitrust and competitiveness.[52]

47 *Baumol*, Contestable Markets: An Uprising in the Theory of Industry Structure, 72 The American Economic Review (1982), 1; *Brozen*, Competition, Efficiency, and Antitrust, 3 Journal of World Trade Law (1969), 659.

48 A decision endorsing workable competition in EU law is Case C-26/76, EU:C:1977:167 – *Metro I*; *Clark*, Toward a Concept of Workable Competition, 30 The American Economic Review (1940), 241.

49 *Yoshizawa*, European Union Competition Policy versus Industrial Competitiveness: Stringent Regulation and Its External Implications, Routledge 2022.

50 *Jorde/Teece, Antitrust Policy and Innovation: Taking Account of Performance Competition and Competitor Cooperation*, 147 Journal of Institutional and Theoretical Economics (1991), 118; *Brozen*, The Antitrust Tradition: Entrepreneurial Restraint, 9 Harvard Journal of Law & Public Policy (1986), 337; *Watkins*, The Economic Philosophy of Antitrust Legislation, The Annals of the American Academy of Political and Social Science (1930), 12.

51 *Smith*, From Competition to Competitiveness: A New EU Industrial Policy?, (Eighth Biennial International Conference of the European Union Studies Association, Nashville, Tennessee, March 2003).

52 *Petit*, "Picking Mergers": The Challenge of Competitiveness in Competition Policy, 45 European Competition Law Review (2024), 385.

2. Indirect approaches to the antitrust-competitiveness nexus

Literature studies antitrust and competitiveness only indirectly. For example, one channel is antitrust's impact on productivity.[53] Many authors find that antitrust enforcement fosters productivity.[54] And there is agreement that "well-designed and well-implemented antitrust policy has a significant impact on TFP growth".[55] Overall, the literature here is limited. But it unequivocally suggests that antitrust can help competitiveness most effectively by enabling the reallocation of resources to productive firms in the long-term.[56]

Antitrust scholarship on efficiency may also be considered as indirectly exploring competitiveness issues. The friendliness of EU antitrust law toward efficiency becomes apparent when compared to the US system. The Treaty of Rome was more permissive to efficient accumulations of market power, recognizing that "control by a single firm over an exceptionally large portion of an industry was not prohibited".[57] Rene Joliet, an early member of the Court of Justice, corroborated this view by endorsing that EU antitrust law viewed efficiency favorably.[58] He argued that, to catch up with the American economy, EU law was designed to welcome firms capable of superior efficiency. Later, his statements were echoed by Pınar Akman, who reasserted that exclusion was originally a non-issue for EU antitrust law, which only concerned itself with the exploitation of market power.[59]

---

53 For a clear exposition, see *Nazzini*, The Foundations of European Union Competition Law: The Objective and Principles of Article 102 TFEU, Oxford University Press 2018.

54 *Ju Hong*, Effects of Competition Policy on Macroeconomic Outcomes, 37 Journal of Economic Integration (2022), 337; *Dierx et al.*, Does EU Competition Policy Support Inclusive Growth?, 13 Journal of European Competition Law & Economics (2017), 225.

55 *Buccirossi et al.*, Competition Policy and Productivity Growth: An Empirical Assessment, 95 The Review of Economics and Statistics (2013), 1324.

56 *Cavenaile/Çelik/Tian*, The Dynamic Effects of Antitrust Policy on Growth and Welfare, 121 Journal of Monetary Economics (2021), 42.

57 *Krause* (n 37), 152.

58 *Joliet*, Monopolization and Abuse of Dominant Position: A Comparative Study of the American and European Approaches to the Control of Economic Power, Martijn Nijhoff 1970.

59 *Akman*, Searching for the Long-Lost Soul of Article 82 EC, 29 Oxford Journal of Legal Studies (2009), 267.

In addition to productivity and efficiency, another thread that links competitiveness with antitrust is innovation. Some scholars argue that competitiveness could benefit if innovation concerns guided antitrust law.[60] For example, antitrust enforcement can boost competitiveness by "unfreezing markets", that is, by forcing inert monopolists to innovate.[61] In addition, antitrust enforcement helps competitiveness by opening up previously monopolized markets or forcing incumbent firms to accommodate new entrants. A clear example is supplementing deregulatory efforts in utilities (*e.g.*, telecoms and energy) with antitrust enforcement, often effectuated through securing commitments from legacy firms.[62]

While competitiveness and antitrust are rarely examined directly, a common theme nonetheless emerges. All commentaries emphasize dynamism and the long-run. The scholarship generally underlines the importance of long-run adaptation, innovation, and productivity growth for economic performance.[63] Even authors leaning toward industrial policy, who see antitrust enforcement as antithetical to competitiveness, base their critique of antitrust on its short-term orientation to the detriment of long-run performance of European firms.[64]

C. Competitiveness, Antitrust, and Legitimacy

Clearly, competitiveness played a central role in European integration. But it was disfavored in antitrust scholarship, featuring rarely and only indirectly. Besides an emphasis on long-term dynamism, there is no indication on how competitiveness-oriented antitrust law would look like. But a broader question must be addressed before. Even if we can conjecture the shape of

60 *Wu*, Taking Innovation Seriously: Antitrust Enforcement If Innovation Mattered the Most, 78 Antitrust Law Journal (2012), 313.

61 *Petit/Schrepel*, Complexity-minded antitrust, 33 Journal of Evolutionary Economics (2023), 541.

62 See generally entries in *Lowe/Marquis*, European Competition Policy Annual: Competition, Regulation, and Public Policies, Oxford University Press 2014.

63 *Ahn*, Competition, Innovation, and Productivity Growth: A Review of Theory and Evidence, OECD Economics Department Working Paper No. 317 (2002).

64 See, *e.g.*, *Cini/McGowan*, Competition Policy in the European Union, Palgrave MacMillan 2008.

competitiveness-oriented antitrust law, should we? Would it be legitimate for EU antitrust law to support competitiveness?[65]

Discussing competitiveness and antitrust in the EU is likely to raise eyebrows. It is still common to see competitiveness equated with traditional industrial policy, and consequently, dismissed without much debate. But doing so ignores the evolution of how economics came to understand competitiveness. Without analyzing these developments, judging the place of competitiveness in EU antitrust law will be misleading.

When talking about competitiveness, traditional economic literature refers to favorable trade performance, specifically in exports.[66] In this context, competitiveness depends on relative industrial costs and the extent of demand in foreign markets. It operates on price-based rivalry, and countries producing cheaper are expected to gain competitive advantage over others. It is a macroeconomic concept, and as such, not directly legible to antitrust law and policy. The aversion of antitrust law toward competitiveness is based on this traditional understanding.[67] Many writers critique that competitiveness may produce "a dangerous obsession" over economic performance.[68] They argue that there are many ways to become price competitive. And some of these are not at all desirable, such as evading labour standards or slacking on environmental protection to slash costs. Price-based competitiveness, it is argued, could also be used as a "political slogan" by countries.[69] It may cause governments to manipulate currencies or provide subsidies irresponsibly. This is why a typical reaction to European competitiveness revolves around old school industrial policy, "champions", and loose state aid regulation.[70]

65 On issues of normative and positive legitimacy in EU law, see *Priban*, A Social Theory of Constitutional Imaginaries: Beyond the Unity of *topos-ethnos-nomos* and its European Context, in Belavusau/Gliszczynska-Grabias (eds.), Constitutionalism Under Stress, Oxford University Press 2020, 175.

66 For a literature review, see *Aiginger*, European competitiveness and sustainable development, 31 Competitiveness Review (2021), 883.

67 *Petit/Neyrinck*, EU Competition Law and Industrial Policy: In Need of a Rethink?, in Merola/Derenne (eds.), GCLC Annual Conference Series 2012, Bruylant 2013, 1.

68 *Krugman*, Competitiveness: A Dangerous Obsession, Foreign Affairs 1994, 28.

69 *Wigger*, Enhancing 'competitiveness' in response to the European crisis, in Jager/Springler (eds.), Asymmetric Crisis in Europe and Possible Futures: Critical Political Economy and Post-Keynesian Perspectives, Routledge 2015, 133.

70 This phenomenon is documented by *Kaseberg/Van Laer*, Competition Law and Industrial Policy: Conflict, Adaptation, and Complementarity, in Patel/Schweitzer

Such an understanding is outdated. The traditional view of competitiveness has been extensively criticized in economic literature. First, traditional factors of competitiveness lack explanatory power. Empirical studies document that accounting only for price-based competitiveness leaves large residuals in trade performance unexplained.[71] Economists explain such gaps with *non-price competitiveness*. Accordingly, competitiveness depends on a broader array of factors, such as product quality and uniqueness, superior technological attributes, and innovation.[72] Indeed, there is a "Schumpeterian emphasis" on economic performance based on factors other than price.[73]

Second, traditional views of price-based competitiveness also suffer from "Kaldor's paradox".[74] Put simply, Kaldor's paradox refers to situations where competitiveness and input costs rise simultaneously. From a traditional perspective, this is an odd result, as price-based competitiveness predicts falling costs. But in modern economies, where countries export diversified and high-quality products, this intuition no longer holds. Somewhat counterintuitively, modern competitiveness demands the ability to sell at *high prices* due to superior quality of exports.[75] Indeed, economists call non-price competitiveness "the high road to industrial success", as opposed to the "low road" based on price competition.[76] In short, performance in non-price competition is taken as the gold standard of modern competitiveness.[77]

(eds.), The Historical Foundations of EU Competition Law, Oxford University Press 2013, 162.

71 *Benkovskis/Wörz*, What Drives Market Share Changes? Price versus Non-Price Factors, ECB Working Paper Series No. 1640 (2014).

72 *European Commission*, Quarterly Report on the Euro Area 16, European Economy Institutional Paper No. 049 (2017).

73 *Keil*, Assessing the role of non-price factors: Shedding new light on the European competitiveness puzzle, 178 Journal of International Economics (2024), 100495; See also, Akçiğit/Van Reenen (eds.), The Economics of Creative Destruction: New Research on Themes from Aghion and Howitt, HUP 2023.

74 *Kaldor*, Conflicts in national economic objectives, 81 The Economic Journal (1971), 1.

75 On this point, see Pascal Lamy, 'Smart policies to maintain European competitiveness' (*Speech at the WTO*, 20 October 2012) https://www.wto.org/english/news_e/sppl_e/sppl255_e.htm (accessed 3 March 2025).

76 *Milberg/Houston*, The high road and the low road to international competitiveness: Extending the neo-Schumpeterian trade model beyond technology, 19 International Review of Applied Economics (2005), 137.

77 *Cezar/Cartelier*, Price and non-price competitiveness: Lessons from global value chains, 224 Bulletin de la Banque de France (2019), 1.

Third, modern economics of competitiveness draws a link between macro- and microeconomic dimensions. Contemporary literature acknowledges that competitiveness is a "multidimensional concept" that encompasses firms and sectors as well as the ability of institutions to support efficient markets, thereby translating into superior economic performance".[78] Firms become competitive when they outrun their rivals by producing attractive products, which then makes their countries competitive by improving terms of trade, attracting investment, and boosting welfare.

The progression of economic literature should urge a reflection on the prior beliefs of antitrust. While many concerns of antitrust law regarding competitiveness are justified, they are also based on outdated scholarship. Indeed, the modern view of European competitiveness is conceived as a future-oriented project based on adaptation and market evolution.[79] As the EC long-acknowledged, competitiveness refers not to "measures designed to keep alive activities that no longer have any prospect of competing in the modern world", but to measures "contribut[ing] to a much more dynamic development."[80] This calls into question whether antitrust law and policy is still rightful in dismissing competitiveness. We may have reached a point that a window to bring competitiveness and antitrust closer has appeared.

Five reasons illustrate why a modern account of competitiveness resonates with antitrust. Competitiveness is a recurrent theme in EU law and an important goal for antitrust law (**I**); the modern understanding of competitiveness is compatible with wider EU objectives (**II**); competitiveness can contribute to market integration (**III**); it relies on a defensible philosophy (**IV**); and it is pragmatic (**V**).

I. Recurrence

Competitiveness as a goal of EU law is well-documented. But this is not to ascribe a domineering goal for the law. Rather, careful analysis suggests that no idea or ideology dominated antitrust law.[81] Instead, antitrust law

78 *Collignon/Esposito*, Competitiveness in the European Economy, Routledge 2014.

79 *Aiginger/Vogel*, Competitiveness: from a misleading concept to a strategy supporting Beyond GDP goals, 25 Competitiveness Review (2015), 497.

80 *European Commission*, The Community's industrial policy (1970) COM(70) 100 final.

81 *Buch-Hansen/Wigger*, The Politics of European Competition Regulation: A Critical Political Economy Perspective, Routledge 2011.

has been a product of compromise and pragmatism, with many forces coalescing around the shaping of the law.[82] As Gerber put it, the "institutional dynamics" of the EU and the substantive richness of antitrust law preclude a "singular voice".[83] This context-driven and pragmatic approach suggests that the law does not stand in the way of policy. Perhaps this is what Oliver Wendell Holmes alluded to by "social desire" as a shared aspiration that the law commits to in a given period.[84]

The permissive attitude of law toward policy can be traced in the history of antitrust. In the beginning of the European project, antitrust prioritized eliminating private barriers to cross-border trade. This was done to secure European integration.[85] Later on, antitrust equipped a more economic lens and targeted consumer welfare. This roughly coincided with "the end of history" when the EU was "peaking": unemployment was lower, financial markets were reasonably liquid, and businesses were relatively mobile.[86] In such an environment, shorter-term goals like consumer welfare probably seemed sensible.[87]

As evidenced above, the lingering "collective legal consciousness" around European competitiveness has resurfaced strongly.[88] Competitiveness remains a central EU objective, and it occupies the top spot in the economic agenda. The new EC's mandate places competitiveness first in the list of policy priorities. The 2024–2029 Strategic Agenda of the EU, promulgated

82 *Van Apeldoorn*, Transnational Capitalism and the Struggle over European Integration, Routledge 2002; *Brook*, In search of a European economic imaginary of competition: fifty years of the Commission's annual reports, 1 European Law Open (2022), 822.

83 *Gerber*, The Goals of European Competition Law – Some Distortions in the Literature, in Zimmer (ed.), The Goals of Competition Law, Elgar 2012, 85.

84 *Holmes*, Law in Science and Science in Law, 12 Harvard Law Review (1899), 443.

85 *Sierra*, Writing Straight with Crooked Lines: Competition Policy and Services of General Economic Interest in the Treaty of Lisbon, in Biondi/Eeckhout/Ripley (eds.), EU Law After Lisbon, OUP 2012, 347.

86 'Peak Europe turns 25: why June 1999 marked the continent's zenith' (*The Economist*, 6 June 2024) https://www.economist.com/europe/2024/06/06/peak-europe-turns-25-why-june-1999-marked-the-continents-zenith (accessed 3 March 2025).

87 *Evans*, The consumer and competition policy: welfare, interest and engagement, in Ezrachi (ed.), Research Handbook on International Competition Law, Elgar 2012, 545. We do not mean to say that consumer welfare is short-termist, but that consumer welfare has been mainly pursued by addressing short-term monopolistic pricing. See, *Melamed/Petit*, The Misguided Assault on the Consumer Welfare Standard in the Age of Platform Markets, 54 Review of Industrial Organization (2019), 741.

88 *Kurkchiyan*, Perceptions of Law and Social Order: A Cross-National Comparison of Collective Legal Consciousness, 29 Wisconsin International Law Journal (2019), 366.

by the European Council, dedicates much space to creating "a prosperous and competitive Europe".[89] The Lisbon Treaty no longer counts "competition" as an objective of EU law but relegates it to a Protocol. While competition retains its value – it remains the method of organizing economic activity in the EU[90] – this change is not purely symbolic either. The subtle amendment has been interpreted as reflecting an instrumentalization of competition in pursuit of a "highly competitive" economy.[91] As noted by a prominent lawyer, it may be time for EU antitrust law to "return to its roots" and reprioritize economic competitiveness.[92]

II. Compatibility

One reason why competitiveness commands a bad reputation in literature is an alleged conflict with fairness or social justice.[93] This claim is overstated and outdated. Competitiveness is not incompatible with broader EU objectives. It is actually an enabling force. As argued powerfully by Servan-Schreiber[94]:

> "*The degree of autonomy, prosperity, and social justice that a country aspires to depends upon its growth rate. A society enjoying rapid growth is free to define its own form of civilization because it can establish its order of priorities. A stagnant society cannot really exercise the right of self-determination.*"

---

89 *European Council*, 'Strategic Agenda: 2024 – 2029' https://www.consilium.europa.eu/media/4aldqfl2/2024_557_new-strategic-agenda.pdf (accessed 3 March 2025).

90 As reaffirmed after the Lisbon Treaty in Case C-52/09 *TeliaSonera Sverige AB* [2011], para. 22. See also, *Pera*, Changing Views of Competition, Economic Analysis, and EC Antitrust Law, 4 European Competition Journal (2008), 127.

91 *Tosato*, The Shape of post-Lisbon Europe, in Micossi/Tosato (eds), The European Union in the 21st Century: Perspectives from the Lisbon Treaty, Oxford University Press 2009, 271.

92 *Bellis*, 'Quelle place encore pour la politique de la concurrence dans l'Union européenne aujourd'hui?' (*IEE-ULB Blog*, 15 April 2024) https://www.iee-ulb.eu/content/uploads/2024/04/Carte-blanche_Jean-Francois-Bellis_1504_final.pdf (accessed 3 March 2025).

93 *Gerard/Lianos*, Reconciling Efficiency and Equity: A Global Challenge for Competition Policy, Cambridge University Press 2019.

94 *Servan-Schreiber* (n 33), 182.

A continent with very ambitious goals like decarbonization, digitalization, and rejuvenation needs to be economically strong. Decades of academic and policy literature suggests that the EU is failing Servan-Schreiber's test. This fact alone is sufficient for taking competitiveness seriously. Nonetheless, the compatibility between competitiveness and other EU objectives withstands deeper scrutiny.[95]

EU law does not envisage the internal market as a purely economic construct, but one that encompasses material and non-material wellbeing.[96] In addition to undistorted competition, the internal market must also supply "sustainable development", "economic growth and price stability", "a highly competitive social market economy", "full employment and social progress", and "a high level of protection and improvement of the quality of the environment". Some of these objectives are broadly in alignment with competitiveness. For instance, competitiveness is very effective in generating economic growth. Similarly, and while it may be too much to ask for antitrust law to decidedly combat inflation, empirical research suggests that a competitive economy incurs slower price increases.[97] Hence, supporting competitiveness via antitrust law is not incompatible with the EU's aim of achieving stable prices.

The compatibility of other objectives, such as employment, social mobility, and environmental protection, with competitiveness is not as readily apparent. For example, competitiveness is often portrayed as conflicting with social mobility.[98] But a competitive, high productivity economy fosters social mobility. Productive firms are known to pay their workers more. In general, sustained empirical work demonstrates the positive relationship

---

95 For another treatment, see *Maggiolino*, 'The Multi-Purpose Approach and Article 102 TFEU' (*Network Law Review,* 3 July 2024) https://www.networklawreview.org/maggiolino-future-brandeis/ (accessed 3 March 2025).

96 *Kaupa, The Pluralist Character of the European Economic Constitution*, Hart 2016.

97 *Clark*, Inflation and the Productivity Decline, 72 The American Economic Review (1982), 149.

98 *Liebert*, Reconciling Market with Social Europe? The EU Under Lisbon Treaty, in Schiek/Liebert/Schneider (eds.), European Economic and Social Constitutionalism after the Treaty of Lisbon, Cambridge University Press 2011, 47. The negative effects of innovation on social mobility is not significant. See, *Aghion/Akçiğit/Bergeaud/Blundell/Hemous*, Innovation and Top Income Inequality, 86 The Review of Economic Studies (2019), 1.

between competitiveness and living standards.[99] The picture is similar for environmental protection. Competitiveness and the environment may conflict, especially when industries perpetuate environmentally harmful practices to remain cost competitive. But as clarified earlier, this is an obsolete understanding of competitiveness. EU law embraces environmental protection.[100] The "cross-cutting nature" of environmental policy was highlighted by the Court of Justice in many cases.[101] In this context, competitiveness cannot compromise the environment. To the contrary, modern competitiveness theory is a key companion of environmental protection. Jurisdictions housing productive firms are resource efficient.[102] Resource efficiency directly contributes to environmental sustainability, as less input is used to create more output. Moreover, it also has carryover effects on competitiveness by freeing up resources that can be used in other activities. This mutually beneficial relationship has been recognized in EU policy. For example, a 1992 Communication from the EC reads:

> *"...the exploitation of positive synergies between industrial competitiveness and protection of the environment is increasingly seen to lie in the introduction of environmentally sound industrial processes and products rather than through remedying unwanted side-effects of existing patterns of activity. They also respond much better to the requirements of international competitiveness by providing a permanent boost to fundamental factors of competitiveness instead of temporary advantage.*[103]

While competitiveness enables broader EU objectives, it is not a panacea.[104] Some policy tensions may persist in a scenario where antitrust supports

99 *Turegano*, Sectoral productivity vis-à-vis the US and heterogeneity within the EU27: the role of firm size distribution and firm demographics, EC Joint Research Centre Technical Report No. 30460 (2020).

100 *Nowag*, Environmental Integration in Competition and Free-Movement Laws, Oxford University Press 2016.

101 See, *e.g.*, Case C-333/2, EU:C:2023:1011 – *European Superleague Company*. But the cross-cutting nature of environmental protection does not imply primacy over other EU objectives. See, on this point, Opinion of AG Geelhoed in Case C-161/04, EU:C:2006:66 – *Austria v. Parliament*, para. 59.

102 *Mazzanti/Zoboli*, Environmental efficiency and labour productivity: Trade-off or joint dynamics?, 68 Ecological Economics (2009), 1182.

103 *European Commission*, Industrial Competitiveness and Protection of the Environment (1992) SEC(92) 1986 final.

104 *Gerbrandy*, Rethinking Competition Law within the European Economic Constitution, 57 Journal of Common Market Studies (2019), 127. We also take note of the broader debates in EU law: see, *e.g.*, *Lindseth*, The Constitutional Imaginary and

competitiveness. For example, competitiveness may cause temporary job losses (or job reallocations).[105] As a result of innovation and technological change, agriculture and manufacturing in developed economies employ fewer people today. Moreover, many productive firms derive their value-added less from labour and more from capital.[106] Thus, there is often a trade-off between competitiveness and short-term employment. A silver lining is that benefits to society of innovation and technological growth outweigh the disadvantages, especially with active labor market policies.[107] Income equality may be another tension point. The research on the relationship between income equality and competitiveness is unsettled.[108] However, pursuing competitiveness can make incomes more unequal in the short-term.[109] As less developed nations are more likely to grow fast, member states with less advanced economies may experience periods of higher inequality when competitiveness is the focus. Official data seem to support this hypothesis.[110] Lastly, competitiveness may also clash with territorial cohesion. EU member states are not created equal; the social and economic disparities between them may prove sticky. Empirical work shows that "promoting a market environment that reallocates resources to the most productive firms" can help lagging geographies progress.[111] But it is also

the "Metabolic" Realities of European Integration, in Komarek (ed.), European Constitutional Imaginaries: Between Ideology and Utopia, Oxford University Press 2023, 199.

105 For example, automation in telecoms eliminated some existing jobs but created more future jobs. See, *Feigenbaum/ Gross*, Answering the Call of Automation: How The Labor Market Adjusted to Mechanizing Telephone Operation, 139 The Quarterly Journal of Economics (2024), 1879.

106 *Autor/Dorn/Katz/Patterson/Reenen*, The Fall of the Labor Share and the Rise of Superstar Firms, 135 The Quarterly Journal of Economics (2020), 645.

107 *Andrews/Saia*, Coping with Creative Destruction: Reducing the Costs of Firm Exit, OECD Economics Department Working Paper No. 1353 (2016).

108 *Aiyar/Ebeke*, Inequality of Opportunity, Inequality of Income and Economic Growth, IMF Working Paper No. 19/34 (2020).

109 This is one of the lessons taught by Nobel Laureate Simon Kuznets' work. See also, *Olson*, Rapid Growth as a Destabilizing Force, 23 The Journal of Economic History (1963), 529.

110 'Living conditions in Europe – income distribution and income inequality' (*Eurostat*, October 2023) https://ec.europa.eu/eurostat/statistics-explained/index.php?title=Living_conditions_in_Europe_-_income_distribution_and_income_inequality&oldid=528159#Key_findings (accessed 3 March 2025).

111 *Andrews/Criscuolo/Gal*, Frontier Firms, Technology Diffusion and Public Policy: Micro-Evidence from OECD Countries, OECD Productivity Working Papers No. 2 (2015).

true that competitiveness concentrates economic activity in certain areas ("agglomeration economies").[112] The relationship between competitiveness and territorial cohesion would therefore raise important questions. It may be necessary that antitrust and cohesion policies enjoy deeper cooperation, perhaps under state aid law.[113]

III. Integration

While firms are crucial drivers of competitiveness, they nonetheless operate in context. This means that the environment in which competition takes place also needs to be considered. In particular, internal market rules contribute to competitiveness by shaping the behavior of firms. These rules expose firms to intensified competition on innovation and quality by facilitating market integration. The ensuing race to secure competitive advantages over rivals incentivizes competitiveness greatly.[114] Furthermore, as markets expand, economic actors specialize in certain activities. For example, there may be *intra-industry* specialization, which occurs when firms within the same industry sell highly differentiated products.[115] Specialization can also occur at the input level, which reduces input costs and increases their quality.[116] This is another way market integration hastens competitiveness.[117]

Non-price competitiveness typically operates on a higher risk appetite. Integrating financial markets and improving access to financing would

112 See generally, *Capello/Nijkamp*, Handbook of Regional Growth and Development Theories, Elgar 2019.

113 Under Article 107 (2) and (3), state aid in pursuit of regional development enjoys flexibility. However, tensions between territorial cohesion and competitiveness continue to surface in state aid law. See, *Colomb/Santinha*, European Union Competition Policy and the European Territorial Cohesion Agenda: An Impossible Reconciliation?, 22 Journal of European Planning Studies 2014, 459.

114 *Shapiro*, Competition and Innovation: Did Arrow Hit the Bull's Eye?, in Lerner/Stern (eds.), The Rate and Direction of Inventive Activity Revisited, University of Chicago Press 2012, 361.

115 For a literature review on the impact of European integration on specialization, see *Sapir*, European Integration at the Crossroads: A Review Essay on the 50th Anniversary of Bela Balassa's "Theory of Economic Integration", 49 Journal of Economic Literature (2011), 1200.

116 *Chaney/Ossa*, Market Size, Division of Labor, and Firm Productivity, 90 Journal of International Economics (2013), 177.

117 *Xifre*, Non-Price Competitiveness Factors—A simple measure and implications for the five largest euro area countries, 44 The World Economy (2021), 3091.

therefore support non-price competitiveness of European firms.[118] There seem to be lingering problems with business funding, though. A 2023 study by the European Investment Bank found that close to half of European businesses cite "availability of funding" as an impediment to investment and growth.[119] This scenario is not that different from 1973[120]:

> *"The Commission intends to promote the creation of a facility for financing by risk capital. Despite the considerable efforts of private financial circles, young European firms with a high growth and innovation capacity often have difficulty in finding sufficient risk capital to finance their growth, particularly when their aim is cross-frontier mergers or cooperation."*

From a legal perspective, non-price competitiveness can be improved by focusing on free movement of capital. Free movement of capital is a part of deep integration. Rather than merely regulating trade, it structures methods of production.[121] As such, it is an important input for non-price competitiveness through innovation.

While market integration is important for competitiveness, it should not be regarded as a one-way street. It is a typical reaction to resort to market integration whenever the topic of competitiveness comes up. But organization theory reminds us that firms "co-evolve" together with their markets.[122] This means that competitive firms can also benefit market integration. Since the political will to embark on an ever-closer Union is not riding high, this function seems doubly important.[123]

Consider technology. Many technologies expand the reach of economic activity. For example, railroads expand a firm's geographic market. By

118 This is well-recognized in economic literature. See, *Aghion/Fally/Scarpetta*, Credit constraints as a barrier to the entry and post-entry growth of firms, 22 Economic Policy (2007), 732.

119 *European Investment Bank*, 'Investment Survey 2023: European Union Overview' (2023) https://www.eib.org/en/publications/20230285-econ-eibis-2023-eu (accessed 3 March 2025).

120 *European Commission*, Memorandum on the technological and industrial policy programme (1973) SEC (73) 1090 final, para. 44.

121 *Snell*, Free Movement of Capital: Evolution as a Non-Linear Process, in Craig/de Burca (eds.), The Evolution of EU Law, Oxford University Press 3rd Edition, 579.

122 *Helfat*, What Does Firm Shaping of Markets Really Mean?, 6 Strategy Science (2021), 360.

123 *Grin*, The Vicissitudes of Market Europe, in Segers/Van Heke (eds.), The Cambridge History of the European Union: European Integration Inside-Out, Cambridge University Press 2023, 235.

lowering information costs, electronic communication systems allow firms to draw from broader pools of labour and finance.[124] The internet greatly expands demand for many businesses by virtually eliminating distribution costs.[125] These gains may be very effective in expanding the scale and scope of trade. For example, evidence suggests that technological development accounted for greater integration in the US than trade liberalization.[126] More generally, firms developing technologies through large R&D spending are more likely to enter foreign markets, thereby furthering integration. This is because R&D expenditures are fixed costs, and they do not depreciate in value when selling across borders, unlike marketing or distribution expenses that tend to be country specific.[127]

Also consider productivity. By facilitating the exit of unproductive rivals, competition concentrates economic activity in highly productive companies.[128] These firms can be leaders of integration. Economic evidence suggests that large, competitive firms enter foreign markets more frequently and effectively.[129] This mode of *integration through competition* was a fundamental premise of the European project.[130] As the Cecchini Report put it, entry and exit are "elixirs of industrial rejuvenation" against "large established firms [who] monopolize the national stage thanks [also] to privileged links with the public powers."[131]

In sum, internal market rules can help firms become competitive by improving opportunities to innovate and specialize. In turn, highly competitive firms can also help market integration by developing trade-facilitating technologies or entering foreign markets. Consequently, a competitiveness-

124 *Koenig*, Technical Change and Superstar Effects, 5 American Economic Review (2023), 207.

125 *Goldfarb/Tucker*, Digital Economics, 57 Journal of Economic Literature (2019), 3.

126 *O'Rourke/Williamson*, Globalization and History: The Evolution of a Nineteenth-Century Atlantic Economy, Cambridge University Press 2000.

127 *Spence*, Industrial Organization and Competitive Advantage in Multinational Industries, 74 The American Economic Review (1984), 356.

128 *Minervini*, Insolvency, Competition, and the Theory of the Firm, 32 European Business Law Review (2021), 743. See also, *Easterbrook*, The Chicago School and Exclusionary Conduct, 31 Harvard Journal of Law & Public Policy (2008), 439.

129 *Bighelli et al.*, European Firm Concentration and Aggregate Productivity, 21 Journal of the European Economic Association (2023), 455. See also, *Rossi-Hansberg/Sarte/Trachter*, Diverging Trends in National and Local Concentration, 35 NBER Macroeconomics Annually (2020), 115.

130 *Scitovsky*, Economies of Scale, Competition, and European Integration, 46 The American Economic Review (1956), 71.

131 *Cecchini et al.* (n 17), 88.

oriented antitrust law would help spur significant progress in market integration, a key objective of the European project.

IV. Philosophy

A significant objection to competitiveness-minded antitrust law can be made on philosophical grounds. Antitrust enforcement in pursuit of competitiveness is outcome oriented. It would protect competition only to support a further goal perceived as desirable. Thus, safeguarding competitiveness makes antitrust law consequentialist. By contrast, many scholarly works and judicial statements argue that antitrust law protects "competition as such".[132] This view is deontological. Protecting competition becomes prized for its own sake and not because it leads to other, presumably desirable, ends.

Essentially, competitiveness-minded antitrust law can be criticized from both angles. The dominant view in EU antitrust law is consequentialist. Latest case law confirms that antitrust law protects competition in service of furthering consumer welfare.[133] Introducing competitiveness into the picture may confuse advocates of consumer welfare. But this need not be. Modern economic theory draws a robust correlation between competitiveness and long-run welfare. Thus, competitiveness and consumer welfare are not incompatible when considered in broader perspectives. One can think of competitiveness as promoting *long-term consumer welfare*.[134]

The deontological criticism is likely to be more convoluted. Such critique finds roots in constitutional law. Legal systems do not permit limitless enjoyment of rights. They constrain rights based on justifications. For example, a property owner can enjoy a right to reside in a home, but may be condemned through tort law for setting their house on fire and jeopardizing the neighborhood. This is because the residents of the area also possess rights, for example the right to safety, that constrain the homeowner's right to freely dispose of property. In the same vein, businesses also

132 See, *e.g., Andriychuk*, The Normative Foundations of European Competition Law, Elgar 2017. See also, Opinion of AG Kokott in Case C-307/18, EU:C:2020:28 – *Generics (UK) and Others.*

133 Case C-377/20, ECLI:EU:C:2022:379 – *Servizio Elettrico Nazionale.*

134 *Teece*, The Dynamic Competition Paradigm: Insights and Implications, 1 Columbia Business Law Review (2023), 375.

have rights. But can they be condemned through antitrust law when they do not use their property to serve competitiveness? After all, does anyone have 'a right to a competitive economy'? If not, pursuing competitiveness via antitrust law, and limiting businesses' property rights in the process, would be morally wrong.[135]

A competitiveness-minded antitrust would not limit firms' right to property unjustifiably. This is because, at least under EU law, citizens arguably have a right to competitiveness. Both TEU and TFEU enshrine citizens' right to welfare and a competitive economy (*e.g.,* TEU 3 and TFEU 173). It must be remembered that the Treaties act as a "constitutional charter" for the EU.[136] It can be argued that EU law is constitutionally mandated to balance businesses' right to property with competitiveness. As noted by Drucker: "society must demand of the corporation that it be able to discharge the specific economic functions which are [the society's] priorities".[137]

If that argument was unpersuasive, let us concede for a moment that limiting property rights in service of competitiveness cannot be defended.[138] This would leave the *status quo* unchanged. But the current application of antitrust law already constrains property rights to boost consumer welfare. Consumer welfare is generally protected by prohibiting monopolistic pricing. However, the economic benefit from doing this is not very large.[139] Therefore, firms' property rights are limited for insignificant gains. This is the "worst of both worlds" scenario for a deontologist, as it makes antitrust law "immoral" for misguided aspirations. If antitrust law is to be enforced at all, it ought to focus on significant, long-term welfare increases.[140]

---

135 *Tucker*, Are Antitrust Laws Immoral?, 1 Journal of Markets & Morality (1998), 75.

136 See, *e.g.,* Opinion 1/17 of the Court [2019]. See also, *Lenaerts*, The Basic Constitutional Charter of a Community Based on the Rule of Law, in Maduro/Azoulai (eds.), The Past and Future of EU Law: The Classics of EU Law Revisited on the 50th Anniversary of the Rome Treaty, Bloomsbury 2010, 295.

137 *Drucker*, Concept of the Corporation, Transaction 6th edn. 1993.

138 For such deontological accounts of antitrust law, see *White*, Rights versus Antitrust: Challenging the Ethics of Competition Law, Agenda 2024; *Ayal*, Fairness in Antitrust – Protecting the Strong from the Weak, Hart 2014.

139 The classic source for this insight is *Harberger*, Monopoly and Resource Allocation, 44 The American Economic Review (1954), 77.

140 *Teece/Pisano*, The Dynamic Capabilities of Firms: An Introduction, 3 Industrial and Corporate Change (1994), 537.

V. Pragmatism

Lastly, one may think odd of using antitrust law to support competitiveness. Antitrust law typically intervenes *ex-post*, while competitiveness depends on productivity, a future-oriented endeavor. Hence, either continuous regulation or perhaps merger law may seem preferable.[141] Indeed, the little attention devoted to competitiveness in antitrust literature mainly focuses on merger control and state aid. Now, these policies are certainly important in supporting competitiveness. But this should not come at the expense of neglecting antitrust rules. It is regrettable that abuse of dominance does not feature much in competitiveness discussions.[142] Antitrust enforcement, and specifically unilateral conduct rules, can prove very effective in supporting competitiveness. As the EC highlighted in a study, "...the range of savings associated with an average antitrust intervention lies above the ranges recorded for an average cartel prohibition (...) or merger intervention".[143] To put it bluntly, antitrust enforcement seems to create more bang for buck. Hence, employing antitrust law to support competitiveness may be a pragmatic way of using limited enforcement resources.

D. Conclusions

European integration always maintained an affinity for economic competitiveness. From Spaak to Draghi, institutions, academics, and policymakers tried to find solutions for Europe's competitiveness deficit. But competitiveness largely failed to penetrate antitrust law and policy discussions. This was mostly because of an outdated understanding of what competitiveness means.

This contribution tried to highlight that modern competitiveness means innovation, productivity, and dynamism. It is not about obsessing over cost-cutting, engaging in unchecked subsidy spending, and protecting legacy industries. As such, it is compatible with EU law and broader Euro-

141 For a brief discussion, see *Stigler*, Mergers and Preventive Antitrust Policy, 104 University of Pennsylvania Law Review (1955), 176.

142 For an exception, albeit from US-based management scholars, see *Jorde/Teece*, Antitrust, Innovation, and Competitiveness, Oxford University Press 1992.

143 *European Commission*, 'Modelling the macroeconomic impact of competition policy: 2022 update and further development' (2023) https://op.europa.eu/en/publication-detail/-/publication/6ec6f2c2-f082-11ed-a05c-01aa75ed71a1 (accessed 3 March 2025).

pean values and objectives. Modern competitiveness relies on a defensible philosophy of promoting long-term welfare, and chimes well with environmental sustainability, social mobility, and economic growth. The permissive nature of antitrust law is unlikely to raise issues in constructing a pragmatic and effective antitrust-competitiveness nexus.

The ideas presented in this contribution are starting points. If the intuition is reasonably correct, then a vast research agenda, concerned with how antitrust law – and not only merger control – can contribute to competitiveness, awaits our field.

Section 19a GWB as a measure of counter-power against "Undertakings with Paramount Significance for Competition across Markets"

*Annika Stöhr**

A. Introduction

The 10th amendment to the German Act against Restraints of Competition ("Gesetz gegen Wettbewerbsbeschränkungen", GWB) was designed by legislators with the objective of "modernize(-ing) antitrust law with regard to the digitalization and globalization of the business world".[1] The necessity for modernization was evidenced by the waning intensity of competition and the accompanying increase in concentration in platform markets and digital ecosystems.[2] The resulting market power problems[3] include the

* Post-doc at the Chair for Economic Theory, Institute of Economics, Ilmenau University of Technology, Germany, Email: annika.stoehr@tu-ilmenau.de.

1 *CDU/CSU/SPD*, Koalitionsvertrag zwischen CDU, CSU und SPD, 19th legislative period, 2018, para. 2755f.

2 Inter alia, *Autor/Dorn/Katz/Patterson/Van Reenen*, Concentrating on the Fall of the Labor Share, 107 American Economic Review (2017), 180; *Gutiérrez/Philippon*, Ownership, Concentration, and Investment, 108 AEA Papers and Proceedings (2018), 432; *Grullon/Larkin/Michaely*, Are US Industries Becoming More Concentrated?, 23 Review of Finance (2019), 697; *De Loecker/Eeckhout/Unger*, Rise of Market Power and the Macroeconomic Implications, 135 The Quarterly Journal of Economics (2020), 561; *De Loecker/Eeckhout*, Global market power, 2021, https://www.janeeckhout.com/wp-content/uploads/Global.pdf (accessed November 4, 2024)https://drive.google.com/file/d/1W7A95XOPOjs9pRxcKa5h0U5kx24-XrGW/view; *Budzinski/Mendelsohn*, Regulating Big Tech: From Competition Policy to Sector Regulation?, 72–73 ORDO (2023), 217, 220f.

3 Inter alia, *Kerber*, Updating competition policy for the digital economy? An analysis of recent reports in Germany, UK, EU, and Australia, 2019, https://papers.ssrn.com/sol3/papers.cfm?abstract_id=3469624 (accessed November 4, 2024); *ACCC*, Digital platforms inquiry. Final report, 2019, https://www.accc.gov.au/system/files/Digital%20platforms%20inquiry%20-%20final%20report.pdf (accessed November 4, 2024); *Barreto/Morita Sakowski/Park*, The First Report of the BRICS Competition Authorities Working Group on the Digital Economy, 3 The Antitrust Chronicle (2019), 66; *Crémer/de Montjoye/Schweitzer*, Competition policy for the digital era, 2019, https://op.europa.eu/en/publication-detail/-/publication/21dc175c-7b76-11e9-9f05-01aa7

"tipping" of markets resulting from the combination of direct and indirect network effects,[4] which is reinforced by natural or strategically created incompatibilities and switching costs,[5] the data power of individual firms that is not or hardly contestable, as well as economies of scope that create opportunities for anti-competitive vertical and conglomerate leveraging, for example in the form of self-preferencing.[6] The efficacy of existing an-

---

5ed71a1/language-en (accessed November 4, 2024); *Furman/Coyle/Fletcher/Marsden/McAuley*, Unlocking digital competition. Report of the digital competition expert panel, 2019, https://assets.publishing.service.gov.uk/media/5c88150ee5274a230219c35f/unlocking_digital_competition_furman_review_web.pdf (accessed November 4, 2024); *Haucap/Kerber/Schweitzer/Welker*, Modernizing the Law on Abuse of Market Power in the Digital Age: A Summary of the Report for the German Ministry for Economic Affairs and Energy, 3 The Antitrust Chronicle (2019), 39; *Schallbruch/Schweitzer/Wambach*, A New Competition Framework for the Digital Economy – Report by the Commission "Competition Law 4.0", 3 The Antitrust Chronicle (2019), 33; *Schweitzer/Welker*, Competition Policy for the Digital Era, 3 The Antitrust Chronicle (2019), 16; *Scott-Morton/et al.*, Committee for the Study of Digital Platforms: Market Structure and Antitrust Subcommittee, Report, 2019, https://research.chicagobooth.edu/-/media/research/stigler/pdfs/market-structure-report.pdf?la=en&hash=E08C7C9AA7367F2D612DE24F814074BA43CAED8C (accessed November 4, 2024); *Steenbergen/Snoep/Barthelmé*, Benelux Competition Authorities on Challenges in a Digital World, 3 The Antitrust Chronicle (2019), 54.

4 *Farrell/Saloner*, Standardization, Compatibility, and Innovation, 16 Rand Journal of Economics (1985), 70; *Katz/Shapiro*, Network Externalities, Competition, and Compatibility, 75 American Economic Review (1985), 424; *Rochet/Tirole*, Platform Competition in Two-Sided Markets, 1 Journal of the European Economic Association (2003), 990; *Rochet/Tirole*, Two-sided markets: a progress report, 37 Rand Journal of Economics (2006), 645; *Caillaud/Jullien*, Competition among Intermediation Service Providers, 34 Rand Journal of Economics (2003), 309; *Armstrong*, Competition in two-sided markets, 37 Rand Journal of Economics (2006), 668; *Budzinski/Mendelsohn* (n 2) 233.

5 *Klemperer*, Competition when Consumers have Switching Costs: An Overview with Applications to Industrial Organization, Macroeconomics, and International Trade, 62 Review of Economic Studies (1995), 515.

6 Inter alia, *Farrell/Katz*, Innovation, Rent Extraction, and Integration in Systems Markets, 48 Journal of Industrial Economics (2000), 413; *Zhu/Liu*, Competing with complementors: An empirical look at Amazon.com, 39 Strategic Management Journal (2018), 2618; *De Cornière/Taylor*, A model of biased intermediation, 50 The RAND Journal of Economics (2019), 854; *De Cornière/Taylor*, Data and Competition: a General Framework with Applications to Mergers, Market Structure, and Privacy Policy, TSE Working Paper February 2020, n. 20–1076; *Hagiu/Teh/Wright*, Should platforms be allowed to sell on their own marketplaces?, 53 The RAND Journal of Economics (2022), 297;; *Bougette/Budzinski/Marty*, Self-Preferencing and Competitive Damages: A Focus on Exploitative Abuses, 67 The Antitrust Bulletin (2022), 190; *Peitz*, How to Apply the Self-Preferencing Prohibition in the DMA, 14 Journal of European Competition Law & Practice (2023), 310.

titrust instruments in addressing these challenges has been demonstrated, prompting a discussion and implementation of various reforms, novel approaches, and instruments worldwide.

A central component of the modernization of German abuse control and one of the most discussed new instruments is Sec. 19a GWB.[7] The legislation introduces a new power criterion, namely the designation of undertakings with so-called "paramount significance for competition across markets" (UPSCAM). The intention behind this is to surmount the limitations and challenges with conventional market power determinations.[8] Furthermore, the possibility is provided to adopt ex-ante measures in order to prevent anti-competitive behavior and enable effective competition. This article examines the initial case practice of the German Federal Cartel Office (FCO) in determining the paramount significance of firms for competition across markets (Sec. 19a (1) GWB, "Stage 1") and prohibiting specific conduct by these companies (Sec. 19a (2) GWB, "Stage 2").

This paper commences with a comprehensive overview of the genesis of Sec. 19a GWB (chapter B.) and the initial cases (chapter C). Chapter D. provides a detailed discussion of the first case practice, the economic arguments employed, and the initial learnings for the FCO. The article concludes with some general policy implications.

B. Objectives and Genesis of the Instrument

Sec. 19a GWB establishes a two-stage procedure for implementing more expedient and efficacious intervention options for the FCO with regard to the abuse of dominance. The objective of this process is to foster legal certainty and ensure the harmonization of competition law within the European context. This kind of a two-stage process is analogous to that

7 See for a comprehensive and interdisciplinary overview *Stöhr/Mendelsohn,* Durchsetzung des § 19a GWB: Erste Erfahrungen und Verhältnis zum Digital Markets Act, in Becker (ed.), Wettbewerb auf digitalen Märkten, Nomos 2025, 265. See also *Budzinski/Gaenssle/Stöhr*, Der Entwurf zur 10. GWB Novelle: Interventionismus oder Laissez-faire?, 46 List Forum für Wirtschafts- und Finanzpolitik (2020), 157; *BKartA*, Press Release: Amendment to the Act against Restraints of Competition, 2021, https://www.bundeskartellamt.de/SharedDocs/Meldung/EN/Pressemitteilungen/2021/19_01_2021_GWB%20Novelle.html (accessed November 4, 2024).

8 *Mendelsohn*, Reconsidering Conglomerates – How are digital conglomerates different from those in the past? Theory and implications, 15 Competition Law Review (2023), 83.

employed in "conventional" cases of abuse of market power. However, Sec. 19a GWB empowers the FCO to determine the "paramount significance for competition across markets" of individual companies in the first stage, which extends beyond the scope of traditional market power. The basis for this determination is a non-exhaustive list of criteria, as set forth in Sec. 19a (1) GWB. The criteria include: (1) the existence of a dominant position on one or more markets, (2) the financial strength of the firm or its access to other resources, (3) vertical and conglomerate integration/activity, (4) the access of the firm to competition-relevant data, and (5) the importance of the firm for/influence on the business activities of third parties, in particular on the upstream and downstream market access of these third parties. These criteria largely correspond to those that apply to the determination of market dominance by an individual company in accordance with Sec. 18 GWB. Nevertheless, the aforementioned criteria are now applied on a cross-market basis. This approach entails a comprehensive examination of the relevant sources of power of digital companies as a whole. To illustrate, a company may occupy a dominant or powerful position in Market A, possess data resources in Market B, and exert relative power over upstream firms in Market C. All of these factors can be taken into account when assessing whether an undertaking is of paramount significance for competition across markets. Furthermore, this can be determined even in the absence of a dominant firm in an identifiable and clearly defined market. The legislator has explicitly stated that the criteria set out in Sec. 19a (1) GWB do not have to be met cumulatively. By evaluating all criteria in each individual case, the concept aims to assess the overall significance of a firm within a digital ecosystem.[9] The list of criteria for Stage 1 includes the presence of a dominant market position, which serves as one indicator of the existence of paramount significance of a firm for competition across markets. This criterion combines traditional criteria for assessing individual market dominance with elements of economic dependence or relative market power, thereby establishing a novel category of market power, which could be referred to as "systemic market power".[10] The determination of paramount significance for competition across markets is limited to a period of five

9 *Budzinski/Gaenssle/Stöhr* (n 7); *Budzinski/Gaenssle/Stöhr*, Outstanding relevance across markets: A new concept of Market Power?, Concurrences N° 3–2020 (2020), 38; German Bundestag of 19.10.2020, printed matter 19/23492, GWB Digitization Act (2020), 73 et seqq.

10 *Budzinski/Gaenssle/Stöhr* (n 7).

years from the date on which it becomes effective. This is intended to guarantee proportionality and legal certainty, including for potential cases and obligations that may arise in Stage 2.[11]

Stage 1 can be described as an expression of the so-called ecosystem theory.[12] The theory posits that the respective firms as a whole are not exposed to sufficient competition (pressure), yet it does not explicitly address the issue of a specific lack of competition in certain markets.[13] This is corroborated by the necessary preliminary step of ascertaining substantial activity on multi-sided or platform markets as defined in Sec. 18 (3a) GWB and the additional criteria set forth in Sec. 19a (1) GWB that substantiate "cross-market significance". From an economic perspective, the market structures encompassed by the ecosystem concept are intricate conglomerate and lateral systems that are challenging to grasp within the conventional frameworks of market power. The existing intermediation power within individual platforms, as well as cross-platform power, can give rise to a system of multiple economic dependencies. This enables a variety of self-preferencing strategies and the leveraging of market power, the strategic creation of incompatibilities, and the creation or strengthening of barriers to market entry, without there being a dominant position of the company in one of the individual markets involved. This makes it more challenging to address these issues using traditional competition law instruments.[14]

In the event that an undertaking is deemed to be of paramount significance for competition across markets, the FCO may, in a subsequent step (Stage 2), prohibit the undertaking in question from engaging in specific conduct that is considered to be particularly harmful to competition (Sec. 19a (2) GWB): (1) the preferential treatment of its own services and goods (self-preferencing) when arranging access to sales and procurement markets, (2) taking measures that hinder third parties in their business activities on procurement or sales markets if the UPSCAM's activities are important for access to these markets, (3) directly or indirectly impeding

11 German Bundestag (n 9), 75.

12 *Heidhues/Kösters/ Kőszegi*, A Theory of Digital Ecosystems, ECONtribute Discussion Paper No. 329 (2024); *Lianos/Eller/Kleinschmitt*, Towards a Legal Theory of Digital Ecosystems, Centre for Law, Economics and Society Research Paper Series: 2/2024 (2024).

13 German Bundestag (n 9); *Hornung*, Ecosystem Concept, the DMA, and Section 19a GWB, 12 Journal of Antitrust Enforcement (2023), 396.

14 *Budzinski/Gaenssle/Stöhr* (n 9); *Haucap/Kerber/Schweitzer/Welker* (n 3).

competitors in a market in which the UPSCAM can rapidly expand its position, even if it is not dominant, (4) creating or increasing barriers to entry or otherwise impede third parties through the processing of competitively sensitive data collected by the UPSCAM, or requiring terms and conditions that permit such processing, (5) denying or impeding the interoperability of products or services or restricting the portability of data, (6) inadequately informing third parties about the scope, quality or success of the service provided or commissioned by the UPSCAM or otherwise making it difficult for them to assess the value of this service, and (7) demanding advantages for the treatment of offers from third parties that are disproportionate to the reason for the demand. These practices are not considered abusive if they can be objectively justified. The burden of proof for such justifications lies with the designated UPSCAM.

C. First Cases

Since the enactment of Sec. 19a GWB in January 2021, the FCO has initiated and partially concluded proceedings against a total of five companies. Alphabet, Amazon, Apple, Meta and Microsoft have already been designated as of paramount significance for competition across markets. Furthermore, proceedings to prohibit certain types of conduct in accordance with Sec. 19a (2) GWB have already been initiated and, in some cases, concluded against the aforementioned companies. These actions were taken concurrently with the ongoing Stage 1 proceedings. Table 1 provides an overview of the status of the proceedings at both Stages.

Table 1: Overview of FCO proceedings on the basis of Section 19a Competition Act – as of March 2025[15]

Firm	Stage 1 - Sec. 19a (1) GWB	Stage 2 - Sec. 19a (2) GWB
Alphabet	Determination of paramount significance for competition across markets completed in December 2021 (legally binding)	- Google News Showcase (completed 12/22) - Google data processing (completed in 10/23) - Google Maps platform and Google Automotive Services (ongoing, statement of objections in 06/23, market test regarding proposed commitments in 12/23)
Meta	Determination of paramount significance for competition across markets completed in May 2022 (legally binding)	- VR glasses/Facebook (ongoing, introduction of Meta account in 11/22)
Amazon	Determination of paramount significance for competition across markets completed in July 2022 (legally binding)	- Price control (ongoing, extended to Sec. 19a (2) GWB in 11/22) - Brandgating (ongoing, extended to Sec. 19a (2) GWB in 11/22)
Apple	Determination of paramount significance for competition across markets completed April 2023 (legally binding)	- App Tracking Transparency Framework (ongoing, initiated 06/22, statement of objections in 02/25)
Microsoft	Determination of paramount significance for competition across markets completed in September 2024	- Currently no examination of specific behavior

I. Alphabet

In the case of Alphabet, the FCO conducted the fastest procedure to date for determining a norm addressee status within the meaning of Sec. 19a (1) GWB. The proceedings were initiated on April 29, 2021, and concluded on December 30 of the same year. The FCO identified Google's search engine as the core product with which the company operates on markets within the meaning of Sec. 18 (3a) GWB to a significant extent in relation to the company's overall activities and in relation to its competitors.[16] In this case,

15 *BKartA*, Proceedings against large digital companies on the basis of Sec. 19a GWB as of March 2025, https://www.bundeskartellamt.de/SharedDocs/Publikation/EN/Downloads/List_proceedings_digital_companies.pdf?__blob=publicationFile&v=17 (accessed March 18, 2025).

16 *BKartA* Decision of 30.12.2021, B7-61/21 – *Feststellung der überragenden marktübergreifenden Wettbewerbsbedeutung von Alphabet/Google*, para 53 et seqq.

the FCO undertook a comprehensive examination of all of the UPSCAM criteria, and determined that Google has a dominant position in the national market for general search services.[17] In addition to this dominant position, there were also indications that the firm held strong positions in adjacent markets, such as markets for search-based advertising and operating systems for mobile devices. However, the FCO did not delineate these markets nor pursue further investigations into potential dominance, as it deemed sufficient dominance to be present in the core market.[18] In defining the market and determining market dominance, the FCO was guided in its conclusions by the findings of the European Commission (most recently in 2018) and other competition authorities and courts. These findings demonstrated that Alphabet did not contest the existence of Google's dominance in these other cases.[19]

Alphabet did not submit any appeals contesting its designation as a norm addressee in accordance with Sec. 19a (1) GWB. Subsequently, the FCO initiated three Stage 2 proceedings. The first investigation pertained to Google News Showcase, which was alleged to have exerted undue pressure and crowded out competitors and to have engaged in discriminatory practices towards participating publishers. The second case focused on data processing conditions and was prompted by concerns arising from Sec. 19a (2) s. 1 no. 4a GWB. The third case pertains to Google Maps and Google Automotive Services, including the alleged imposition of restrictions on the combination of Maps with third-party map services. These proceedings were not conducted in isolation but were integrated into larger, more comprehensive abuse proceedings. The initial two cases have already been concluded with commitments from Google, while the proceedings concerning Maps and Google Automotive Services are still ongoing following an initial warning and the preliminary legal assessment of the FCO in June 2023.[20]

17 *BKartA* (n 16), para 62.

18 *BKartA* (n 16), para 231.

19 *BKartA* (n 16), para 235 et seqq.; *European Commission* 18.07.2018, AT.40099 – Google Android, Rn. 674ff.; *European Commission* 27.06.2017, AT.39740 – Google Search (Shopping), Rn. 271ff., confirmed by ECJ ruling of 10.11.2021, T-612/17 – Google and Alphabet / Commission (Google Shopping).

20 *BKartA* Decision of 21.12.2022, V-43/20 – *Fallbericht: Kartellrechtliche Prüfung von "Google News Showcase"; BKartA,* Press release: Statement of objections issued against various of Google's practices in connection with Google Automotive Services and Google Maps Platform, 2023, https://www.bundeskartellamt.de/SharedDocs/Meldung/EN/Pressemitteilungen/2023/21_06_2023_Google.html (accessed November 4, 2024); *BKartA* (n 16).

II. Meta

On January 28, 2021, just a few days after the 10th Amendment to the GWB came into force, the FCO initiated the first proceedings under Sec. 19a (1) GWB against the company Meta Platforms. These proceedings built on the abuse proceedings that had been ongoing since December 2020 due to the linking of the use of the virtual reality goggles Oculus with a Facebook profile.[21] The decision to designate Meta as the norm addressee pursuant to Sec. 19a (1) GWB was issued on May 2, 2022. In this designation, the FCO identified Facebook as a relevant core service with which Meta holds a dominant position on the national market for social networks with a private user base.[22] The identification of significant activities on markets within the meaning of Sec. 18 (3a) GWB was primarily based on Meta's activities in the domain of social media, including platforms such as Facebook, Instagram, Facebook Messenger, and WhatsApp. These platforms were deemed to exhibit the characteristics of a multi-sided market or network, particularly in view of their business models. In the course of the proceedings, all criteria set forth in Sec. 19a (1) GWB for a potential UPSCAM position were examined and found to be present. This included the dominant position of the core service Facebook and a strong market position of Meta in the area of social media advertising, as defined in Sec. 19a (1) s. 2 no. 1 GWB.[23] Meta did not contest its designation as an UPSCAM within the meaning of Sec. 19a (1) GWB. Concurrently, however, the company explicitly indicated that this did not necessarily signify its concurrence with the entirety of the FCO's findings and conclusions.[24]

With regard to Stage 2, the legal proceedings initiated against Meta in 2020 due to the integration of Facebook and Instagram services with Oculus (now known as "Quest 2") provided the foundation for these sub-

---

21 *BKartA*, Press release: First proceeding based on new rules for digital companies – Bundeskartellamt also assesses new Section 19a GWB in its Facebook/Oculus case, 2021, https://www.bundeskartellamt.de/SharedDocs/Meldung/EN/Pressemitteilungen/2021/28_01_2021_Facebook_Oculus.html (accessed November 4, 2024).

22 *BKartA* Decision of 02.05.2022, B6-27/21 – *Überragende marktübergreifende Wettbewerbsbedeutung von Meta/Facebook*, para 117, 123.

23 *BKartA* (n 22), para 83 et seq., 123.

24 *BKartA*, Press release: New rules apply to Meta (formerly Facebook) – Bundeskartellamt determines its "paramount significance for competition across markets", 2022, https://www.bundeskartellamt.de/SharedDocs/Meldung/EN/Pressemitteilungen/2022/04_05_2022_Facebook_19a.html (accessed November 4, 2024).

sequent proceedings.[25] In response to the concerns raised by the FCO regarding competition, Meta introduced the so-called "Meta account" in August 2022. This account enables users to utilize Oculus glasses without the prerequisite of registering with Instagram or Facebook, a feature that was made available in January 2023. In this regard, it is imperative that users be afforded the autonomy to determine whether to link the services in an uninhibited and impartial manner. However, the FCO has underscored that the matter is not yet fully resolved, as the legality of potential cross-service data processing remains undetermined.[26]

III. Amazon

The proceedings to ascertain whether Amazon constitutes a norm addressee as defined in Sec. 19a (1) GWB were initiated by the FCO on May 18, 2021, and the decision was issued on July 5, 2022. In this case, the designation was confirmed by the German Federal Court of Justice (BGH) in April 2024, as Amazon had filed an appeal against the FCO's decision.[27] A preliminary hearing was conducted in June 2023.[28] In addition to the issues raised by Amazon regarding the obstacles to the application of Sec. 19a GWB (potential notification obligations at the EU level and the relationship to the Digital Markets Act) arising from higher-ranking legislation, the firm questioned the market definition conducted by the FCO and the market dominance identified on the national market for the provision of online marketplace services for commercial traders.[29] The Competition

25 *BKartA* (n 22).

26 *BKartA* Decision of 23.11.2022, B6–55/20 – *Fallbericht: Verknüpfung von Meta Quest (vormals Oculus) mit dem Facebook-Netzwerk (Meta).*

27 *BGH*, Press Release No. 097/2024: Federal Court of Justice confirms Amazon's paramount significance for competition across markets, 2024, https://www.bundesgerichtshof.de/SharedDocs/Pressemitteilungen/DE/2024_en/2024097.html (accessed November 4, 2024).

28 *BGH*, Press Release: Verhandlungstermin am 27. Juni 2023 um 11.30 Uhr, Saal E 101, in Sachen KVB 56/22 (Amazon.com, Inc. – Feststellung der überragenden marktübergreifenden Bedeutung für den Wettbewerb), 2023, https://www.bundesgerichtshof.de/SharedDocs/Pressemitteilungen/DE/2023/2023099.html (accessed March 18, 2025).

29 *BKartA* Decision of 05.07.2022, B2–55/21 – *Feststellung einer überragenden marktübergreifenden Wettbewerbsbedeutung von Amazon*, para 87; *Legal Tribune Online*, BGH verhandelt über Kartellverfahrensbeschwerde. Hat Amazon eine "überragende marktübergreifende Bedeutung"?, 2023, https://www.lto.de/recht/hintergruende/h/b

Senate of the BGH has upheld the FCO's decision, declaring Amazon to be of paramount significance for competition across markets under Sec. 19a (1) GWB. This ruling represents the first final decision on an appeal concerning a declaratory decision under this section, underscoring Amazon's expansive operations in multi-sided markets and its strategic potential to influence competition. Furthermore, the ruling observed that Sec. 19a (1) GWB functions concurrently with the European Union's Digital Markets Act (DMA) without conflict, as it constitutes a national competition law provision.[30]

In addition to conducting its own investigations, the FCO had also considered the findings of other competition authorities in determining Amazon to be an UPSCAM. These authorities had previously identified dominant positions held by Amazon on other geographic markets for the provision of marketplace services or intermediary services via online marketplaces.[31] Concurrently, the FCO's decision indicates that even in the absence of a dominant position held by Amazon on the market for the provision of online marketplace services for commercial traders, the company would nevertheless possess considerable market power. It is also noteworthy that the criterion of market dominance or existing market power, as outlined in Sec. 19a (1) GWB, does not necessarily have to be met for the existence of an UPSCAM position to be established.[32] In addition to a comprehensive examination of the existence of a dominant market position held by Amazon, all other criteria outlined in Sec. 19a (1) GWB were also examined in this case and found to be present.

The Stage 2 proceedings in accordance with Sec. 19a (2) GWB were conducted concurrently with the proceedings before the BGH and are still ongoing. Two ongoing proceedings concerning the abuse of algorithmic price control mechanisms and the potential discrimination of marketplace traders with regard to the admission or exclusion of traders from the sale of branded goods were extended in November 2022 to Sec. 19a (2) GWB.[33]

---

gh-kvb5622-amazon-kartellrecht-kartell-bundeskartellamt-beschwerde-bgh-marktmacht-plattform-digital/ (accessed November 4, 2024).

30 *BGH* (n 28).

31 *BKartA* (n 29), para 263 et seqq.

32 *BKartA* (n 29).

33 *BKartA*, Press release: Extension of ongoing proceedings against Amazon to also include an examination pursuant to Section 19a of the German Competition Act (GWB), 2022, https://www.bundeskartellamt.de/SharedDocs/Meldung/EN/Pressemitteilungen/2022/14_11_2022_Amazon_19a.html (accessed November 4, 2024).

IV. Apple

The BGH recently delivered a ruling on the matter of whether Apple can be regarded as a norm addressee within the meaning of Sec. 19a (1) GWB. The court upheld the determination previously issued by the FCO in April 2023, a decision that had been contested by Apple. The BGH had already provided its preliminary views during the initial hearing in January 2025, generally aligning with the FCO, though with certain reservations concerning its interpretation of market dominance and switching barriers. Apple presented its case, employing several arguments, including the interplay between Sec. 19a (1) GWB and the DMA, contesting the company's characteristic as a digital platform, and data-related aspects of market dominance. The final decision of the BGH on the case was delivered in March 2025.[34] The (to date) longest-running Stage 1 proceedings commenced on June 21, 2021. In a manner analogous to the circumstances surrounding the Amazon case, the FCO initially determined that Apple occupied a dominant position in the mobile hardware markets based on the iPhone, iPad, and Apple Watch products. This position is further reinforced by the technical exclusion of alternative offerings with regard to central platform markets for mobile operating systems and software distribution. Consequently, Apple is also dominant in the relevant markets with the iOS operating system and the App Store. For all three markets, the FCO determined that, even in the absence of market dominance, Apple occupied a powerful position in the relevant markets with the iOS operating system and the App Store.[35] This conclusion was reached subsequent to a comprehensive examination of the entire list of criteria set out in Sec. 19a (1) GWB, which revealed the presence of all UPSCAM characteristics.

Even prior to the conclusion of the Stage 1 proceedings, the FCO initiated further proceedings against Apple in accordance with Sec. 19a (2) GWB. The App Tracking Transparency Framework, introduced by the

34 *SCiDA*, A Report from the Court Room Part II: Apple's paramount significance for competition across markets on trial, 2025, https://scidaproject.com/2025/01/30/a-report-from-the-court-room-part-ii-apples-paramount-significance-for-competition-across-markets-on-trial/ (accessed January 31, 2025); *BGH*, Press Release: Bundesgerichtshof bestätigt Apples überragende marktübergreifende Bedeutung für den Wettbewerb, 2025, https://www.bundesgerichtshof.de/SharedDocs/Pressemitteilungen/DE/2025/2025053.html (accessed March 18, 2025).

35 *BKartA* decision of 03.04.2023, B9–67/21 – *Feststellung der überragenden marktübergreifenden Wettbewerbsbedeutung von Apple*, para 233 et seq.

firm in 2021, is currently under investigation to determine whether it may potentially constitute self-preferencing. This is due to the fact that the user choices in question pertain solely to the utilization of their data in third-party products (apps).[36]

V. Microsoft

The most recently concluded Stage 1 proceedings (September 30, 2024) pertain to Microsoft and have been ongoing since March 28, 2023. The determination acknowledges the extensive digital ecosystem of Microsoft, which encompasses a range of significant markets, including PC operating systems (Windows), productivity software (Office), cloud services (Azure), gaming (Xbox), and professional networking (LinkedIn). As the FCO asserts, Microsoft's ecosystem has become a crucial part of the IT infrastructure for businesses, government agencies, and individuals, reinforced by technical interconnections and complementary offerings that extend its influence across multiple sectors. This network of interrelated products has enabled Microsoft to establish strong market positions both in traditional domains and in emerging areas such as cloud services and artificial intelligence (AI), particularly through its collaboration with OpenAI. Microsoft's ecosystem advantage allows it to offer a wide range of integrated solutions, which can potentially influence competition by fostering dependencies and limiting interoperability for third-party developers who must align their products with Microsoft's standards. Despite being designated as a gatekeeper under the EU's DMA, Microsoft's obligations are limited in scope, applying only to specific services such as Windows and LinkedIn. The FCO's Sec. 19a GWB designation explicitly extends this regulatory oversight to Microsoft's broader ecosystem, thereby addressing potential anti-competitive practices that fall outside the scope of the DMA.[37]

36 *BKartA*, Press release: Bundeskartellamt reviews Apple's tracking rules for third-party apps, 2022, https://www.bundeskartellamt.de/SharedDocs/Meldung/EN/Pressemitteilungen/2022/14_06_2022_Apple.html (accessed November 4, 2024).

37 *BKartA*, Press release: Examination of Microsoft's significance for competition across markets, 2023, https://www.bundeskartellamt.de/SharedDocs/Meldung/EN/Pressemitteilungen/2023/28_03_2023_Microsoft.html (accessed November 4, 2024); *BKartA*, Press Release: Microsoft also subject to extended abuse control pursuant to Section 19a GWB – Bundeskartellamt determines paramount significance across

At the time of writing, the FCO had not initiated any Stage 2 proceedings. However, the press release regarding the designation decision explicitly names the latest developments at the EU level regarding the separation of the Teams application from Microsoft's Office program and the takeover of games developer Activision Blizzard as matters of interest for the authority.[38]

D. Learnings from first Case Practice

I. Stage 1

The recently introduced instrument under Sec. 19a GWB is designed to address potentially anti-competitive practices by firms that leverage diverse digital business models. This is similar to the objectives of the EU's DMA. However, Sec. 19a GWB differs substantially from the DMA in terms of the criteria used to assess and designate firms as having “paramount significance for competition across markets”. In accordance with the DMA, a company’s designation as a so-called “gatekeeper” is based on clear, quantifiable thresholds. In particular, the DMA stipulates that a firm qualifies as a gatekeeper if it (a) has a significant impact on the internal market, evidenced by a minimum annual Union turnover of EUR 7.5 billion over the past three financial years, or an average market capitalization of at least EUR 75 billion in the last financial year, with operations across at least three EU Member States; (b) provides core platform services that serve as critical gateways for businesses to access end users, demonstrated by the company’s service reaching at least 45 million monthly active EU users and 10,000 yearly active EU-based business users in the last financial

---

markets, 2024, https://www.bundeskartellamt.de/SharedDocs/Meldung/EN/Pressemitteilungen/2024/30_09_2024_Microsoft_19a.html (accessed November 4, 2024).

38 *European Commission*, Press release: Commission clears acquisition of Activision Blizzard by Microsoft, subject to conditions, 2023, https://ec.europa.eu/commission/presscorner/detail/%20en/ip_23_2705 (accessed November 4, 2024); *European Commission*, Press release: Commission opens investigation into possible anticompetitive practices by Microsoft regarding Teams, 2023, https://ec.europa.eu/commission/presscorner/detail/en/ip_23_3991 (accessed November 4, 2024); *Linde*, blogs.microsoft.com, Microsoft announces changes to Microsoft 365 and Office 365 to address European competition concerns, https://blogs.microsoft.com/eupolicy/2023/08/31/european-competition-teams-office-microsoft-365/ (accessed November 4, 2024); *BKartA* 2024 (n 37).

year; and (c) enjoys a stable, entrenched market position, or is expected to achieve such a position imminently, evidenced by consistently meeting these thresholds over three financial years (Art. 3 DMA). This cumulative, data-driven approach ensures that firms with a significant and established market presence are designated as gatekeepers. In contrast, the UPSCAM determination process of Sec. 19a GWB is not characterized by the presence of definitive, quantitative criteria. Rather, the assessment is based on a wide range of qualitative factors, none of which are obligatory, cumulative, or assigned a specific weight in determining a firm's standing. This structure allows the FCO a considerable degree of discretion in its determinations. Consequently, the process may be viewed as exhibiting increased flexibility but also reduced predictability. While the DMA's criteria provide a transparent threshold-based framework, however worthy of discussion they may be, Sec. 19a GWB's reliance on qualitative, non-exhaustive factors can create an environment of ambiguity, as the FCO has room to interpret and prioritize factors based on the specifics of each case. The only mandatory requirement under Sec. 19a GWB is that the firm must operate in multi-sided or network markets. This is a necessary condition for a firm to be considered for UPSCAM designation, regardless of whether its substantial cross-market importance is directly linked to platform-based services. Overall, the justifications for the determinations of an UPSCAM-position, as evidenced in the decisions by the FCO, exhibit notable differences in terms of the weighting assigned to individual factors. With regard to the FCO's case practice with respect to the individual criteria, the following initial observations can be made:

(1) *existence of a dominant position on one or more markets*: While definitive proof of a dominant market position is not a prerequisite for determining an UPSCAM-position, the FCO has nevertheless examined this factor in each of the cases thus far. Furthermore, this factor may be of significant consequence when the paramount significance for competition across markets is observed in a platform or network market within a digital ecosystem. Moreover, strong (but not necessarily dominant) market positions can be taken into account as well. It is therefore not necessary to precisely delineate all affected submarkets. A strong market position of the firm under investigation in at least one

core market is generally sufficient to fulfill the criterion of Sec. 19a (1) s. 2 n. 1 GWB.[39]

(2) *financial strength of the firm or its access to other resources*: In its interpretation of Sec. 19a (1) s. 2 n. 2 GWB, the FCO makes reference to the ecosystem concept. Specifically, the examination considers the extent to which the company under investigation has the corresponding financial strength or other resources that can be used across markets and thus to expand or secure an ecosystem. All capabilities available to the firm are taken into account, with a focus on the company's innovation potential. Potentially self-reinforcement effects are also considered.[40]

(3) *any vertical and conglomerate integration/activity*: Sec. 19a (1) s. 2 n. 3 GWB has the objective of capturing the distinctive characteristics of digital ecosystems, extending beyond the vertical or conglomerate user-side connection of the services and products offered. The FCO's analyses focus on the extent to which these connections facilitate competitive advantages or control over market access for the firm in question. The assessment of vertical and/or conglomerate connections does not result in a differential weighting; rather, it represents the corresponding "breadth" and "depth" of the services and products connected to the core market.[41]

(4) *access of the firm to competition-relevant data*: The FCO considers the potential data power in accordance with Sec. 19a (1) s. 2 n. 4 GWB to be of considerable relevance, whereby data is considered a separate resource (in addition to the resources examined in Sec. 19a (1) s. 2 n. 2 GWB) with great significance for the formation and strengthening of an ecosystem. The term "data" is interpreted in a broad sense, encompassing any information accessible to the firm. In the context of "shareable inputs", which can be utilized across services and devices within an ecosystem, the FCO assesses access to competition-relevant data across markets and evaluates both the quantity and quality of data in various forms.[42]

(5) *importance of the firm for/influence on the business activities of third parties, in particular on the upstream and downstream market access of*

39 See for example *BKartA* (n 29), para 87; *BKartA* (n 35), para 233 et seqq.
40 See for example *BKartA* (n 16), para 53 et seqq.
41 *BKartA* (n 16).
42 See for example *BKartA* (n 22), para 117, 123.

these third parties: Sec. 19a (1) s. 2 n. 5 GWB addresses the rule-setting and intermediation power of firms – and thus, once again, the possibility of either creating or strengthening an ecosystem. Notwithstanding the stipulation that the individual criteria are not to be weighted, the FCO explicitly states in its explanations that the potential dependencies of other market participants can be an essential characteristic of the norm addressee position pursuant to Sec. 19a (1) GWB. This is due to the resulting opportunities to shape (or distort) the competitive process in a manner that benefits the firm. The criterion only requires that the activity of the (potential) norm addressee be significant with respect to third parties' access to procurement and sales markets, but not that it possess any market power that goes beyond this.[43]

It is of particular significance that the stipulation that a dominant market position must be determined has been repealed. In this regard, Sec. 19a GWB attempts to encompass concentrations of power that either exceed traditional market dominance (i.e., establish cross-market power) or are caused by factors beyond prices (such as data, access, attention, etc.). In the absence of a precise market definition[44] and the determination of a dominant market position, it was previously exceedingly challenging to discern the presence of abusive market structures and behavior. The new approach allows the FCO to take action on the basis of alternative criteria and other forms or sources of economic power, thereby enhancing the capacity of competition law to address the distinctive features of digital ecosystems and the concentrations that emerge in these markets. However, a dominant market position has been identified in all cases falling under Sec. 19a GWB to date.

Despite the FCO's comprehensive treatment of the entire list of Stage-1-criteria in relative detail, the relationship between these criteria and their respective weighting remains unclear. It is conceivable that the necessary specification will only become evident in the course of subsequent (judicial) proceedings. While the review findings to date may be convincing, they are, at times, somewhat vague and lacking in specificity. Two firms

---

43 See for example *BKartA* (n 16).

44 On the discussion of market definition in merger control see, *Markovits,* On the Inevitable Arbitrariness of Market Definitions, 47 The Antitrust Bulletin (2002), 571; *Kaplow*, Why (Ever) Define Markets?, 124 Harvard Law Review (2010), 437; *Schwalbe,* e-Competitions Market definition in the digital economy (2019), Art. No. 91832; *Robertson*, Competition Law's Innovation Factor – The Relevant Market in Dynamic Contexts in the EU and the US, Hart 1st edn. 2020.

have already initiated legal proceedings against their determination as UPSCAM, both of which were decided in favor of the FCO's decision and reasoning. In both cases, the firms have contested the existence of a dominant market position. It remains questionable whether the finding of paramount significance for competition across markets can be considered fully convincing in the absence of a determination of market dominance. Furthermore, the necessary level of substantiation and additional criteria that must be met in cases where market power is not established remain unclear.

II. Stage 2

Sec. 19a (2) GWB provides an exhaustive list of the types of conduct that may be prohibited by the FCO following the determination of an UPSCAM. Notably, the prohibition is ex-nunc in nature. It is noteworthy that the FCO is not required to demonstrate concrete harm or specific anti-competitive effects in order to enforce these prohibitions. This allows for the preemptive regulation of potentially harmful conduct. In contrast, gatekeepers under the DMA are subject to a predefined set of obligations and prohibitions that apply uniformly across core platform services. Unlike the approach taken by Sec. 19a GWB, which addresses firms' conduct on a case-by-case basis, the DMA sets out explicit and direct compliance obligations, as outlined in Articles 5–7. These articles mandate, for example, that gatekeepers refrain from practices such as combining user data without consent (Art. 5), restricting business users' ability to offer better terms on third-party platforms (Art. 5), and prohibiting preferential treatment of their own services over competitors (Art. 6). Additionally, Article 7 emphasizes the importance of ensuring interoperability between communication services provided by gatekeepers and other platforms. In essence, the obligations set forth in the DMA and the prohibited conduct to be established by the FCO under Sec. 19a GWB are largely analogous in nature and draw upon existing case law pertaining to major platform firms. However, with regard to the enforcement and sanctioning mechanisms, Sec. 19a GWB is deficient. The legislation does, however, include procedural options for managing anti-competitive conduct, such as structural and behavioral remedies under Sec. 32 GWB and the possibility for interim measures (Sec. 32a GWB) or commitments (Sec. 32b GWB), but it lacks a robust enforcement framework with direct sanctions comparable to the DMA's regime.

Table 2 provides a more detailed overview of the current and completed Stage-2-cases, including the types of conduct addressed in each case.

Table 2: Theories of harm of the proceedings pursuant to Sec. 19a (2) GWB – as of March 2025[45]

Case (firm)	Current status of the proceedings	Addressed conduct pursuant to Sec. 19a (2) GWB
Microsoft	No examination of specific behavior as of March 2025	
Google News Showcase (Alphabet)	– Completed (12/22) without formal commitment decision – Monitoring the implementation of the following measures in a separate follow-up procedure: • Non-integration of Google News Showcase into Google Search • Adjustment of showcase contracts and negotiations on ancillary copyright – No confirmation of the suspected restriction of press publishers' access to the Google News Showcase service	– Self-preferencing within the meaning of Sec. 19a (2) s. 1 n. 1 GWB through planned integration of the Showcase service in the general Google search – Through this planned integration, also examination of the existence of a measure hindering other companies in their business activities within the meaning of Sec. 19a (2) s. 1 n. 2 GWB – Claiming undue advantages within the meaning of Sec. 19a (2) s. 1 n. 7 GWB in the contracts with publishing houses

45 *BKartA*, Press Release: Proceedings against Google for possible restrictions of competition in map services (Google Maps Platform), 2022, https://www.bundeskartellamt.de/SharedDocs/Meldung/EN/Pressemitteilungen/2022/21_06_2022_Google_Maps.html (accessed November 4, 2024); *BKartA* Decision of 21.12.2022, V-43/20 – *Fallbericht: Kartellrechtliche Prüfung von "Google News Showcase"*; *BKartA*, Press release: Statement of objections issued against various of Google's practices in connection with Google Automotive Services and Google Maps Platform, 2023, https://www.bundeskartellamt.de/SharedDocs/Meldung/EN/Pressemitteilungen/2023/21_06_2023_Google.html (accessed November 4, 2024); *BKartA*, FAQs relating to the "Google News Showcase" proceeding, 2022, https://www.bundeskartellamt.de/SharedDocs/Publikation/EN/Others/FAQ_GoogleNews_Showcase.pdf?__blob=publicationFile&v=3 (accessed November 4, 2024); *BKartA* (n 15); *BKartA*, Press release: Improvements for publishers when using Google News Showcase, 2022, https://www.bundeskartellamt.de/SharedDocs/Meldung/EN/Pressemitteilungen/2022/21_12_2022_Google_News_Showcase.html (accessed November 4, 2024); *BKartA* (n 21); *Hornkohl*, competitionlawblog.kluwercompetitionlaw.com, Brand Gating: German Competition Authority Once Again Launches An Investigation Into Amazon (and Apple), 2020, http://competitionlawblog.kluwercompetitionlaw.com/2020/11/06/brand-gating-german-competition-authority-once-again-launches-an-investigation-into-amazon-and-apple (accessed November 4, 2024); *BKartA* (n 26).

Case (firm)	Current status of the proceedings	Addressed conduct pursuant to Sec. 19a (2) GWB
Google Data Processing (Alphabet)	– Completed (10/23) with following commitments: • Obligation to either introduce new options or specify the data processing conditions • Transparent design of the options in such a way that users can make a voluntary, informed and unambiguous decision • Application/design coherent with the DMA with regard to the collected data and (cross-service) data processing operations	– Data processing conditions vis-à-vis end users that provide for the possibility of cross-service processing of user data without giving end users sufficient choice, in this respect exploitative behavior vis-à-vis users, which is regularly accompanied by an obstruction of other companies, within the meaning of Sec. 19a (2) s. 1 n. 4 a) GWB
Google Maps platform (Alphabet)	– Ongoing – Preliminary legal assessment in connection with Google Automotive Services (06/23)	– Restriction of the combination of own services with third-party services • Potentially reference to Section 19a (2) s. 1 n. 3 GWB or Sec. 19a (2) s. 1 n. 5 GWB
Google Automotive Services (Alphabet)	– Ongoing – Preliminary legal assessment and warning in connection with Google Maps platform (06/23)	– Bundling of automotive infotainment services • Potentially reference to Sec. 19a (2) s. 1 n. 2 GWB or Sec. 19a (2) s. 1 n. 3 GWB – Participation in advertising revenue from the use of Google Assistant agreed with some vehicle manufacturers on the condition that only Google Assistant is installed as a voice assistant in the infotainment platform • Potentially reference to Sec. 19a (2) s. 1 n. 7 GWB – Obstruction of market access through contractual provisions that oblige licensees to set Google services as standard or to display them on the screen before other applications • Potentially reference to Sec. 19a (2) s. 1 n. 2 GWB – Impediment or refusal of interoperability of the infotainment platform with third-party services • Potentially reference to Sec. 19a (2) s. 1 n. 5 GWB
Price control (Amazon)	– Ongoing – Extension of an existing procedure to Sec. 19a GWB (11/22)	– Obstruction of third-party sellers through algorithmic review of their pricing on the Amazon marketplace and initiation of measures or account blocking in the event of "excessive" prices • Potentially reference to Sec. 19a (2) s. 1 n. 2 GWB or Sec. 19a (2) s. 1 n. 4 GWB

Case (firm)	Current status of the proceedings	Addressed conduct pursuant to Sec. 19a (2) GWB
Brandgating (Amazon)	- Ongoing - Extension of an existing procedure to Sec. 19a GWB (11/22)	- Obstruction of marketplace traders by Amazon's agreements with (brand) manufacturers concerning the admission or exclusion of traders for the sale of (brand) products • Potentially reference to Sec. 19a (2) s. 1 n. 1 GWB or Sec. 19a (2) s. 1 n. 2 GWB
App Tracking Transparency Framework (Apple)	- Ongoing - Initiated (06/22)	- Self-preferential treatment within the scope of the regulations on app tracking of third-party apps • Potentially reference to Sec. 19a (2) s. 1 n. 1 GWB
VR glasses/ Facebook (Meta)	- Ongoing - Extension of an existing procedure to Sec. 19a GWB (01/21) - With the introduction of the meta-account (11/22), permission was granted to also sell VR glasses in Germany; proceedings on the permissibility of cross-service data processing are ongoing	- Connection of the use of the Facebook account and Oculus/Meta Quest offers within the meaning of Sec. 19a (2) s. 1 n. 3a) GWB - Through this connection of services, also cross-service processing of data within the meaning of Sec. 19a (2) s. 1 n. 4a) GWB

In the cases that have not yet been concluded, the FCO makes only unspecific reference to the conduct set forth in Sec. 19a (2) GWB. The potential specific norm assignments (number references) incorporated into table 2 were derived from the descriptions of the business practices to be addressed included in the corresponding press releases. Furthermore, Alphabet's conduct with regard to Google Maps and Google Automotive Services has been listed separately for the sake of clarity, whereas these are addressed collectively by the FCO.

It is not yet evident that the FCO is focusing on particular forms of anti-competitive behavior or specific patterns in case practice, which may be explained by the limited number of proceedings that have been initiated thus far. In consideration of the specific potential norm assignments posited here pertaining to proceedings that have not yet been concluded, instances of abuse within the meaning of Sec. 19a (2) s. 1 n. 2 GWB have thus far been addressed most frequently in four cases. Conversely, the strategic creation of non-transparency of business-relevant information within the meaning of Sec. 19a (2) s. 1 n. 6 GWB has not yet been specifically addressed in any case.

The initial proceedings of Stage 2 of Sec. 19a GWB are noteworthy for two key reasons. Firstly, in contrast to the application of the DMA, some of the cases have been integrated into ongoing abuse proceedings.

Secondly, first "successes" have already been documented in the form of commitments and prompt changes in the firms' behavior. In the two concluded proceedings concerning Alphabet and the advanced proceedings concerning Meta, the firms demonstrated a willingness to cooperate with the FCO, either by accepting commitments or by offering them. In the case of Google News Showcase, the FCO has even elected to forego a formal commitment decision. However, these "successes" may be somewhat deceptive. The commitments and behavioral changes exhibited by Alphabet and Meta are somewhat "*low hanging fruit*", as they pertain to practices that have been acknowledged as the new rules of fair competition in the digital age, a recognition that has been influenced by recent rulings[46] or a prevailing consensus in the relevant literature[47]. It remains to be seen whether analogous outcomes can be attained in cases involving a lack of comparable agreement or evidence, or where firms demonstrate a lesser degree of cooperation. In light of the proceedings before the Federal Court of Justice concerning the designation as UPSCAM's, it appears improbable that commitments will be forthcoming from Apple and Amazon. In this context, it can be contended once more that Sec. 19a GWB is deficient in terms of its enforcement and sanctioning mechanisms. In general, it seems reasonable to suppose that a certain degree of success can be achieved with relative ease and expediency, which may contribute to a more open competitive climate. However, it appears improbable that substantial and particularly structural changes in digital markets and ecosystems will be realized.

---

46 An example of such a development is the Facebook decision of the FCO, which involved all instances, *BKartA* Decision of 06.02.2019, B6–22/16 – *Untersagung der Zusammenführung von Nutzerdaten aus verschiedenen Quellen (Facebook)*; *OLG Düsseldorf* Decision of 26.08.2019, Kart 1/19 (V); *BGH* Decision of 23.06.2020, KVR 69/19; *CJEU* Decision of 04.07.2023, Case – C252/21- *Meta Platforms Inc. v Bundeskartellamt.*

47 *Colangelo/Maggiolino*, Data accumulation and the privacy–antitrust interface: insights from the Facebook case, 8 International Data Privacy Law (2018), 224; *Budzinski/Grusevaja,/Noskova*, The economics of the German investigation of Facebook's data collection, 5 Market and Competition Law Review (2021), 43; *Kerber/Zolna*, The German Facebook Case: The Law and Economics of the Relationship between Competition and Data Protection Law, 54 European Journal of Law and Economics (2022), 217; *König*, Stärkung des Wettbewerbs- und Datenschutzes gegenüber marktbeherrschenden Onlineplattformen, 41 NJW (2023), 2979.

E. Conclusion

Sec. 19a GWB is explicitly designed to address the challenges posed by digital ecosystems and platform markets that are dominated by a few large firms. By designating certain companies as having "paramount significance for competition across markets", Sec. 19a GWB empowers the FCO to preemptively restrict practices that could impede competition. This framework diverges from conventional approaches to competition law, which frequently can only intervene after anti-competitive harm has been presented. From an economic perspective, Sec. 19a addresses the complexities of digital markets, where multi-sided network effects, data power, and vertically integrated services can result in entrenchment of dominance, the creation of barriers to entry, and the facilitation of self-preferencing practices that limit market dynamism and consumer choice. In doing so, Sec. 19a GWB often addresses not only matters of competition but also (indirectly) issues of data protection, areas which frequently overlap in digital markets and may give rise to interconnected market failures. In digital ecosystems, a firm's market dominance frequently intersects with issues of privacy and information access, which can reinforce each other, thereby complicating the separation of these policy domains. This interplay complicates the formulation of regulatory responses, as addressing anti-competitive conduct may simultaneously impact privacy protections and vice versa. It would be advantageous for future proceedings under Sec. 19a GWB to draw upon case history, particularly in instances where competition and privacy concerns are intertwined, as exemplified by the German Facebook case.[48] Based on economic theory, this phenomenon represents a convergence of multiple market failures. This intersection is generally under-researched. Insights from welfare economics, particularly the "theory of the second best"[49], indicate that addressing one type of market failure does not necessarily lead to an overall increase in market efficiency if other market failures remain unaddressed. In digital markets, attempts to address issues of market dominance may potentially exacerbate effects on data protection – and vice versa – or give rise to unintended consequences at the policy level. These interaction effects require a comprehensive approach to enforcement, as case practice focused exclusively

---

48 *Kerber/Zolna* (n 47).

49 *Lipsey/Lancaster*, The General Theory of Second Best, 24 Review of Economic Studies (1956), 11.

on addressing a single market failure may yield unintended (side-)effects. Consequently, the pursuit of welfare-enhancing outcomes in digital markets necessitates an examination of the cumulative effects and interconnections of multiple market failures. In light of the ongoing Stage 2 proceedings under Sec. 19a GWB, it is imperative to consider these interaction effects. The current proceedings have not yet thoroughly addressed these intersections. It would be beneficial in the future to acknowledge and incorporate these insights into the enforcement of competition law, which could result in more balanced and sustainable outcomes.

The unclear relationship between Sec. 19a GWB and the DMA was discussed from many sides at an early stage. Among other things, the respective scope of application and the question of the legal nature of Sec. 19a GWB as regulatory or competition law were questioned. In examining the relationship between Sec. 19a GWB and the DMA, it becomes evident that while both instruments share certain objectives and can complement each other – acting as specific competition law and competition law regulation, respectively, in parallel – there are also notable differences in their approaches.[50] In contrast to the DMA's structured and immediate obligations for designated gatekeepers, Sec. 19a GWB operates on a case-by-case basis for the Stage 2 proceedings, allowing the FCO greater flexibility but also introducing legal uncertainty for firms. Moreover, Sec. 19a GWB does not provide for direct sanctions for non-compliance, instead relying on structural or behavioral remedies, which could limit the effectiveness of enforcement in cases where firms resist voluntary commitments. The introduction of explicit guidelines and sanctions for non-compliance could enhance the effectiveness of Sec. 19a GWB. However, as demonstrated by the arguments presented by Amazon and Apple in the respective appeal proceedings, the relationship between the DMA and Sec. 19a GWB remains ambiguous. Additionally, there is a risk of regulatory fragmentation due to the concurrent application of national and European legislation. In general, there is a considerable degree of flexibility, both legally and practically, for national competition authorities to collaborate with the Commission

50 For an assessment of the legal nature of the instrument and the subsequent connection to the DMA see *Wolf/Brüggemann,* Agenda 2025: The digital markets act and section 19a GWB, 2022, https://www.d-kart.de/en/blog/2022/07/19/agenda-2025-der-digital-markets-act-und-%C2%A719a-gwb/ (accessed January 31, 2025), as well as *Bauermeister*, Section 19a GWB as the German 'Lex GAFA' – lighthouse project or superfluous national solo run?, 15 Yearbook of Antitrust and Regulatory Studies (2022), 75, and *Hornung* (n 13).

in the context of competition enforcement. A similar approach could be advantageous within the framework of the DMA and Sec. 19a GWB, as it could facilitate learning-by-doing and ensure the continued relevance of the regulatory framework. To address this, coordination is necessary to avoid duplication and regulatory fragmentation. However, the FCO's proceedings should be given serious consideration as important reference points for monitoring the behavior of digital Gatekeepers.[51]

In summary, Sec. 19a GWB empowers the FCO to address instances of multi- and cross-market dominance, thereby aligning with contemporary economic theories on digital ecosystems. This approach can facilitate a more comprehensive understanding of market power by accounting for the cumulative impact of digital firms' activities across multiple markets. Nevertheless, the practical effectiveness of Sec. 19a GWB is contingent upon the consistent and transparent application by the FCO, as well as its capacity to adapt to evolving market dynamics. Future amendments, such as those proposed by the Monopolies Commission in summer 2024, could enhance Sec. 19a GWB by refining the criteria for UPSCAM determination and strengthening its enforcement mechanisms, ultimately aligning it more closely with the economic realities of digital ecosystems[52]. As further case practice unfolds, insights from both Sec. 19a GWB and the DMA may help refine regulatory strategies, supporting a balanced approach to fostering innovation while preventing anti-competitive behavior.

---

51 *Alexiadis/et al.*, Coherence versus Fragmentation: Institutional Challenges to EU Digital Markets Regulation, 24 Bus. L. Int'l (2024), 233; *van den Boom/et al.*, Digital Regulation Synthesis: Comparative Analysis of the DMA, Sec. 19a and the DMCCA, SCiDA Discussion Paper (1) (2024); *Graef*, Regulating Digital Platforms: Streamlining the Interaction between the Digital Markets Act and National Competition Regimes, in Graef/van der Sloot (eds.), The legal consistency of technology regulation in Europe 2024, Hart Publishing, 157.

52 In its 2024 Annual Report, the Monopolies Commission proposes amendments to Sec. 19a GWB. It wants to include an 'economic test concept for digital ecosystems' in the regulation. To this end, the catalogue of criteria for determining the 'paramount significance across markets' of an undertaking (Sec. 19a (1) s. 2 GWB) should either be completely rewritten or at least supplemented by further criteria, *Monopolkommission*, XXV. Biennial Report by the Monopolies Commission: Competition 2024, Summary, 2024, https://www.monopolkommission.de/images/HG25/HG25-Summary.pdf (accessed March 18, 2025).

Rethinking Remedy Design in EU Competition Law Enforcement

Elaine Dunne[*]

A. Introduction

The enforcement of competition law within the European Union (EU) is a cornerstone of its policy framework, aimed at ensuring a fair and dynamic internal market. At the heart of this framework are the Treaty on European Union (TEU) and the Treaty on the Functioning of the European Union (TFEU), which establish the principles and legal basis for maintaining competition. The TEU envisages an internal market that is 'highly competitive', while the TFEU by means of *inter alia* Articles 101 and 102 prohibits anti-competitive practices that 'have as their object or effect the prevention, restriction or distortion of competition.'[1] The European Commission (the "Commission"), as the guardian of these treaties, is vested with substantial powers to investigate and remedy anti-competitive practices. Regulation 1/2003,[2] a pivotal regulation in this context, grants the Commission a range of tools to restore competition.

According to the law as it stands, the Commission has a certain discretion with regard to the kind of remedies to impose to address anti-competitive practices. In principle, remedies can be grouped into (i) behavioural or structural remedies pursuant to Regulation 1/2003; and (ii) cease-and-desist or market-shaping remedies.[3] Prior experience suggests that behavioural remedies that are market-shaping in nature have, in some cases, been ineffective. Examples in this regard include *Microsoft* and *Google Shopping*[4]. Moreover, the idiosyncrasies of digital markets further

---

* Elaine is a trainee solicitor with the corporate team of DLA Piper, Dublin.

1 Consolidated version of the Treaty on the Functioning of the European Union OJ C 326/47, Art. 101.

2 Council Regulation (EC) No 1/2003 of 16 December 2002 on the implementation of the rules on competition laid down in Articles 81 and 82 of the Treaty (Text with EEA relevance).

3 *Ibáñez Colomo*, The New EU Competition Law, Hart Publishing 2023.

4 Case T-612/17, EU:T:2021:763 – *Google LLC v. European Commission.*

complicates the design of effective remedies (due to the fast-paced nature of these markets and the difficulty in predicting future market dynamics). Furthermore, in light of the constitutional principles of proportionality, legal certainty and legitimate expectation, this paper argues that the Commission must balance these principles with the need for effective enforcement. Against this backdrop, the paper proposes an iterative or staggered approach to remedy design, incorporating ex-post review mechanisms to ensure the ongoing effectiveness of remedies.

The paper begins with an overview of the legal framework governing remedy design, including an analysis of the Commission's powers under Regulation 1/2003. The writer then reviews the existing remedial practices and consider the (in)effectiveness thereof. The paper will then explore the future of remedy design, critically assessing the constraints that influence remedy design. It will ultimately be suggested that notwithstanding the constitutional constraints, the broad power conferred on the Commission 'to bring the infringement effectively to an end',[5] thereby impliedly permitting the imposition of positive or negative obligations to restore the competitive process, enhanced by the wide margin of discretion conferred on the Commission in terms of the application of the general principles of EU law in competition enforcement, should be further utilised and leveraged to combat anti-competitive practices in emerging markets.

B. The Competition Law Enforcement Framework of EU Regulation 1/2003

It flows from a finding of the existence of an infringement that competitive conditions have been disrupted. A remedy by definition strives to set right an undesirable situation. In the context of competition law, that is to 'halt the illegal conduct and stop the anticompetitive effects that flow from it'.[6] The design of an appropriate remedy is, of course, on a case-by-case basis and is dependent on the theory of harm identified. The restoration of competitive conditions is contingent upon the adoption and imposition of suitably designed remedies. Regulation 1/2003 sets forth what the adoption and imposition of remedies seeks to achieve. That is, to 'bring the infringement

5 Consolidated version of the Treaty on the Functioning of the European Union OJ C 326/47, Art 7(1).

6 Bostoen/van Wamel, Antitrust Remedies: From Caution to Creativity, 14 Journal of European Competition Law & Practice (2023), 540, 541.

effectively to an end'.[7] The Commission is conferred the power to bring any such infringement to an end pursuant to Regulation 1/2003. Article 7 thereof permits the Commission, upon determining that a breach of Articles 101 or 102 TFEU has occurred, 'to require the undertakings...concerned to bring such infringement to an end. For this purpose, it may impose on them any behavioural or structural remedies which are proportionate to the infringement committed and necessary to bring the infringement effectively to an end.'[8] Article 9 offers an alternative. If the Commission forms the opinion *prima facie* that an infringement has occurred, and an undertaking the subject of said opinion offers commitments that adequately address the concerns identified by the Commission, 'the Commission may by decision make those commitments binding on the undertakings.'[9] It should be noted, however, that article 9 is not available in cases concerning hardcore cartels or those cases in which the Commission intends to impose a fine. Further, an important power is found in article 8 of Regulation 1/2003. Thereunder, the Commission is permitted to take interim measures to combat practices that are *prima facie* anti-competitive. While in the context of merger control, under the European Union Merger Regulation ("EUMR"), the Commission is granted the power to declare a concentration incompatible with the internal market and shall prohibit a concentration which would significantly impede effective competition ("**SIEC**") in the internal market or a substantial part of it as a result of the creation or strengthening of a dominant position.[10] Similar to Article 9 of Regulation 1/2003, under the EUMR the Commission is also empowered to accept commitments from the undertakings concerned and thereby approve the concentration subject to such conditions.[11] It is worth noting that the assessment of a proposed concentration is an *ex-ante* effort and therefore, the provisions of the EUMR are invoked *ex-ante*, while the provisions of Regulation 1/2003

7 Consolidated version of the Treaty on the Functioning of the European Union OJ C 326/47, Art 7(1).

8 Consolidated version of the Treaty on the Functioning of the European Union OJ C 326/47, Art 7(1).

9 Consolidated version of the Treaty on the Functioning of the European Union OJ C 326/47, Art 9(1).

10 Council Regulation (EC) No 139/2004 of 20 January 2004 on the control of concentrations between undertakings (the EC Merger Regulation) (Text with EEA relevance), art 1(3).

11 Council Regulation (EC) No 139/2004 of 20 January 2004 on the control of concentrations between undertakings (the EC Merger Regulation) (Text with EEA relevance), Art 8(2).

are invoked *ex-post* when a disruption in the market is suspected to have occurred.

Essentially, 'once liability has been established, re-establishing the conditions for effective competition is the ultimate objective of competition law and remedies are the means to achieve this goal.'[12] In its submission to the OECD under Session IV of the Global Forum on Competition, the EU submits that the objective of a remedy can be threefold; a remedy should '(i)...re-establish the situation as it was before the infringement; (ii)... re-establish the situation as it would be absent the infringement; (iii)... re-establish the competitive process, i.e restore the conditions for a competitive and contestable market.'[13] The notion of re-establishing the competitive process is demonstrated by the case of *Akzo*.[14] In this case, ECS had lost customers to Akzo, due to Akzo's predative pricing strategy. A remedy such as cease-and-desist would not suffice, as such a remedy would not change the situation or remedy the effects of the anti-competitive conduct. Such a remedy is designed to simply terminate the anti-competitive conduct and would not re-establish the competitive process. Instead, the remedy actually imposed, which placed a prohibition on Akzo in respect of its price offering in specified circumstances, enabled ECS 'to re-establish the situation that existed before the dispute.'[15] Similarly in *Commercial Solvents*[16] the CJEU upheld a remedy imposed by the Commission that required commercial solvents to supply a specified quantity of a raw material to another undertaking, on the grounds that this was necessary to protect the undertaking from the consequences of the infringement. The court rejected the applicant's argument that the Commission had acted ultra vires. The court held that the regulation should be read as permitting the Commission not only to require the undertaking to bring the infringement to an end, but also as granting the Commission the power to 'to do certain

12 Lowe/Maier-Rigaud, Quo vadis antitrust remedies, in Hawk (ed.), Fordham Competition Law Institute, Huntington: Juris Publishing 2008, 597.

13 OECD Global Forum on Competition, Remedies and Commitments in Abuse Cases – Contribution from the European Union DAF/COMP/GF(2022)5 https://one.oecd.org/document/DAF/COMP/GF(2022)5/en/pdf accessed 2 April 2024 [16].

14 Case C-62/86, EU:C:1991:286 – *AKZO Chemie BV v Commission of the European Communities.*

15 Ibid; Katharina Voss, Between Enforcement and Regulation A Study of the System of Case Resolution Mechanisms Used by the European Commission in the Enforcement of Articles 101 and 102 TFEU (2019) Stockholm University, 67.

16 Case 6 and 7/73, *Commercial Solvents and ICI v Commission.*

acts or provide certain advantages which have been wrongfully withheld' to 'make good' the infringement.[17] Moreover, in *Magill*,[18] the court upheld the legality of the Commission's decision requiring the applicants to licence the use of protected IP to third parties on grounds that it was necessary to restore competitive conditions, and was proportionate to that objective.[19] Dubbed by Forrester as 'a child of Magill',[20] the case of *Microsoft*[21] goes even further in imposing an onerous obligation, requiring 'several hundred Microsoft engineers…research how the relevant server software functioned, describe that in some 10,000 electronic pages'[22] as part of the effort to fulfil the terms of the compulsory licencing remedy imposed. Forrester, opining on the acceleration and unpredictability shift that has occurred in the field of competition law in less than 20 years, notes that 'we have moved from anything being surprising to everything being possible.'[23]

The delicate balancing act of designing and imposing a remedy that is proportionate, yet effective, continues to prove itself as a difficult task. The challenge for the Commission lies in ensuring compliance with its mandate to impose a remedy that does not prove 'ineffectual or even illusory'[24], while simultaneously respecting general principles of EU law. Further, the design of an adequate remedy does not in itself ensure that the goal of bringing the infringement to an end will ensue, rather, it remains the task of the Commission to ensure effective implementation of a remedy, no matter how carefully designed. The challenge is more prevalent than ever before in evolving, dynamic markets and in particular, for the digital economy. *Google Shopping*[25] serves as a pertinent example of this challenge. Despite

17 Case 6 and 7/73, *Commercial Solvents and ICI v Commission*; Arianna Andreangeli, Between Economic Freedom and Effective Competition Enforcement: the impact of the antitrust remedies provided by the Modernisation Regulation on investigated parties' freedom to contract and to enjoy property (2010) 6(2) The Competition Law Review 225, 227.

18 C-242/91P ECRI-743 *RTE and ITP v Commission.*

19 Ibid; Andreangeli (n 15) 227.

20 Ian Forrester K.C, 'Magill revisited' in Inge Govaere, Reinhard Quick and Marco Bronckers (eds), *Trade and Competition Law in the EU and Beyond* (Edward Elgar 2011).

21 Case T-201/04 *Microsoft Corporation v Commission [*2004] ECR II-2977.

22 Forrester (n 20), 388.

23 ibid.

24 Case 792/79 R EU:C:1980:18 *Camera Care v European Communities*; *Bostoen/van Wamel* (n 4) 543.

25 Case T-612/17 ECLI:EU:T:2021:763 *Google LLC v. European Commission.*

the European Commission's efforts to address Google's abuse of market dominance by favouring its own comparison-shopping service, the remedy imposed has been criticised for its ineffectiveness.[26] The remedy did not sufficiently restore competition, as rival comparison-shopping services remained less visible and continued to suffer from reduced traffic. This highlights the tendency towards 'market shaping' remedies that may not fully address the underlying issues. Ibanez Colomo opines that the application of Articles 101 and 102 has been characterised by 'market-shaping' intervention. Central to the application of modern EU competition law, 'market-shaping' enforcement is now 'at the heart of the system.'[27] The era of digitisation has necessitated this shift towards 'market shaping' remedies where 'activities tend to revolve around a bottleneck' and 'remedies of the oligopoly era are often ineffective.'[28] Ultimately, 'market-shaping' enforcement exposes the competition law system to the limits of what it can meaningfully and realistically achieve.'[29] Thus, the writer is of the view that an understanding of the relevant challenges and the necessary considerations is vital to appreciate the constraints and limitations upon remedy design, implementation and monitoring.

C. Existing Remedial Practices

I. The legal remedial framework

Pursuant to regulation 1/2003, the Commission can impose behavioural or structural remedies to bring an infringement to an end. A structural remedy, generally speaking, involves the break-up of an undertaking to effectively divide up the competition into the hands of different competitors. Behavioural remedies on the other hand are, at least theoretically, not as invasive. Behavioural remedies generally involve the imposition of

26 *Hoppner*, 'Google's (Non-) Compliance with the EU Shopping Decision' (2020) https://papers.ssrn.com/sol3/papers.cfm?abstract_id=3700748 (accessed 12 May 2024) Philip Marsden, 'Google Shopping for the Empress's New Clothes – When a Remedy Isn't a Remedy (and How to Fix it) (2020) 11 Journal of European Competition Law and Practice 553; Ibáñez Colomo, *The New EU Competition Law*, Hart Publishing 2023, 189.

27 Ibáñez Colomo (n 26) 41.

28 Ibáñez Colomo (n 26) 41.

29 Ibáñez Colomo (n 26) 41.

mandatory and/or prohibitory obligations on an undertaking with respect to their behaviour in the market.[30] Separately, Article 9 decisions concern commitments offered by an undertaking against whom the commission intends to make a finding of an infringement, which if accepted by the Commission, are made legally binding on the undertaking.[31] Further, pursuant to Article 8 of Regulation 1/2003, the Commission is empowered to adopt interim measures to prevent 'irreparable damage' to competition.[32] The adoption of interim measures requires there to be a level of urgency attached to the situation.[33] The Commission must be satisfied that there is a *prima facie* infringement, and that damage is sufficiently foreseeable, before it can adopt interim measures pursuant to article 8. Article 8 provides that interim measures may only be adopted by the Commission acting on its 'own initiative' and thus, interim measures may not be imposed where they are requested by complainants. The fast-paced nature of the digital economy has increased the likelihood that anti-competitive conduct may cause 'serious and irreparable damage'[34] and consequently, the utilisation of Article 8 measures is likely to increase. Ruiz Feases opines that the reignition of the use of interim measures in *Broadcom*[35] is evidence 'of a renovated appetite for this tool.'[36]

II. Application of the legal framework in practice

While remedies imposed must respect general principles of EU law, at the same time, we have seen that the Commission is conferred a broad range of powers pursuant to Regulation 1/2003 and is afforded a wide margin

30 OECD Global Forum on Competition, Remedies and Commitments in Abuse Cases – Contribution from the European Union DAF/COMP/GF(2022) 5 https://one.oecd.org/document/DAF/COMP/GF(2022)5/en/pdf (accessed 2 April 2024) [14].

31 Regulation 1/2003 (n 2), Art. 9.

32 Regulation 1/2003 (n 2), Art 8; OECD, Working Party No. 3 on Co-operation and Enforcement Interim Measures in Antitrust Investigations – Note by the European Union DAF/COMP/WP3/WD(2022) 2 https://one.oecd.org/document/DAF/COMP/WP3/WD(2022)13/en/pdf#:~:text=In%20line%20with%20Article%208,be%20seriously%20and%20irreparably%20damaged.(accessed 21 May 2024).

33 OECD (n 32) 3.

34 OECD (n 32) 3.

35 Commission Decision of 16 October 2019, Broadcom, Case AT.40608.

36 Ruiz Feases, Sharpening the European Commission's tools: interim measures (2020)16 (2–3) European Competition Journal 404, 405.

of discretion with respect to the application of these powers. Notwithstanding, commentators suggest that the vast majority of remedies adopted by the Commission are cease-and-desist orders[37] or are the result of the commission adopting a 'principles-based approach'.[38] As such, 'they do not prescribe a specific conduct to be adopted by the infringing undertakings.'[39] Rather, the infringing undertaking is left to its own devices to determine the appropriate action to remedy the infringement. Research of cases from 2004 to 2018 in respect of Article 7 decisions found that in all cases a cease-and-desist order was issued. Unfortunately, however, only a very limited number of cases included 'specific additional remedies' over and above the cease-and-desist order.[40] The shortcomings in the mere issuing of cease-and-desist orders and the 'principles-based approach' are demonstrated by the *Google Shopping* case.[41] Google was found to have abused its dominant position by engaging in self-preferencing practices by giving 'prominent placement'[42] to its shopping services above that of its competitors, on the google search engine results. An *ex-post* analysis of this case highlighted the ineffectiveness of the 'principles-based approach' remedy, which was not subject to *ex-post* review, notwithstanding Google's failure to take compliance measures.[43] Google, left to its own devices to implement measures to remedy it's infringement, implemented measures described by commentators as 'meritless'.[44] Google's interpretation of the Commission's decision meant that google merely restructured its business, but did

37 OECD (n 30) [13].

38 Ibáñez Colomo, Remedies in EU Antitrust Law (2024) 21 Journal of Competition Law & Economics.

39 Ibáñez Colomo (n 38).

40 Loertscher/Maier-Rigaud, On the Consistency of the European Commission's Remedies Practice' in Damien Gerard and Assimakis Komnios (eds.) Remedies in EU Competition Law (Kluwer Law International B.V. 2020) 81.

41 Case T-612/17 ECLI:EU:T:2021:763. Google LLC v. European Commission.

42 Persch, 'Google Shopping: The General Court takes its position' (2021), https://competitionlawblog.kluwercompetitionlaw.com/2021/11/15/google-shopping-the-general-court-takes-its-position/ (accessed 12 May 2024).

43 *Hoppner*, 'Google's (Non-) Compliance with the EU Shopping Decision' (2020) https://papers.ssrn.com/sol3/papers.cfm?abstract_id=3700748 (accessed 12 May 2024).

44 *Hausfeld*, 'Antitrust remedies in digital markets: lessons for enforcement authorities from non-compliance with EU Google decisions'(2020) https://www.hausfeld.com/nl-nl/what-we-think/competition-bulletin/antitrust-remedies-in-digital-markets-lessons-for-enforcement-authorities-from-non-compliance-with-eu-google-decisions/ (accessed 12 May 2024).

not actually remedy the infringement at all. Instead, 'Google designed, tested, implemented, and maintained a mechanism that neither brought the anti-competitive conduct nor its effects to an end but had the same object and effect as the identified abuse.'[45] Admittedly, the Commission's preference for a 'principles-based approach' to intervention is understandably founded in its concern to ensure that remedial measures imposed are proportionate.[46] Moreover, such an approach, through for example, simple cease-and-desist orders merely require the undertaking concerned to bring the infringement to an end, thus, monitoring is not required on the part of the Commission.[47] However, adopting a 'principles-based approach' as a form of intervention is considered by Ibanez Colomo as a 'suboptimal' enforcement technique.[48] *Google Shopping* involved further intricacies as the Commission, due to its unfamiliarity with the design of the product, left the design of the remedy to Google and the 'remedy' was therefore 'incapable of providing sufficient legal certainty, either to the addressee or to third parties.'[49] The 'principles- based approach' undermines legal certainty, as such an approach fails to 'provide full clarity about whether the firm has effectively met the obligations to which it is subject.'[50] For example, in *Google Shopping*, 'several years after the finding of infringement, third-party rivals, and their advisers, continued to claim that the dominant undertaking had failed to abide by the principle of equal treatment and that additional modifications to the search engine's operation were necessary.'[51] Ultimately, Ibanez Colomo opines that if the 'principles-based approach' were 'abandoned in favour of one that consistently specified in detail and with clarity...the obligations with which undertakings have to comply', competition law enforcement 'would be more effective and would provide greater legal certainty'.[52]

45 Hausfeld (n 44).

46 Bostoen/van Wamel (n 6) 547.

47 Ibáñez Colomo, 'Regulatory' and 'Antitrust' Remedies in EU Competition Law' in Damien Gerard and Assimakis Komnios (eds) Remedies in EU Competition Law (Kluwer Law International B.V. 2020) 97.

48 Ibáñez Colomo, 'Remedies in EU Antitrust Law' (2024) 21 Journal of Competition Law & Economics, 33 https://ssrn.com/abstract=5028492 (accessed 5 January 2025).

49 Ibáñez Colomo (n 48) 38.

50 Ibáñez Colomo (n 48) 38.

51 Ibáñez Colomo (n 48) 38.

52 Ibáñez Colomo (n 48) 33.

III. Proposed directions for future remedial practices

In spite of the assumed concerns from the Commission's perspective, the writer suggests that the foregoing discussion pertaining to the broad construction of the Commission's powers, and the wide interpretation of the application of the general principles of EU law to the application of those powers, should somewhat alleviate those concerns. It is suggested that the preceding discussion should highlight the inefficiencies from a competition perspective, of the failure by the Commission to fully utilise the scope of the powers conferred on it. Perhaps more importantly, the consideration of the resistance on the part of the Commission towards adopting more pro-active measures, and the inadequacies surrounding cease-and-desist orders and the 'principles-based approach' on the enforcement of competition law, should re-enforce the importance of utilising the full extent of the powers conferred on the Commission by the EU's remedial framework. Ultimately, it is submitted that 'competition can only be meaningfully protected if authorities are in a position to adopt, where necessary, measures that go beyond ordering that infringements be brought to an end'[53] and in many instances, the nature of the product design and the remedy imposed warrant enhanced compliance measures to ensure continuous compliance and monitoring.[54]

Moreover, it is submitted that a downfall in the current remedial practice of the Commission is the lack of *ex-post* review of the implementation and effectiveness of remedies imposed. One such example where the Commission's enforcement remedy faced challenges due to the lack of *ex-post* review is the case of *Microsoft*.[55] In 2013, the European Commission fined Microsoft €561 million for failing to comply with a previous ruling that required the company to offer users a choice of web browsers in addition to its own Internet Explorer. Microsoft had committed to providing a browser choice screen to European Windows users, allowing them to easily select and install alternative browsers. However, some two years later in 2011, it was discovered that Microsoft had failed to include the browser choice screen in its Windows 7 Service Pack 1 update, affecting millions of

53 Ibáñez Colomo (n 48) 17.
54 Ibáñez Colomo (n 48) 24.
55 Case T-167/08 ECLI:EU:T:2012:32 *Micorsoft Corp. v European Commission.*

users.[56] The Commission launched an investigation and ultimately found Microsoft to be in breach of its 2009 commitments. The lack of an effective *ex-post* review meant that the violation continued for some two years, and consequently affected millions of consumers.[57] Perhaps even more alarming is the fact that the failure of the Commission to conduct any form of *ex-post* review meant that the violation came to their attention via external information and complaints.[58] Irrespective of the fact that Microsoft acknowledged the error and apologised, by the time the issue came to light, millions of users had already been affected, undermining the effectiveness of the remedy. This example underscores the importance of implementing *ex-post* review mechanisms and monitoring procedures, as an element of the EU's competition law enforcement framework, to detect and address non-compliance and remedy failures, to ensure that undertakings adhere to their obligations and that consumers benefit from competitive markets.

D. The Future of Remedy Design

I. Constitutional Constraints Influencing Remedy Design

Commentators have suggested that the lack of definitive criteria as to what constitutes an effective remedy is unsurprising given that 'effectiveness is a neutral, fluid and relative'[59] concept. This lacuna, if you will, suggests that in order for the Commission to fulfil its mandate to ensure the effectiveness of remedies, it must be in a position to implement remedies that are *inter alia* 'fluid and relative'.[60] This notwithstanding, constitutional considerations from an EU perspective impose restraints on the extent to which the Commission can go in designing, and re-visiting remedies. In this regard, general principles of EU law must be afforded due consideration and adequately respected. Key of those general principles to competition law enforcement include *inter alia* proportionality, legal certainty and legitimate expectation.

---

56 *European Commission Press Release*, 'Antitrust: Commission opens proceedings against Microsoft to investigate possible non-compliance with browser choice commitments' (Brussels, 17 July 2012) https://ec.europa.eu/commission/presscorner/detail/en/IP_12_800 (accessed 13 May 2024).

57 *European Commission Press Release* (n 56).

58 *European Commission Press Release* (n 56).

59 Bostoen/van Wamel (n 6) 543.

60 Bostoen/van Wamel (n 6) 543.

Proportionality is enshrined in article 5(4) TEU which stipulates that 'the content and form of a Union measure shall not exceed what is necessary to achieve the objectives of the treaties.'[61] A remedy is proportionate if it goes no further than is necessary to achieve the desired objective, i.e. brings to an end the infringing conduct and restores competitive conditions. A broad discretion is afforded to the Commission in this context, however, since public interest considerations are afforded high priority by both the EU legislature and the courts. The jurisprudence of the courts suggests that a party claiming that a remedy imposed is disproportionate bears the burden of proving such, and moreover, this burden is a high one.[62] For example, in *Commission v Lundbeck*[63] the CJEU upheld the Commission's decision imposing fines and remedies on pharmaceutical companies for entering into agreements that delayed the market entry of generic drugs. In upholding the Commission's decision, the CJEU highlighted the importance of effective competition enforcement in the pharmaceutical sector due to the significant harm caused by the anticompetitive behaviour. Similarly, the case of *SGL Carbon AG v Commission*[64] the CJEU held that 'so far as the appellant's argument relating to the freedom to conduct business and the right to property is concerned, it is sufficient to note that those principles are subject to public-interest restrictions and that they cannot be relevant in the context of setting a fine for an infringement of Community competition law.'[65] It can be deduced therefrom, that the CJEU is committed to safeguarding competition, even if it requires remedies that might seem disproportionate in certain contexts.[66] The objective of promoting competition justified intervention, even if it resulted in restrictions on the dominant firm's property rights or commercial freedom. It is submitted that the afore considered jurisprudence demonstrates the CJEU's willingness to prioritise the objectives of competition law enforcement over strict adherence to proportionality when addressing serious anticompetitive behaviour.

Further, in support of the proposition that the principle of proportionality is not an overwhelming constraint on the Commission, commentators

61 TEU art 5(4).

62 Hellström/ Maier-Rigaud/Wenzel Bulst, Remedies in European Antitrust Law (2009) 76 Antitrust Law Journal 43, 49.

63 Case C 591/16 ECLI:EU:C:2021:243 *P Commission v Lundbeck.*

64 Case C-308/04 P E.C.R. I-5977 *SGL Carbon AG v. Commission*; Hellström/Maier-Rigaud/Bulst (n 62) 50.

65 Hellström/Maier-Rigaud/Bulst (n 62) [108].

66 Hellström/Maier-Rigaud/Bulst (n 62).

have laid emphasis on the text of article 7(1) regulation 1/2003, namely that 'structural remedies can only be imposed either where there is no equally effective behavioural remedy or where any equally effective behavioural remedy would be more burdensome for the undertaking concerned than the structural remedy.'[67] A remedy must be effective.[68] Article 7(1) mandates that 'structural remedies can only be imposed where there is no *equally* effective behavioural remedy is a logical consequence of effectiveness' and thus, the provision demands that the remedy that is most effective must prevail.[69] Therefore, commentators opine that 'proportionality is only second to effectiveness: it cannot justify ineffective remedies.'[70] Moreover, proportionality takes on a different 'extent and content'[71] depending on the legal basis upon which the Commission bases its decision, whether that be Article 7, 8, or 9 of Regulation 1/2003.[72] For example, in the case of *Alrosa*,[73] the court determined that the principle of proportionality is somewhat weakened where Article 9 commitment decisions are concerned. The court justifies this by arguing that in such cases, an undertaking is freed from being found to have formally breached EU competition law.[74]

Additionally, the principle of legal certainty requires 'on the one hand, that rules of law must be clear and precise and, on the other, that their application must be foreseeable by those subject to them.'[75] Importantly, however, *vis-à-vis* today's dynamic markets, it is difficult to predict the future and thus, albeit that due respect must be afforded to the principle of legal certainty, existing rules must be capable of being adapted, extended and applied to new abuses in evolving or emerging markets. Thus, a balance needs to be struck 'between creating certainty in rules to be easily applied and the need to create general rules that can be applied to many

67 Bostoen/van Wamel (n 6) 545.
68 Bostoen/van Wamel (n 6) 545.
69 Bostoen/van Wamel (n 6) 545.
70 Bostoen/van Wamel (n 6) 544.
71 Case C-441/07 P EU:C:201 *European Commission v Alrosa Company Ltd.*
72 Regulation 1/2003 (n 2).
73 European Commission v Alrosa Company Ltd (n 71).
74 European Commission v Alrosa Company Ltd (n 71); Voss, The Principle of Equality: A Limit to the Commission's Discretion in EU Competition Law Enforcement? (2013) Global Antitrust Review, 154.
75 Case C-201/08 EU:C:2009:539 *Plantanol GmbH & Co KG v Hauptzollamt Darmsta*; Voss, Between Enforcement and Regulation A Study of the System of Case Resolution Mechanisms Used by the European Commission in the Enforcement of Articles 101 and 102 TFEU (2019) Stockholm University, 56.

situations.'[76] Commentators suggest that the broad margin of discretion afforded to the Commission due to the scope of *inter alia* articles 101 and 102, together with the adoption of soft law guidance, arguably offends against the principle of legal certainty. However, the broad discretion conferred on the Commission is again highlighted by the jurisprudence of the courts, where challenges to, in particular, the calculation of fines, have withstood scrutiny by the judiciary,[77] and thus, 'the exact criteria where the principle of legal certainty would be considered infringed…remains unclear.'[78]

Moreover, the related general principle of legitimate expectation also prevails in competition law enforcement.[79] Undertakings to whom legislation and soft law instruments are addressed are entitled to expect that such law and policy will continue to be applied and interpreted in the same manner and thus, to form a legitimate expectation as to how it may affect them. Similar to other general principles, however, the jurisprudence suggests that the principle cannot be relied upon 'in an absolute manner'.[80] Rather, a party invoking the principle bears a high burden of proof to claim protection on the grounds of legitimate expectation. One such example is the case of *Archer Daniels Midland Co v Commission of the European Communities*.[81] In that case, the Commission imposed a fine by reference to fining guidelines that were adopted by the Commission after the investigation had been opened, and thus the Commission were effectively applying the fining principles retrospectively. The court noted that the Commission was not estopped from increasing fines if it was necessary to do so for the proper implementation of EU competition policy.[82] The court further noted that an undertaking cannot rely on the principle of legitimate expectation to suggest that the Commission cannot impose a fine that exceeds the level of fines previously imposed, and by reference to different guidelines.[83] The court considered that it was not unforeseeable that the Commission may review the level of fines to ensure the proper implementation of competi-

76 Voss (n 75).
77 Voss (n 75).
78 Voss (n 75) 57.
79 Voss (n 75).
80 Voss (n 75) 58.
81 Case T-329/01 EU:T:2006:268 *Archer Daniels Midland Co v Commission of the European Communities*.
82 (n 81).
83 (n 81).

tion law and policy.[84] By analogy, the writer suggests that *vis-à-vis* rapidly changing, dynamic markets, effective implementation of competition law and policy demands that the Commission be afforded a wide margin of discretion to ensure that its mandate; to bring competition law infringement to an end, is fulfilled.

While the general principles of EU law such as proportionality, legal certainty and legitimate expectation are undoubtedly a constitutional restraint upon remedy design and implementation and so must be observed, it is the view of the writer that the foregoing analysis of the jurisprudence in relation to the general principles and their ability to impact as constitutional restraints on remedy design and implementation suggest that 'competition law enforcement is characterised by a wide margin of discretion afforded to the Commission.'[85] Thus, while admittedly the power of the Commission is circumscribed to a degree by the general principles, the writer suggests that the jurisprudence of the CJEU is support for the proposition that this circumscription is not so overwhelming such that the Commission is estopped from adapting and evolving it's remedial practices, to tackle infringements of competition law, in rapidly growing and changing markets. Moreover, cases such as *Akzo* and *Commercial Solvents* serve as a reminder of the extent of the Commission's prerogative, which extends beyond merely ending anti-competitive practices, but which also extends to imposing positive or negative obligations on undertakings to counter the effects of its anti-competitive conduct. It is ultimately suggested that this power, enhanced by the wide margin of discretion conferred on the Commission in terms of the application of the general principles of EU law in competition enforcement, should be further utilised and leveraged to combat anti-competitive practices in emerging markets. Ibanez Colomo cites *Ufex*[86] in support of the argument for restorative intervention, wherein the court held 'the 'anti-competitive effects continue after the practices which caused them have ceased', the Commission 'remains competent' to 'act with a view to eliminating or neutralising' such effects.'[87]

84 (n 81). [49].
85 Voss (n 75) 58.
86 C-119/97 P EU:C:1999:116 *Union Française de l'Express (Ufex) v Commission.*
87 Ibáñez Colomo, Remedies in EU Antitrust Law 2024) 21 Journal of Competition Law & Economics, 12.

II. Should the emphasis on competition law remedies decrease as regulation becomes more prevalent?

The conventional view is that regulation operates *ex-ante*, and competition law *ex post*. EU competition law consists of *ex-ante* and *ex-post* tools. It may be argued by opponents to the reform of remedy design in competition law to target in particular, digital markets, that it is unnecessary *vis-à-vis* regulation, such as the Digital Markets Act ("DMA").[88] It may be purported that competition concerns can be addressed 'from a regulatory perspective, superseding traditional antitrust enforcement.'[89] The view, however, that reforms to remedy design practices and procedures are redundant where regulation will tackle the challenges in such markets, is challenged by this writer. Regulation in isolation is not a panacea and *vice versa*. Regulation and competition law should not be viewed as mutually exclusive. The notion that competition law and regulation 'live in two separate worlds' is not reflective of reality. Rather, the two can, and do, co-exist and operate in parallel. The recent introduction of the DMA is demonstrative. The DMA seeks to control the activities of 'large online digital platforms, who by virtue of the DMA, are christened 'gatekeepers' by the Commission. Such a label carries with it enhanced obligations, both mandatory and prohibitory, on the part of such online platforms with respect to their behaviour in the market. The criteria for identifying platforms upon whom gatekeeper status should be conferred is set out in the DMA,[90] while the jurisdiction to confer such status rests exclusively with the Commission.[91] The preamble to the DMA explicitly states that the application of the Act

88 Regulation (EU) 2022/1925 of The European Parliament and of The Council of 14 September 2022 on contestable and fair markets in the digital sector and amending Directives (EU) 2019/1937 and (EU) 2020/1828 (Digital Markets Act) (Text with EEA relevance) OJ L 265/1.

89 Lancieri/ de Silva Pereira Neto, Designing Remedies For Digital Markets: The Interplay Between Antitrust and Regulation (2021) 18(3) Journal of Competition Law & Economics, 613, 621–622.

90 Regulation (EU) 2022/1925 of The European Parliament and of The Council of 14 September 2022 on contestable and fair markets in the digital sector and amending Directives (EU) 2019/1937 and (EU) 2020/1828 (Digital Markets Act) (Text with EEA relevance) OJ L 265/1, Art 3.

91 Regulation (EU) 2022/1925 of The European Parliament and of The Council of 14 September 2022 on contestable and fair markets in the digital sector and amending Directives (EU) 2019/1937 and (EU) 2020/1828 (Digital Markets Act) (Text with EEA relevance) OJ L 265/1, Art 3(4).

is without prejudice to the application of competition rules. Moreover, the preamble highlights that the DMA seeks to pursue an objective different to that pursued by competition law.[92] Albeit that the DMA has a different legal basis, it is submitted that the objectives are not as different as they are portrayed to be.[93] The DMA operates as a very useful regulatory tool at the Commission's disposal to regulate digital markets *ex-ante*. It is surmised by this writer that the DMA operates in reality, as an extension of competition law; an *ex-ante* tool in the Commission's competition toolkit, akin to a behavioural remedy. It's scope, however, is limited. While Schroeter and Hoyng consider the DMA as an *ex ante* instrument of competition law,[94] Commissioner Vestager states that the DMA 'is not a competition law instrument'.[95] This writer is inclined to side with the former view. In fact, albeit that the DMA operates under a different legal basis, this writer argues that the DMA is a *de facto* competition instrument. Ultimately, however, rather than striving to draw a stark line between competition law and regulation, the sentiments of commentators[96] that the two should be considered as complimentary tools which work in tandem; which operate in synergy and complement one another, is echoed by this writer.

Makris notes that this desire to clearly delineate between competition law and regulation has culminated in the view that by acting proactively, competition law strays into the territory of regulation and is thereby 'incompatible with its nature.'[97] The line between competition law and regulation is arguably blurred, when one considers the reality that behavioural remedies are effectively *ex-ante* measures and thus, 'are placed at the borderline with market regulation'.[98] Makris ultimately submits that 'we should recognize

---

92 Regulation (EU) 2022/1925 of The European Parliament and of The Council of 14 September 2022 on contestable and fair markets in the digital sector and amending Directives (EU) 2019/1937 and (EU) 2020/1828 (Digital Markets Act) (Text with EEA relevance) OJ L 265/1 (11).

93 Belle Beems, The DMA in the broader regulatory landscape of the EU: an institutional perspective' (2023) 19 (1) European Competition Journal 1–29, 16.

94 Beems (n 93) 20.

95 Speech Margrethe Vestager, 'Competition in a Digital Age' (European Internet Forum, 17 March 2021); Beems (n 93) 4.

96 Beems (n 93) 20.

97 Makris, Responsive Competition Law Enforcement: Lessons from the Greek Competition Authority (2023) 46(2) World Competition, 206.

98 Botta/Wiedemann, EU Competition Law Enforcement vis-à-vis Exploitative Conducts in the Data Economy Exploring the Terra Incognita' Working Paper, Max Planck Institute for Innovation and Competition Research Paper No. 18–08, 70.

the artificiality of juxtaposing competition law with regulation on the basis that the former is only applied *ex post* and in a prescriptive manner.'[99] By the same token, Ibãnez Colomo acknowledges that it is 'somewhat misleading' and 'artificial'[100] to suggest that there must be a clear division between competition remedies and regulatory remedies.[101] Competition law and regulation have long operated in parallel with one another, and so the operation of the DMA in conjunction with competition law is not an alien concept. Sectors such as telecoms and energy are demonstrative. In *Deutsche Telekom*,[102] EU competition law was applied notwithstanding that sector specific regulation was in force. *Deutsche Telekom* concerned a dominant undertaking in the telecommunications sector which was subject to an obligation to deal under specified conditions. The sector specific regulation had not made provision for managing the margin squeeze that occurred. *Deutsche Telekom* illustrates how EU competition law and sector-specific regulation work in tandem. Competition law fills the lacunae that regulation cannot pre-empt. Competition law occupies a 'gap-filling' role acting as a sort of safety net, intervening when regulation may not easily achieve the desired intervention.[103] 'Whenever such gaps emerge, Articles 101 and 102 TFEU maybe be able to address them, even if partially or imperfectly.'[104]

Similarly, the DMA cannot compensate for every eventuality and thus, the importance of intervening in the form of competition law and designing appropriate enforcement remedies, in particular for digital markets, is not dissipated by the application of the DMA. The blurring of the line between competition law and regulation is driven by the need for a cohesive approach to managing the complexities of modern digital markets. Both aim to ensure fair competition and consumer protection, but the dynamic and intertwined nature of market challenges necessitates a more integrated and flexible application of both disciplines. Ultimately, 'in order to regulate big tech, regulatory initiatives cannot be considered in isolation'[105] thus,

99 Ibáñez Colomo (n 87) 92.
100 Ibáñez Colomo (n 87) 92.
101 Ibáñez Colomo (n 87) 92.
102 Case C-280/08 P Deutsche Telekom v European Commission [2010] ECLI:EU:C:2010:212.
103 Pablo Ibáñez Colomo, The New EU Competition Law (Hart Publishing 2023) 154.
104 Ibáñez Colomo (n 103) 92.
105 Belle Beems, 'The DMA in the broader regulatory landscape of the EU: an institutional perspective' (2023) 19 (1) European Competition Journal 1–29, 29.

competition law will continue to co-exist alongside regulation in digital markets. Therefore, the design of appropriate remedies still remains relevant *vis-à-vis* modern markets.

III. Responsive Enforcement

In light of the reality that regulation and competition law operate in parallel and neither is subordinate to the other in the context of the protection of competition, the validity of the argument for responsive enforcement of competition law, and by extension remedy design, remains paramount. The earlier part of this paper suggests, by implication, that the success of competition law is best measured by the success of remedies and consequently, is dependent on 'effective enforcement by well-equipped authorities'.[106] Cases such a *Google* and *Microsoft* highlight how the failure to ensure proper enforcement ultimately jeopardised the effectiveness of the remedies imposed.

It is suggested, supported by the foregoing considerations, that the notion that competition law should be confined to the *ex-post* sphere is archaic. Modern competition law provides for 'a wide array of enforcement tools of varied intensity and develop strategies that go beyond the narrow contours of the crime-tort enforcement model'.[107] Rather, 'they have the tools to apply the law 'responsively' and they often aspire to be 'responsive enforcers'.'[108] The preceding discussion suggests that the Commission, despite having substantive tools at its disposal, has failed to fully utilise and maximise the potential of the application of those tools.

As we have seen from the foregoing analysis, competition law, in permitting the Commission to impose mandatory or prohibitory obligations in an effort to undo the effects of an infringement, has extended the Commission's powers beyond merely imposing a cease-and-desist remedy. Equally, it has been suggested that the court has applied a wide interpretation to the application of general principles of EU with respect to the utilisation of these extensive powers. However, it is respectfully submitted that there is little appetite on the part of enforcers to (1) impose an appropriate remedy beyond merely cease-and-desist and (2) ensure the implementation

106 Beems (n 105).
107 Makris (n 97) 206.
108 Makris (n 97) 206.

and effectiveness of any remedy imposed. While it is submitted that the jurisprudence of the CJEU in respect of the application of the Commission's powers should provide some comfort and assurance, the position of the Commission with respect to its obligations under general principles of EU law, as well as the particular challenges presented by remedy design, such as the risk of under or over enforcement, is appreciated.[109] Ultimately, *vis-à-vis* such challenges and faced with growing and emerging fast paced markets, it is suggested by this writer, informed by the opinions of various commentators,[110] that an iterative or staggered approach to remedy design is required in modern competition law enforcement, in particular to effectively regulate 'big tech' and the digital economy. It is submitted that this iterative system of remedy design should be supported by the introduction of *ex-post* review as a feature of EU competition law and policy, to assess the adequacy and effectiveness of remedies imposed. This in turn, will inform decisions by enforcers as to whether more stringent measures should be imposed, or conversely, the alteration or removal of measures that, upon review of their effects, went further than was necessary to achieve their aim.

Ultimately, this proposal envisages a staggered approach to remedy design whereby remedies are subject to *ex-post* review according to timelines.[111] If upon review, it realises that the initially imposed remedy transpires to be ineffective, 'it can be adapted based on the lessons learned.'[112] Similarly, it has been suggested that the enforcement authority may initially 'impose a more lenient behavioural remedy that leaves a broader discretion to the defendant as regards its implementation. However, to ensure that the defendant effectively implements this original remedy, the authority may simultaneously impose a more stringent (e.g. pro-active or structural remedy) that applies automatically in case the infringement has not ended within a certain time limit.'[113] Such an approach would arguably remedy the defects in enforcement that arose in cases such as *Google* and *Microsoft*. It is submitted that as such, a non-binary approach would help to avoid the pitfalls of over-regulation, which can stifle innovation and under-regulation, and in turn fail to address competitive harms. Iterative adjustments ensure

109 Makris (n 97) 208.
110 Makris (n 97) 208; Bostoen/van Wamel (n 6); Hellström, Maier-Rigaud and Bulst (n 62).
111 Bostoen/van Wamel (n 6) 550.
112 Bostoen/van Wamel (n 6) 550.
113 Hausfeld (n 44).

a balanced intervention that protects competition. Informed by Bary and De Bure who opine that 'behavioural commitments are "rigid", and they do not match the peculiarities of modern digital markets, characterized by disruptive innovation and sudden changes of the market structure. A competition issue that requires a behavioural remedy today might be outdated in a few years' time, due to the entry of a new competitor in the market that can quickly acquire market power due to the release of an innovative product',[114] Botta and Wiedmann have called for the use of active review clauses in commitment decisions.[115]

Ultimately, 'the risk of remedies becoming outdated…is mitigated when the remedies themselves can evolve.'[116] An iterative process allows for initial remedies to be adapted based on their effectiveness. The enforcement authority may begin with a lenient behavioural remedy, but simultaneously impose a stricter remedy to be activated if the infringement is not resolved within a specified period. The ability of an enforcement authority to escalate or de-escalate its intervention is supported by Makris who advocates for the implementation of sunrise and sunset clauses, noting that 'sunset clauses can phase out a remedy when the competition problem has been addressed, while sunrise clauses may compel authorities to revisit the effectiveness of the remedy in light of new market circumstances.'[117] This strategy aims to balance between over-regulation, which can inhibit innovation, and under-regulation, which may not adequately address competitive harms. Nevertheless, it is crucial to stress that it is by no means intended that such an approach should be construed as a licence to impose effectively useless remedies in the first instance, where more stringent measures are clearly warranted. It is suggested that by adopting an iterative or staggered approach, the Commission would not be considered to be acting *ultra vires, vis-à-vis* the provisions of Regulation 1/2003.

Writing in 2010 addressing the sixth international forum on Competition in Seoul, then Director General for Competition European Commission Alexander Italianer opined that:

114 De Bure/ Bary, 'Disruptive innovation and merger remedies: How to predict the unpredictable?' Concurrences (2017) https://www.concurrences.com/en/review/issues/no-3-2017/articles/disruptive-innovation-and-merger-remedies-how-to-predict-the-unpredictable; (accessed 17 April 2025); Bostoen/van Wamel (n 6) 550.

115 Bostoen/van Wamel (n 4) 550.

116 Bostoen/van Wamel (n 4) 550.

117 Makris (n 97) 240.

> 'competition law enforcement is a flexible tool that we have strived to modernise constantly. We have proven capable of analysing complex markets in a dynamic way. Our tools have served us well in the past and I believe they will also serve us well in the new digital era.... All we need to do is to see how best to apply our principles to the digital sphere and to increasingly converging markets.'[118]

Similarly, this writer is of the view that Regulation 1/2003 provides an adequate legal basis for an iterative or staggered approach to remedy design. As discussed throughout this paper, Article 7 empowers the Commission to impose remedies necessary to address infringements of EU competition law. The Article 7 effectiveness requirement 'lays down a lower limit' in that the Commission is obliged to '*at least* ensure that the remedies it imposes are effective.'[119] Thus, arguably implicit in Article 7 is the permission to monitor and review remedies, as the effectiveness of remedies initially imposed may be called into question, and their ability to meet their intended objective(s) may fall short with the passage of time, and the shift in markets. Further, pursuant to Article 9(2),[120] if market conditions change or if the initial commitments prove to be ineffective, the Commission can reopen the case. This provides a clear legal basis for the review and adaptation of remedies, ensuring they remain effective over time. Moreover, inherent in Article 23(2),[121] which permits the Commission to impose fines for non-compliance with commitments or remedies, is the legal basis for *ex-post* monitoring or review in order to detect such non-compliance.

Furthermore, it is submitted that an iterative or staggered approach would be likely to comply with the general principles of EU law. For example, the principle of proportionality, which as previously discussed, requires that the remedies imposed should not be excessive and should be no more burdensome than necessary, considering the nature and gravity of the infringement, supports a staggered approach. By starting with less intrusive measures and escalating, if necessary, the Commission thereby ensures that remedies are proportionate and are gradually adjusted to

118 *Italianer,* Directorate General for Competition EU Commission, Safeguarding and promoting competition in the age of digital convergence (15 September 2010) 6th International Competition Forum Seoul, Session on digital convergence and competition issues.

119 Bostoen/van Wamel (n 4) 543.

120 Regulation 1/2003 (n 2), art 9(2).

121 Regulation 1/2003 (n 2), art 23(2).

achieve compliance without imposing undue burdens. In fact, the use of review clauses was explicitly approved as enhancing the proportionality of measures by the Commission in *Deutsche Lufthansa AG v Commission.*[122] The court opined that review clauses 'give expression to the principle of proportionality inasmuch as they allow... the waiver, modification or substitution of the commitments if it is demonstrated that the latter are no longer necessary or proportionate'.[123]

It is acknowledged that with a staggered approach, it is crucial to have a clear framework and criteria for when and how adjustments will be made. This provides legal certainty to the parties involved. It is submitted that this can be achieved by a number of measures. One such option is to make provision in the original decision for the automatic application of a more stringent remedy, in the event that the initial remedy fails to bring the originally identified infringement to an end within a specified time limit.[124] Thus, the more stringent remedy is made known to the undertaking at the outset. The initial decision should allow for iterative adjustments based on the monitoring results. This means being open to refining the remedy as new information becomes available or as market conditions change. To safeguard legal certainty, the decision should clearly specify the conditions under which adjustments will be made, such as failure to meet competitive benchmarks or significant changes in market dynamics. Speaking in the context of merger control, Bougette, Budzinski and Marty note that remedies may 'age badly'[125] as 'the market environment may have outdated them post-merger'.[126] This challenge is ever greater in the context of digital markets. The failure to re-visit remedies and 'the use of static models of competition law enforcement can result in insufficient and occasionally

122 Case T-712/16 EU:T:2018:269 *Deutsche Lufthansa AG v Commission.*

123 Bostoen/van Wamel (n 6) 551; Case T-712/16 EU:T:2018:269 *Deutsche Lufthansa AG v Commission* [53].

124 Hausfeld, Antitrust remedies in digital markets: lessons for enforcement authorities from non-compliance with EU Google decisions'(2020) https://www.hausfeld.com/nl-nl/what-we-think/competition-bulletin/antitrust-remedies-in-digital-markets-lessons-for-enforcement-authorities-from-non-compliance-with-eu-google-decisions/ (accessed 12 May 2024).

125 Bougette/Budzinski/Marty, In The Light Of Dynamic Competition: Should We Make Merger Remedies More Flexible? (2023) 28(181) Ilmenau University of Technology Institute of Economics, 12.

126 Bougette/Budzinski/Marty (n 125).

excessive or inefficacious remedies, particularly in rapidly evolving and dynamic markets.'[127]

Importantly, in the interests of transparency it is suggested that 'evaluation ex post should…consider the objective and constraints that were faced by the decision maker ex-ante...In other words the metric ex post should be consistent with the decision-making problem ex ante.'[128] Anticipated arguments include that undertakings may face uncertainty regarding their compliance obligations, as initial lenient remedies could later be replaced with more stringent ones. This uncertainty can impact business planning and operations. To counter this, however, the proposal envisages clear timelines and criteria for reviews to provide undertakings with predictable frameworks. Clear communication of the potential for stricter remedies, the conditions under which they will be applied and by confining the second review to the same investigative competencies as the initial review, the right of undertakings to legal certainty is arguably balanced with the objective of safeguarding competition in the market. While the ultimate design of such reform is beyond the scope of this paper, it is suggested that there be a time window within which to activate the second review, 'for instance, between 3 and 7 years after the original…decision. Given the changing nature of market environments and the idea that this should not become a permanent regulatory supervision, longer time periods seem to be unfeasible. The alternative to a time window would be a fixed point in time (e.g., after 5 years) which looks less flexible.'[129]

It is anticipated that opponents to such a staggered approach are likely to argue that there is a greater risk that authorities might initially impose remedies that are too lenient, failing to adequately address significant competition concerns. However, this proposal stresses that lenient remedies should not be used where stringent measures are clearly warranted. Clear guidelines and criteria for selecting initial remedies can help ensure that they are appropriately robust. The *ex-post* review mechanism and remedy adjustment serves as a fail-safe, enabling adjustments to be made if the initial measures prove insufficient.

As discussed in the earlier section of this paper, the Commission is afforded a wide latitude with respect to the application of the general

127 Bougette/Budzinski/Marty (n 125) 9.

128 Neven/Zenger, Ex post evaluation of enforcement: a principal-agent perspective (DG Competition, European Commission) 8.

129 Neven/Zenger (128) 14.

principles, to the invocation of its powers pursuant to Regulation 1/2003. Ultimately, this wide latitude, combined with the principles underpinning a staggered approach to remedy design and the compliance thereof with the general principles, supports the writer's contention that such an approach would likely withstand a challenge as to its compatibility with the general principles of EU law. The proposed staggered approach to remedy design in EU competition law aims to provide a balanced and flexible enforcement mechanism. While there are valid concerns regarding complexity, uncertainty, and resource demands, these can be mitigated through clear guidelines and transparency. By ensuring that initial remedies are not overly lenient and by incorporating a mechanism for iterative adjustments, it is submitted that this approach can effectively address competitive harms while avoiding the extremes of over-and under regulation.

IV. Further Recommendations

While an iterative or staggered approach to remedy design may seem effective in theory, in order for it to prove effective in practice, a substantive *ex-post* review mechanism must be integrated into the competition law enforcement framework and practice. As highlighted by Lancieri and de Silva Pereira Neto, 'it took the Commission more than 14 months to find out that Microsoft inadvertently removed a browser selection screen imposed as a remedy in the Microsoft browser investigation—no one noticed the "remedy" was gone.'[130] Thus, the implementation failure by the undertaking, and the simultaneous neglect by the authorities to detect this failure, meant that the remedy did not produce any effects on the market. It is opined that a substantive *ex-post* review mechanism would have highlighted this failure in a timely manner, and informed remedial action to address the anti-competitive conduct promptly thereafter. Lancieri and de Silva Pereira Neto identify 'the monitoring of how the remedy is being implemented and the adaptation of the intervention to new data on its impacts on markets' as a key aspect of remedy design.[131]

130 Lancieri/ de Silva Pereira Neto, Designing Remedies For Digital Markets: The Interplay Between Antitrust and Regulation (2021) 18(3) Journal of Competition Law & Economics, 613, 614.

131 Lancieri/ de Silva Pereira Neto (n 130) 651.

As noted by Lancieri and de Silva Periera Neto, 'even an authority that is well-positioned to identify problems and to design remedies can still be ill-suited to oversee the remedy's implementation.'[132] It is this writer's proposition that this is true of the European Commission. The Commission lacks the internal resources to conduct effective monitoring of the implementation and effectiveness of remedies. In light of the foregoing considerations pertaining to the existing legal framework within which *ex-post* monitoring may be conducted, it is suggested that in order to properly comply with its mandate and leverage its wide margin of discretion in terms of its powers and their application, the Commission must invest in its monitoring resources and integrate a substantive *ex-post* review mechanism. As an element of this integration, this writer proposes the creation of an internal unit, akin to the role of the monitoring trustee, as a dedicated unit within DG Competition, responsible for monitoring compliance with remedies.

To embrace a more adaptable approach is to 'compel' the Commission to expend and 'allocate resources towards gathering information regarding the efficacy of remedies.'[133] In the same way the Commission 'has invested in improving its epistemic capacity, by creating the position of Chief Competition Economist in 2003 and by setting up internal checks and balances demonstrate its emphasis on problem-solving and delivering results',[134] the creation of the position of the internal monitoring trustee, would further advance the Commission's responsive enforcement agenda. In line with the proposed staggered or iterative approach to remedy design, commentators suggest that 'authorities should at first use milder means and more lenient enforcement mechanisms. It is recognised, however, 'that these techniques can only produce positive results if more severe measures lurk in the background and can be used successfully. It is the existence and effective use of such 'big guns' that renders voluntary compliance effective.'[135] It is suggested that a monitoring trustee would serve as the 'big guns'. If undertakings are alert to the fact that they are subject to surveillance by a monitoring arm of DG Competition, compliance is arguably more likely.

---

132 Lancieri/ de Silva Pereira Neto (n 130) 651.

133 Bougette/ Budzinski/Marty, In the Light of Dynamic Competition: Should We Make Merger Remedies More Flexible? (2023) 28(181) Ilmenau University of Technology Institute of Economics, 12.

134 Makris (n 97) 226.

135 Makris (n 97) 226.

Furthermore, even where compliance is not an issue, but market dynamics have shifted, detection of the inadequacy of a remedy imposed to restore competitive conditions, has a greater likelihood of capture. Ultimately, *vis-à-vis* dynamic, ever evolving markets, 'it becomes increasingly evident that competition law intervention must be multi-levelled and multi-fashioned and that remedies are key in solving competition problems. Remedies are key also because what matters at the end of the day is whether competition law intervention improved the state of competition in the market. For this reason, competition authorities are increasingly using a wide array of tools and engage in *ex ante* and *ex post*, prescriptive and proscriptive enforcement.'[136]

The creation of the role of the monitoring trustee within DG Competition, responsible for monitoring compliance with remedies envisages a dedicated unit responsible for continuous and real-time monitoring of the effectiveness of imposed remedies. A specialised unit or role within DG Competition would bring focused expertise to the task of monitoring and evaluating remedies, improving the overall effectiveness and efficiency of enforcement actions. A dedicated role could establish formal channels for receiving feedback from stakeholders, including competitors, consumers, and market participants, ensuring that their insights inform the ongoing assessment of remedies. Regular reporting on the effectiveness of remedies and the outcome of reviews would increase transparency, helping to build trust among stakeholders. While the intricacies are beyond the scope of this paper, the role should have a clear mandate and sufficient operational independence to make unbiased assessments and recommendations. This would include the authority to initiate reviews and propose adjustments to remedies.

While the creation of a specialised role or unit within DG Competition is novel, the concept of the monitoring trustee is not. The EU already uses monitoring trustees in specific cases, particularly in merger control and antitrust cases where complex remedies are involved. These trustees are appointed to oversee the implementation of commitments by undertakings to ensure compliance with the Commission's decisions. They act as the "eyes and ears" of the Commission, providing regular reports on the progress and effectiveness of the remedies. Moreover, it is submitted that the in-house monitoring trustee will assist in overcoming the limitations presented by

136 Makris (n 97) 226.

the appointment of an external trustee.[137] In *Microsoft*, the court found that the Commission could not confer powers on an external monitoring trustee, those powers that were reserved for the Commission.[138] An internal unit would operate under the direct authority of the DG Competition and the European Commission. This means that it would inherently possess the legal powers and authority reserved for the Commission, avoiding the legal complications associated with delegation of these powers externally.

Finally, it is submitted that the current legal framework is positioned to accommodate an in-house monitoring trustee. The EUMR[139] is demonstrative. The Commission has used external monitoring trustees in merger cases to oversee compliance with remedies. This precedent can serve as a foundation for expanding the concept to an in-house role. Moreover, it is submitted that the enabling nature of Regulation 1/2003 grants the Commission investigatory powers and the ability to impose remedies, which it is suggested, could be interpreted to act as a legal basis for the establishment of internal mechanisms for monitoring compliance. Alternatively, in specific cases, the Commission could include provisions in its decisions that establish the role and powers of an in-house monitoring trustee as part of the remedies package. This would create a case-by-case legal basis for the role. While there is no explicit legal basis for an in-house monitoring trustee within the current EU competition law framework, there are pathways to establish such a role by the Commission, whether that be on a case-by-case basis, by legislative interpretation, or alternatively, by applying the practice analogously with the precedent set under the EUMR. By leveraging its existing powers and engaging in a transparent process, the European Commission can establish a robust legal foundation for an in-house monitoring trustee, enhancing the effectiveness and adaptability of competition remedies in dynamic markets.

137 *Morris*, 'Microsoft: paying the price' https://uk.practicallaw.thomsonreuters.com/7-376-3974?transitionType=Default&contextData=(sc.Default)&firstPage=true (accessed 15 August 2024).

138 Case T-201/04 ECR II-3601 *Microsoft v Commission* [1268].

139 Council Regulation (EC) No 139/2004 of 20 January 2004 on the control of concentrations between undertakings (the EC Merger Regulation) (Text with EEA relevance).

E. Conclusion

The enforcement of competition law within the EU, as guided by the principles set forth in the TEU and TFEU, aims to preserve the integrity and dynamism of the internal market. A remedy by definition strives to set right an undesirable situation. In the context of competition law, that is to 'halt the illegal conduct and stop the anticompetitive effects that flow from it'.[140] The restoration of competitive conditions is contingent upon the adoption and imposition of suitably designed remedies. Regulation 1/2003 sets forth what the adoption and imposition of remedies seeks to achieve. That is, to 'bring the infringement effectively to an end'.[141]

The regulatory framework equips the European Commission with a broad array of remedial powers to address anti-competitive practices, ranging from structural and behavioural remedies to interim measures. These remedies, designed on a case-by-case basis, are intended not only to halt illegal conduct but also to restore competitive conditions effectively.

As discussed, the challenges in remedy design are multifaceted, encompassing the need to ensure proportionality, legal certainty, and the protection of legitimate expectations. Despite these constitutional constraints, the jurisprudence of the CJEU reflects a commitment to prioritizing the effectiveness of competition law enforcement. Cases such as *Akzo*, *Commercial Solvents*, and *Microsoft* illustrate the Commission's extensive prerogative in imposing remedies that go beyond merely ending anti-competitive practices, extending to proactive measures that counteract the effects of such conduct. However, the use of cease-and-desist orders, as evidenced by the Commission's historical practices, raises concerns about the adequacy and effectiveness of such remedies in rapidly evolving markets, particularly in the digital economy. The *Google Shopping* case exemplifies the limitations of leaving infringing undertakings to their own devices to remedy violations, highlighting the need for more specific and enforceable remedial measures, as well as reinforcing the need for oversight and review of the implementation and efficacy of measures.

Looking forward, the writer suggests that the Commission must balance its discretionary powers with the evolving nature of markets and the imperative to design remedies that not only comply with EU legal principles, but also effectively restore competition. This necessitates a more nuanced

140 Bostoen/ van Wamel (n 6) 541.

141 Regulation 1/2003 (n 2), Art 7(1).

approach that leverages the Commission's wide margin of discretion while ensuring robust monitoring and enforcement mechanisms to achieve the ultimate goal of maintaining a competitive and dynamic market environment for the benefit of consumers. The ongoing evolution of competition law enforcement practices will require continued adaptation and vigilance to address new and emerging challenges in the global marketplace. In this respect, the writer has proposed the creation of a monitoring unit within DG Competition, akin to the role of the external monitoring trustee.

Ultimately, the writer advocates for a more proactive and comprehensive approach to remedy design, one that considers the full scope of potential market impacts and prioritises the restoration of genuine competitive conditions. The desire to find a definitive, one-off solution is universal.[142] It submitted, however, that rather than viewing the need to review a remedy as a failure, that an iterative or more flexible approach is in fact reflective of a successful regime. Ultimately, it has become 'increasingly evident that competition law intervention must be multi-levelled and multi-fashioned and that remedies are key in solving competition problems. Remedies are key also because what matters at the end of the day is whether competition law intervention improved the state of competition in the market. For this reason, competition authorities are increasingly using a wide array of tools and engage in ex ante and ex post, prescriptive and proscriptive enforcement.'[143] Supported by the wide margin of discretion granted to the Commission and the jurisprudence of the CJEU, the writer is of the view that an iterative approach to remedy design will be crucial in maintaining the integrity and effectiveness of EU competition law enforcement in the face of evolving, dynamic markets.

142 Lancieri/de Silva Pereira Neto, Designing Remedies for Digital Markets: The Interplay Between Antitrust and Regulation (2022) Journal of Competition Law & Economics 613, 651.

143 Makris (n 97) 227.

Part III:
Competition Law, Crisis and Geoeconomics

State aid and international crises: balance between market's intervention and integrity?

Nicole Deneka[*]

A. Introduction

In response to international crises – such as the financial crisis of 2007–2009, the COVID-19 pandemic, or Russia's aggression against Ukraine – the European Commission introduced temporary frameworks for state aid, which specifically adapted state aid rules to the prevailing circumstances. These frameworks were intended to enable Member States to more effectively support entities affected by these crises.

For instance, during the financial crisis, the European Commission approved restructuring aid for the Royal Bank of Scotland[1], which was on the verge of collapse in late 2008. The UK government provided state aid to RBS through a £45.5 billion recapitalization, along with guarantees and liquidity measures. In return, the European Commission approved the aid under the condition that RBS undertake a comprehensive restructuring plan, including divestments, asset reductions, and behavioral commitments to limit market distortions. However, by 2017, the UK sought to replace this commitment with an alternative package of measures, including funding for challenger banks and investments in financial technology.[2] The European Commission ultimately approved this alternative, concluding that it would effectively remedy the market distortions caused by the state aid to RBS while fostering competition in the UK's SME banking sector.[3]

---

* PhD Candidate in Legal Sciences, University of the National Education Commission, Krakow, Poland.

1 Further as: **RBS**.

2 European Commission, https://ec.europa.eu/commission/presscorner/detail/en/ip_17_863 (accessed: 10 January 2025).

3 European Commission Decision (EU) 2018/119 of 18 September 2017 on State aid SA.47702 (2017/C) (ex 2017/N) — United Kingdom — Alternative package to replace the commitment for the Royal Bank of Scotland to divest the Rainbow business (notified under document C(2017) 6184.

In discussions about the justification for introducing such special frameworks regarding state aid during crises, some emphasize the need for greater flexibility in state aid law and the ability to adapt it to changing social and economic conditions. On the other hand, there is concern that introducing additional frameworks in this area may lead to excessive distortion of competition and inefficient use of public funds.[4]

The purpose of this paper is to explore the aim of the adjustments made in state aid law during international crises concerning the European Union's market. The proper design and implementation of state aid rules are crucial for protecting competition, as government intervention in the economy can disrupt its proper functioning and negatively impact the business activities of individual entities. Such interference can further exacerbate existing market distortions, underscoring the importance of ensuring appropriate framework in this area. This paper seeks to determine the aim of these frameworks during international crises by analyzing relevant frameworks. In particular, it seeks to answer the question: 'What are the primary objectives of the state aid frameworks introduced during international crises?'. Furthermore, this paper examines how the European Commission can balance the need for rapid state aid interventions during crises with the long-term preservation of competition and fairness in the EU's internal market.

The paper is organized into five sections: an Introduction, three main sections, and a Conclusion. The Introduction outlines the paper's structure, presents the research question, and emphasizes its significance in the context of modern competition law. The first main section provides a general overview of state aid law and its objectives. The second section discusses the most critical legal frameworks introduced in response to the three major crises of the past fifteen years. The final section attempts to answer the research question posed at the beginning of the paper. The Conclusion summarizes the key information presented throughout the paper.

---

4 *D'Sa*, "Instant" State Aid Law in a Financial Crisis – A U-Turn?, 8 *European State Aid Law Quarterly* (2009), 139, 141; *Maczkovics*, How Flexible Should State Aid Control Be in Times of Crisis?, 19 *European State Aid Law Quarterly* (2020), 271, 275.

B. State aid law: general prohibition, exceptions and crisis adaptations

State aid is a form of support granted by Member States to undertakings that can potentially distort competition in the EU's internal market. While such aid may serve important objectives, it constitutes an intervention in free market mechanisms and must be carefully regulated to prevent undue market distortions. The European Union's general prohibition on state aid, established under Article 107(1) of the Treaty on the functioning of the European Union[5], reflects its commitment to maintaining fair competition within the internal market. This prohibition ensures that market forces, rather than state intervention, primarily drive economic activity.

In the context of crises, such as the 2007–2009 financial crisis or the COVID-19 pandemic, the challenges of balancing state aid with competition principles become particularly acute. The European Commission has introduced temporary frameworks to provide Member States with the flexibility to respond to crises while maintaining the fundamental principles of the internal market. For example, during the financial crisis, state aid played a critical role in stabilizing the financial sector, but such interventions were subject to strict conditions to minimize long-term market distortions. Similarly, during the COVID-19 pandemic, the European Commission authorized targeted aid to ensure liquidity and employment support while preserving fair competition.

While the EU Treaties do not provide a precise definition of state aid, the concept is guided by four main criteria derived from Article 107(1) TFEU:

a) the granting of aid by a Member State or through state resources;
b) the distortion or threat of distortion to competition;
c) the conferral of an advantage to certain undertakings or the production of specific goods; and
d) an impact on trade between Member States.

From the above, it follows that for a measure to be considered state aid, there must be an actual or potential distortion of competition within the EU's internal market. Moreover, in order to determine whether an economic advantage exists, it is recommended to conduct the so-called private vendor test.[6] This test involves assessing whether, under the same

5 Official Journal of the European Union (2016/C 202/01), further as: **TFEU**.
6 *Plender*, Definition of Aid, in Biondi/Eeckhout/Flynn (eds.), The Law of State Aid in the European Union, Oxford University Press 1st edn. (2004), 31, 32.

conditions, a private investor of similar size, operating under typical market conditions, would make a similar investment decision. If the test shows that the entity representing the member state would act in the same way as a private investor in a comparable situation, it is considered that no state aid is present.[7]

While the prohibition of state aid is a cornerstone of EU competition policy, certain forms of aid may serve broader objectives and can be deemed compatible with the internal market. For example, Article 107(2) TFEU explicitly allows aid to address natural disasters or exceptional occurrences. Additionally, Article 107(3) TFEU provides scope for the European Commission to approve aid for specific purposes, such as promoting economic development in disadvantaged regions or addressing serious economic disturbances, as seen during crises.

In summary, the prohibition of state aid serves as a safeguard for competition but also allows for flexibility in exceptional circumstances. The European Commission's temporary frameworks during crises illustrate how this flexibility can be operationalized to balance immediate economic needs with long-term market stability. This nuanced approach underscores the importance of targeted and proportionate measures to address the challenges posed by crises while maintaining the integrity of the EU's internal market.

This approach is consistent with the EU's longstanding commitment to liberal economics, an area in which according to S. Meunier it has long positioned itself as a leader.[8] The principles of liberal economics[9], particularly the emphasis on non-intervention by states, underpin the rationale for the EU's general prohibition on state aid.

Nevertheless, these restrictive rules governing the provision of state aid are designed to minimize instances where distortions might occur. At the same time, it does not seem feasible to completely eliminate the prohibition on state aid or to apply it in a blanket manner without allowing for any exceptions.

---

7 European Commission Notice on the notion of State aid as referred to in Article 107(1) of the Treaty on the Functioning of the European Union, Official Journal of the European Union (2016/C 262/01).

8 *Meunier*, Managing Globalization? The EU in International Trade Negotiations, 45(4), Journal of Common Market Studies (2007), 905–926.

9 *Gehrke*, EU Open Strategic Autonomy and the Trappings of Geoeconomics, 27, European Foreign Affairs Review (2022), 62.

Adopting either of these extreme approaches could fundamentally disrupt the functioning of the EU internal market—whether by eliminating state intervention entirely or by permitting unrestricted intervention. In the case of full state intervention, Member States could potentially abuse such measures to favor domestic undertakings, leading to inequalities within national, regional, or even broader areas of the internal EU market. However, the rationale for a complete prohibition on state aid also requires further explanation.

One might argue that since the very act of granting state aid leads to a distortion of competition, or at least carries a high risk of doing so, a total ban on state aid would eliminate these distortions. While this would indeed prevent disruptions caused by state aid, it could also result in situations where, in the absence of state support, certain market disturbances—such as those seen during the 2007–2009 financial crisis, the COVID-19 pandemic, or Russia's aggression towards Ukraine—could not be mitigated. Therefore, the aim of state aid law should also include the ability to respond to the surrounding economic and social realities by appropriately regulating the conditions under which state aid can be granted, particularly in such extraordinary circumstances.

In the following sections of this paper, particular attention will be given to the issues related to the 2007–2009 financial crisis, the COVID-19 pandemic, and Russia's aggression towards Ukraine. These events have been chosen due to the extensive and detailed frameworks that were developed by the European Commission in response to these crises. The paper will delve into how these frameworks were designed to address the specific challenges posed by the above-mentioned crises.

C. State aid law during international crises

I. Financial crisis of 2007–2009

The international financial crisis of 2007–2009 had a profound impact on various sectors of the global economy, with its effects lingering for many years beyond the immediate crisis period. In response to this unprecedented economic turmoil, the European Commission adopted seven temporary crisis communications. These communications were crucial in outlining the criteria under which state aid, granted by Member States, could be considered compatible with the internal market according to Article 107(3) (b) TFEU with a specific focus on the financial sector during the crisis.[10] This particular Article of the TFEU provides an exceptional allowance for state aid aimed at remedying a serious disturbance in the economy of a Member State.

The European Commission justified the adoption of such a substantial number of frameworks by pointing to the rapidly evolving nature of the crisis and the continuous changes that occurred as the situation developed.[11]

Above-mentioned temporary crisis communications include:

a) Communication on the application of State aid rules to measures taken in relation to financial institutions in the context of the current global financial crisis ('2008 Banking Communication') (OJ C 270, 25.10.2008, p. 8);
b) Communication on the recapitalisation of financial institutions in the current financial crisis: limitation of aid to the minimum necessary and safeguards against undue distortions of competition ('Recapitalisation Communication') (OJ C 10, 15.1.2009, p. 2);
c) Communication from the European Commission on the treatment of impaired assets in the Community financial sector ('Impaired Assets Communication') (OJ C 72, 26.3.2009, p. 1);
d) Communication on the return to viability and the assessment of restructuring measures in the financial sector in the current crisis under the State aid rules ('Restructuring Communication') (OJ C 195, 19.8.2009, p. 9);
e) Communication from the European Commission on the application, from 1 January 2011, of State aid rules to support measures in favour of financial institutions in the context of the financial crisis ('2010 Prolongation Communication') (OJ C 329, 7.12.2010, p. 7);
f) Communication from the European Commission on the application, from 1 January 2012, of State aid rules to support measures in favour of

10 Communication from the European Commission on the application, from 1 August 2013, of State aid rules to support measures in favour of banks in the context of the financial crisis, Official Journal of the European Union (2013/C 216/01), further as: Banking Communication, para. 1.

11 Communication from the European Commission on the application, from 1 August 2013, of State aid rules to support measures in favour of banks in the context of the financial crisis, Official Journal of the European Union (2013/C 216/01), further as: Banking Communication, para. 2.

financial institutions in the context of the financial crisis ('2011 Prolongation Communication') (OJ C 356, 6.12.2011, p. 7), and the newest
g) Banking Communication.

The forms of state aid covered by these frameworks included: state capital support for banks, guarantees on bond issuances, aid in the form of recapitalization, support during liquidation processes, and emergency loans.

Interestingly, despite the fact that the financial crisis, as mentioned earlier, affected various areas of the economy, the European Commission chose to introduce frameworks exclusively for the financial sector. This approach has been a point of contention among some scholars, who argue that the financial sector received a form of special treatment, with substantial amounts of aid being directed solely to this one sector.[12] An opposing viewpoint in this regard was based on the assertion that aid provided to banks during the financial crisis is unequivocally beneficial, even without the need for compensatory measures.[13]

This may be attributed to the fact that the stability of the financial sector is often seen as crucial to the broader economy, and its collapse could have far-reaching consequences beyond the sector itself. The European Commission *expressis verbis* named financial stability as an 'overarching objective (…) whilst ensuring that State aid and distortions of competition between banks and across the Member States are kept to the minimum', in its response to financial crisis.[14]

According to the European Commission that financial stability in particular should mean both ensuring that banking institutions still are able to provide adequate lending and preventing negative spill-over effects in the banking system caused by failure of the credit institutions.[15]

Financial stability is the key element of the European Commission's assessment of state aid, as declared in para. 7 of the Banking Communication. Additionally, in the same context, it was emphasized that the European Commission needed to carry out this assessment with consideration of how the crisis was evolving and changing over time. This highlighted the risk of fragmentation within the EU's internal market—a situation where the deepening of the crisis might occur predominantly in specific regions of the

12 *D'Sa* (n4) 144.
13 *Ahlborn/Piccinin*, The Application of the Principles of Restructuring Aid to Banks during the Financial Crisis, European State Aid Law Quarterly (2010), 61.
14 Banking Communication, para. 7.
15 Banking Communication, para. 7.

EU. Such fragmentation could potentially weaken the economic integration of the EU, as significant disparities in the economic conditions of these regions could emerge, leading to increasingly divergent economic outcomes across the European Union.[16]

As noted in the Introduction, one prominent example of crisis aid involved the RBS in the United Kingdom. Beyond RBS, the case of Commerzbank serves as an example of the European Commission's approach to approving state aid during the 2007–2009 financial crisis. Faced with severe financial difficulties exacerbated by the crisis, Commerzbank was supported through multiple rounds of state aid provided by Germany under its Financial Market Stabilisation Fund[17]. The European Commission reviewed and approved these measures in several key decisions, ensuring they were compatible with Article 107(3)(b) TFEU (before Article 87(3)(b) of the Treaty establishing the European Community[18]).

The first measure was notified to the European Commission in December 2008. Germany proposed an €8.2 billion recapitalization of Commerzbank through SoFFin, aimed at addressing serious disturbances in the German economy. The European Commission approved this measure on 12 December 2008, recognizing its necessity to stabilize a key financial institution and prevent broader disruptions in the banking sector.[19] In European Commission's view this recapitalization was aligned with the principles outlined in the Banking Communication, particularly regarding proportionality and the minimization of distortions of competition.[20]

However, as the financial crisis deepened, additional aid became necessary. In January 2009, Germany notified the European Commission of its intention to provide Commerzbank with a €10 billion guarantee. This measure was approved by the European Commission on 9 January 2009, emphasizing its compliance with the Recapitalisation Communication's conditions for burden-sharing and proportionality. The guarantee was es-

16 Banking Communication, para. 7.

17 Further as: **SoFFin.**

18 Official Journal of the European Union (2002/C325).

19 European Commission Decision (EU) 2008/625 of 12 December 2008 on State aid N 625/2008 – Germany – Rescue package for credit institutions. Official Journal of the European Union, C 143, 24 June 2009, p. 1.

20 European Commission Decision (EU) 2008/625 of 12 December 2008 on State aid N 625/2008 – Germany – Rescue package for credit institutions. Official Journal of the European Union, C 143, 24 June 2009, p. 1.

sential to bolster confidence in the bank's solvency and ensure its continued ability to provide credit to the German economy.

To address Commerzbank's long-term viability and reduce its dependence on state aid, Germany submitted a comprehensive restructuring plan, which the European Commission approved on 7 May 2009[21]. The plan included several key elements aimed at restoring the bank's financial health while limiting potential distortions of competition. Burden-sharing was a central feature of the plan, requiring shareholders to absorb losses and prohibiting dividend payments until the aid was repaid. Executive remuneration was also capped, ensuring that those managing the bank bore part of the responsibility for its recovery.

The restructuring plan also imposed significant structural commitments to reduce Commerzbank's market presence and prevent undue competitive advantages. These measures included the divestment of Eurohypo, a subsidiary specializing in real estate and public sector finance, as well as a substantial reduction in risk-weighted assets. Commerzbank's balance sheet was to be reduced by approximately 45 %, ensuring a more focused and sustainable operational model. Additionally, the plan required Commerzbank to withdraw from certain high-risk business activities, aligning its operations with the principles of sound financial management.

The European Commission emphasized the importance of monitoring mechanisms to ensure compliance with the approved restructuring plan. Germany committed to submitting regular progress reports, allowing the European Commission to assess whether the agreed measures were being implemented effectively. This oversight was critical to ensuring that Commerzbank's recovery would not lead to long-term distortions in the internal market.[22]

The Commerzbank case highlights the European Commission's dual objectives during the financial crisis: stabilizing systemically important banks to protect financial stability while imposing conditions to preserve fair competition. By approving the state aid with stringent conditions and long-term monitoring, the European Commission demonstrated its commitment to safeguarding the internal market while responding to the extraordinary challenges posed by the crisis. These large-scale interventions demonstrate

21 Commission Decision (EU) 2009/3708 of 7 May 2009 on State aid N 244/2009 – Commerzbank – Germany, C(2009) 3708 final.

22 Commission Decision (EU) 2009/3708 of 7 May 2009 on State aid N 244/2009 – Commerzbank – Germany, C(2009) 3708 final.

both the scope of government action and the European Commission's insistence on safeguards to uphold competition within the internal market.

However, the Tercas case[23] highlights the limits of state aid control in situations where financial assistance originates from private industry mechanisms rather than state resources. In this case, the Fondo Interbancario di Tutela dei Depositi, a privately managed deposit guarantee scheme, intervened to support Banca Tercas, a failing bank under special administration, to facilitate its acquisition by Banca Popolare di Bari. The European Commission ruled in 2015 that this intervention constituted unlawful state aid, arguing that it involved state resources and was imputable to the Italian state.[24] However, the General Court annulled the decision in 2019, concluding that FITD's intervention was purely private, and the Court of Justice of the European Union upheld this ruling in 2021. The Court reaffirmed that aid granted by private banking consortia without state control does not fall under EU state aid rules, even if public authorities supervise the mechanism.[25]

The Tercas ruling contrasts with Commerzbank, where the use of state resources required strict European Commission oversight to prevent competitive distortions. While Commerzbank demonstrates the European Commission's insistence on safeguards when public funds are used, Tercas establishes the judicial limits of state aid rules in cases involving purely private financial interventions. Together, these cases define the balance between financial stability measures and EU competition law, illustrating the European Commission's role in crisis management while reinforcing the judiciary's role in setting clear boundaries for state aid enforcement.

After the financial crisis concluded, the European Union took some additional measures to safeguard the financial sector from potential disruptions. These measures included the establishment of the European Systemic Risk Board and the adoption of the Bank Recovery and Resolution Directive[26].

---

23 Joined Cases T-98/16, T-196/16 and T-198/16, EU:T:2019:167 – Italy and Others v European Commission, Judgment of 19 March 2019.

24 European Commission Decision 2016/1208 of 23 December 2015 on State aid granted by Italy to the Bank Tercas (Case SA.39451 (2015/C) (ex 2015/NN)) (OJ 2016 L 203, p. 1).

25 Court of Justice of the European Union, Press Release No 30/21, Luxembourg, 2 March 2021, https://curia.europa.eu/jcms/upload/docs/application/pdf/2021-03/cp210030en.pdf (accessed: 27 January 2025).

26 Directive 2014/59/EU of the European Parliament and of the European Council of 15 May 2014 establishing a framework for the recovery and resolution of cred-

Additionally, the creation of the Banking Union, with its mechanisms such as the Single Supervisory Mechanism and the Single Resolution Mechanism, further strengthened the sector's resilience.[27] However, the European Commission acknowledged that these actions were not the final steps in securing financial stability.[28]

The Special Report of the European Court of Auditors also highlights that the EU's initiatives in this area have contributed to making banking institutions more resilient, with a general improvement in their condition observed until the onset of the COVID-19 pandemic.[29]

II. COVID-19 pandemic

The Temporary Framework for State aid measures to support the economy in the current COVID-19 outbreak[30] was first adopted on 19 March 2020 and amended six times[31]. The aim of COVID-19 Communications stated by the European Commission was enabling 'Member States to use the full

---

it institutions and investment firms and amending European Council Directive 82/891/EEC, and Directives 2001/24/EC, 2002/47/EC, 2004/25/EC, 2005/56/EC, 2007/36/EC, 2011/35/EU, 2012/30/EU and 2013/36/EU, and Regulations (EU) No 1093/2010 and (EU) No 648/2012, of the European Parliament and of the European Council, Official Journal of the European Union, L 173/190, further as: Directive 2014/59/EU.

27 *European Court of Auditors*, 'Special Report on EU State Aid for Banks, Report No. 21/2020', Publications Office of the European Union (2020), https://www.eca.europa.eu/lists/ecadocuments/sr20_21/sr_state_aid_en.pdf (accessed: 5 August 2024), further as: Special report of ECA, 11–13.

28 Special report of ECA, 13.

29 Special report of ECA.

30 Communication from the European Commission Temporary Framework for State aid measures to support the economy in the current COVID-19 outbreak, Official Journal of the European Union (2020/C 91 I/01), further as: COVID-19 Communication or with amendments: COVID-19 Communication.

31 Last amendment: Communication from the European Commission Sixth Amendment to the Temporary Framework for State aid measures to support the economy in the current COVID-19 outbreak and amendment to the Annex to the Communication from the European Commission to the Member States on the application of Articles 107 and 108 of the Treaty on the Functioning of the European Union to short-term export-credit insurance, Official Journal of the European Union (2021/C 473/01), further as: COVID-19 Framework.

flexibility foreseen under State aid rules to support the economy in the context of the coronavirus outbreak'[32].

Most of the measures provided for in the COVID-19 Framework were available for use until 30 June 2022, with certain exceptions. However, some specific measures, such as investment support and solvency support, were allowed to be extended and utilized for a longer period—until 31 December 2023. Additionally, certain forms of aid under this framework were subject to transformation into other types of aid. For instance, it was possible to switch from loans and guarantees to direct grants as the needs of businesses and the economic situation evolved.[33]

The main aim of this framework was to ensure the continuity of the economic activity despite the negative socio-economic impact of COVID-19 pandemic in European Union and enable the market's recovery from its consequences, specifically taking into consideration the green and digital transitions.[34]

According to the European Commission, the proper application of state aid control was intended to ensure that the support measures provided effectively improved the situation of entities impacted by the COVID-19 pandemic while minimizing distortions of competition within the EU's internal market.

The COVID-19 Communications introduced additional measures for state aid granted under Article 107(2)(b), (3)(b) and (c) TFEU in response to the negative effects of the pandemic. These measures included, among others:

a) liquidity support,
b) state loans,
c) state guarantees,
d) R&D support,
e) investment for innovations (testing and production of product crucial during pandemic),
f) recapitalization.

In publications on state aid, it is also noted that the COVID-19 Communications included provisions regarding aid granted, both directly and indi-

32 COVID-19 Framework, para. 1.
33 https://competition-policy.ec.europa.eu/state-aid/coronavirus/temporary-framework_en (accessed: 8 August 2024).
34 COVID-19 Framework, para. 2.

rectly, to financial institutions.[35] According to paragraph 6 of the COVID-19 Framework, aid granted by Member States under Article 107(3)(b) TFEU, which was channelled through banks as financial intermediaries, benefited those undertakings directly. Such aid was not intended to preserve or restore the viability, liquidity, or solvency of banks. Similarly, aid granted by Member States to banks under Article 107(2)(b) TFEU to compensate for direct damage suffered due to the COVID-19 outbreak did not aim to preserve or restore the viability, liquidity, or solvency of any institution or entity. Consequently, such aid would not be classified as extraordinary public financial support under Directive 2014/59/EU or under Regulation 806/2014 of the European Parliament and of the European Council[36] and would also not be assessed under the State aid rules applicable to the banking sector.

It is worth to note that the aviation sector was one of the most severely impacted industries during the pandemic due to prolonged travel restrictions and reduced consumer confidence. The COVID-19 Framework was used extensively to provide targeted aid to major airlines, ensuring their survival while imposing conditions to minimize distortions of competition.

A notable example is Lufthansa, which received a €6 billion rescue package from the German government in 2020. This package consisted of equity injections and silent participations under the Temporary Framework. The European Commission approved the measure under Article 107(3)(b) TFEU, recognizing the systemic importance of Lufthansa for Germany's economy and its role in maintaining vital connectivity across Europe[37].

To ensure compliance with EU state aid rules, the European Commission imposed several conditions on Lufthansa:

a) Lufthansa was required to divest valuable slots at key airports, including Frankfurt and Munich, to foster competition and provide opportunities for competing airlines,

35 E.g.: Special report of ECA, 17; *Buendía/Dovalo*, State Aid Versus COVID-19: The Commission Adopts a Temporary Framework, European State Aid Law Quarterly (2020), 7.

36 Regulation (EU) No 806/2014 of the European Parliament and of the European Council of 15 July 2014 establishing uniform rules and a uniform procedure for the resolution of credit institutions and certain investment firms in the framework of a Single Resolution Mechanism and a Single Resolution Fund and amending Regulation (EU) No 1093/2010, Official Journal of the European Union (L 225/1).

37 European Commission, https://ec.europa.eu/commission/presscorner/detail/hu/ip_20_1179 (accessed: 30 January 2025).

b) restrictions were placed on dividend payments and executive remuneration until the aid was repaid, ensuring that shareholders and management bore part of the restructuring costs,
c) Germany committed to submitting a restructuring plan to the European Commission, outlining how Lufthansa would return to long-term viability without continued reliance on state aid.[38]

Similarly, Air France-KLM received over €10 billion in aid from the French government, including loans and guarantees. In approving this measure, the European Commission emphasized that the aid was necessary to address the airline's liquidity needs and maintain critical air transport services within and beyond Europe. Conditions imposed on Air France-KLM included environmental commitments, such as reducing domestic flights where viable rail alternatives existed, and behavioral restrictions, such as limits on acquisitions.[39]

However, the legality of COVID-19 aid to Air France-KLM has been the subject of judicial scrutiny before the General Court. In a judgment issued on 20 December 2023, the General Court annulled the European Commission's approval of state aid granted by France to Air France and the Air France-KLM group[40]. The measures were intended to help the airline recover from the impact of COVID-19 restrictions, but Ryanair challenged the aid package, arguing that it distorted competition in the European aviation market.[41]

The General Court ruled that the European Commission had erred in defining the beneficiaries of the state aid, finding that both KLM and the broader Air France-KLM group had, at least indirectly, benefited from the financial support. The General Court pointed to the capital, functional, and economic links between Air France and KLM, as well as the contractual framework of the aid measure, concluding that the European Commission had failed to assess the full scope of the advantage conferred by the aid. This ruling reaffirmed the principle that state aid must be assessed not only

38 European Commission, https://ec.europa.eu/commission/presscorner/detail/hu/ip_20_1179 (accessed: 30 January 2025).
39 European Commission, https://ec.europa.eu/commission/presscorner/detail/en/ip_24_3704 (accessed: 30 January 2025).
40 Case T-494/21, EU:T:2023:831 – Ryanair and Malta Air v European Commission, Judgment of 20 December 2023.
41 https://www.lawsociety.ie/gazette/top-stories/2023/december/court-annuls-backing-for-air-france-measures/ (accessed: 29 January 2025).

based on its direct recipients but also its wider economic effects on linked entities within corporate groups.[42]

These examples illustrate how the COVID-19 Framework facilitated targeted interventions to stabilize vital industries during the pandemic while seeking to maintain compliance with EU state aid principles. The measures were designed not only to support the recovery of airlines but also to safeguard competition and align with broader EU policy objectives, such as environmental sustainability. However, subsequent judicial scrutiny of these measures, particularly in the General Court's ruling on Air France-KLM's state aid, has highlighted challenges in ensuring that aid remains proportionate, non-discriminatory, and appropriately targeted.

The Air France-KLM ruling underscores the ongoing tension between emergency economic support and the need to uphold fair competition within the EU's internal market. While the European European Commission sought to balance rapid intervention with structural conditions, such as environmental commitments and behavioral restrictions, the General Court's annulment of certain approvals suggests that in some cases, the assessment of aid beneficiaries and market impact may not have been sufficiently rigorous. This judicial intervention reinforces the importance of ensuring that crisis-era aid does not create long-term distortions, particularly in highly competitive sectors like aviation.

III. Russia's aggression towards Ukraine

The European Commission also responded promptly to Russia's aggression towards Ukraine, which escalated significantly in February 2022, by issuing a communication on the state aid rules applicable in relation to this conflict. Recognizing the severe impact of the war, the European Commission aimed to provide Member States with the necessary tools to support their economies while maintaining the integrity of the internal market.

The first document published in this context was the Temporary Crisis Framework for State Aid measures to support the economy following the aggression against Ukraine by Russia[43], issued on 23 March 2022. This

42 Case T-494/21, EU:T:2023:831 – Ryanair and Malta Air v European Commission, Judgment of 20 December 2023.

43 Official Journal of the European Union (2022/C 131 I/01), further as: Aggression Framework.

framework was designed to complement the existing state aid rules, allowing Member States to grant aid to address the extraordinary challenges posed by the conflict.[44]

Subsequently, the European Commission adopted an amendment to the Aggression Framework on 20 July 2022, which focused on enabling Member States to grant temporary support measures in the areas of renewable energy and the decarbonization of production processes.[45]

Another amendment[46] was introduced on 28 October 2022, based on surveys answered by Member States and taking into account the energy market situation and the significant increase in energy prices.[47] This amendment was aimed at providing Member States with additional flexibility to address the soaring energy costs and support businesses and consumers affected by the energy crisis exacerbated by the conflict.

The European Commission's focus on sectors critical to the transition to a net-zero economy led to the issuance of another communication, titled the Temporary Crisis and Transition Framework for State Aid measures to support the economy following the aggression against Ukraine by Russia.[48] This framework was subsequently amended twice[49], with particular emphasis on changes impacting the agriculture and aquaculture sectors.[50]

The primary objective of these frameworks, as stated by the European Commission, was to mitigate the negative socio-economic consequences

---

44 https://competition-policy.ec.europa.eu/state-aid/temporary-crisis-and-transition-framework_en (accessed: 14 August 2024).

45 Communication from the Commission Amendment to the Temporary Crisis Framework for State Aid measures to support the economy following the aggression against Ukraine by Russia, Official Journal of the European Union (2022/C 280/01).

46 Communication from the Commission Temporary Crisis Framework for State Aid measures to support the economy following the aggression against Ukraine by Russia, Official Journal of the European Union (2022/C 426/01), further as: Aggression Framework II.

47 https://competition-policy.ec.europa.eu/state-aid/temporary-crisis-and-transition-framework_en (accessed: 14 August 2024).

48 Official Journal of the European Union (2023/C 101/03).

49 First amendment: Amendment to the Temporary Crisis and Transition Framework for State Aid measures to support the economy following the aggression against Ukraine by Russia, Official Journal of the European Union (C/2023/1188).
Second amendment: Second amendment to the Temporary Crisis and Transition Framework for State Aid measures to support the economy following the aggression against Ukraine by Russia, Official Journal of the European Union (C/2024/3113).

50 https://competition-policy.ec.europa.eu/state-aid/temporary-crisis-and-transition-framework_en (accessed: 14 August 2024).

of the aggression within the European Union by preserving economic activities and jobs.[51] The framework aimed to provide targeted support to sectors and industries that were not only affected by the conflict but also essential to the EU's long-term environmental and economic goals. By facilitating state aid in these critical areas, the European Commission sought to ensure that the transition to a net-zero economy could continue despite the disruptions caused by the conflict, while also addressing immediate economic challenges faced by Member States.[52]

As some researchers point out, the aim of the Aggression Framework's aid measures was to inject the market with adequate liquidity while simultaneously encouraging companies to implement green initiatives, such as the adoption of renewable energy sources and the development of sustainable transportation methods.[53]

For instance, in certain cases, Member States have the option to grant aid to companies facing insolvency due to the impact of Russia's aggression against Ukraine (provided that these impacts are not the result of sanctions imposed on those companies[54]) under Article 107(3)(b) TFEU.[55] In such cases, when the European Commission conducts its assessment of the planned aid, it considers factors such as the necessity of the aid, its appropriateness, and its proportionality.[56]

These three characteristics—necessity, appropriateness, and proportionality—are repeatedly emphasized by the European Commission in its communications. The European Commission specifically notes that it is the responsibility of Member States to demonstrate that the aid measures notified to the European Commission under Article 107(3)(b) TFEU, in connection with Russia's aggression against Ukraine, are necessary, appropriate, and proportionate to improve the situation in that Member State.[57]

The energy sector, being significantly impacted by the conflict, became a focal point of the European Commission's frameworks. One notable example involves Germany's aid to Uniper SE, a major energy provider

51 Aggression Framework II, para. 7.

52 https://competition-policy.ec.europa.eu/state-aid/temporary-crisis-and-transition-framework_en (accessed: 14 August 2024).

53 *Drăgoi*, How the Russian-Ukrainian war has shaped the state aid policy in EU, Global Economic Observer (2024), 30.

54 Aggression Framework, paras. 52–54.

55 Aggression Framework, para. 31.

56 Aggression Framework, para. 32.

57 Aggression Framework, para. 51.

and importer of Russian gas, which faced a liquidity crisis due to the steep reduction in gas supplies following Russia's aggression. Germany was allowed to grant €34.5 billion in state aid to Uniper under the Aggression Framework[58].

The European Commission approved the measure under Article 107(3)(b) TFEU, emphasizing that the aid was necessary to address severe economic disturbances caused by the energy crisis. To limit distortions of competition and ensure the proportionality of the aid, the European Commission imposed several conditions, including:

a) Uniper was required to divest assets, such as a portion of its power generation portfolio, to address market imbalances caused by the aid;
b) the company was prohibited from engaging in aggressive pricing practices and barred from acquiring competitors;
c) Germany committed to submitting periodic progress reports to the European Commission to ensure compliance with these conditions.[59]

The Uniper case exemplifies the European Commission's approach to balancing the need for immediate support with long-term market integrity, particularly in the energy sector, where disruptions could have widespread economic and social consequences.

The response to the crisis caused by Russia's aggression against Ukraine allows Member States to grant aid under three different articles of the TFEU: the previously used Article 107(3)(b) TFEU (which covers, for example, liquidity support for companies), as well as Articles 107(2)(b) and 107(3)(c) TFEU.[60] This broad scope of articles provides Member States with more flexibility in addressing the specific challenges posed by the conflict.

---

58 European Commission, https://ec.europa.eu/commission/presscorner/detail/en/ip_22_7830 (accessed: 29 January 2025).

59 European Commission, https://ec.europa.eu/commission/presscorner/detail/en/ip_22_7830 (accessed: 29 January 2025).

60 Aggression Framework, paras. 25–26, 34–39 and 40.

D. Comparative perspective of crisis frameworks

I. The aim of crisis frameworks

'The objective of State aid control is to allow Member States to provide State aid to address genuine market failures while preventing the distortions of competition that state intervention can cause'.[61] This position remains truly in line with the temporary crisis communications issued so-far by the European Commission.

According to the Introduction to the Banking Communication, the purpose of creating this document was to ensure 'financial stability while minimizing distortions of competition between banks and across Member States in the single market' within the framework.[62]

Moreover, in European Commission's opinion the COVID-19 Framework 'seeks to ensure an appropriate balance between the positive effects of the aid measures granted to undertakings and any potential negative effects on competition and trade in the internal market'[63].

In the context of the crisis caused by Russia's aggression towards Ukraine, European Commission claimed that 'the targeted and proportionate application of EU State aid control serves to ensure that national support measures are effective in helping undertakings and workers affected by the current crisis. EU State aid control also ensures that the EU internal market is not fragmented and that the level playing field stays intact. The integrity of the internal market is crucial to withstand external pressures and to avoid subsidy races, where Member States with deeper pockets can outspend their neighbours, to the detriment of cohesion within the Union'[64].

The temporary frameworks introduced during each crisis were designed to address immediate economic disruptions, yet their scope and duration varied significantly. During the financial crisis of 2007–2009, the European Commission's response focused on short-term stabilization, primarily through recapitalization and guarantee measures for banks. These measures were intended to be phased out as soon as financial conditions improved, with strict conditions ensuring that banks receiving aid implemented restructuring plans to restore long-term viability.

---

61 *Ahlborn/Piccinin* (n 13) 51–52.

62 Banking Communication, para. 2.

63 COVID-19 Framework, para. 2.

64 COVID-19 Framework, para. 25.

In contrast, the COVID-19 pandemic prompted a more adaptive and medium-term approach, as the crisis affected a broader range of sectors beyond financial institutions. Initially framed as a temporary response, the COVID-19 framework evolved to include solvency support and investment incentives for green and digital transitions, reflecting the pandemic's prolonged impact on economies.

The response to Russia's aggression against Ukraine marks a further shift toward long-term structural adjustments, with the Temporary Crisis and Transition Framework extending support beyond immediate liquidity concerns to renewable energy development and decarbonization processes. This evolution in approach demonstrates a growing flexibility in the European Commission's state aid policy, moving from reactive stabilization to proactive economic transformation.

II. Short-term objectives

In every temporary crisis communication, the European Commission consistently emphasized the need to balance the short-term objectives, which vary depending on the specific crisis, with the integrity of the internal market.

These short-term goals, as previously mentioned, differ significantly depending on the nature of each crisis. For instance, during the 2007–2009 financial crisis, the European Commission repeatedly underscored the paramount importance of financial stability.

In contrast, in the context of Russia's aggression against Ukraine, the European Commission's priorities shifted towards more targeted support, emphasizing the need to effectively assist undertakings and workers directly impacted by the conflict. The goal here was to mitigate the socio-economic disruptions caused by the war, ensuring that businesses could continue to operate and that jobs were preserved despite the challenging circumstances.

Meanwhile, during the COVID-19 pandemic, the European Commission adopted a broader approach, focusing on the positive impacts of the aid provided in response to the crisis.

In each of these cases, while the specific short-term objectives varied, the underlying principle remained the same: to provide the necessary support to address the immediate crisis, while carefully managing the potential long-term effects on the internal market and ensuring that competition in the EU is maintained.

Some researchers argue that achieving the right balance between the positive and negative effects of aid can be particularly challenging during times of crisis.[65] But what constitutes the necessary balance between state aid and competition of the EU's internal market? We should view the balance in case of state aid as the point, where the significant distortion of the competition does not occur in case of aiding the necessary support, i.e. the proportionality between positive and negative effects of granted aid is maintained.[66]

III. State aid distribution

The implementation and distribution of crisis aid has also varied significantly across crises and sectors. During the financial crisis, aid was heavily concentrated in the financial sector, with major beneficiaries including RBS and Commerzbank, reflecting the systemic importance of banks to economic stability. By contrast, COVID-19 aid was more widely distributed, targeting airlines, hospitality, and SMEs, with Lufthansa and Air France-KLM receiving substantial financial assistance under strict competitive safeguards. In the case of Russia's aggression, the focus shifted toward energy-intensive sectors, as seen in Germany's €15 billion aid package for Uniper SE, a key energy supplier facing liquidity challenges due to reduced gas supplies. This measure included structural and behavioral conditions to prevent competitive imbalances. The varying allocation of aid across crises reflects the different economic priorities of Member States and the European Commission, as well as the need to adapt state aid measures to the specific challenges posed by each crisis.

Procedural handling and monitoring

A crucial element in finding the right balance between state aid and competition, particularly during international crises, has been the effective

65 *Buendía/Dovalo* (n 35) 4.

66 Also described as 'balancing exercise between the negative impact of aid in terms of distortion of competition, on the one hand, and its positive effect of achieving a public policy objective, on the other' – *OECD*, Competitive Neutrality Toolkit: Promoting a Level Playing Field, OECD Publishing (2024), 66, https://doi.org/10.1787/3247ba44-en (accessed: 18 August 2024).

monitoring of state aid distribution. This has became especially significant when considering the frameworks established in response to such crises. For example, in the case of the financial crisis, as specified in documents like the Banking Communication, Member States were required to submit regular and detailed reports to the European Commission. These reports needed to cover the operation of all bank support programs that had been approved by the European Commission under the framework designed to address the crisis.[67]

These reports were not just formalities; they played a vital role in ensuring transparency and accountability. Member States were expected to provide comprehensive information, including specifics about each individual bank that was undergoing liquidation. The purpose of this rigorous reporting requirement was twofold. First, it allowed the European Commission to closely monitor the liquidation processes of banks, ensuring that these were carried out in strict accordance with the established framework. This oversight was crucial in maintaining the integrity and objectives of the framework, which aimed to stabilize the financial sector without undermining the broader goals of the European Union.

Also in case of COVID-19 Communications the monitoring and reporting activities by Member States were deemed necessary. Member States with certain exceptions – had to publish relevant information about granted aid, maintain detailed records for 10 years, and submit annual reports to the European Commission. Member States also were obliged to publish above-mentioned information on a dedicated platform within 12 months of granting the aid. It was also necessary for the Member States to prepare, until the end of 2020, a list of implemented state aid measures based on the COVID-19 Communications.[68]

Similarly to earlier crisis communications, the European Commission ensured that proper monitoring and reporting obligations were included for state aid granted in connection with Russia's aggression against Ukraine. This includes the requirement for Member States to publish information on individual aid granted once certain thresholds are exceeded (10,000 EUR for the agriculture and aquaculture sectors or 100,000 EUR in other cases)[69]. Such information must remain publicly accessible for 12 consecutive

67 Banking Communication, para. 87.
68 Banking Communication, para. 34–37.
69 Banking Communication, para. 54.

months from the date the aid is granted.[70] Additionally, Member States are required to submit annual reports to the European Commission summarizing the aid granted each year.[71] Information regarding the aid must generally be retained for 10 years from the date it was granted.[72] Importantly, the European Commission can request relevant information about the granted aid from a Member State at any time.[73]

The process of monitoring state aid is crucial to ensuring that, despite the inherent unpredictability of crises, the aid granted during such times remains consistent with the principles of competition within the EU's internal market.

This 'need for close European coordination of national aid measures'[74] as described by the European Commission, underscores the importance of a coordinated and transparent approach. It ensures that while Member States are responding to immediate and pressing economic challenges, they do so in a way that does not undermine the integrity of the internal market or create unfair advantages that could distort competition across the European Union. Effective monitoring helps to maintain a level playing field, even in the midst of crisis, by ensuring that all aid measures are proportionate, appropriate, and aligned with EU competition goals.

E. Conclusion – finding the balance

Michael Honoré referred to the process of the European Commission drafting state aid rules in response to the COVID-19 crisis as 'constructing the railway with the train already on it'. However, this metaphor could just as easily apply to the European Commission's approach to any crisis, reflecting the unprecedented and rapidly evolving nature of these situations, where rules and frameworks had to be developed and adapted in real-time as new challenges emerged.[75]

For this reason, during highly unpredictable and economically perilous situations such as the 2007–2009 financial crisis, the COVID-19 pandem-

70 Banking Communication.
71 Banking Communication, para. 55.
72 Banking Communication, para. 56.
73 Banking Communication.
74 As mentioned in the Aggression Framework.
75 *Honoré*, State Aid and COVID-19 – Hot Topics, European State Aid Law Quarterly (2020), 111.

ic, and Russia's aggression against Ukraine, it is both crucial and more challenging than usual to maintain the balance between the principles of competition within the EU's internal market and the support provided to specific businesses or sectors by Member States through state aid.

The European Commission's approach to state aid during crises has consistently emphasized the delicate balance between addressing immediate, crisis-specific needs and preserving the integrity of the EU's internal market. Across various crises—whether the 2007–2009 financial crisis, the COVID-19 pandemic, or Russia's aggression against Ukraine—the European Commission has tailored its objectives to the particular challenges at hand, focusing on financial stability, targeted support for affected businesses and workers, and the broader positive impacts of aid measures. However, the underlying principle guiding all these efforts remains steadfast: to ensure that while providing necessary and timely support, the long-term stability and fairness of the internal market are not compromised.

This balance can be achieved not only through the European Commission's notification procedure and the general assessment of a given aid measure before it is granted, but also through the detailed monitoring of state aid provided by Member States—even several years after the aid has been granted. On this basis, the European Commission can not only review and adjust existing state aid rules but also draw lessons for the future. These insights will enable the European Commission to develop new state aid rules more effectively, even in times when 'the train will already be on the railway'.

Geopolitics and Competition Law: An Odd Couple or a Match Made in Heaven?

Sophie Bohnert[*]

A. Introduction

The competitive race metaphor aptly describes not only the dynamics between businesses, but also between geopolitical actors. Just as firms vie for market share, geopolitical actors compete to attract foreign trade and investment as well as to achieve regulatory leadership, technological superiority, and military dominance. In today's era of great power rivalry and increasing international polarization and fragmentation, there have been calls for '*multi-policy strategies, combining fiscal policies to incentivize domestic production, trade policies to penalize anti-competitive behavior abroad and foreign economic policies to secure supply chains*'.[1] In other words, there is a growing literature arguing for a broader, more structural approach to protecting the geopolitical interests of the European Union ('EU') by promoting a closer integration of competition, industrial, and trade policies.[2]

The current debate is reminiscent of the well-known debate on whether competition enforcement should take into account certain public interest considerations that go beyond the core economic objectives of EU competition law. The current orthodoxy is that EU competition law should not

---

* Sophie Bohnert was previously affiliated with the Institute for International and European Law at the Vienna University of Economics and Business, where she worked as a teaching and research assistant from October 2018 until September 2024. This article reflects the author's personal academic work and views, and was written in a strictly private capacity.

1 *Draghi*, 'A Competitiveness Strategy for Europe (Part A)' (2024), 12 https://commission.europa.eu/document/97e481fd-2dc3-412d-be4c-f152a8232961_en (accessed 22 March 2025).

2 See, e.g., *Caffarra*, 'Power, Not Price: On the Antitrust Agenda for the "Next World Order"' *CPI Columns* (2024), https://www.pymnts.com/cpi-posts/power-not-price-on-the-antitrust-agenda-for-the-next-world-order/ (accessed 22 March 2025); *Caffarra/Kilic*, 'Re-Joining Trade with Antitrust' *VOXEU COLUMN* (2024), https://cepr.org/voxeu/columns/re-joining-trade-antitrust (accessed 22 March 2025).

directly promote a particular public interest objective. There must be a 'carve-out' from the application of EU competition law insofar as an 'undertaking' pursues a public interest objective in a manner that triggers antitrust scrutiny.[3] Therefore, some have argued that the European Commission ('EC') should recalibrate its interpretation of the notion of 'consumer welfare', the '*guiding principle of competition law and policy*'[4] and the lowest common denominator for the coherent application of competition law, to allow for the integration of certain public policy objectives into its competitive assessments. In the past, the EC and some commentators[5] have refused to do so, citing the supposed purity, stability, clarity, and exhaustiveness of competition law in its adherence to economic principles, as well as shortcomings in terms of legal competence and technical expertise.[6] Against this background, one might ask whether this time the EC would be willing to give competition policy and enforcement a greater role in advancing the EU's geopolitical ambitions and in addressing the EU's competitiveness challenge. Put another way, is there scope in the regulatory framework designed to create a level playing field for businesses to be harnessed to promote the EU's geopolitical objectives in the 'global race' for economic, political, technological, and moral leadership among geopolitical actors?

This paper argues that the geopolitical considerations embodied in and channeled through EU foreign trade policy and law are fundamentally different from most other public policy considerations. The paper asserts that there are two main reasons for this: First, foreign trade policy and law are 'on the same team' as competition policy and law, albeit different in substantive scope and normative objectives, in that they seek to promote

3 *Dunne*, Public Interest and EU Competition Law, 65 Antitrust Bulletin (2020), 256, 261.

4 *Vickers*, Competition Policy and the Consumer Welfare Standard, 13 Journal of Antitrust Enforcement (2025), 6, 6.

5 See, e.g., 'Why US Antitrust Law Should Not Emulate European Competition Policy: Hearing before the United States Senate Committee on the Judiciary, Subcommittee on Antitrust, Competition Policy, and Consumer Rights' (2018), https://laweconcenter.org/wp-content/uploads/2018/12/GAM-Oral-Only-Senate-Antitrust-Subcommittee-Testimony-12-19-2018.pdf (accessed 22 March 2025). For a general discussion of the antagonizing positions, see *Ezrachi/Stucke*, The Fight Over Antitrust's Soul, 9 Journal of European Competition Law & Practice (2018), 1, 1.

6 For a discussion of these concerns in relation to the question whether competition law enforcement should incorporate data protection and privacy concerns, see *Costa-Cabral/Lynskey*, Family Ties: The Intersection between Data Protection and Competition in EU Law, 54 Common Market Law Review (2017), 11, 13.

market integration.[7] Such considerations are therefore rather economic than non-economic in nature.

Second, it is generally accepted that EU competition law and free movement law are complementary. While free movement law seeks to remove state barriers to trade between the EU Member States, competition law seeks to prevent private economic actors from re-erecting these barriers. Although free movement law and foreign trade law operate in different contexts, the same logic of complementarity could be applied to EU competition law and foreign trade law. To the extent that it seeks to remove state barriers to trade, foreign trade law can be seen as the, perhaps less ambitious, 'big brother' of free movement law.[8] This is supported by the fact that the legal architecture of free movement law, which is based on the principles of market access and non-discrimination, was strongly inspired by and designed in accordance with the principles of free trade and economic integration of the General Agreement on Trade and Tariffs ('GATT') of 1947,[9] a multilateral international agreement governing international trade in goods.[10]

The paper goes on to argue that '*competition policy cannot be pursued in isolation, as an end in itself, without reference to the legal, economic, political and social context*'.[11] This is not to suggest that public policy considerations should be introduced into substantive competition assessments without a clear legal basis. Rather, this paper shows that the EU Treaties do not treat their different policy areas as 'silos'. Commentators agree that these policies are interrelated and that several Treaty provisions support, if not legally require, a 'more integrated approach'. More specifically, this paper proposes

7 See, e.g., *Calliess*, Grundlagen des Wettbewerbsrechts, in Säcker (ed.), Münchener Kommentar zum Wettbewerbsrecht, vol. 1, CH Beck 4th edn. 2023, para. 739.

8 Both fields of law aim to regulate economic exchanges. However, their scope is different: While internal market law seeks to ensure the free movement of goods, services, people, and capital within the EU, foreign trade law facilitates international trade and ensures that EU companies have access to markets outside the EU.

9 General Agreement on Tariffs and Trade 1994 ('GATT'), 15 April 1994, Marrakesh Agreement Establishing the World Trade Organization, Annex 1A, 1867 U.N.T.S. 187.

10 *de Búrca/Scott*, The Impact of the WTO on EU Decision-Making, in de Búrca/Scott (eds.), The EU and the WTO: Legal and Constitutional Issues, Hart Publishing 2001, 1, 2.

11 *European Commission*, 'XXIInd Report on Competition Policy' (1992), 13 https://op.europa.eu/en/publication-detail/-/publication/d406e5bd-53a6-4642-b7f9-00c2abb4d01b (accessed 22 March 2025).

that these '*policy-linking clauses*'[12] create a horizontal obligation for the EU to adopt a holistic approach to policy making and policy implementation and give rise to a collective responsibility of the College of Commissioners.[13]

Against this background, this paper contends that the 'more economic approach', with its focus on market efficiency and consumer welfare as the current enforcement paradigm of EU competition law, puts the brakes on the closer alignment of competition, industrial, and trade policies as part of an overall strategy. This paper suggests that the adoption of the more economic approach and the concomitant '*scientification*'[14] of competition law has led to '*antitrust isolationism*'[15] that manifests itself in policy and institutional 'silos'. This paper argues that the choice of enforcement paradigm reflects a political preference that may be subject to change.[16] As a result, competition law's claim to objectivity and universality is unwarranted.[17] As competition, industrial, and trade policies evolve to address broader issues such as inequality, geopolitical challenges, and sustainability, the EC may need to rethink its preoccupation with economic efficiency and may legitimately choose to adopt a 'more integrated approach' across policy areas.[18]

This paper is organized as follows: Section B sets the context for the discussion by describing the current geopolitical landscape. It then explains why the EU's lack of competitiveness in many strategic sectors is not only a fundamental economic challenge but also a strategic one. Section C discusses why competition and trade are cut from the same cloth and why many geopolitical considerations are different from most other public policy considerations. Section D discusses how competition and trade pol-

12 *Wardhaugh*, Competition Law in Crisis, Cambridge University Press 2022, 29.

13 *Wardhaugh* (n 12), 30.

14 *Andriychuk*, Between Microeconomic and Geopolitics: On the Reasonable Application of Competition Law, 85 Modern Law Review (2022), 598, 608.

15 *Fox*, The End of Antitrust Isolationism: The Vision of One World, University of Chicago Legal Forum (1992), 221, 221 (coining the term and defining it as '*the view that antitrust law is separate from trade law and other policies at its interface, as well as the view that each nation's antitrust law is separate from other nations' antitrust law*').

16 *Katz*, The Chicago School and the Forgotten Political Dimension of Antitrust Law, 87 University of Chicago Law Review (2020), 413, 416.

17 See, e.g., *Ezrachi*, Sponge, 5 Journal of Antitrust Enforcement (2017), 49, 49 (arguing that the view that competition law '*must be based on economic considerations and reject external social, or political objectives*' and '*embodies a sense of purity is merely an illusion*').

18 *Caffarra*, 'Power, Not Price' (n 2).

icy parted ways in the 1990s with the adoption of the 'more economic approach' to competition enforcement and its implications. Section E explains why a compartmentalized approach to competition and trade policy implementation and enforcement is misguided and proposes a 'more integrated approach' as a way forward. Section F concludes.

B. Background

The question of whether EU competition policy and law enforcement should play a greater role in advancing the EU's geopolitical ambitions and in addressing the EU's competitiveness challenge is a timely one. A recent report by Mario Draghi, President of the European Central Bank, calls for industrial, competition, and trade policies to be '*aligned as part of an overall strategy*'[19] in the context of an increasingly hostile geopolitical climate and weakening productivity growth. The following section explains some of the key terms used in this paper. It also describes the current geopolitical landscape and sketches the contours of the EU's competitiveness challenge.

I. The Shift in the Geopolitical Landscape

'Geopolitics' is the study of how countries use territorial, military, and political resources to influence the global balance of power. It examines how geographical factors influence politics, power, and international relations.[20] 'Geoeconomics' is the study of how polities use trade, investment, and other economic policies as a means of exercising power and influence in international relations. It is concerned with the economic strategies used by polities to achieve geopolitical goals.[21] While geoeconomics is often seen as a tool of geopolitics, economic priorities can drive political decisions. Economic factors can be both a cause and a consequence of power struggles between polities. Economic strength can underpin geopolitical power by providing the means to influence, coerce, or cooperate with other polities.

19 *Draghi* (n 1), 13.

20 *Deudney*, 'Geopolitics', *Encyclopædia Britannica* (2024), https://www.britannica.com/topic/geopolitics (accessed 22 March 2025).

21 *Luttwak*, From Geopolitics to Geo-Economics, 20 The National Interest (1990), 17, 19.

It determines the way in which polities interact with each other, whether through alliances, competition, or conflict.[22]

In everyday language, the term 'competition' refers to a situation where someone is trying to win something or to be more successful than someone else.[23] Competition can occur between entities such as companies and between polities[24] such as States and trading blocs, and it can be about achieving any exclusive goal. In economics, competition refers to the process by which market participants compete for the attention of consumers, for example, by offering cheaper or better-quality products to increase their market share.[25]

The concept of 'competition' is central to market economies. It serves as a decentralized means of allocating scarce resources to those who value them the most based on price mechanisms. It ensures that goods and services are produced in response to actual demand. This represents a contrast to planned economies, where the allocation of resources is directed by central government authorities. As a result, market competition is believed to lead to an efficient allocation of resources, greater consumer choice, and dynamic innovation and growth.[26]

The term 'competition' is also widely used in the study of international relations: States and other international actors engage in international rivalry. These actors seek to gain advantage, often over others perceived as challenging or threatening, through the self-interested pursuit of contested goods such as power, security, wealth, influence, and status.[27] '*Great power rivalry*'[28] or '*great power competition*'[29] is a specific sub-category of

---

22 *Mallin et al.*, Introduction: Explanation, critique and critics of geoeconomics, 57 EPA: Economy and Space (2025), 93, 93.

23 'Competition', *Oxford English Dictionary* (2023), https://www.oed.com/dictionary/competition_n?tab=meaning_and_use (accessed 22 March 2025).

24 The term 'polity' is used in a geopolitical sense. It refers to nation-states and supranational entities.

25 *Bain*, 'Competition', *Encyclopædia Britannica* (2024), https://www.britannica.com/money/monopoly-economics#ref243879 (accessed 22 March 2025).

26 *Whish/Bailey*, Competition Law, Oxford University Press 10th edn. 2021, 6.

27 *Mazarr et al.*, 'Understanding the Emerging Era of International Competition', *RAND* (Research Report) (2018), 5 https://www.rand.org/pubs/research_reports/RR2726.html (accessed 22 March 2025).

28 *Kroening*, The Return of Great Power Rivalry, Oxford University Press 2020.

29 *DiCicco/Onea*, 'Great-Power Competition', *Oxford Research Encyclopaedia of International Studies* (2023), https://oxfordre.com/internationalstudies/display/10.1093/acrefore/9780190846626.001.0001/acrefore-9780190846626-e-756?d=%2F10.1093%2Fac

international competition. It is understood as the '*permanent, compulsory, comprehensive, and exclusive contest for supremacy in one or more regions, domains, or fields among those states considered to be the major players in the international system at a given time*'.[30] The intensity of the competitive dynamic fluctuates over time. Similarly, the competitive dimensions and their relative importance may be subject to change.[31]

The confluence of China's rise, Russia's comeback, and the relative disengagement of the United States ('US') from the international scene is characteristic of a new era of great power rivalry. The US National Security Strategy of October 2022 states that the global community is '*in the midst of a strategic competition to shape the future of the international order*'.[32] This strategic rivalry is not only about the shape of the international system as such. It also has military, economic, and technological dimensions.

For several decades, the EU has prioritized economic integration and the expansion of its network of free trade agreements, while largely neglecting power politics. Indeed, '*the era of geopolitical stability under US hegemony allowed the EU largely to separate economic policy from security considerations* (...)'.[33] However, the political economy has changed dramatically since the beginning of the European integration project: The US is no longer the dominant power in the international system and has relinquished its role as the world's policeman. As a result, the EU can no longer rely on the US to guarantee its security. Consequently, the EU can no longer afford to ignore the role of power politics and has recently come out of the woodwork to experience a '*geopolitical awakening*'.[34] In 2019, the then newly elected President of the EC, Ursula von der Leyen, announced the inauguration of the first '*geopolitical Commission*'.[35]

---

refore%2F9780190846626.001.0001%2Facrefore-9780190846626-e-756&p=emailA0AJOd4jxyXYc (accessed 22 March 2025).

30 *DiCicco/Onea* (n 29).

31 *DiCicco/Onea* (n 29).

32 *The White House*, 'National Security Strategy' (2022), https://bidenwhitehouse.archives.gov/wp-content/uploads/2022/10/Biden-Harris-Administrations-National-Security-Strategy-10.2022.pdf (accessed 22 March 2025).

33 *Draghi* (n 1), 9.

34 *Bergmann*, 'Europe's Geopolitical Awakening', *Foreign Affairs* (2020), https://www.foreignaffairs.com/articles/europe/2020-08-20/europes-geopolitical-awakening (accessed 22 March 2025).

35 *President-Elect von der Leyen*, 'Speech in in the European Parliament Plenary on the Occasion of the Presentation of her College of Commissioners and their Programme'

Today's geopolitical challenges are linked to the economic core of European integration, not just to foreign and security policy. A significant number of EU policies require a reorientation that takes account of power relations and addresses the EU's vulnerabilities in a holistic manner. As a result, the EU needs to act with the necessary vigor and determination on a number of interlinked fronts at the same time, including its digital and technological, environmental, trade and investment, and industrial policies. For example, as former EC-Vice President and Competition Commissioner Margrethe Vestager noted, '*with the global race for the technologies we need the most, technology is challenging* [the EU's] *economic security*'.[36]

The EU also needs to take action to strengthen its digital sovereignty. This includes creating a European-based digital infrastructure, including 5G telecommunications networks, that is resilient, secure, and sustainable. The EU must also foster a competitive data industry within its borders. Today's world is driven by technology and '*those who lead are those who control the most critical technologies and their supply chains*'.[37] In line with the 'European Green Deal' and the objectives set out in the Paris Agreement, the EU is committed to a green transition towards a carbon-neutral economy.[38]

As regards the broader geopolitical climate, the EU faces an increasingly multipolar world order. The World Trade Organization's ('WTO') multilateral trading system and the virtue of rules-based free trade as such are increasingly being challenged, including by a resurgence of US isolationism. The rapid rise of hybrid economic systems, most notably China's '*neo-mercantilism*',[39] '*steroids model of growth*',[40] and its '*murky relationship between state and private sector*',[41] have given rise to a discourse on the potential distortion of competitive dynamics by foreign subsidies, renewed lamentations

(2019), https://ec.europa.eu/commission/presscorner/detail/en/SPEECH_19_6408 (accessed 22 March 2025).

36 *Vestager*, 'A Lecture on Technology and Politics' (2024), https://ec.europa.eu/commission/presscorner/detail/en/SPEECH_24_1927 (accessed 22 March 2025).

37 *Vestager* (n 36).

38 *European Commission*, 'The European Green Deal' (Communication) COM (2019) 640 final, 11 December 2019.

39 *Collins/O'Brien*, Neo-Mercantilism in Action: China and Small States, 60 International Politics (2023), 635, 635.

40 *Jin*, China's Steroids Model of Growth, in Catão/Obstfeld (eds.), Meeting Globalization's Challenges, Princeton University Press 2019, 77, 77.

41 *The Economist*, 'The New Order of Trade' (2021), https://www.economist.com/special-report/2021/10/06/the-new-order-of-trade (accessed 22 March 2025).

about the lack of 'European champions', and calls for measures to make global value chains more resilient.[42]

II. The EU's Competitiveness Challenge

All these challenges outlined above are directly or indirectly linked to the EU's competitiveness.[43] The EU seems to be struggling to maintain its industrial base and capacity, mainly due to low innovation output performance. The EU is experiencing difficulties in maintaining its competitive edge vis-à-vis countries such as China and the US, in particular in key sectors such as the development of artificial intelligence. As a result, the EU risks losing its reputation as a global manufacturing and industrial powerhouse.[44]

This has prompted the French, German, Italian, and Polish Economy Ministers to call for far-reaching reforms of EU competition policy and law in a joint letter of 4 February 2020 to then Competition Commissioner Vestager.[45] This letter is a follow-up to the 'Franco-German Manifesto for a European Industrial Policy fit for the 21st Century' of 19 February 2019,[46] in which the French and German Economy Ministers proposed a reform of the European Merger Regulation[47] to better accommodate efforts to create

42 *Behboodi*, Competition Law and Trade Policy: "Never the Twain Shall Meet"? 84 Antitrust Law Journal (2021), 127, 128 (observing that '*changing patterns of trade and, in particular, the rise of a new economic model in China, with massive interlocking state-trading enterprises dominating export markets, pose a threat to the integrity of functioning competitive markets targeted by those enterprises*').

43 *Gros*, 'Europe's Geoeconomic Competitiveness Challenge' *Project Syndicate* (2024), https://www.project-syndicate.org/commentary/decline-of-eu-relative-economic-power-raises-geopolitical-risks-by-daniel-gros-2024-05 (accessed 22 March 2025).

44 *Gehrke/Medunic*, 'Fortune Favours the Bold: Upgrading the EU's Geoeconomic Strategy' *ECFR* (Policy Brief) (2024), https://ecfr.eu/publication/fortune-favours-the-bold-upgrading-the-eus-geoeconomic-strategy/ (accessed 22 March 2025).

45 'Joint Letter by the French, German, Italian, and Polish Economy Ministers' (2020), https://www.politico.eu/wp-content/uploads/2020/02/Letter-to-Vestager.pdf (accessed 22 March 2025).

46 'A Franco-German Manifesto for a European Industrial Policy Fit for the 21st Century' (2019), https://www.bmwk.de/Redaktion/DE/Downloads/F/franco-german-manifesto-for-a-european-industrial-policy.pdf%3F__blob%3DpublicationFile%26v%3D2 (accessed 22 March 2025).

47 Council Regulation (EC) No 139/2004 of 20 January 2004 on the control of concentrations between undertakings [2004] OJ L24/1.

'European Champions'. This manifesto can be seen as a direct response to the blocking of the Siemens-Alstom merger,[48] which the EC said would be harmful to European consumers.[49]

The joint letter included a proposal that the European Council should have the right to veto the EC's merger decisions in '*well-defined cases, subject to strict conditions*'.[50] It also recommended that the current EC Notice on market definition be updated to take account of global and potential competition in order to give greater consideration to the economic challenges posed by China. The letter was published at a time when the EC was stepping up its efforts to implement a more centralized industrial policy.[51] The letter called for an evaluation and modernization of the EC Guidelines on the assessment of horizontal mergers. It also highlighted the need for a more effective and efficient competition toolbox to better address potential abuses by non-EU undertakings, including state-owned or subsidized enterprises.[52]

Importantly, the signatories called for immediate action. However, former Competition Commissioner Vestager presented them with a long-term timetable for competition law reform.[53] Since then, the EC has issued a revised Notice on market definition on 22 February 2024,[54] which provides specific guidance on the application of market definition concepts in certain circumstances, including digital markets, innovation-intensive industries, and clarifications on dynamic and forward-looking assessments. A recent statement by then EC President-elect von der Leyen in the plenary of the European Parliament suggests that the French, German, Italian, and Polish Economy Ministers may perhaps soon get what they asked for: '[W]*e*

48 *Siemens/Alstom* (Case M.8677) Commission Decision 2019/C 300/07 [2019] OJ C300/14.

49 *Braun et al.*, 'EU Big Four Press Vestager to Clear Path for Champions' *Politico* (2020), https://www.politico.eu/article/eu-big-four-france-germany-italy-poland-press-executive-vice-president-margrethe-vestager-to-clear-path-for-champions/ (accessed 22 March 2025); *Behboodi* (n 42) 154.

50 'Joint Letter by the French, German, Italian, and Polish Economy Ministers' (n 45).

51 *Braun et al.* (n 49).

52 'Joint Letter by the French, German, Italian, and Polish Economy Ministers' (n 45).

53 *Braun et al.* (n 49).

54 Commission Notice on the definition of the relevant market for the purposes of Union competition law [2024] OJ C2024/1645.

need a competition policy that supports companies to scale up. Europe must be the home of opportunity and innovation'.[55]

C. Foreign Trade and Competition Law: Cut from the Same Cloth

This section argues that the geopolitical considerations embodied in and channeled through EU foreign trade policy and law are different from most other public policy considerations. First, to the extent that it seeks to liberalize market access, foreign trade policy is aligned with competition policy in promoting market integration, making it an economic policy. Second, EU foreign trade law and competition law are complementary, just as EU competition law and free movement law are complementary.

I. On the Same Team

Broadly speaking, competition policy encompasses all policies that affect market competition in a polity. This understanding is not limited to policies that regulate anticompetitive practices by firms, but can extend to policies on deregulation, privatization, foreign direct investment, and public procurement. In the broadest sense, the term can also include trade and industrial policy.[56] When used in this paper, the term 'competition policy' does not include trade and industrial policy.

Foreign trade policy refers to all policies that shape international trade flows between polities.[57] Like competition policy, trade policy has the potential to promote productivity growth through the international division of labor, to contribute to the reduction of global income inequality, and to enable the democratization of economic opportunity.[58] However, trade

55 *von der Leyen*, 'Statement at the European Parliament Plenary by President Ursula von Der Leyen, Candidate for a Second Mandate 2024–2029' (2024), https://enlargement.ec.europa.eu/news/statement-european-parliament-plenary-president-ursula-von-der-leyen-candidate-second-mandate-2024-2024-07-18_en (22 March 2025).

56 *Sweeney*, Globalisation of Competition Law and Policy: Some Aspects of the Interface between Trade and Competition, 5 Michigan Journal of International Law (2004), 375, 379.

57 *Velut*, Trade Policy, in Wright (ed.), International Encyclopaedia of the Social & Behavioral Sciences, Elsevier 2nd edn. 2014, 485, 485.

58 *Motta*, The Relationship between Trade and Competition in a Globalized Economy, 84 Antitrust Law Journal (2021), 169, 169.

policy rarely achieves its full potential because free trade is very difficult to maintain in the real world. Governments often adopt protectionist policies in favor of domestic industries and erect tariff and non-tariff barriers to trade.[59]

Competition policy and trade policy share a common denominator: Both seek to remove barriers to trade in order to promote trade liberalization and market integration. More specifically, they both seek to encourage the mobility of capital, goods, and sometimes even labor. Open and competitive markets are thought to deliver the best results. However, real markets are prone to imperfections. Therefore, corrective policies are needed.[60]

While both policy areas share a common line of attack, the law implementing them tends to operate in two '*parallel universes*'[61] and there are important differences in the relevant enforcement mechanisms and remedies. Competition law addresses anticompetitive behavior by private firms. Its application tends to be territorial, and it is typically enforced by independent enforcement agencies. EU competition law has always pursued several parallel objectives, namely market efficiency, (consumer) welfare, commercial or economic freedom and freedom to compete, effective competitive structure and protection of competitors, fairness, market integration, and the protection of the competitive process. Empirical analysis shows that while all of these objectives have always been present throughout the history of EU competition law, the significance of each may vary over time.[62] Competition law works through prohibitions, fines, and/or behavioral or structural remedies.[63]

Much of foreign trade law, by contrast, is primarily concerned with liberalizing market access and removing or reducing state barriers to trade such as tariffs, import quotas, sanitary and phytosanitary measures, and technical barriers to trade. Trade rules are usually enforced by international bodies composed of representatives of national governments. Disputes are often settled by negotiation.[64] Trade policy is usually implemented through

59 *Motta* (n 58), 169.
60 *Motta* (n 58), 169.
61 *Epstein*, The Other Side of Harmony: Can Trade and Competition Laws Work Together in the International Marketplace? 17 American University International Law Review (2002), 343, 345.
62 *Stylianou/Iacovides*, The Goals of EU Competition Law: A Comprehensive Empirical Investigation, 42 Legal Studies (2022), 620, 623.
63 Epstein (n 61), 345.
64 Epstein (n 61), 345.

bilateral or multilateral trade agreements.[65] Foreign trade law frames market access in terms of the right of exporters to enter a foreign market. Consumers can benefit from the resulting reduction in barriers to international trade in goods and sometimes even services and from the international division of labor, which can ultimately reduce prices and increase choice and quality.[66]

In sum, although the two regulatory frameworks involve different actors with fundamentally different perspectives, types of inquiry, methods of dispute resolution, and legal principles, they are nonetheless on the same team in seeking to promote market integration.

II. Two Sides of the Same Coin

1. Theories on Interaction between Competition and Trade

There are two theoretical models of the interaction between trade and competition. One theory portrays the two areas of law as substitutes, the other as complements.[67] A theory of trade and competition law as substitutes starts from the insight that trade liberalization may render competition law superfluous. The basic idea is this: The existence of barriers to entry makes it possible to maintain cartels and other forms of restrictive behavior, and competition law must therefore intervene. Free trade, on the other hand, helps to maintain market competition because it encourages entry by foreign firms and thus limits market power.[68]

---

65 Note that there are also preferential trading schemes that entail one-sided, non-reciprocal trade preferences granted by developed countries to developing ones, with the goal of helping them to increase exports and spur economic development. In the EU, unilateral arrangements include the 'Generalized Scheme of Preferences', the 'Generalized Scheme of Preferences Plus', and 'Everything but Arms'.

66 Epstein (n 61), 345 (noting that international trade law is more directly '*aimed at opening markets to exporters of member countries, not at optimizing marketplace efficiencies and consumer benefits*'); *Sweeney* (n 56), 415 (observing that the '*trade conception of market access is not necessarily about enhancing welfare*').

67 *Bradford/Chilton*, Trade Openness and Antitrust Law, 62 The Journal of Law and Economics (2019), 29, 32. See also *Noonan*, The Emerging Principles of International Competition Law, Oxford University Press 2008, 144; *Motta* (n 58) (observing that in an ideal world, '*free trade would be the main instrument of competition policy*').

68 *Büthe*, The Politics of Market Competition: Trade and Antitrust in a Global Economy, in Martin (ed.), The Oxford Handbook of the Political Economy of International Trade, Oxford University Press 2015, 213, 215.

The first argument that supporters make in favor of relying on free trade to ensure market competition is that foreign competitors face a number of trade costs. The fact that these firms are able to compete after incurring these costs suggests that they are more efficient and therefore a more effective disciplining force than domestic firms.[69] Proponents further argue that trade liberalization and the consequent deterrent effect of imports on anticompetitive behavior obviate the need for intervention.[70]

However, there are several arguments against seeing free trade as a substitute for competition policy. First, a large part of international trade takes place in oligopolistic industries.[71] Second, competition policy may well be designed not only to maximize economic efficiency but also to serve other objectives.[72] Third, the idea that free trade can substitute for competition policy assumes that domestic industries are powerless to resist the liberalization efforts of policymakers. While it is true that genuine trade liberalization is possible, commentators suggest that previously well-protected industries have the material capacity and incentives to find other forms of protection to undermine liberalization efforts.[73] Finally, it is questionable whether competition policy can effectively replace trade policy. In the face of trade barriers such as exceptionally high tariffs, foreign entry is unlikely no matter how competitive the markets of the importing State may be.[74] Some further argue that the argument rests on the assumption that enforcement agencies are only concerned with market efficiency. This assumption overlooks the fact that competition law enforcement may be influenced by political considerations, since it implies a reliance on public authority to impose limits on the exercise of market power by private parties.[75]

The proposition that policymakers seeking to constrain market power can use both policies to achieve the same ends is the basis of a theory of trade and competition law as complementary policy areas.[76] These policy areas are indeed '*mutually reinforcing*'.[77] This is because trade openness can increase the rents resulting from anticompetitive behavior, such as a cross-

69 *Bradford/Chilton* (n 67), 32.
70 *Bradford/Chilton* (n 67), 32.
71 *Büthe* (n 68), 216.
72 *Büthe* (n 68), 216.
73 *Büthe* (n 68), 217.
74 *Bradford/Chilton* (n 67), 33.
75 *Büthe* (n 68), 217.
76 *Behboodi* (n 42), 135; *Motta* (n 58).
77 *Bradford/Chilton* (n 67), 33.

border cartel. It also reduces the likelihood of detection in cross-border cases. As a result, trade liberalization may increase the likelihood of anti-competitive behavior. Therefore, policymakers may seek to impose stricter antitrust laws to prevent private economic operators from re-establishing barriers to trade.[78]

2. Competition and Free Movement in the Internal Market

The rules on free movement and competition (together with the economic rights enshrined in the EU Charter of Fundamental Rights)[79] form the '*normative basis of the EU economic constitution*'.[80] The rules on free movement and competition are seen as interdependent, as they are the two main instruments for creating an EU internal market based on a free market economy and competition: While the rules on free movement address the *public* obstacles to transnational business activities, the rules on competition address the *private* obstacles to cross-border economic activities.[81]

These two sets of rules share a common goal: to create and maintain the EU's single market.[82] The Spaak Report, which served as the basis for the negotiations leading to the Treaties establishing the European Communities, laid the foundations for the process of economic integration. It was clear that the creation of a common market would require the integration of national markets through the removal of government barriers to trade and the establishment of a customs union. However, it was feared that restrictions by private companies would frustrate the purpose of the single market. As a result, the Spaak Report called for the inclusion of rules on cross-border competition.[83]

---

78 *Bradford/Chilton* (n 67), 33.

79 *Calliess* (n 7), para. 739.

80 *Szyszcak*, Competition and the Liberalised Market, in Shuibhne (ed.), Regulating the Internal Market, Edward Elgar 2006, 87, 101.

81 *Mataija*, Private Regulation and the Internal Market, Oxford University Press 2016, 116.

82 *Calliess* (n 7), para. 785.

83 'Rapport des chefs de délégation aux ministres des Affaires étrangères, comité intergouvernementale crée par la conférénce de Messine' (1956), 16 http://aei.pitt.edu/996/1/Spaak_report_french.pdf (accessed 22 March 2025) ('*Le premier fait dont il convient de tenir compte, c'est la dimension atteinte par les entreprises, ou l'usage des ententes entre entreprises et, par suite, les pratiques de monopole, les facultés de discrimination, les possibilités de répartition du marché. Des règles de concurrence qui s'imposent aux entreprises sont donc nécessaires pour éviter que des doubles prix*

The complementarity of competition law and free movement law and their overlapping objectives have been repeatedly confirmed by the case law of the EU Courts. Early competition law cases on vertical restraints invoked the same market integration rationale as free movement cases.[84] The archetypal example is *Consten & Grundig*, where the Court held that '*an agreement (...) which might tend to restore the national divisions in trade between Member States might (...) frustrate the most fundamental objections of the Community. The Treaty, whose preamble and content aim at abolishing the barriers between States, and (...) could not allow undertakings to reconstruct such barriers. Article* [101(1)] *is designed to pursue this aim (...)*'.[85] Exactly the same wording can be found in more recent competition law cases such as *GlaxoSmithKline*.[86]

At the same time, there are judgments in free movement law that echo the wording of competition law cases. A prominent example is the definition of measures having an effect equivalent to quantitative restrictions prohibited by Art 34 TFEU.[87] The phrase '*all trading rules enacted by Member States which are capable of hindering, directly or indirectly, actually or potentially, intra-Community trade*'[88] in *Dassonville* was taken almost verbatim from *Consten & Grundig*[89] and *Société Technique Minière*.[90] Perhaps the most explicit statement of the common objectives of competition and free movement rules can be found in *Leclerc*.[91] The Court held that the objective of establishing a market characterized by the free movement of goods '*is secured inter alia by* [Art 34 TFEU] *prohibiting restrictions on*

---

aient le même effet que des droits de douane, qu'un dumping mette en danger des productions économiquement saines, que la répartition des marchés se substitue à leur cloisonnement.').

84 *Mataija* (n 81), 122.

85 Joined Cases 56 and 58/64, EU:C:1966:41 – *Consten and Grundig v Commission*, 299, 340.

86 Joined Cases C-501/06 P, C-513/06 P, C-515/06 P and C-519/06 P, EU:C:2009:610 – *GlaxoSmithKline v Commission*, para. 61.

87 *Mortelmans*, Towards Convergence in the Application of the Rules on Free Movement and on Competition? 38 Common Market Law Review (2001), 613, 623.

88 Case 8/74, EU:C:1974:82 – *Procureur du Roi v Benoît and Gustave Dassonville*, para. 5.

89 *Consten and Grundig v Commission* (n 85), 341.

90 Case 56/65, EU:C:1966:38 – *Société Technique Minière (LTM) v Maschinenbau Ulm GmbH (MBU)*, para. 7.

91 Case 231/83, EU:C:1985:29 – *Cullet v Leclerc*.

intra-Community trade and by [Art 101 TFEU] *on the rules on competition* (...)'.[92]

3. Expanding the Argument: Parallels Between Free Movement and Foreign Trade

Complementarity between competition and trade rules exists not only at the EU level but also at the international level. This becomes clear when one considers the parallels between the EU rules on free movement of goods and services and foreign trade in terms of objectives, economic rationale, and legal principles, despite important differences in structure, ambition, context, and institutional set-up. In terms of objectives and economic rationale, both sets of rules aim to reduce trade barriers based on the economic theory of comparative advantage.[93] In terms of legal principles, both internal market law and parts of external trade law emphasize the elimination of discriminatory practices in order to ensure fair and equal treatment of market participants. One of the key principles of internal market law is non-discrimination, in particular on grounds of nationality. In foreign trade, the EU is bound by international trade rules, in particular by the multilateral framework of the WTO. The most-favored nation and national treatment principles aim to ensure that the EU does not discriminate between trading partners and treats imported products in the same way as 'like' domestic products.[94]

The parallels are even more striking when one considers the evolution of the rules governing the free movement of goods and services and foreign trade, to the extent that the latter seeks to liberalize market access, from a historical perspective. The beginnings of European integration and the GATT of 1947 as the most prominent and admittedly also most successful example of an international economic integration project can both be traced back to '*the desire of political leaders after the Second World War*

92 *Cullet v Leclerc* (n 91), para. 11.

93 *Gains et al.*, Comparing Two Trade Liberalisation Regimes, in Gains et al. (eds.), Liberalising Trade in the EU and the WTO, Cambridge University Press 2012, 3, 6.

94 *Cottier/Oesch*, Direct and Indirect Discrimination in WTO and EU Law, in Gains et al. (eds.), Liberalising Trade in the EU and the WTO, Cambridge University Press 2012, 141, 143 ('*Both the WTO and the European Union are founded upon the principle of non-discrimination, taming the sovereign rights of states to select and choose their preferences within the international community with respect to the importation of products, both goods and of services.*').

to promote mutual economic benefit and international cooperation through liberalization of trade to prevent recurrence of the autarkical economic competition leading to political and ultimately armed conflict during the 1930s'.[95] As de Búrca and Scott note,[96] EU free movement law is heavily inspired by and modeled on the principles of free trade and economic integration of the GATT, making the EU's Common Market '*a sort of mini-GATT*'.[97]

The historical perspective also provides additional arguments for a complementary reading of competition and trade rules at the international level.[98] In particular, the post-war international trade negotiations and the Havana Charter,[99] the draft founding document for the International Trade Organization ('ITO'), included measures to protect competition in world trade. The draft Havana Charter would have required the members of the proposed ITO to, among other things, take '*appropriate*' measures to prevent private commercial enterprises with '*effective control of trade*' from '*restrain*[ing] *competition, limit*[ing] *access to markets, or foster*[ing] *monopolistic control in international trade*'[100] when such conduct would adversely affect production and trade and impede the achievement of the Charter's objectives. However, the ITO never came into being due to opposition from the US Congress. Since then, global antitrust initiatives have failed.[101] Although a working group on the interaction between trade and competition policy was established at the 1996 WTO Ministerial Conference in Singapore, the issue was dropped from the work program for the Doha Round.[102]

In sum, EU free movement law and foreign trade law both aim to promote free trade and market integration, albeit in different contexts. Further-

95 *Gains et al.* (n 93), 8.

96 *de Búrca/Scott* (n 10), 2 (observing that '*the EEC's common market was modelled partly on the GATT, and many of the EC Treaty provisions clearly reflect this. Interesting comparisons can be drawn between the similar EC and GATT rules on matters such as internal taxation, discriminatory and non-discriminatory trade restrictions*').

97 *Larik*, Much More Than Trade: The Common Commercial Policy in a Global Context, in Evans/Loutrakos (eds.), Beyond the Established Legal Orders, Bloomsbury 2011, 13, 18.

98 *Fox*, Competition Law and the Agenda for the WTO: Forging the Links of Competition and Trade 4 Pacific Rim Law & Policy Journal (1995), 1, 2. See also *Epstein* (n 61), 354.

99 'The Havana Charter for an International Trade Organization' (1948), https://www.worldtradelaw.net/document.php?id=misc/havana.pdf (accessed 22 March 2025).

100 Havana Charter (n 99), Art 46.

101 *Fox* (n 98), 4.

102 *Motta* (n 58).

more, the analysis shows that a complementary reading of free movement and competition rules is justified not only within the EU. Such a reading can also be extended to the interaction between competition and foreign trade rules at the international level.

D. The 'More Economic Approach': When Competition and Trade Law Parted Ways

While the previous section has concluded that competition policy and law, on the one hand, and foreign trade policy and law, on the other hand, are interrelated, this section notes that '*the mainstream thinking about free movement and competition law has split into different directions, especially as competition law has progressed and developed*'.[103] The adoption of the 'more economic approach' to competition law enforcement and the influence of US antitrust scholarship have led to a more prominent role for consumer welfare and market efficiency in EU competition law enforcement.[104] This section criticizes the 'more economic approach' to EU competition law enforcement because it has favored incoherent policies.

I. The Making of the 'More Economic Approach'

In the mid-1990s, the EC's enforcement practice underwent a significant change with the introduction of the so-called 'more economic approach'. The 'more economic approach' is an umbrella term for a number of developments, often involving a reinterpretation of the basic concepts of EU competition law by the EC. It has affected all three pillars of EU competition law. Ibáñez Colomo identifies '*legitimacy considerations*'[105] as the main driving force behind this remodeling. More specifically, the changes in the EC's enforcement practice were prompted by the perceived need to

103 *Mataija* (n 81), 120.

104 *Mataija* (n 81), 120.

105 *Ibáñez Colomo*, Whatever Happened to the "More Economics-Based Approach"? 11 Journal of European Competition Law & Practice (2020), 473, 473. See also *Ibáñez Colomo*, The New EU Competition Law, Hart Publishing 2023, 49 (observing that the European Commission '*addressed what can be termed a legitimacy crisis in competition policy by adjusting the substantive and institutional dimensions of the system*').

align itself with mainstream economics.[106] While economic analysis has always been present in competition law enforcement, this shift responded to criticism that the EC's previous approach had been too formalistic.[107]

The EC has always pursued a variety of objectives in enforcing EU competition law. These parallel objectives include market efficiency, (consumer) welfare, commercial or economic freedom and freedom to compete, effective competitive structure and protection of competitors, fairness, market integration, and the protection of the competitive process. Empirical analyses show that the importance of each of these objectives may vary over time. In short, competition law has been used to pursue a variety of objectives set out in the EU Treaties,[108] while taking into account certain public interest concerns.[109]

With the advent of the 'more economic approach', the EC began to increasingly emphasize the maximization of 'consumer welfare' or 'allocative efficiency' in its institutional practice.[110] A quantitative analysis by Stylianou and Iacovides, which among other things analyzes the number of sources associated with a given goal on a year-to-year basis, confirms that a plurality of goals has always been pursued in EU institutional practice. While

---

106 *Ibáñez Colomo* (n 105), 473.

107 *Witt*, The European Court of Justice and the More Economic Approach to EU Competition Law – Is the Tide Turning? 64 Antitrust Bulletin (2019) 172, 174.

108 *Witt* (n 107), 177.

109 See, e.g., Case C-309/99, EU:C:2002:98 – *Wouters and Others*, 1577, 1653 (holding that restrictions on free competition may be justified by legitimate public policy concerns, such as ensuring the impartiality of the legal profession, provided that the measures are necessary and proportionate); Case C-519/04 P, EU:C:2006:492 – *Meca-Medina and Majcen v Commission*, 6991, 7006 (holding that the rules of sporting bodies may be subject to EU competition law if they have economic effects, which must be legitimate and proportionate); Case C-67/96, EU:C:1999:430 – *Albany*, 5751, 5863 (holding that agreements concluded in the context of collective bargaining between employers and employees with a view to achieving recognized social policy objectives do not fall within the scope of EU competition law); Case C-1/12, EU:C:2013:127 – *OTOC* (holding that a regulation adopted by a professional association establishing a system of compulsory training for its members falls within the scope of EU competition law and restricts competition in a prohibited manner in so far as it restrains competition in a substantial part of the relevant market and imposes discriminatory conditions to the detriment of competitors); Case C-136/12, EU:C:2013:489 – *Consiglio nazionale dei geologi (Italian geologists)* (holding that the 'dignity of a profession' may be a legitimate objective for determining professional remuneration, since it may be necessary to ensure the quality of the services provided by geologists).

110 *Zelger*, Restrictions of EU Competition Law in the Digital Age, Springer 2023, 19.

not necessarily suggesting that some goals take precedence over others, the empirical evidence shows an increase in the prevalence of sources associated with consumer welfare and efficiency from the 2000s onwards, both in the institutional practice of the EC and the EU Courts.[111] It is against this background that the understanding of competitive harm has evolved: For a restriction of competition to be considered anticompetitive, there must be a likely reduction in consumer welfare (i.e., for firms' conduct to be illegal, there must be a negative net effect on output and prices).[112] Another implication is that only economic efficiency gains can outweigh anticompetitive effects.[113]

II. The Purported Purity of the 'More Economic Approach'

Importantly, the 'more economic approach' is accompanied by a '*claim to objectivity and universality*'.[114] The apparent strict adherence to economic principles is often mistakenly equated with an enforcement model that is free from political considerations and interference. However, as Caffarra notes, the choice of enforcement model always '*embodies a political view of antitrust*'.[115] The 'more economic approach' is inspired by US antitrust scholarship, particularly the so-called Chicago School. This is a school of thought that argues that economic efficiency should be the sole objective of competition law. Consumer welfare is understood as the ability of consumers to purchase products and services at lower prices.[116]

Critics note that this narrow view of consumer welfare is not reflected in the legislative history of most antitrust laws. For example, the US Sherman Act was enacted to promote a variety of economic and non-economic

---

111 *Stylianou/Iacovides* (n 62), 636.

112 *Easterbrook*, Chicago on Vertical Restrictions, 3 Competition Law International (2007), 3, 3.

113 *Witt* (n 107), 183.

114 *Fiebig/Gerber*, The Causes and Consequences of the Neo-Brandeisian Antitrust Movement in the United States, 19 Zeitschrift für Wettbewerbsrecht (2021), 460, 469.

115 *Caffarra* (n 2). See also *Büthe* (n 68) (observing that '*effective competition policy is inherently deeply political, since it entails the use of political power to constrain or even redistribute economic power*'); *Katz* (n 16), 416 (observing that '*the choice to prefer the ideas and arguments associated with one school over another is political because it determines the direction of the law and fosters certain legal outcomes* [...]').

116 *Fiebig/Gerber* (n 114), 473.

objectives, such as the redistribution of wealth, the protection of small and medium-sized enterprises, the protection of economic freedom, and the prevention of the accumulation of economic power.[117] In the same vein, EU competition law was initially adopted to promote market integration in particular.[118] Similarly, competition laws in Germany and Japan were enacted after the Second World War to prevent the re-emergence of the cartels and industrial conglomerates that the Allies believed had contributed to the countries' ability to wage war.[119]

Against this background, some commentators argue that the suggestion '*that competition law should only be concerned with consumer welfare and/or efficiency amounts to usurping legislation enacted for other purposes*'.[120] In fact, consumers do not only care about price. They also care about the quality, variety, and innovative nature of the product. The neoclassical view of competition policy and competition law as an exact science with universal truths has its limits.[121] It is true that competition law typically refers to the laws governing private anticompetitive behavior. It is also true that most competition law regimes share some key provisions. However, the precise architecture and content of the law are largely determined by competition policy, which differs from polity to polity.[122] Moreover, for reasons that may be internal or external to competition policy, enforcement agencies and courts may give varying degrees of priority to different aspects of competition policy.[123]

---

117 Neo-Brandeisians consistently argue that the legislative purpose of antitrust law goes well beyond consumer welfare in purely economic terms. See, e.g., *Khan*, Amazon's Antitrust Paradox, 126 Yale Law Journal (2017), 710, 743; *Stucke*, Reconsidering Antitrust's Goals, 53 Boston College Law Review (2012), 551, 578.

118 *Blockx*, The Limits to the "More Economic Approach" to Antitrust, 42 World Competition (2019), 476, 489.

119 *Steenbergen*, Competition and Trade Policy and the Challenge of Globalization, in Govaere et al. (eds.), Trade and Competition Law in the EU and Beyond, Edward Elgar 2011, 3, 9; *Bourgeois/Tuominen*, The Nexus between Competition, Industrial and Trade Policies, in Merola et al. (eds.), Competition Law in Times of Crisis, Bruylant 2013, 539, 540.

120 *Blockx* (n 118), 491.

121 *Andriychuk* (n 14), 603.

122 *Sweeney* (n 56), 379.

123 *Andriychuk* (n 14), 603.

III. Implications of the 'More Economic Approach': Policy and Institutional 'Siloing'

Today's global economic order gives rise to complex dynamics between competition and foreign trade that can be difficult to address in a coherent manner, particularly under the current antitrust enforcement paradigm. The latter contributes to an isolation from other policy areas, which is reinforced by institutional 'siloing'. Competition policy and law, on the one hand, and trade policy and law, on the other, have largely developed separately and have been treated as conceptually distinct.[124] However, an interpretation of the EU Treaties shows that these policies cannot be separated and that their coherent implementation requires a holistic approach.[125]

Organizational 'siloing' occurs when there is a '*lack of interaction between parts of an organization, such as between colleagues in different departments beyond their immediate co-workers*'.[126] In public administration, institutional 'siloing' refers to '*a hierarchical organization which seeks to maximize vertical coordination at the expense of horizontal coordination*'.[127] Organizational silos can be found in the authorities responsible for implementing and enforcing trade and competition rules. They tend to be highly specialized and typically institutionally separate from each other.[128]

For example, the EC is organized into policy departments called Directorates-General ('DGs'). They are responsible for different policy areas. While this specialization is beneficial in terms of focus and expertise, it creates a risk of fragmentation and poses challenges for the horizontal and vertical coordination within the EC. As a result, this organizational structure can have a negative impact on policy coherence. Once established, these silos are difficult to break down. Individual DGs develop their own organizational identity, underpinned by the logic of portfolio, purpose, and affiliation, which they are keen to preserve.[129]

---

124 *Fox*, Blind Spot: Trade and Competition Law – the Space Between the Silos, 24 German Law Journal (2023), 269, 270.

125 See Section E.I below.

126 *Vantaggiato et al.*, Breaking out of Silos: Explaining Cross-Departmental Interactions in Two European Bureaucracies, 28 J European Public Policy (2020) 1, 2.

127 *Scott/Gong*, Coordinating Government Silos: Challenges and Opportunities, 1 Global Public Policy and Governance (2021), 20, 20.

128 *Behboodi* (n 42), 128.

129 *Chatzopoulou*, Resilience of the Silo Organizational Structure in the European Commission, 61 Journal of Common Market Studies (2023), 545, 547.

Competition authorities, by the very nature of their work and like any other public authority, can be quite susceptible to a silo mentality.[130] While formal decisions on competition violations are taken by the College of 27 Commissioners responsible for all EU policies, which helps to mitigate the risk of incoherent decision-making to some extent, the practical importance of this institutional feature should not be overestimated.[131] Caffarra even suggests that some competition authorities have long cultivated a kind of 'exceptionalism' and have historically paid very little attention to normatively distinct but logically related policy areas such as industrial policy, trade, and data protection. The logical underpinning of this distancing from other policy areas is said to be linked to the role of economic analysis as a determining factor.[132]

E. The Case for a 'More Integrated Approach'

This section argues that the EU Treaties contain provisions that encourage, if not legally require, a 'more integrated approach' to policymaking and enforcement. This section further suggests that the current enforcement paradigm in EU competition law reflects political preferences that may be subject to change over time due to shifts in the political economy. Indeed, the enforcement paradigm of EU competition law has not remained constant. The adoption of the 'more economic approach' was a response to calls to bring competition enforcement in line with mainstream economics. More recently, with the rise of 'Big Tech', there seems to be an emerging consensus on 'fairness' as a guiding principle.

---

130 *Jenny*, The Institutional Design of Competition Authorities: Debates and Trends, in Jenny/Katsoulacos (eds.), Competition Law Enforcement in the BRICS and in Developing Countries, Springer 2016, 1, 19.

131 *Ezrachi* (n 17), 54.

132 *Caffarra*, 'Antitrust and the Political Economy: Part 2', *VOXEU COLUMN* (2024), https://cepr.org/voxeu/columns/antitrust-and-political-economy-part-2 (accessed 22 March 2025).

I. Policy-Linking Clauses in the EU Treaties

The question of whether the EU Treaties address the link between competition and trade has been debated by several commentators.[133] The consensus among these commentators is that none of these policies operate in hermetically sealed silos. Advocates of a more integrated approach base this claim on the following provisions: Art 9 TFEU provides that '[i]*n defining and implementing its policies and activities the Union shall take into account requirements linked to the promotion of a high level of employment, the guarantee of adequate social protection, the fight against social exclusion, and a high level of education, training and protection of human health*'. This provision was originally introduced by the Treaty of Amsterdam. It should be read in conjunction with Art 3(3) TEU[134] and Protocol No 27 on the internal market and competition.[135]

Some commentators refer to Art 3(3) TEU in conjunction with Art 9 TFEU as the '*social clause*',[136] the rationale of which is to counterbalance the dominance of market-related objectives in policymaking.[137] The strong legislative emphasis on the market policy dimension reflected in the internal market rationale can, to some extent, be explained by Scharpf's 'asymmetry thesis'. The thesis suggests that the EU Treaties, in particular their policy processes, decision rules, and institutions more generally,

---

133 *Fox* (n 15), 224; *Steenbergen* (n 119), 15; *Bourgeois/Tuominen* (n 119), 550.

134 Art 3(3) TEU provides that '[t]*he Union shall establish an internal market. It shall work for the sustainable development of Europe based on balanced economic growth and price stability, a highly competitive social market economy, aiming at full employment and social progress, and a high level of protection and improvement of the quality of the environment. It shall promote scientific and technological advance. It shall combat social exclusion and discrimination, and shall promote social justice and protection, equality between women and men, solidarity between generations and protection of the rights of the child. It shall promote economic, social and territorial cohesion, and solidarity among Member States. It shall respect its rich cultural and linguistic diversity, and shall ensure that Europe's cultural heritage is safeguarded and enhanced*'.

135 Protocol No 27 reads as follows: '*Considering that the internal market set out in Article 3 of the Treaty on European Union includes a system ensuring that competition is not distorted, (...). To this end, the Union shall, if necessary, take action under the provisions of the Treaties, including under Article 352 of the Treaty on the Functioning of the European Union*'. Pursuant to Art 51 TEU, the Protocols and Annexes shall form an integral part of the Treaties.

136 *Bourgeois/Tuominen* (n 119), 550.

137 *Bourgeois/Tuominen* (n 119, 550.

are biased in favor of negative integration (i.e. market liberalization) but provide weaker mechanisms for positive integration (i.e. the creation of common market-correcting policies on, for example, social, environmental, and public health issues). In particular, market competences benefit from a more robust institutional and legal base, providing the EU with the means to legislate and enforce effectively in these areas. In contrast, non-market competences often rely on Member State action or are constrained by stricter decision-making requirements, making them more fragmented and less enforceable at the EU level.[138] Art 9 TFEU has traditionally been used by the EU Courts as a reference point when dealing with the application of free movement law and competition law.[139] The creation of the internal market is at the top of the list of objectives in Art 3(3) TEU. Protocol No 27 refers to competition policy as one of the elements of market integration. At the same time, the creation of the internal market is intertwined with other equally important objectives.[140] These include balanced economic growth, price stability, a highly competitive social market economy, full employment and social progress, a high level of protection and improvement of the quality of the environment, and the promotion of scientific and technological progress.[141]

At the same time, the 'asymmetry thesis' has lost some of its persuasiveness over the years. In fact, the EU has acquired many explicit market-correcting competences in the course of the integration process.[142] Moreover,

138 See, generally, *Scharpf*, Governing in Europe: Effective and Democratic? Oxford University Press 2011. For a discussion of the challenges that the 'asymmetry' thesis poses for social policymaking, see *Scharpf*, The Asymmetry of European Integration, or Why the EU Cannot be a "Social Market Economy" 8 Socio-Economic Review (2010), 211, 211. Note that recent scholarship suggests that the 'asymmetry thesis' no longer accurately depicts reality in that domestic welfare mechanisms have remained relatively stable and EU tools to pursue social and redistributive objectives have emerged. See van den *Brink/Dawson/Zglinski*, Revisiting the Asymmetry Thesis: Negative and Positive Integration in the EU', 32 Journal of European Public Policy (2025), 209, 209.

139 *Bourgeois/Tuominen* (n 119), 550.

140 *Steenbergen* (n 119), 16 (observing that '[t]*he Treaties do not clearly define a hierarchy of objectives*').

141 *Bourgeois/Tuominen* (n 119), 550.

142 *Boeger*, Minimum Harmonisation, Free Movement and Proportionality, in Syrpis (ed.), The Judiciary, the Legislature and the EU Internal Market, Cambridge University Press 2012, 62, 62 (noting that these legal bases often allow only partial harmonization and do not prohibit the Member States from maintaining or adopting stricter national regulatory standards).

the EU legislator has often been able to mitigate the effects of competence constraints by relying on Art 114 TFEU, the legal basis for the '*approximation of the provisions laid down by the law, regulation and administrative action in Member States which have as their object the establishment and functioning of the internal market*'. It is available as a means of achieving the objectives set out in Art 26 TFEU. This legal basis gives the EU legislator a wide margin of discretion.[143] As a result, the EU legislator can rely on this legal basis to enact market-correcting legislation. Provided that the legislation removes (future) barriers to trade, Art 114 TFEU can be used even if non-market objectives such as consumer protection or public health are a '*decisive*' policy motive.[144] As a result, Art 114 TFEU has become the legal basis for a large number of legislative acts that pursue policy objectives that are not necessarily directly related to the establishment of the internal market.[145]

Another policy-linking argument can be found in the provisions on monetary and economic policy which clearly state that the EU's policies are to be conducted '*in accordance with the principle of an open market economy with free competition*'.[146] A similar commitment to the principles of open and free competition is enshrined in Art 170(2) TFEU, which deals with trans-European networks.[147] Furthermore, Art 173(1) TFEU states that '[t]*he Union and the Member States shall ensure that the conditions necessary for the competitiveness of the Union's industry exist*'. According to Bourgeois and Tuominen, there is an inevitable link here with the EU's trade policy as enshrined in Arts 205 to 207 TFEU, since EU industry should be given the opportunity to achieve high levels of income both in the EU and abroad.[148]

---

143 Case C-257/06, EU:C:2009:795 – *Roby Profumi*, para. 14; Case C-324/99, EU:C:2001:682 – *DaimlerChrysler*, para. 32.

144 Case C-376/98, EU:C:2000:544 – *Germany v European Parliament and Council (Tobacco Advertising I)*, para. 99.

145 *de Witte*, A Competence to Protect, in Syrpis (ed.), The Judiciary, the Legislature and the EU Internal Market, Cambridge University Press 2012, 36, 36.

146 Art 119(1) and (2) and Art 120 TFEU.

147 Art 170(2) TFEU provides that '[w]*ithin the framework of a system of open and competitive markets, action by the Union shall aim at promoting the interconnection and interoperability of national networks as well as access to such networks. It shall take account in particular of the need to link island, landlocked and peripheral regions with the central regions of the Union*'.

148 *Bourgeois/Tuominen* (n 119), 552.

Against this background, commentators argue that competition is not an end in itself, but rather a means to pursue the objectives listed in Art 9 TFEU. Competition policy and industrial policy are seen as complementary, together forming the framework that provides for the structural conditions necessary for economic success in a globalized economy. Similarly, trade policy cannot be implemented in isolation. Although explicit references to EU trade policy are sparse and somewhat ambiguous, Art 9 TFEU mentions the broad term 'policies'. This necessarily includes trade policy. Moreover, the EU's industrial strategies typically contain elements that are inextricably linked to trade.[149] In sum, it is reasonable to suggest that '[t]*he trade/free competition principle is at the core of* [EU] *law*'.[150]

Overall, '*there are constitutional reasons not to view the EU's competition (...) regime as somehow ring-fenced from the rest of the Treaties' other goals and provisions*'.[151] More specifically, these policy-linking clauses seem to impose horizontal obligations onto the EU institutions to promote and respect policy coherence. More precisely, it is the collective responsibility of the EC to embrace a holistic approach.[152]

II. A New Enforcement Paradigm in the Making?

Approaches to policy implementation and enforcement paradigms are not constant but may change in response to shifts in the political economy. Back in the 1970s, for example, the EC championed a more integrated approach. In its 1970 memorandum on industrial policy, the EC stated that

> [t]here is an urgent need to extend the solidarity of the Community countries to the other fields under public responsibility where international economic rivalry is felt today; these include investment, competition, technology and patents, the object being, as in respect of trade, not to create a closed and inward looking Community but to step up the

149 *Bourgeois/Tuominen* (n 119), 552.
150 *Fox* (n 15), 224.
151 *Wardhaugh* (n 12), 32.
152 *Wardhaugh* (n 12), 32.

efforts to co-operate on equal terms, and therefore profitably, with the large partners outside the Community.[153]

Against this background, the adoption of the 'more economic approach' constitutes somewhat of an outlier and a departure from the decade-long integrated thinking about competition, industrial, and trade policy. Commentators observe that this enforcement paradigm can be traced back to the political economy of the 1980s and in particular the 'Reagan era' in the US, which is characterized by laissez-faire attitudes and pro-business policies.[154]

Today, the most prominent change in the political economy is the rise of Big Tech.[155] Relying solely on likely harm to consumer welfare as a trigger or justification for enforcement action has already proved inadequate in the face of the competitive peculiarities of digital markets.[156] Ibáñez Colomo argues that the move towards the 'more economic approach' in the late 1990s and early 2000s may have been a response to the then pervasive preoccupation with over-enforcement and 'false positives'. This obsession with avoiding enforcement errors began to gradually loosen its grip on the antitrust community in the early 2010s, as many stakeholders came to realize with the benefit of hindsight that the competition disciplines had been subject to regulatory capture by large corporations, on the one hand, and intellectual capture on the other.[157] The '*pro-corporate efficiency paradigm*'[158] that had dominated antitrust thinking had, according to some, failed to deliver the promised economic growth and to address distributional concerns. Indeed, the advocacy of the 'more economic approach' has led enforcement agencies to turn a blind eye to increasing market concentration[159] and has provided corporate lawyers with a seemingly inexhaustible stream of 'efficiency defenses'.[160]

---

153 European Commission, 'The Community's Industrial Policy' (Commission Memorandum to the Council) COM (70) 100 final, 18 March 1970.

154 *Fiebig/Gerber* (n 114), 463; *Caffarra* (n 2).

155 *Fiebig/Gerber* (n 114), 470.

156 *Ibáñez Colomo* (n 105), 68.

157 *Ezrachi* (n 17), 70; *Ibáñez Colomo, New Competition Law* (n 105), 66.

158 *Caffarra/Kilic* (n 2).

159 *Caffarra* (n 132) (observing that the economic principles '*tend to support a pro-incumbent assessment*').

160 *Caffarra* (n 132) (observing that there is '*a proliferation of these exculpatory narratives, as a set of adaptable narratives that economists pull out on request*'); *Caffarra/Kilic* (n 2).

It is suggested that these changes in the political economy have already triggered a paradigm shift in antitrust thinking. This emerging consensus is structured around the idea of 'fairness', abandoning the narrow focus on 'consumer welfare' in strictly economic terms. This new enforcement paradigm also discards 'throughput legitimacy' in favor of 'output legitimacy'. That is, enforcement is endowed with legitimacy based on its ability to help achieve a politically desirable result.[161]

In today's multi-polar, multi-crisis world, the mutually reinforcing relationship between trade and competition could gain traction as another widely recognized shift in the political economy. The nexus between competition and trade policy is particularly evident as they face similar challenges. First, both policies have for a long time been shaped by neoliberal thinking. This neoliberal orientation has led to a 'fetishization' of market efficiency. The 'consumer welfare standard' has become the 'holy grail' of the antitrust community and 'market liberalization' is its trade counterpart.[162] Globalization critics claim that international trade competition and its obsession with market efficiency have led to a race to the bottom in labor and environmental standards. While the antitrust community is moving away from the 'more economic approach' and its focus on allocative efficiency, the trade community is recognizing the need to 'green' international trade and investment agreements and to address concerns about health, biodiversity, and labor standards.[163]

Second, public interest considerations are no longer a 'no-go area' for neither antitrust nor trade lawyers. Antitrust has begun to shed its pro-big business bias and has become more sensitive to distributional issues.[164] Similarly, trade liberalization is increasingly becoming a means to address income inequality and the unequal distribution of economic opportunity, rather than an end in itself.[165]

While a competitive market economy is a necessary condition for companies to grow at home and subsequently succeed abroad, there are two

161 *Ezrachi/Stucke* (n 5), 1; *Ibáñez Colomo* (n 105), 68.

162 *Tai*, 'Connecting Trade, Competition and Industrial Policy: Conversation with Ambassador Katherine Tai' (2024), https://thecapitolforum.com/resources/connecting-trade-competition-and-industrial-policy-conversation-with-ambassador-katherine-tai/ (accessed 22 March 2025).

163 *Tai* (n 162).

164 *Fiebig/Gerber* (n 114), 466 (citing '*deference to big business*' as one of the reasons for the rise of Neo-Brandeisians).

165 *Tai* (n 162).

considerations that challenge this conventional wisdom. First, because of global value chains and just-in-time manufacturing, cartels, oligopolies, or monopolies in one part of the world can disproportionately affect global trade patterns and markets elsewhere. Second, private undertakings have to compete with state-owned or state-financed undertakings. This poses unprecedented challenges for competition, trade, and investment policies. It also raises, amongst others, the question of whether otherwise anticompetitive mergers should be allowed to enable the creation of 'National Champions' to enhance the competitiveness of the national economy.[166]

As discussed above, trade and competition are two sides of the same coin. Enforcement agencies in the EU and the US have woken up to the fact that lax antitrust enforcement has led to unprecedented levels of market concentration. At the same time, the cherished notion that domestic dominant companies should be allowed to do as they please in order to fend off foreign (i.e., mostly Chinese) competitors has been called into question: Having to put up with foreign dominant undertakings does not support the proposition that domestic dominant undertakings should be allowed to abuse their market power at home.[167] New structuring principles such as 'fairness' suggest that antitrust is no longer just about efficiency in purely economic terms. Enforcement agencies on both sides of the Atlantic are eager to tackle market concentration and the undue exercise of market power by dominant undertakings in order to counter corporate and related political dominance.[168]

This anti-monopoly agenda cannot be successfully implemented without a complementary trade policy. In other words, trade policy must not be designed in such a way as to torpedo and negate domestic antitrust policy by continuing to allow large multinational corporations to do as they please. For decades, trade liberalization has aided and abetted the expansion of corporate power from domestic to foreign markets. The '*idolization of*

166 *Behboodi* (n 42), 146.

167 *Caffarra*, 'Antitrust and the Political Economy: Part 1' *VOXEU COLUMN* (2024), https://cepr.org/voxeu/columns/antitrust-and-political-economy-part-1 (accessed 22 March 2025).

168 *Teachout/Khan*, Market Structure and Political Law: A Taxonomy of Power, 9 Duke Journal of Constitutional Law & Public Policy (2014), 37, 69 (claiming that '*market power is political power*').

market efficiency'[169] has rigged the rules of global trade to the benefit of already dominant market players and industrialized economies.[170]

The rise of anti-monopoly thinking can be traced back to the so-called 'Neo-Brandeisian movement' in US antitrust. The ideas of the Neo-Brandeisians are more radical than those of the post-Chicago scholars. Whereas the post-Chicago movement argued that economic theory should guide antitrust enforcement, the Neo-Brandeisian movement rejects the normative role of economic theory as a determining factor. They do not call for a complete abandonment of the use of economic tools in antitrust. Rather, proponents argue for a more restrained use of economic analysis. According to the Neo-Brandeisian view, existing law is a mirror of existing social power structures. The choice of economic thinking to guide US antitrust is therefore anything but apolitical. Some proponents of the Neo-Brandeisian school of thought go so far as to argue that antitrust should be an instrument for advancing non-economic policy goals.[171]

The cross-fertilization between competition and trade policy and law is evidenced by the adoption of several 'hybrid' instruments. International trade considerations are increasingly being injected into areas previously addressed only by EU State aid and merger control legislation, and vice versa. For example, the Foreign Subsidies Regulation[172] is based on the EU's exclusive trade competence under Art 207 TFEU and, to the extent that it '*might affect the right of establishment and the free movement of goods and services within the Union*',[173] the shared internal market competence under Art 114 TFEU, while having several features that make it reminiscent of more traditional competition law instruments.[174] Its procedure and institutional set-up are similar to those under state aid and competition law. Under the Foreign Subsidies Regulation, there is a system of pre-notification and subsequent investigation by the EC, as well as the possibility for the EC

169 *Tai* (n 162).

170 *Tai* (n 162).

171 *Fiebig/Gerber* (n 114), 477.

172 Regulation (EU) 2022/2560 of the European Parliament and of the Council of 14 December 2022 on foreign subsidies distorting the internal market [2022] OJ L330/1.

173 European Commission, Proposal for a Regulation of the European Parliament and the Council on Foreign Subsidies Distorting the Internal Market, COM (2021) 223 final, 5 May 2021.

174 For a discussion on the choice of legal basis for the Foreign Subsidies Regulation, see *Smela Wolski*, Legal Basis for the Proposal for a Regulation on Foreign Subsidies Distorting the Internal Market, 21 European State Aid Law Quarterly (2022) 153, 159.

to initiate investigations on its own initiative.[175] The mere fact that several features of the Foreign Subsidies Regulation suggest that it is a competition law instrument does not, of course, have a decisive impact on the choice of legal basis. Rather, the choice of legal basis in EU law is subject to objective factors that are amenable to judicial review, including the aim and content of the measure.[176] Where a measure pursues two objectives or has two components, the 'center of gravity test' will normally serve as a means of identifying the main or predominant objective or component and thus a single legal basis.[177] However, where a measure simultaneously pursues several objectives or has several components which are inextricably linked, without one being incidental to the other, such a measure will exceptionally have to be based on different corresponding legal bases.[178]

Similarly, the International Procurement Instrument[179] is based on the EU's exclusive trade competence under Art 207 TFEU. However, the instrument essentially addresses competition concerns. It aims to 'level the playing field' by regulating the access of third-country economic operators, goods, and services seeking access to EU public procurement or concession markets.[180]

III. How to 'Remarry' Competition and Trade

Record levels of concentration in certain markets suggest that the choice of economic efficiency as the polestar in trade and competition may have been a wolf in sheep's clothing. A 'more integrated approach' is needed, both in terms of substance and institutions. In terms of substance, policymakers need to pursue their trade, competition, and industrial policy agenda more holistically in order to meet the current geopolitical challenges. This

175 *Blockx/Mattiolo*, The Foreign Subsidies Regulation: Calling Foul While Upping the Ante? 28 European Foreign Affairs Review (2023), 53, 58.

176 Case C-155/07, EU:C:2008:605 – *Parliament v Council*, para. 34.

177 *Parliament v Council*, para. 35.

178 *Parliament v Council*, para. 36.

179 Regulation (EU) 2022/1031 of the European Parliament and of the Council of 23 June 2022 on the access of third-country economic operators, goods and services to the Union's public procurement and concession markets and procedures supporting negotiations on access of Union economic operators, goods and services to the public procurement and concession markets of third countries [2022] OJ L173/1.

180 *Dawar*, The EU 2022 International Procurement Regulation Enters in to Force Reciprocity, 57 The Journal of World Investment & Trade (2023), 139, 155.

requires a more integrated approach to policymaking and enforcement that takes into account the interactions and mutually reinforcing dynamics between these policy areas. This will ensure that trade, competition, and industrial policy are not just about lower prices, but also about building a more democratic society and creating a level playing field that allows the economies of the Global South to catch up.[181]

In terms of institutions, authorities need to be able to pool their expertise and capabilities and must take measures to counteract silo mentality. This does not necessarily mean rationalizing and consolidating enforcement authorities. Rather, it is sufficient to find ways to institutionalize coordination. At the international level, this means that the International Competition Network, an already existing global body dedicated exclusively to competition law enforcement, could establish a working group on the interaction between trade and competition law and its impact on enforcement. Alternatively, new international agreements under the auspices of the WTO or other multilateral or bilateral agreements should provide for a structure that allows competition authorities and trade authorities to establish and uphold a smooth dialogue. This close integration would allow them to share information, identify hybrid and disguised competitive restrictions, and initiate joint enforcement action.[182]

F. Conclusion

Calling for a 'more integrated approach' to policy implementation and enforcement does not mean that competition law should be subordinated to strategic trade policy or used to address all of the EU's strategic vulnerabilities. Indeed, this paper does not mean to suggest that geopolitical considerations should be integrated into substantive competition law without a clear legal basis. The more considerations are taken into account, the greater the risk of 'muddying the waters' and making the objectives of EU competition law murky. As Easterbrook notes, '[w]*hen everything is relevant, nothing is dispositive*'.[183]

It would be misguided to suggest that competition law is a universal panacea that should address each and every policy issue. Competition en-

181 *Caffarra/Kilic* (n 2).

182 See already *Fox* (n 124), 279.

183 *Easterbrook*, The Limits of Antitrust, 63 Texas Law Review (1984), 1, 12.

forcement is not always appropriate for trade policy interventions. Where a particular action has a clear trade focus, the appropriate response is to adopt trade measures. For example, in international trade, dumping and unfair subsidies – which often resemble illegal practices under EU competition rules – can harm domestic producers. Dumping is similar to predatory pricing by exporters, and imports often benefit from government subsidies. As a result, domestic companies seek protection from foreign competition. However, competition law, which typically aims to protect the competitive process and is not designed for extraterritorial application, may not be the appropriate tool to address this issue. Instead, the use of trade remedies, such as anti-dumping and countervailing measures, may be more appropriate.[184]

Calling for a 'more integrated approach' means alerting the competent authorities to the link between trade, competition, and industrial policy. Indeed, former Competition Commissioner Vestager said that she did '*not see the competition portfolio as a lonely portfolio. On the contrary, competition is central to the things we want to create both in and for Europe*'.[185] Similarly, Draghi notes that there is a '*lack of coordination across policies*' at the EU level and observes that '[i]*ndustrial policies today (...) comprise multi-policy strategies, combining fiscal policies to incentivize domestic production, trade policies to penalize anti-competitive behavior abroad and foreign economic policies to secure supply chains*'.[186] Against this background, it may be time to reconsider the existing competition law enforcement paradigm. A recalibrated approach should be more sensitive to trade and perhaps even industrial policy considerations. This may involve a reassessment of how to deal with 'European Champions' or rather the lack thereof, a more rigorous enforcement approach to 'killer acquisitions', and the consideration of concerns related to foreign direct investment, foreign subsidies falling outside the WTO framework, and strategic value chain considerations. The EU has already started to promote greater policy coherence and integration

184 *Bourgeois*, Antitrust and Trade Policy: Peaceful Coexistence – European Community Perspective, 17 International Business Lawyer (1989), 58, 61.

185 *Vestager*, 'Hearing of the Commissioner-Designate for Competition Margrethe Vestager before the European Parliament' (2014), https://multimedia.europarl.europa.eu/en/video/hearing-of-margrethe-vestager-denmark-commissioner-designate-for-competition-extracts-from-the-statement-by-margrethe-vestager_I093061 (accessed 22 March 2025).

186 *Draghi* (n 1), 12.

through, for example, the adoption of the Foreign Subsidies Regulation and the International Procurement Instrument.[187]

In the US, there were also signs of greater awareness of the link between trade, competition, and industrial policy under the Biden administration. In October 2023, the US Trade Representative ('USTR') decided to withdraw the US from the WTO negotiations on electronic commerce. These negotiations were aimed at establishing international disciplines to protect cross-border data flows, prohibit data localization mandates, and protect US source code from compulsory disclosure to foreign governments. Unsurprisingly, this decision was met with disapproval by Big Tech, as it potentially deprives these companies of the ability to generate even greater revenues from data flows. This suggests that the USTR and the US competition authorities were indeed talking to each other in an effort to align US foreign trade policy with the '*trust-busting*'[188] agenda of competition policy at home.[189]

187 *Majcher*, '"Open Strategic Autonomy": Towards the Geopoliticisation of EU Competition Law?' *Kluwer Competition Law Blog* (2020), https://competitionlawblog.kluwercompetitionlaw.com/2020/11/20/open-strategic-autonomy-towards-the-geopoliticisation-of-eu-competition-law/ (accessed 22 March 2025).

188 The original 'trust busting' policy was pursued by former US President Theodore Roosevelt who revived the then defunct US Sherman Act by bringing suit against the Northern Securities Company and 43 other major corporations. See *Cooper*, 'The Square Deal of Theodore Roosevelt', *Encyclopedia Britannica* (2024), https://www.britannica.com/biography/Theodore-Roosevelt/The-Square-Deal (accessed 18 March 2025).

189 *Caffarra* (n 2); *Caffarra/Kilic* (n 2).

Competition law as *'a continuation of policy with other means'*? The application of the Foreign Subsidies Regulation to concentrations

*Pierfrancesco Mattiolo**

A. Introduction

The Foreign Subsidies Regulation (Regulation (EU) 2022/2560, hereafter 'FSR' or 'the Regulation')[1] is one of the tools that has been developed by the EU as part of its shift to the paradigm of 'open strategic autonomy'.[2] As Ursula von der Leyen assumed the office of President of the European Commission for the first time in 2019, her 'geopolitical commission' was tasked with reviewing EU trade policy to account for the different political and economic conditions.[3] Its new trade policy was 'open, sustainable, and assertive':[4] the EU remains committed to multilateralism and willing to trade with everyone, while developing new autonomous tools to enforce multilateral and bilateral agreements and better defend its economy from aggressive trade practices, such as subsidies. The FSR represents the autonomous 'third-best option' for addressing subsidy-related imbalances in the global trade system – since fully open solutions do not seem politically viable.[5] Stemming from trade considerations, the FSR has nevertheless

* PhD Candidate and a Graduate Teaching and Research Assistant in European and International Economic Law at the University of Antwerp, Belgium.

1 Regulation (EU) 2022/2560 of the European Parliament and of the Council of 14 December 2022 on foreign subsidies distorting the internal market (FSR) [2022] OJ L330/1.

2 *Mattiolo*, Concordia discors? The Foreign Subsidies Regulation and increased subsidization in the EU under the open strategic autonomy model, in Fechter/Wiesenthal (eds.), The Age of Open Strategic Autonomy (2025), 157, 157–161.

3 *Mattiolo*, A new phase of geopolitical merger control? On the foreign subsidies regulation and other recent developments in EU (geo)economic law, in Idriz/Kassoti/Larik (eds.), The legal implications of the EU's geopolitical awakening (2025), 17, 19.

4 European Commission, 'Trade policy review: an open, sustainable and assertive trade policy' (Communication) COM(2021) 66 final.

5 Ministry of Economic Affairs and Climate Policy of the Netherlands, 'Dutch government assessment of White Paper on foreign subsidies' (Contribution to the public

found its place in the toolbox administered by the Directorate-General for Competition (DG COMP).

Subsidies represent a 'growing source of trade tensions'[6] and have been on the rise in the last years among the G20 economies and, especially, the three larger economies: the US, China and the EU.[7] While China dominates the FSR unofficial narrative, driving its conception and perhaps enforcement as the main granter of foreign subsidies, European companies may have also to face the unintended consequences of the 'friendly fire', namely the US Inflation Reduction Act (IRA).[8] Interestingly, as we will see, most of the FSR very first cases are in 'green' sectors, the same ones that the Biden Administration wanted to bolster on American soil via the IRA. The protection of these sectors from Chinese competition appears necessary, to both the EU and the US, not only for their increasing economic relevance, but also for strategic purposes, so as to reduce dependence on a 'rival' in key sectors and, in a broader perspective, 'de-risking'.[9]

If 2019 marked a paradigm shift for EU trade policy in the face of geoeconomic upheaval,[10] it was also a significant year for competition policy, though for almost the opposite reason. When presented with the Siemens-Alstom acquisition, the Commission prohibited it, deeming it potentially harmful to competition,[11] notwithstanding political pressure from the French and German governments. The decision, published in February 2019, sparked a lively debate on whether competition law was hindering the creation of 'European champions' capable of competing with larger US and Chinese companies—and whether such champions were desirable. One of the 'geoeconomic' arguments raised by the critics of the *Siemens-Alstom* decision was that the Commission did not consider the challenge posed

---

consultation on the White Paper on Foreign Subsidies) (2020), 1–2 https://ec.europa.eu/info/law/better-regulation/have-your-say/initiatives/12452-White-Paper-on-Foreign-Subsidies/public-consultation_en (accessed 4 August 2024).

6 *Evenett/Fritz*, Subsidies and Market Access: Towards an Inventory of Corporate Subsidies by China, the European Union and the United States, CEPR Press 2021, 12–19.

7 *Evenett/Fritz* (n 6), 12–15.

8 Public Law 117–169 – An act to provide for reconciliation pursuant to title II of S. Con. Res. 14 (Inflation Reduction Act).

9 *Brinza et al*, EU-China relations: De-risking or de-coupling – the future of the EU strategy towards China, EPRS Study PE 754.446 (2024), 1–2.

10 *Mattiolo* (n 3), 18–21.

11 *Siemens/Alstom* (Case M.8677) Commission Decision [2019] OJ C/2019/300.

by Chinese train makers backed by subsidies, in particular CRRC.[12] As of today, the rules remain unchanged, and the debate continues, as evidenced by proposals in favour of greater consolidation in the two reports authored by Enrico Letta and Mario Draghi on the future of the internal market[13] and European competitiveness,[14] respectively. Even so, there is still no consensus on reforming merger control to account for external competition.

In short, from 2019 up to today, the EU has been looking at its policies, including competition, through this 'geopolitical lens' more and more. As put by President von der Leyen herself in the Mission Letter to Executive Vice-President-designate Teresa Ribera, 'competition policy should also reflect the growing importance of resilience in the face of geopolitical [...] threats [...] and of unfair competition through subsidies'.[15] Political and strategic considerations joined purely economic rationales in the design and enforcement of EU tools. This shift influenced the FSR's objectives as well, extending beyond restoring the 'level playing field' to include deterring foreign penetration into the European economy and preventing the offshore relocation of production and technology through mergers and acquisitions supported by foreign subsidies.[16] As this chapter argues, the FSR complements traditional EU competition law tools, i.e. State aid rules and merger control, to include issues that those tools could not, by design and long-standing practice, address.

In the broader context of this volume, the 'big question' that this contribution raises is whether competition law has become – borrowing a

---

12 *De Vries/De Best*, The Emergence of the Foreign Subsidies Regulation, 1 Mededingingsrecht in de Praktijk (2024), 14, 14.

13 *Letta*, 'Much more than a market' (Report) (2024) https://www.consilium.europa.eu/media/ny3j24sm/much-more-than-a-market-report-by-enrico-letta.pdf (accessed 10 January 2025).

14 *Draghi*, 'The future of European competitiveness – A competitiveness strategy for Europe' (Report) (2024) https://commission.europa.eu/document/download/97e481fd-2dc3-412d-be4c-f152a8232961_en?filename=The%20future%20of%20European%20competitiveness%20_%20A%20competitiveness%20strategy%20for%20Europe.pdf (accessed 25 October 2024).

15 Von der Leyen/European Commission, 'Mission Letter to Teresa Ribera Rodríguez, Executive Vice-President-designate for a Clean, Just and Competitive Transition' (Mission Letter to Commissioner-designate) (2024), 5 https://commission.europa.eu/document/download/4047c277-f608-48d1-8800-dcf0405d76e8_en?filename=Mission%20letter%20-%20%C5%A0EF%C4%8COVI%C4%8C.pdf (accessed 25 September 2024).

16 European Commission, 'White Paper on levelling the playing field as regards foreign subsidies' (White Paper), COM(2020) 253 final, 7.

famous quote of Prussian military thinker Carl von Clausewitz, and moving from warfare to *lawfare* – 'a mere continuation of policy with other means' ('...*eine bloße Fortsetzung der Politik mit anderen Mitteln*'). The term 'policy' could also be changed with 'politics' as a translation of the German *Politik* – notwithstanding the ignorance of the author when it comes to the German language. The key issue is that, while law is expected to pursue a predetermined set of goals, through predetermined procedures and powers, under the pretence of legal certainty and objectivity, these expectations may be bent by this political turn The fact that the second von der Leyen Commission expressed its willingness to 'vigorously enforce the Foreign Subsidies Regulation, including by proactively mapping the most problematic practices that could lead to competition distortions',[17] makes investigating the FSR's boundaries even more relevant.

This chapter examines the FSR, with a particular focus on its procedure for mergers and acquisitions. It explores the Commission's capacity to oversee transactions involving foreign entities by comparing the FSR's framework with that of Regulation (EC) 139/2004 (the EU Merger Regulation, or EUMR). This analysis seeks to determine how these regulatory instruments interact and whether the FSR is more capable of incorporating both economic and other policy considerations. Additionally, the study investigates the relationship between the FSR and Foreign Direct Investment (FDI) Screening, a mechanism primarily managed by Member States with limited EU-level coordination. The intersection of these regulatory tools is particularly interesting, as the FSR could play a role in scrutinising investments from companies with ties to foreign governments – albeit from a radically different perspective. Given that a single transaction may be subject to scrutiny under multiple legal regimes, this raises concerns for investors. To illustrate these complexities, the case of the Chinese company CNRC's acquisition of a stake in the Italian firm Pirelli in 2015 will be examined. This discussion ultimately seeks to determine whether EU competition law is evolving to protect new strategic interests or whether legal principles are yielding to broader political considerations.

17 Von der Leyen/European Commission (n 15), 7.

B. The FSR: a refresher

The FSR establishes three procedures – one general *ex officio* and two special ones, respectively for concentrations and public procurement – and a set of common provisions. The Regulation was integrated by an Implementing Regulation 2023/1441, which defined further rules on notifications and procedure.[18]

I. Notions: foreign subsidy, distortion

Article 3(1) of the Regulation defines a foreign subsidy as a 'financial contribution' granted by a third country directly or indirectly, which confers a benefit selectively on one or more undertakings active in the internal market. Readers versed in competition and trade law may recall, respectively, the similar notion of State aid in Article 107 of the Treaty on the Functioning of the European Union (TFEU)[19] and some elements of the ASCM's industrial subsidy.[20] To define a financial contribution, Article 3(2) provides a non-exhaustive list of operations that would fall under the scope of the Regulation, based on their object and subject. On this latter aspect, the FSR targets subsidies given either by a foreign government or a private enterprise that may be under its influence.

Foreign subsidies are not unwelcome per se, but only when they generate or may generate a 'distortion', as defined in Article 4, so by improving the position of one undertaking active in the internal market, affecting negatively, the competition in the internal market.[21] The Commission verifies the existence of or the potential for a distortion using the parameters indicated by Article 4(1), or by detecting one of the subsidies that are presumed by the Regulation as 'unlikely'[22] or 'most likely distortive'.[23] By January

18 Commission Implementing Regulation (EU) 2023/1441 of 10 July 2023 on detailed arrangements for the conduct of proceedings by the Commission pursuant to Regulation (EU) 2022/2560 of the European Parliament and of the Council on foreign subsidies distorting the internal market (FSR Implementing Regulation) [2023] OJ L177/1.

19 Consolidated Version of the Treaty on the Functioning of the European Union (TFEU) [2012] OJ C326/47, Art. 107.

20 *Mattiolo* (n 3), 27–28.

21 The FSR's distortion mirrors the same concept in TFEU Art. 107.

22 FSR Art. 4(2).

23 FSR Art. 5.

2026, in line with Article 46, the Commission should publish guidelines to clarify which criteria and indicators are used to determine an improvement in the competitive position of the subsidised undertaking and a negative effect on competition, whether potential or actual, in the internal market.[24]

II. Procedures and participation of private parties

When the Commission learns of a potentially distortive foreign subsidy, it can start an *ex officio* procedure. In the case of concentrations and public tenders, their two specialised procedure may be started upon notification from the concerned undertaking, unless such operations fail to meet the thresholds and requisites of the two specialised procedures. In those cases, or when the notification is not performed, the Commission can still act *ex officio*.[25] The FSR does not provide for third parties to formally act as complainants – the initiative is always taken by the Commission *motu proprio*. However, the Commission can receive 'any information'[26] from private parties about a potentially distortive subsidy and choose to launch an investigation.[27,28]

The three procedures share a common structure, articulated in two phases. In the first phase, the 'preliminary review', the Commission considers whether a foreign subsidy and a distortion under the FSR exist.[29] If both conditions are satisfied, the procedure moves to phase two and an 'in-depth investigation' is started. The Commission informs the concerned undertaking and then publishes a summary notice in the Official Journal, allowing interested third parties and companies to provide additional information

---

24 European Commission, 'Call for evidence for the Foreign Subsidies Guidelines' (Call for Evidence) Ref. Ares(2025)1757107, 2.

25 *Hornkohl*, The EU Foreign Subsidy Regulation – What, Why and How?, in Hillebrand Pohl et al (eds), Weaponising Investments II, Springer Nature Switzerland 2024, 1, 18–19.

26 FSR Art. 35(2).

27 *Hornkohl*, The role of third parties in the enforcement of the Foreign Subsidies Regulation: complaints, participation, judicial review and private enforcement, 8 Competition Law & Policy Debate (2023), 30, 35–36.

28 *Carlier/Mattiolo*, 'The Foreign Subsidies Regulation – One Year in Review: Challenges and Ways Ahead?' (*CELIS Institute Blog*, 13 December 2024) https://www.celis.institute/posts-celis-2019/the-foreign-subsidies-regulation-one-year-in-review-challenges-and-ways-ahead/ (accessed 17 March 2025).

29 FSR Art. 10.

on the distortive subsidy or on its eventual positive effects.[30] During the investigation, it may impose *interim* measures to avoid an 'irreparable damage to competition on the internal market'.[31,32]

III. Possible outcomes

Within 18 months after the start of the in-depth investigation, the Commission adopts a decision, either with redressive measures or no objections. The available redressive measures are not fully defined by the Regulation, which provides only a non-exhaustive list of examples in Article 7(4). In this regard, the FSR and State aid law differ significantly. The primary remedy in State aid practice is the repayment of aid to the granting Member State, with other measures used only in exceptional circumstances.[33] By contrast, it may be difficult to monitor the recovery of a foreign subsidy – although not impossible, as the Commission can still accept it as a commitment from the undertaking if it can verify that the recovery has occurred.[34]

Some of these suggested remedies, such as the obligation to offer access to newly acquired infrastructure, license assets or publish R&D results,[35] may serve both the traditional purposes of competition law – ensuring fair competition and protecting consumer welfare – and, indirectly, strategic considerations, such as ensuring that key infrastructure and technological assets do not fall into the hands of foreign agents. Outside Article 7's list, the Commission may deploy measures from other fields of EU law, such as competition law, if compatible with the FSR's rules and situations. Fines too can be used only in certain cases under the FSR, while they are a key weapon of antitrust law. Fines are provided by the FSR to punish misconduct or negligence by the undertaking during the investigation;[36] or, for concentrations, when the undertaking fails to notify a notifiable

30 *Hornkohl* (n 27), 36–37.

31 FSR Art. 12.

32 *Mattiolo* (n 3), 29–30.

33 *Hornkohl*, Protecting the Internal Market from subsidisation with the EU State aid regime and the Foreign Subsidies Regulation: two sides of the same coin, 14 Journal of European Competition Law & Practice (2023), 137, 149.

34 FSR Art. 7(6).

35 FSR Art. 7(4).

36 FSR Art. 17.

concentration or implements the concentration before receiving clearance from the Commission (the so-called 'gun jumping'). Similar to Article 14(2) EUMR, Article 26(3) FSR allows for a fine of up to 10 % of the turnover. An undertaking may also avoid a decision with redressing measures by offering commitments suitable to address the distortion. The Commission may accept and make such commitments binding via decision.[37,38]

IV. The balancing test: the Commission's discretion in 'considering other positive effects'

If the subsidy is found to be distortive, under Article 6(1) the Commission *may* conduct a 'balancing test' between its positive and negative effects during the in-depth investigation.[39] The formulation of Article 6(1) frames the balancing test as a discretionary exercise by the Commission, although the following paragraph states the Commission '*shall* take into account the assessment'[40] of Article 6(1) when it adopts redressive measures or accepts commitments. Article 6(2) seems to require the Commission to perform the balancing test before limiting the rights of the undertaking, but the scope of this obligation remains unclear. In any case, the balancing test can only lead to a more favourable decision for the undertaking: either a decision with no objections, more lenient measures or less stringent commitments.[41] For this reason, if the Commission had full discretion to choose whether or not to perform the balancing test before adopting an unfavourable decision, this could lead to inconsistent treatment, with some companies missing the opportunity for a more favourable decision. The upcoming Guidelines will clarify how Article 6 is applied by the Commission, and the positive effects that are considered.[42] The publication of a final decision by the Commission may also provide clarity, as it should outline the reasoning behind its balancing in such decisions:[43] as of March 2025, the first case closed after

37 FSR Art. 7(2).

38 *Mattiolo* (n 3), 31.

39 *Hornkohl*, The EU Foreign Subsidy Regulation – What, Why and How?, in Hillebrand Pohl et al (eds), Weaponising Investments II, Springer Nature Switzerland 2024, 1, 21–22.

40 FSR Art. 6(2).

41 FSR Recital 21.

42 European Commission (n 24), 2.

43 FSR Recital 21.

an in-depth investigation, e&-PPF Telecom (discussed in paragraph C.I.3), resulted in a decision with commitments, but the Commission has still to make the decision public and its press release made no mention of the balancing test.[44]

Moving back to Article 6(1), the balancing test is performed 'on the basis of information received', as also illustrated by Recital 21.[45] The Commission considers the positive effects demonstrated by the evidence provided by the Member States and private parties,[46] and the investigated undertaking.[47] In the test, the negative effects – i.e., the distortion – are balanced against the positive ones. If the Commission is investigating a most likely distortion under Article 5(1), the Recital states that 'positive effects are less likely to outweigh negative effects' – perhaps, a presumption that may be overcome by the Commission itself or rebutted by the undertaking.

But what positive effects does the Commission consider? The Regulation prioritises[48] the 'development of the relevant subsidised economic activity on the internal market'. Indeed, the negative and positive economic effects are balanced '*while* considering other positive effects'; and these 'other positive effects' relate to 'relevant policy objectives, in particular those of the Union'.[49] This current formulation of what is considered in the FSR balancing test appears to be a middle ground between the even broader 'EU interest test', originally proposed in the White Paper on levelling the playing field as regards foreign subsidies,[50] and the purely economic balancing included in the Draft FSR Regulation.[51][52]

The Guidelines to be published by January 2026 will probably clarify the range of positive effects that may be considered by the Commission. Until then, the indications left by the Commission must suffice. Recital 21 states that 'other positive effects should be taken into account, where

44 European Commission, 'Commission Conditionally Approves the Acquisition of Parts of PPF Telecom by E&, under the Foreign Subsidies Regulation' (Press release) IP/24/4842 https://ec.europa.eu/commission/presscorner/detail/en/ip_24_4842 (accessed 25 November 2024).

45 *Hornkohl* (n 39), 11.

46 FSR Recital 21.

47 *Hornkohl* (n 39), 12.

48 *Hornkohl* (n 39), 12.

49 FSR Art 6(1).

50 European Commission, 'White Paper on levelling the playing field as regards foreign subsidies' (White Paper), COM(2020) 253 final, 7.

51 *Hornkohl* (n 39), 13–14.

52 *Mattiolo* (n 3), 28.

appropriate, in order to avoid that the balancing gives rise to unjustified discrimination'. By mentioning this hypothetical discrimination, the Recital implies that the FSR balancing test should reasonably lead to the same outcome as another similar tool – State aid, most probably. The Recital goes on to cite environmental and social protection, as well as the promotion of research and development, as examples of policy objectives under which positive effects may be recognised – objectives that also constitute grounds for justification under State aid law. The Commission provided further elaboration in the initial clarifications published in July 2024, adding that it considers 'more generally [...] certain positive effects on the internal market [...] acknowledged under the EU State aid rules'.[53] In other words, the FSR balancing test should remain consistent with State aid practice, and undertakings and professionals may find further guidance there on how Article 6 operates. Finally, the fact that the Commission looks 'in particular' to the policy objectives 'of the Union' raises two further questions. Will the FSR balancing test consider EU objectives that have never been considered in State aid practices? What role, if any, do the commendable policy objectives of the third country providing the subsidy play?

To summarise, the boundaries of the balancing test remain unclear and are of great interest to practitioners and scholars. The Commission enjoys broad discretion in balancing a wide range of positive effects. The current uncertainties are partially alleviated by the fact that the balancing test can only result in a more favourable outcome for the undertaking. Based on the methodology used and the policy objectives pursued by the Commission, Article 6 has the potential to 'continue other policies by means of competition law.'

53 European Commission, 'Initial clarifications on the application of Article 4(1), Article 6 and Article 27(1) of Regulation (EU) 2022/2560 on foreign subsidies distorting the internal market' (Commission Staff Working Document) SWD(2024) 201 final, 6.

C. The FSR concentrations procedure and its interaction with merger control

I. The concentrations procedure

1. A tool to gather data and inform other policies?

Under Article 20 of the FSR, a concentration occurs when a merger, an acquisition or a full-function joint venture produce 'a change of control on a lasting basis'. This concentration becomes notifiable if two thresholds are surpassed: (i) at least one of the merging companies, the target of the acquisition or the joint venture is established in the Union and generates an aggregate EU turnover of at least € 500 million; (ii) the financial contributions received by all the involved companies from third countries,[54] in the three years before the start of the acquisition process, are below € 50 million.[55] According to the FSR's letter, and as confirmed by the Commission itself,[56] an undertaking must notify all financial contributions *ex* Article 3(2) and not foreign subsidies *ex* Article 3(1). Compared to a bare financial contribution, a foreign subsidy must also confer a benefit and be selective to fall in the FSR scope. In other words, a company should notify also contributions provided on market terms that do not confer a benefit in an FSR sense and non-selective measures,[57] like the lowering of general corporate taxes[58]. This provision makes the scope of notifiable concentrations much broader than the scope of the foreign subsidies incompatible with the FSR. Consequently, the amount of notifiable operations may be much higher than the amount of operations that fall in the general, yet narrower, scope of Art. 3(2) and that may lead to an FSR procedure. Additionally, Article 20 does not mention distortion, so non-distortive financial contributions also concur with the threshold.[59] This is less surprising since it is up to

54 Financial contributions from multiple foreign countries can concur to meet the second threshold for a single concentration.

55 FSR Art. 20(3).

56 Directorate-General for Competition of the European Commission, 'Competition FSR Brief – Issue 1' (2024), 2 https://competition-policy.ec.europa.eu/document/download/22197012-2036-4b1e-8b02-0eb8b2d6e666_en?filename=kdar24001enn_competition_FSR_brief_1_2024_100-days-of-FSR-notification-obligation.pdf (accessed 1 August 2024).

57 Directorate-General for Competition of the European Commission (n 56), 2.

58 *Hornkohl* (n 39), 25–26.

59 *Bauermeister*, A Tool to Investigate M&A Transactions with Regard to Foreign Financial Contributions, 25 Zeitschrift für europarechtliche Studien (2022), 477, 483.

the Commission to determine, during its investigation, if a financial contribution qualifies as a foreign subsidy and may produce a distortion.

A possible explanation for the different calibration of Articles 3 and 20 is that, by broadening the scope of the notification obligation, the Commission wants to gather more information and ensure that no potential foreign subsidy goes undetected. The Commission considers in its assessment only those subsidies that may have distorted the concentration specifically; all other financial contributions included in the notification could be used for other purposes, such as another FSR procedure or under other trade defence tools. After all, the lack of transparency and data on foreign industrial subsidies is one of the EU's grievances towards the WTO framework,[60] so the FSR could become a source of useful information for planning policies and enforcement in other areas, such as trade defence.[61] For undertakings, sometimes organised across the globe and in hundreds of subsidiaries, complying with the notification requirement may represent quite a cost: in terms of administrative burden, but also disclosure of sensitive information to the European watchdog.

2. The notification: obligations and first data

Undertakings must notify the Commission of a concentration which satisfies the aforementioned thresholds prior to their implementation.[62] If the undertaking does not comply with the notification obligation, the Commission can start an *ex officio* procedure or order the notification.[63] As with the EUMR,[64] companies can pre-notify the concentration and dialogue with the Commission so as to make sure that the formal notification is correctly filed.[65] To do so, the undertaking requests the Commission to allocate a specific team to their case (in the jargon of the Commission's FSR unit, case team allocation request, CTAR). A CTAR may not necessarily result in a formal notification, as the pre-notification dialogue may reveal

60 *Blockx/Mattiolo*, The Foreign Subsidies Regulation: Calling Foul While Upping the Ante?, 28 European Foreign Affairs Review (2023), 53, 72.
61 *Mattiolo* (n 3), 32–33.
62 FSR Art. 21.
63 FSR Art. 21(4).
64 Council Regulation (EC) No 139/2004 of 20 January 2004 on the control of concentrations between undertakings (EUMR) [2004] OJ L24/1.
65 FSR Implementing Regulation, Annex I para. 8.

that the concentration is not notifiable.[66] To submit the formal notification, the company files a 'notification form of a concentration', or Form FS-CO, which was included by the Commission in Annex I to the FSR Implementing Regulation. The form asks for all the information necessary for the Commission to verify if the concentration meets the thresholds and determine the impacts on the internal market.[67]

After the notification, the concentration cannot be implemented during a standstill period that lasts until the expiration of its terms or a favourable decision by the Commission.[68] As mentioned before, 'gun-jumping' may result in a fine of up to 10 % of the aggregate turnover and the dissolution of the concentration, if the investigation has a negative outcome. The standstill period allows the Commission to investigate the concentration, following the two-phase procedure (preliminary review, then in-depth investigation). The preliminary review may not reveal sufficient elements to move to the in-depth phase: in that case, the Commission simply informs the notifying companies of the end of the preliminary review, without adopting a decision, so that the parties can proceed with the concentration at the end of the standstill period (25 working days).[69] The final decision, after the in-depth investigation, can accept commitments, clear the transaction (no-objection decision) or prohibit it.[70] In other words, the only redressive measure available is the 'nuclear option': stopping the acquisition. So, the Commission's powers are somewhat less diverse at the end of the concentrations procedure, as compared to the *ex officio* review. This choice, which mirrors the EUMR,[71] may be explained by the fact that different redressive measures may render the concentration unpalatable to the undertakings and require the companies to drastically reconsider the operation. The Commission may still accept the commitments offered spontaneously by the undertaking.

Between the entry into force of the FSR and the end of January 2024, so in a little more than three months, the Commission has already received

66 Directorate-General for Competition of the European Commission (n 56), 1–2.
67 FSR Implementing Regulation, Annex I.
68 FSR Art. 24–25.
69 Directorate-General for Competition of the European Commission (n 56), 2.
70 FSR Art. 25 (3).
71 *Hornkohl* (n 39), 28–29.

and started processing 53 pre-notifications,[72] way more than the expected 33 cases per year foreseen in the FSR Impact Assessment.[73]

Cases analysed by the Commission under the FSR concentrations procedure in the first 100 days of enforcement.

Total cases pre-notified to the Commission (CTARs)	53
Cases formally notified	14
Cases fully assessed by the Commission	9
In-depth investigation started	0
Procedure interrupted since the notifying parties decided to not proceed with the transaction	1
Cross-border EU-non-EU transaction	33
Cross-border transaction within the EU	7
Cross-border transaction outside the EU	7
Transaction within an EU Member State	6

Source: European Commission[74]

This preliminary data confirms the hypothesis that the broader scope of the notification obligation leads to a high number of procedures started (the number of CTARs, 53 in the first 100 days) in the absence of a (potentially distortive) foreign subsidy (the number of in-debt investigations, zero in the first 100 days). Additionally, if the financial contributions were qualified as foreign subsidies, they were not found distortive by the Commission.[75] Most of the notified financial contributions are capital injections, equity contributions and loans granted by financial institutions deemed attributable to a third country. Approximately one-third of the pre-notifications were made by investment funds. Other frequent contributions have a purely public nature, such as State guarantees, project grants and tax benefits for R&D and investment projects.[76] Finally, the notifications originate from a variety of sectors.

72 Directorate-General for Competition of the European Commission (n 56), 1.
73 European Commission, 'Impact Assessment Accompanying the Proposal for a Regulation of the European Parliament and of the Council on foreign subsidies distorting the internal market' (Impact Assessment Report) SWD(2021) 99 final, 53.
74 Directorate-General for Competition of the European Commission (n 56), 1–2.
75 Directorate-General for Competition of the European Commission (n 56), 2.
76 Directorate-General for Competition of the European Commission (n 56).

Economic sectors by number of cases opened under the concentrations procedure (as of 30 March 2025).

Manufacture	43
Electricity, gas and water supply (...)	18
Construction	8
Wholesale and retail trade (...)	29
Transport and storage	10
Information and communication	11
Finance and insurance	23
Real estate	3
Professional, legal and administrative services (...)	9
Health and social work	3
Entertainment	2
Total number of cases opened:	135[77]

Source: European Commission[78]

3. The first in-depth investigation and decision: *e&-PPF Telecom*

In June 2024 the Commission opened its first in-depth investigation under the concentrations procedure, following the notification from the Emirates Telecommunications Group (e&) of the acquisition of PPF Telecom – in particular, of the latter's activities and assets in Bulgaria, Hungary, Serbia and Slovakia.[79] Three financial contributions were deemed potentially distortive foreign subsidies by the Commission: an unlimited guarantee from the government of United Arab Emirates (UAE), performed by exempting e& and other Emirati State owned enterprises (SOE) from domestic insolvency law, which in turn facilitates obtaining credit from financial institutions; a loan not in line with market conditions granted by a group of banks linked to the UAE government; finally, financial contributions in the form

77 Notifying undertakings may be active in more than one sector; therefore, a single case may be counted under multiple sectors.

78 Directorate-General for Competition of the European Commission, 'COMPCases Database' (*competition-cases.ec.europa.eu*, 30 March 2025) https://competition-cases.ec.europa.eu/search?caseInstrument=InstrumentFS&caseTypesFS=FSConcentration&sortField=caseLastDecisionDate&sortOrder=DESC (accessed 30 March 2025).

79 *Emirates Telecommunications Group/PPF Telecom Group* (Case FS.100011) Summary Notice concerning the initiation of an in-depth investigation [2024] C/2024/3970.

of contracts awarded to e& – expectably, from the UAE, but potentially also by other third countries, as the Commission was not explicit on the matter.[80] According to the Commission, the first two contributions fall in the list of most likely distortive subsidies of Article 5(1). While this categorisation seems self-evident for the unlimited guarantee, based on Article 5(1)(b), this is less straightforward for the loan, which the Commission preliminary considered to fall under Article 5(1)(d), i.e., a 'foreign subsidy directly facilitating a concentration'. The Commission probably had enough elements to link the loan to the acquisition. The next step, for the Commission, was to verify if the subsidies received by e& negatively affected the acquisition process by putting its competitors for the acquisition (if present) at a disadvantage or enabling an operation that would have been impossible otherwise; or if the resulting entity may compete, in the future, from an advantageous position in the internal market.[81]

The procedure was closed in September 2024, with the Commission adopting a decision with commitments.[82] As of March 2025, the decision has still to be made public.[83] The in-depth investigation established that e& had indeed received foreign subsidies, but they were not distortive of the acquisition process, as the Emirati company was the sole potential acquirer and able to perform the operation even by relying on its sole resources. On the other hand, the subsidy was potentially distortive 'post-transaction', as the resulting entity would have been able to expand 'its activities beyond what an equivalent economic operator would engage absent the subsidies'. Therefore, e& had to offer commitments that it would (i) not deviate from

80 *Emirates Telecommunications Group/PPF Telecom Group* (n 79), 1–2.

81 *Emirates Telecommunications Group/PPF Telecom Group* (n 79), 1–2.

82 European Commission (n 44).

83 A provisional version of the decision was published in April 2025 https://ec.europa.eu/competition/foreign_subsidies/cases/202514/FS_100011_979.pdf>(accessed 10 May 2025). While the full decision's contents are not explored in this contribution, which was finalised in March 2025, the reader may find an extensive analysis of the decision in *Hornkohl/Mattiolo*, The Concept of 'Distortion in the Internal Market' in the Foreign Subsidies Regulation - From the Legacy of State Aid Law to the First Case Practice, available online at https://papers.ssrn.com/sol3/papers.cfm?abstract_id=5247472 (accessed 15 May 2025), and, a briefer one, in *Hornkohl/Mattiolo*, 'Learnings from the first FSR Phase II merger decision: The Commission publishes a provisional public version of the commitment decision in e&/PPF' (*competitionlawblog.kluwercompetitionlaw.com*, 15 April 2025) https://competitionlawblog.kluwercompetitionlaw.com/2025/04/15/learnings-from-the-first-fsr-phase-ii-merger-decision-the-commission-publishes-a-provisional-public-version-of-the-commitment-decision-in-e-ppf/ (accessed 15 May 2025)

ordinary UAE bankruptcy law, (ii) not finance PPF's activities in the EU internal market, with certain exceptions to be reviewed by the Commission, (iii) perform intra-group transactions at market terms and (iv) inform the Commission of future acquisitions not notifiable under the FSR. The commitments are implemented under the monitoring of an independent trustee based in Germany and the supervision of the Commission, for a duration of 10 years, which is extendable to five additional years if the Commission decides so.[84]

While waiting for the decision to be published, some preliminary considerations are possible. The Commission indeed considers the possible distortions to the corporate control market and the ones to the product market in two different steps of its logical process – the matter is further discussed in paragraph C.III.2. The commitments necessary to obtain the Commission's approval can be considerable and lasting (e.g., ten years), requiring further supervision by the Commission. Procedure-wise, as observed by some practitioners, the decision came before the end term for the in-depth investigation but after a long pre-notification phase, suggesting that pre-notification engagement can expedite the whole procedure – standing that under the FSR it is not possible to reach a decision 'in Phase I' (i.e., preliminary review), as it may happen under the EUMR, and the Commission has to move to the in-depth phase.[85]

II. The EU Merger Regulation (EUMR): a refresher

Regulation 139/2004 reformed the EU framework for merger control, which was first established with Regulation 4064/89. At the end of the '80s, the establishment of the Single Market pushed the European Communities to centralise the review. The new unified market was expected to encourage new concentrations, and maintaining merger control at the national level would have entailed, for a single cross-border operation, being scrutinised in multiple Member States, under different standards.[86] This need was

84 European Commission (n 44).

85 *Yannouchos/Barrantes Díaz*, 'Learnings from the first FSR clearance subject to commitments: the e&/PPF case' (*cliffordchance.com*, 26 September 2024) https://www.cliffordchance.com/insights/resources/blogs/antitrust-fdi-insights/2024/09/learnings-from-the-first-fsr-clearance-subject-to-remedies.html (accessed 13 January 2025).

86 *Levy*, EU Merger Control: from Birth to Adolescence, 26 World Competition (2003), 195, 195–198.

addressed by providing for a 'one-stop shop', i.e. the Commission, with exclusive competence for all concentrations with an 'EU dimension'. A concentration under the EUMR scope coincides with a 'change of control on a lasting basis'[87] or with the creation of a full-function joint venture, and assumes an EU dimension when it surpasses certain turnover thresholds.[88] Without an EU dimension, a concentration falls under the jurisdiction of the national authorities. This two-level distribution of adjudication has a certain degree of flexibility, as cases can be referred from a national authority to the Commission[89] and vice versa,[90] under certain circumstances.[91]

The key obligation for companies under the EUMR is to notify the Commission of the concentration and not proceed with the operation until the latter has authorised it. Upon receiving the notification, the Commission has 25 working days[92] to verify whether the concentration falls under the EUMR's scope and consider its potential effects (the so-called 'Phase I investigation'). Then, the Commission can declare, by decision, the concentration compatible with the internal market,[93] allowing the companies to finalise the operation; or, if it has 'serious doubts as to' the concentration's 'compatibility with the common market',[94] the Commission initiates a more thorough investigation that may last up to 90 working days ('Phase II investigation').[95] Hence, investigations under both the EUMR and the FSR have a two-phase structure. Under the EUMR, the undertaking may also offer commitments to allay the potential concerns of the Commission and facilitate a positive and swift conclusion of the proceeding;[96] this possibility represents another aspect in common with the FSR.[97]

The test performed by the Commission aims to verify that the concentration does not produce a *significant impediment to effective competition*

87 EUMR Art. 3(1).

88 *Boyce/Lyle-Smythe*, Merger Control, in Bailey/John (eds.), Bellamy & Child: European Union Law of Competition, Oxford University Press 8th edn. 2018, 594, 595–597.

89 EUMR Art. 4(4).

90 EUMR Art. 4(4).

91 Commission Notice on Case Referral in respect of concentrations [2005] OJ C56/02.

92 EUMR Art. 10(1).

93 EUMR Art. 6.

94 EUMR Art. 6(1)(c).

95 *Boyce/Lyle-Smythe* (n 88), 596.

96 *Boyce/Lyle-Smythe* (n 88), 684–693.

97 FSR Art. 7.

(SIEC test),[98] offering a sort of 'preventive' protection of the same interests guarded by Article 102 and 101 TFEU. When the EUMR cannot be used to examine an operation *ex ante* because it falls below the Regulation's thresholds, Article 102 TFEU can be used *ex post* instead, as enunciated in the *Towercast* judgement.[99] In line with the core underlying principle of EU competition law, the objective of the EUMR and its enforcement is 'to protect consumer welfare by maintaining a high degree of competition in the common market'.[100] So, the Commission concretely looks, deploying economic analysis and theories of harm,[101] at the potential effects of the concentrations on prices, quality, availability of products,[102] and how the merger may affect the innovation ecosystem.[103] If a joint venture between two companies is notified, the Commission also checks if this may lead to the coordination of behaviour of the two independent undertakings and if that collides with Article 101 TFEU.[104]

III. Overlapping between the FSR and the EUMR

Undertakings negotiating a concentration must consider whether the operation falls within the scope[105] of the two regulations and, if applicable, notify under one or both procedures. The concentration may fall under the scope of the FSR concentrations procedure, if the involved undertakings have received, combined, 'financial contributions' for more than 50 million euros from foreign governments in the three years preceding the opera-

98 EUMR Art. 2.

99 Case C-449/21, EU:C:2023:207, *Towercast v Autorité de la concurrence and Ministère de l'Économie*, para. 41.

100 *Monti*, 'The Future for Competition Policy in the European Union' (Speech, London, 7 September 2001) https://ec.europa.eu/commission/presscorner/detail/en/speech_01_340 (accessed 8 August 2024).

101 *Zenger/Walker*, Theories of Harm in European Competition Law: A Progress Report, in Bourgeois/Waelbroeck (eds.), Ten Years of effect-based Approach in EU Competition Law (2012), 185, 2–5.

102 *Boyce/Lyle-Smythe* (n 88), 596.

103 Guidelines on the assessment of horizontal mergers under the Council Regulation on the control of concentrations between undertakings (Horizontal Mergers Guidelines) [2004] OJ C31/5, para. 38.

104 *Boyce/Lyle-Smythe* (n 88), 596.

105 Based on the turnover thresholds set, respectively, by EUMR Art. 1(3) and FSR Art. 20(3)(a).

tion.[106] In case the operation falls under both procedures, the undertaking submits two notifications that are handled by the Commission separately.[107] As mentioned before, in the first 100 days of FSR enforcement, the Commission reported that 42 of the 53 pre-notified concentrations were also notified under the EUMR.[108] Alternatively, if not at the EU level via the EUMR, the concentration may fall under the scope of national merger control procedures,[109] as it happened to five of the 53 first cases.[110]

While discussing the matter of the respective scopes, it is interesting to observe the different remedies for operations under threshold. For merger control, national competition authorities could either act *ex post* under Art. 102 TFEU, coherently with the *Towercast* judgement,[111] or use the 'call-in' powers of the national authorities, with the possibility to refer the case to the Commission under Article 22 EUMR, as long as they respect the rules set by Court of Justice in *Illumina/Grail*.[112] The *Towercast* path, in particular, empowers third parties to file complaints and initiate public enforcement.[113] Whereas the FSR provides no formal powers for third parties, since the only remedy for below threshold concentrations is the *ex officio* procedure, as discussed in paragraph B.II.

1. Before the FSR: tackling foreign subsidies in merger control

If a concentration can be assessed under different tools, the innovative impact of the FSR becomes evident by examining whether—and how—merger control has addressed the significant impediment to effective competition caused by foreign subsidies. One example can be found at the national level: the decision by the German *Bundeskartellamt* on the CRRC-Vossloh deal in 2020.[114][115] CRRC, a Chinese SOE that produces trains, sought to ac-

106 FSR Art. 20(3).
107 *Hornkohl* (n 39), 31–32.
108 Directorate-General for Competition of the European Commission (n 56), 2.
109 *Bauermeister* (n 59), 483–484.
110 Directorate-General for Competition of the European Commission (n 56), 2.
111 Case C-449/21, EU:C:2023:207, *Towercast v Autorité de la Concurrence.*
112 Case C-611/22 P., EU:C:2024:677, *Illumina Inc. v European Commission.*
113 *Fischer*, Double-checking mergers: *Ex-ante* and *ex-post* competition law enforcement and its implications for third parties, 15 Journal of European Competition Law & Practice (2024), 428, 430–435.
114 Bundeskartellamt, Decision of April 27, 2020, Case B4–115/19—*CRRC/Vossloh.*
115 *Hornkohl* (n 39), 33–34.

quire Vossloh Locomotives, a subsidiary of the historic German firm Vossloh AG, which is primarily active in manufacturing railway components. The German Authority examined, as part of its SIEC test,[116] how CRRC had benefited from substantial subsidies that would not be permitted under EU State aid rules. These subsidies, in turn, enabled the company to lower its prices and strengthen its market position, as evidenced by several trade defence decisions by the Commission. Even so, the acquisition was ultimately cleared due to Vossloh's weakened position and the presence of competitors in the market.[117]

Thus, the German competition authority was able to consider, within a merger control procedure, the impact of a company operating in a State-controlled economy.[118] However, the *Bundeskartellamt* itself would point out the limits of EU law on this matter,[119][120] a concern echoed by the Biennal Report of the *Monopolkommission* on Chinese State capitalism, which called for the introduction of a new instrument – the future FSR.[121] Before the deal with Vossloh, CRRC had already animated the policy debate in occasion of the *Siemens/Alstom* case in 2019 and was later the object of the first FSR in-depth investigation in 2024, in the context of a public tender for electric trains in Romania.[122] The procedure, under the FSR public procurement module, was never concluded, as CRRC withdrew its bid.[123]

116 *Christiansen*, The SIEC Test in German Merger Control, in Heine/Budzinski, Wettbewerb, Recht und Wirtschaftspolitik, Nomos 2024, 159.

117 *Hornkohl*, Do we really need the EU Foreign Subsidy Regulation? CPI Antitrust Chronicle (May 2023), 1, 6.

118 *Hornkohl* (n 39), 32.

119 Bundeskartellamt, Decision of April 27, 2020, Case B4–115/19—*CRRC/Vossloh*.

120 *Reinhold/Weck*, Welcome to the Jungle! Identification of Foreign Subsidies Under the New EU Foreign Subsidies Regulation, 23 European State Aid Law Quarterly (2024), 22, 34.

121 *Mattiolo* (n 3), 22–23.

122 European Commission, 'Commission opens first in-depth investigation under the Foreign Subsidies Regulation' (Press release) IP/24/887 (2024) https://ec.europa.eu/commission/presscorner/detail/en/ip_24_887 (accessed 10 March 2024).

123 *Bermingham*, 'Chinese rail company CRRC withdraws Bulgarian bid amid EU inquiry' *South China Morning Post* (27 March 2024) https://www.scmp.com/news/china/article/3256843/chinese-rail-company-crrc-withdraws-bid-bulgarian-public-tender-amid-eu-inquiry (accessed 29 March 2024).

2. The assessments of the FSR and the EUMR compared

If the same concentration triggers two different notifications, how does the assessment differ between the two procedures? Under the Foreign Subsidies Regulation (FSR), the first distinction lies in the materials examined by the Commission: the parties must submit not only details of the transaction but also any foreign financial contributions received. Based on this information, the Commission determines whether a foreign subsidy exists and whether it is distortive, both before and after the concentration.[124] In other words, the distortion test in the FSR concentrations procedure follows a two-step test. (i) Has the subsidy distorted the corporate control market? (ii) Could the subsidy distort the product market in which the undertaking will operate if the concentration is approved? This structure, which emerged in the e&/PPF case,[125] may be further clarified in the 2026 Guidelines. If the Commission intends to impose redressive measures or accept commitments, it then performs the balancing test. The assessment is limited to the concentration in question,[126] meaning only subsidies that impact the concentration are considered; other foreign financial contributions disclosed in the notification are ignored (at least, in the procedure at hand).[127] If the Commission aligns its FSR methodology with State aid law, this will influence deeply the Regulation's assessment.[128]

As just mentioned, the market that may distorted could be either the one for corporate control or the products market in which the undertaking is (or will be) active.[129] For the corporate control market, the Commission could follow two different theories of harm to demonstrate how the subsidy has distorted or may distort competition: (i) one undertaking prevailed on one competitor thanks to the subsidy or (ii) the concentration would not be concluded without the subsidy, regardless of the presence or not of a competitor. Both theories present some limits for the Commission: the first would exclude from the FSR application purely bilateral operations, without competition; the latter may be inconsistent with the words of Article 4, as the subsidy may not 'affect competition' or 'improve the competitive

124 *Mattiolo* (n 3), 36.
125 European Commission (n 74); FSR Art. 25(1).
126 FSR Art. 19.
127 *Reindl/Van Damme*, The EU Foreign Subsidies Regulation, Concurrences 2024, 65.
128 *Mattiolo* (n 3), 37.
129 *Reindl/Van Damme* (n 127), 64.

position' when there is no competitor.[130] The Commission may look also at the products market since the notification form requires the undertaking to illustrate the activities and products of the involved companies, as long as they overlap, possibly due to the fact that a subsidy may be considered distortive if it reinforces a dominant position.[131] Considering how the products market will look after the concentration may bring the FSR assessment closer to the EUMR's one.

On the opposite side, the Commission has the burden of proof in the SIEC test and there are no presumptions.[132] Using the words of Court in *CK Telecoms*, the SIEC test requires the Commission to 'demonstrate, by means of a sufficiently cogent and consistent body of evidence, that it [the significant impediment] is more likely than not'.[133] Therefore, the EUMR review may be much more intense than the FSR one on this aspect and bound to purely economic considerations. In general terms, the substantive assessment conducted by the Commission in the EUMR aims to test if the concentration is 'compatible with the common market'.[134] While Recital 23 adds that the assessment is performed 'within the general framework of the achievement of the fundamental objectives' outlined in Article 3 of the Treaty on the European Union, the EUMR was written in a way to minimise the pursuit of policy goals other than the defence of competition.[135] Article 2(1) presents a non-exhaustive[136] list of the elements that

130 *Reindl/Van Damme* (n 127), 65–66.

131 *Reindl/Van Damme* (n 127), 66.

132 *Whish/Bailey*, Competition Law, Oxford University Press 10th edn. 2021, 909.

133 Case C-376/20 P., EU:C:2023:561, *European Commission v CK Telecoms UK Investments Ltd.*, para. 87.

134 *Boyce/Lyle-Smythe* (n 88), 702.

135 In this sense, it can be useful to consider the words of the two incumbent Commissioners at the time of the first (1989) and second (2004) EU Merger Regulation. Leon Brittan, Competition Commissioner in 1989 wrote, as quoted in Levy (n 86): 'I was determined that the Merger Regulation should not be used as a way of imposing an industrial policy on Europe, although there were quite a number of participants in the debate who wanted to do just that. Whether it was because they wished to create European champions, or wanted to allow social considerations to have an important impact, they wanted the wording of the Regulation to be sufficiently broad for the Commission to be able to consider matters going well beyond the effects of the merger on competition in the relevant market. In the end, the supporters of an industrial policy were effectively beaten back, and the Regulation gives clear primacy to the competition criterion, with only the smallest nod in the direction of anything else'. For Mario Monti, Competition Commissioner in 2004, see the speech referred at n 100.

136 *Boyce/Lyle-Smythe* (n 88), 701–702.

the Commission must consider in the SIEC test, such as the structure of the concerned markets, the presence of actual or potential competitors and the position of the consumers. In most cases, the SIEC test consists of demonstrating that the concentration may create or strengthen a dominant position, which the Commission considers a 'primary form of competitive harm'.[137] To define the concept of 'dominance', the General Court has been following[138] the well-known formulation of the *Hoffmann-La Roche* case, i.e., 'a position of economic strength' that allows an undertaking to 'behave to an appreciable extent independently of its competitors, its customers and ultimately of the consumers', thus preventing 'effective competition being maintained on the relevant market'.[139]

Yet, the SIEC assessment of the current EUMR is not limited to simply assessing the presence of dominance by one undertaking, as it was in the 1989 Regulation.[140] Also, situations of 'collective dominance' in oligopolistic markets can qualify under the EUMR:[141] a concentration may lead to a market where few undertakings can 'become aware of common interests and (...) cause prices to increase without having to enter into an agreement or resort to a concerted practice',[142] so outside the scope of Article 101 TFEU. More generally, the SIEC test does not require to demonstrate the creation or strengthening of a dominant position[143] and can consider the characteristics of the market to conclude that competition would be negatively affected by a concentration. Interestingly, the circumstance that the acquirer is ultimately controlled by a foreign government may be relevant for the SIEC test: if the acquirer does not operate as a single economic entity but in coordination with other SOEs, this may result in *de facto* vertical or horizontal integration, affecting competition negatively. This concern led the Commission to raise the matter in EUMR cases involving

137 Horizontal Mergers Guidelines, para. 2.
138 Case T-102/96, ECLI:EU:T:1999:65 – Gencor Ltd v Commission.
139 Case 85/76, ECLI:EU:C:1979:36 – Hoffmann-La Roche & Co. AG v Commission, para. 4.
140 *Boyce/Lyle-Smythe* (n 88), 707–708.
141 Horizontal Mergers Guidelines, para. 4.
142 Case T-102/96, ECLI:EU:T:1999:65, *Gencor Ltd v Commission*, para. 38.
143 Horizontal Mergers Guidelines, para. 23.

Chinese SOEs,[144] such as the CNRC-Pirelli case[145] – which is discussed later.

3. Procedural aspects: time and regimes of disclosure

Even if the two procedures have roughly similar time limits and are both started by a notification, they may advance at a different pace,[146] and with suspensions (in case of requests for information or inspections) or extensions granted for one procedure not affecting the other.[147] A concentration may be cleared first under the FSR but still wait for the conclusion of the EUMR assessment. Considering some hypotheses, during Phase I of the EUMR, if a Member State requests a referral or the undertaking offers a commitment, the Commission receives an extension of 10 working days, a possibility not present in the FSR. The Commission will need to find a way to coordinate the two procedures and their remedies, beyond the current text of the Regulations,[148] supposing that the lack of synchronisation constitutes a problem, after all.

Another difference between the EUMR and the FSR is that the Commission discloses less information during the latter's procedure. The notifications or the closing of preliminary investigations are not published to avoid disclosing sensitive information on the foreign financial contributions received by the notifying parties. Only if the Commission decides to open an in-depth investigation, by adopting a decision *ex* Article 10(3), the main elements behind its determination are published as a summary notice in the Official Journal of the European Union.[149]

These last paragraphs have outlined the overlap between the FSR and the EUMR. As discussed, foreign subsidies were already considered – albeit with limitations – by merger control authorities even before the FSR. While the assessments under the two regulations differ, both remain fundamentally economic in nature. However, the FSR may introduce non-economic

144 *Svetlicinii*, Chinese state owned enterprises and EU merger control, Routledge 2021, 54–61.

145 *CNRC/Pirelli* (Case M.7643) Commission Decision [2015] C(2015) 4608 final.

146 *Blockx*, The proposal for an EU Regulation on foreign subsidies distorting the internal market: how will it impact corporate mergers and acquisitions?, in de Jong et al (eds), The Rise of Public Security Interests in Corporate Mergers and Acquisitions, Wolf Legal Publishers 2022, 141, 149–154.

147 *Hornkohl* (n 39), 35.

148 *Hornkohl* (n 39), 34–35.

149 Directorate-General for Competition of the European Commission (n 56), 2.

policy objectives through the balancing test, though only after assessing potential positive economic effects. In contrast, the EUMR remains firmly rooted in the traditional goals of competition law.

D. The FSR concentrations procedure and interaction with FDI screening

I. The EU FDI Screening framework and the challenges for its Europeanisation

If a concentration involves a non-EU undertaking, the operation may fall under the scope of a national FDI law if it poses a risk to national security. Since national security is an 'essential State function' and a 'sole responsibility' of Member States,[150] FDI screening is operated at the Member State level and coordinated across the EU by the FDI Screening Regulation (Regulation (EU) 2019/452, hereafter 'FDI Regulation').[151,152] The Regulation sets the essential elements, but national legislation can lead to differences in the enforcement. Since the FDI Regulation does not impose on Member States to have a screening mechanism in the first place, nor to consider the same factors in assessing risk, there are notable differences among national mechanisms.[153] Some Member States do not screen,[154] while others are more proactive: how shut the door to the internal market is depends on national FDI laws, even though trade policy is an EU-exclusive competence.[155] This gap is considered a liability for the economic security of the bloc,[156]

150 Consolidated Version of the Treaty on the European Union [2012] OJ C326/13, Art. 4(2).
151 Regulation (EU) 2019/452 of the European Parliament and of the Council of 19 March 2019 establishing a framework for the screening of foreign direct investments into the Union (FDI Regulation) [2019] OJ L79I/1.
152 *Mattiolo* (n 3), 38–39.
153 European Court of Auditors, 'Screening foreign direct investments in the EU' (Special report) 27/2023, 30–40 https://www.eca.europa.eu/ECAPublications/SR-2023-27/SR-2023-27_EN.pdf (accessed 20 August 2024).
154 European Commission (n 4), 20.
155 TFEU Art. 3(1).
156 European Court of Auditors (n 153), 1.

and the Commission has been recommending a deeper 'Europeanisation' of FDI screening.[157]

The Commission proposed in January 2024 the reform of the FDI Regulation,[158] in the context of its Economic Security Package,[159] and signalled its will to swiftly adopt the new text in the Mission Letter to the new Commissioner for Trade *and Economic Security* Maroš Šefčovič.[160] Šefčovič's updated job title, now including 'economic security', represents another symptom of the increasingly geoeconomic approach to trade in Brussels. Even so, under the current institutional architecture and political climate, it seems difficult for the Commission to reduce the autonomy of Member States in investment screening.[161] The revised FDI Regulation would require all Member States to establish an investment screening mechanism and consider certain parameters of 'likely negative impact on security and public order'.[162] Among these parameters, if an undertaking[163] involved in the investment 'is likely to pursue a third country's policy objectives',[164] the investment should be considered to have a likely negative impact and, therefore, be either prohibited or authorised with the imposition of mitigating circumstances; unless another EU or national tool can address the

157 *Bohnert*, 'FDI Screening Regulation 2.0: Towards Greater Regulatory Convergence?' (*CELIS Institute Blog*, 2 June 2024) https://www.celis.institute/celis-blog/fdi-screening-regulation-2-0-towards-greater-regulatory-convergence/ (accessed 14 July 2024).

158 European Commission, 'Proposal for a Regulation of the European Parliament and of the Council on the screening of foreign investments in the Union and repealing Regulation (EU) 2019/452 of the European Parliament and of the Council' (Regulation Proposal) 2024/0017(COD).

159 European Commission, 'Commission proposes new initiatives to strengthen economic security' (Press release) IP/24/363 https://ec.europa.eu/commission/presscorner/detail/en/ip_24_363 (accessed 23 August 2024).

160 Von der Leyen/European Commission, Mission Letter to Maroš Šefčovič, Commissioner-designate for Trade and Economic Security, Commissioner-designate for Interinstitutional Relations and Transparency (Mission Letter to Commissioner-designate), 8 https://commission.europa.eu/document/download/4047c277-f608-48d1-8800-dcf0405d76e8_en?filename=Mission%20letter%20-%20%C5%A0EF%C4%8COVI%C4%8C.pdf (accessed 25 September 2024).

161 *Bohnert* (n 157).

162 European Commission (n 158), Art. 13.

163 According to Art. 13(a)(e) of the Proposal (n 157), this subject may be 'the foreign investor, a natural person or entity controlling the foreign investor, the beneficial owner of the foreign investor, any of the subsidiaries of the foreign investor, or any other party owned or controlled by, or acting on behalf or at the direction of the foreign investor'.

164 European Commission (n 158), Art. 13(4)(e).

risk.[165] Since many subsidised companies may also pursue the objectives of the foreign governments that fund them, an FDI screening authority may consider that the FSR addresses the same risk.

The Proposal also qualifies intra-EU investments by EU entities controlled by non-EU investors as FDI,[166] similar to how the FSR's scope encompasses all 'undertaking engaging in an economic activity in the internal market,'[167] regardless of where their shareholders are based. If the foreign investor or its subsidiary in the EU is directly or indirectly controlled by a third country, 'including through ownership structure, significant funding, special rights or state-appointed directors or managers',[168] the receiving Member State may clear the investment, but must notify the Commission and the other Member States through the Regulation's cooperation mechanism.[169] One additional affinity between the Commission's FDI Proposal and the FSR is the shared double legal basis: the functioning of the internal market *ex* Article 114 TFEU and the common commercial policy *ex* Article 207 TFEU.[170]

II. Overlapping and interactions between the FSR and the (current) FDI screening framework

26 of the first 53 FSR concentrations procedures were associated with an FDI screening procedure in one Member State.[171] In line with the new tenet of shaping competition policy 'in the face of geopolitical threats',[172] it may be possible for the Commission to use its wide discretion in enforcing the FSR to target specific countries or protect certain EU industries. For instance, the Commission may choose to start or abstain from investigating the subsidies based on their country of origin, or reverse a negative assessment during the balancing test. Investors from certain countries are

165 European Commission (n 158), Art. 14.
166 *Bohnert* (n 157).
167 FSR Art. 1.
168 European Commission (n 158), Art. 5(1)(b)(i).
169 European Commission (n 158), Art. 5.
170 European Commission (n 158), Art. 10.
171 Directorate-General for Competition of the European Commission (n 56), 2.
172 Von der Leyen/European Commission (n 15), 5.

especially concerned about this possibility,[173] and the Commission often repeats it enforces the FSR 'country-blind'.[174]

Under the current FDI Regulation, to determine whether an investment poses a threat to security, the national authority can consider certain factors, such as the fact that 'the foreign investor is directly or indirectly controlled by the government, including state bodies or armed forces, of a third country, including through ownership structure or significant funding.'[175] This same situation is similar to Article 3 FSR, so a brownfield investment may be notified under both a national FDI mechanism and the FSR concentrations procedure. On the contrary, a greenfield investment may only fall under the scope of FDI screening and a later FSR *ex officio* procedure, so it does not require an FSR notification, making greenfield investments potentially easier to implement for foreign investors with governmental ties.

It could be argued that the FSR allows the Commission to scrutinise foreign investments at the EU level when public funding is involved, with some degree of flexibility, offering a limited ersatz to sidestep the Member States' reluctance toward the Europeanisation of FDI screening.[176] The answer seems negative: the two tools may overlap, but remain different at an essential level, from their assessment to their goals. It is also difficult to compare the FSR with FDI screening, as the latter is quite fragmented between Member States. While a few years of FSR enforcement may clarify and reassure foreign investors on its range, as long as the FDI screening remains only loosely coordinated between Member States, there is where investors will face more challenges and uncertainty. Still, the FSR remains an additional scrutiny to incoming brownfield investments: in the upcoming years, researchers should observe whether this aspect pushes companies to opt for greenfield operations instead, so as to remain under the radar of the Commission, at least for some time – an *ex officio* procedure could be potentially opened at a later stage. If FDI screening, currently distributed

173 China Chamber of Commerce to the EU, 'Position document attached to the Consultation questionnaire' (Contribution to the public consultation on the White Paper on Foreign Subsidies) 2020, https://ec.europa.eu/info/law/better-regulation/have-your-say/initiatives/12452-White-Paper-on-Foreign-Subsidies/public-consultation_en (accessed 6 June 2024).

174 *Laprévote/Lin*, Between State Aid, Trade and Antitrust: The Mixed Procedural Heritage of the Foreign Subsidies Regulation and the Overarching Principle of Non-Discrimination, 25 Zeitschrift für europarechtliche Studien (2022), 443, 450–452.

175 FDI Regulation Art. 4(2).

176 *Mattiolo* (n 3), 40.

over almost thirty national systems, moved to the EU level, this would facilitate the coordination between this tool and the FSR within the Commission. Another critical aspect is how such interaction may result in an 'over-securitisation' of the scrutiny over acquisitions, sacrificing openness on the altar of autonomy.[177]

E. An example of the overlapping between the EUMR, FDI screening and (in abstracto) the FSR: the Pirelli saga

As mentioned, the FSR, the EUMR and FDI screening may overlap, potentially leading to uncertain and long procedures. The fate of the Chinese company CNRC and its acquisition of a share of the Italian tyre maker Pirelli offers a cautionary tale.

In July 2015, the Commission cleared the acquisition of Italian tyre manufacturer Pirelli by CNRC, a subsidiary of ChemChina.[178] Both CNRC and ChemChina are Chinese SOEs, with the latter reporting to the Central State-owned Assets Supervision and Administration Commission (Central SASAC), a government agency. In reviewing the merger, the Commission examined whether ChemChina operated as an independent economic entity or as part of a single economic unit comprising the network of Chinese SOEs active in vertically- or horizontally-integrated markets.[179] The Commission had already explored the issue in previous cases concerning Chinese SOEs, taking into consideration factors such as interlocking directorships and the potential sharing of commercially sensitive information.[180] After examining the potential vertical integration between the merging parties and other SOEs with similar obligations towards the Central SASAC, the Commission determined that the proposed transaction would not significantly impede competition in the relevant markets, therefore it was not necessary to establish the independence of ChemChina from the Central SASAC.[181]

177 *Mattiolo* (n 3), 41.
178 *CNRC/Pirelli* (n 145).
179 *CNRC/Pirelli* (n 145), 3–6.
180 *China National Bluestar/Elkem* (Case COMP/M6082) Commission Decision [2011] C(2011) 2429 final.
181 *CNRC/Pirelli* (n 145), 3–6.

In the footnotes of the decision, the Commission reconstructed also the capital operations carried out by CNRC to acquire Pirelli, highlighting the involvement of a Chinese sovereign fund, but without considering whether that constituted a subsidy to facilitate the operation.[182] Three years later, in the context of an anti-subsidy procedure against Chinese tyre makers, the Commission would reconstruct fully the involvement of Beijing, via its SOEs and subsidies, in the Pirelli acquisition.[183] The fact that the acquirer was a foreign SOE was not relevant for the EUMR assessment, in line with the principle of non-discrimination between private and publicly-owned companies, and between domestic and foreign ones. This hints that a core change in the EUMR nature was required to enable this tool to address the matter of foreign subsidies as well.

In 2015, the Italian Government could not screen the investment, as the scope of its then FDI law, the so-called 'golden power',[184] was limited to a few strategic sectors.[185] In 2023, the situation was different: CNRC (controlling 37 % of Pirelli's shares) agreed to change its shareholders' agreement with a Chinese sovereign fund (controlling 9 % of Pirelli), but the modification was this time screened by the Italian Government.[186] Thanks to the legislative amendments of the previous years,[187] Rome was able to exercise its golden power to a wider set of circumstances. The Government cleared the new shareholders' agreement but imposed safeguard measures to ensure Italian control over the top management and part of the compa-

182 *CNRC/Pirelli* (n 145), 4–6.

183 Commission Implementing Regulation (EU) 2018/1690 of 9 November 2018 imposing definitive countervailing duties on imports of certain pneumatic tyres [2018] OJ L283/1; *Svetlicinii* (n 144), 73–74.

184 Decreto Legge 15 marzo 2012, n 21, Norme in materia di poteri speciali sugli assetti societari nei settori della difesa e della sicurezza nazionale, nonché per le attività di rilevanza strategica nei settori dell'energia, dei trasporti e delle comunicazioni.

185 *Picotti*, 'Pirelli: dal takeover cinese del 2015 al golden power del 2023' (*Osservatorio Golden Power*, 01 February 2024) https://www.osservatoriogoldenpower.eu/pirelli-dal-takeover-cinese-del-2015-al-golden-power-del-2023/ (accessed 12 October 2024).

186 *Bertolino*, 'Pirelli, soci cinesi in movimento dopo il golden power. I piani di Brembo' *Corriere della Sera* (online, 10 September 2023) https://www.corriere.it/economia/aziende/23_ottobre_09/pirelli-soci-cinesi-movimento-il-golden-power-piani-brembo-5b8b859c-6687-11ee-aea2-f54ec62808b3.shtml (accessed 27 October 2024).

187 *Sabatino*, The 'Golden Power' on Foreign Investments in EU Law in the Light of Covid Crisis, 18 European Company Law (2021), 189, 192.

ny's know-how,[188] neutralising the initiative of the Chinese shareholders,[189] which later renounced the agreement altogether.[190] The main argument behind the Government's decision was that Pirelli possesses technologies of strategic importance, whose misuse could endanger users' privacy and national security.[191]

With the benefit of hindsight, it may be argued that the CNRC-Pirelli acquisition, while passing the EUMR procedure, would have definitely triggered an FSR scrutiny, if the latter was already in place. In particular, the FSR concentrations procedure would have led the Commission to assess, in the first place, whether the acquisition was enabled by Chinese foreign subsidies, harming other potential acquirers. As mentioned, the Commission would incidentally mention this issue in the context of the EUMR and anti-subsidy[192] procedures, yet without the power to make any legal determination under any of them. Today, the potential distortion on the tyre market would be assessed under both the FSR and EUMR, although in different way, with the former examining the impact of the subsidies, rather than the resulting market structure. On the other hand, the Italian FDI law allows for a stronger, and more discretionary, assessment of national security risks.

The Pirelli saga shows that the industrial plans of a foreign investor may be challenged under different procedures, at different levels, and even at different moments. As the Italian FDI Screening law in this case, even an FSR procedure could be activated *ex officio* for a concentration that was already cleared under the EUMR (or an FDI regime) and was not scrutinised under the FSR concentrations procedure – perhaps because it did not qualify under its thresholds,[193] or because the investment was a

188 Presidenza del Consiglio dei Ministri, 'Golden power' for Pirelli: green light from the Government with provisions to protect strategic asset' (Press release) https://www.governo.it/en/articolo/golden-power-pirelli-green-light-government-provisions-protect-strategic-asset/22952 (accessed 25 October 2024).

189 *Picotti* (n 185).

190 *Bertolino* (n 186).

191 Presidenza del Consiglio dei Ministri (n 188).

192 'Anti-subsidy procedure' refers to a procedure based on Regulation (EU) 2016/1037 of the European Parliament and of the Council of 8 June 2016 on protection against subsidised imports from countries not members of the European Union (codification) (BASR) [2016] OJ L156/55.

193 *Dackö/Brodin/Arlebo*, The FDI Screening Mechanisms and the Draft EU Foreign Subsidy Regulation – Potential Conflicts of Interests and in Application, 25 Zeitschrift für europarechtliche Studien (2022), 505, 516–517.

greenfield initiative. Coordinated enforcement of the three procedures may avoid this burdensome and precarious, although off-chance, situation.

F. Conclusion: can the FSR be used to continue 'policy with other means'?

Given that a single concentration may trigger two (or even three) procedures at both the EU and national levels, potentially with contradictory outcomes,[194] one may ponder whether the FSR was the ideal solution and what its added value truly is. Incorporating the matter of foreign subsidies in the EUMR would have probably generated the same questions and uncertainty that is connected with every new reform, while the adoption of the FSR allows to leave the EUMR untouched. Addressing subsidies in FDI screening would have effectively turned them into a security issue; that is, one to be evaluated primarily through political and national lenses. On the opposite, the FSR conducts an economic assessment, first and foremost. It may have some utility for an economic security agenda or allow for geopolitical considerations (in setting enforcement priorities and balancing *ex* Article 6), but the fact that DG COMP was tasked with its enforcement hints that economic considerations will dominate the FSR assessment, taking stock of the experience matured in State aid and merger review. Finally, bundling together different situations affected by subsidies in one sole tool as the FSR, instead of two 'add-ons' to the EUMR and the FDI Regulation, may lead to a homogeneous approach to regulating this specific phenomenon – without forgetting the trade defence tools that regulate subsidies on goods, such as the BASR and the Basic Anti-Dumping Regulation (Regulation (EU) 2016/1036).

On the use of the FSR in the EU's geopolitical manoeuvres, the Commission designed the tool so that it is 'origin-neutral', and its officials reiterated that nationality is not a determinant for their assessment,[195] therefore it could be expected that the tool will be used consistently and not selectively. It may argued that the FSR offers a different treatment when compared to State aid law since, in the latter, the Commission engages with Member States: companies do not need to bear the burden of defending the legality of the aid they would receive, as their Member States do that for them. On the contrary, the Commission enforces the FSR on undertakings, which

194 *Mattiolo* (n 3), 40.
195 A leitmotiv of the presentations on the FSR given by DG COMP in public fora.

have to bear the costs of the procedure. An assessment in this sense is yet premature and requires observing how aligned the FSR and State aid enforcement will be.

Even so, it is not peculiar that a tool that targets foreign subsidies will be enforced especially on companies hailing from State capitalist economies. The first thought is China: while the EU institutional narrative on the FSR stays clear from mentioning it, the political context and legislative history of the FSR shows that the trade relationship with Beijing has been a central question for EU decision-makers in these last years. Many of the FSR first investigations have involved subsidiaries of Chinese companies: the already mentioned CRRC procurement case in Romania, two cases on public tenders for solar panels, again in Romania,[196] and an *ex officio* investigation on wind turbine suppliers.[197] Yet, the first in-depth investigation under the concentrations procedure involved an Emirati company and SOEs. In other words, not only China, but also other Socialist economies and State capitalist countries in the Gulf or South East Asia[198] may be more exposed to the FSR. So, does the FSR discriminate[199] against certain economic models? Perhaps not: countries that are considered paragons of the market economy can deploy massive subsidies as well, as the US IRA exemplified. Finally, if we look at the sectors where the FSR made the news – electric trains, renewable energies, telecommunication,... –, we see mostly strategic sectors. Yet, this may be due by the Commission's focus in its early days of enforcement, but as its resources and experience with the tool grow, we may see a broader, more general, coverage of sectors.

We clarified that the FSR scrutiny is economic, not a security or geopolitical one as in FDI screening. So, is the FSR, and competition law with

196 European Commission, 'Commission opens two in-depth investigations under the Foreign Subsidies Regulation in the solar photovoltaic sector' (Press release) IP/24/1803 https://ec.europa.eu/commission/presscorner/detail/en/ip_24_1803 (accessed 10 April 2024).

197 WindEurope, 'EU starts investigation into Chinese wind turbines under new Foreign Subsidies Regulation' (Press release) https://windeurope.org/newsroom/press-releases/eu-starts-investigation-into-chinese-wind-turbines-under-new-foreign-subsidies-regulation/ (accessed 5 May 2024).

198 *Sabatino*, The emerging trends of the modernization of state-controlled economy in the ASEAN space. The case of Indonesian State-Owned Enterprises, 1 Rivista di Diritti Comparati (2023), 286, 286–290.

199 The reader should intend the verb 'discriminate' here in a non-technical way. To raise a question of WTO compatibility is outside the scope of the present contribution.

it, 'a continuation of policy (or politics) with other means'? Arguably, yes. However, their overarching objective is to safeguard the EU's 'competitiveness',[200] rather than to directly advance national security or geopolitical aims.[201] 'Revamping competition' to bolster the bloc's competitiveness could be part of a broader economic security and geopolitical strategy, as the Report from former Italian Prime Minister Mario Draghi has highlighted.[202] The Report discusses the issue of foreign subsidies frequently and recommends that the FSR is enforced 'effectively and result(s) in the intended benefits for EU consumers and businesses',[203] echoing the economic approach traditionally at the basis of competition law.[204] So, competition law could remain competition law and the FSR can be a tool to restore the level playing field in the general interest of companies and consumers, instead of a weapon for lawfare against rivals.[205] They would still be useful to the EU to achieve its ambitious, and vital, goals of competitiveness and economic security, in front of an increasingly unstable global scenario.

---

200 *Draghi* (n 14).

201 Selcukhan Unekbas discusses the question with excellent clarity in the chapter 'Competitiveness and Antitrust Law: Between Feasibility And Desirability' of this very volume.

202 *Draghi*, 'The future of European competitiveness – In-depth analysis and recommendations', 298–306 https://commission.europa.eu/document/download/ec1409c1-d4b4-4882-8bdd-3519f86bbb92_en?filename=The%20future%20of%20European%20competitiveness_%20In-depth%20analysis%20and%20recommendations_0.pdf (accessed 25 October 2024).

203 *Draghi* (n 14), 302.

204 The Draghi Report (n 202, 302) continues: 'Otherwise, not only would the credibility of the EU as a regulator be hurt, but economic damages would also follow, such as the reduced appetite of multinational companies to invest in Europe'.

205 While this contribution examines the geopoliticisation of competition law from the perspective of the FSR alone, the reader can find a broader (and more acute) analysis in Sophie Bohnert's chapter, 'Geopolitics and Competition Law: An Odd Couple or a Match Made in Heaven?', in this volume.

Part IV:
EU Competition Law Beyond the EU

Competition Copycats: The Brussels Effect and the Diffusion of the EU's Social Values

Richard Bunworth (LL.B (Dubl), BCL (Oxon), MA (KCL)[*]

A. Introduction

The Brussels Effect[1] describes the means by which the laws of the EU diffuse beyond its boundaries, thereby ensuring an application of its rules that goes far beyond the Union and its Member States. This has granted the EU a global level of influence that exceeds its economic power, as other jurisdictions choose to align with it for various reasons.[2] The Brussels Effect is particularly significant in competition law, where the EU's influence on the development of the law internationally has been extremely pronounced over the last three decades.[3] This occurred in tandem with the waning influence of the more free market-oriented, less interventionist approach of the US, which newly established competition regimes seem to be spurning in favour of the EU's system.[4]

---

* Assistant Professor, Trinity College Dublin and solicitor (qualified to practise in Ireland, England and Wales).

1 The phrase is often attributed to the work of Anu Bradford in the competition law context. Anu Bradford, 'The Brussels Effect' (2012) 107 Northwestern University Law Review 1.

2 Bradford (n 1) 39. Bradford contends that there are five key factors which are crucial to the application of the Brussels Effect; (i) the market size and wealthy consumer base of the Single Market; (ii) institutions within the Union (primarily the European Commission and the Courts) with the expertise and capacity to introduce novel policies; (iii) a political will to develop stringent regulatory standards to set global trends; (iv) creating rules which are based on the actual consumers being in the EU, rather than where the product is made (for example, food and product safety); and (v) companies voluntarily extending the regulatory requirements of the strictest regulator to their global operation. See Anu Bradford, *The Brussels Effect: How the European Union Rules the World* (Oxford University Press 2020) 25–53.

3 Anu Bradford et al., 'The Global Dominance of European Competition Law Over American Antitrust Law' (2019) 16 Journal of Empirical Legal Studies 731; Thomas Geoghegan, 'Brussels or Bust' (2023) 67 The Baffler 38, 45.

4 Bradford et al. (n 3) 734.

There are many reasons explaining the preference of other jurisdictions in following the EU's approach to competition law over that of the US which are touched upon in section three. However, the purpose of this paper is to argue that the EU should seek to capitalise on its influence over the shaping of competition policy through the Brussels Effect by imbuing it with the values of the Union going beyond the traditional, solely economic focus of the discipline. Pursuant to Article 3(5) TEU, the Union is required to 'uphold and promote its values and interests and contribute to the protection of its citizens' in its interaction with the wider world.[5] As part of this role, it will be argued that the EU should introduce the social values which it seeks to promote and protect into competition law, with the ambition that they would disseminate organically through replication by jurisdictions beyond the Union.

The chapter places particular emphasis upon equality and sustainability, which are both core to the constitutional social values of the Union and which are increasingly linked to the enforcement of competition rules.[6] This is most evident in relation to environmental protection, where the Commission has integrated consumer preferences for environmentally sustainable products in a number of recent cases.[7] However, there are also

5 Consolidated Version of the Treaty on European Union [2008] OJ C115/13, Art. 3(5) (Treaty on European Union).

6 For a discussion of the interaction between competition enforcement and equality, see Jonathan B. Baker and Steven C. Salop, 'Antitrust Competition Policy and Inequality' (2015) 104 Georgetown Law Review 1; Daniel A. Crane, 'Antitrust and Wealth Inequality' (2016) 101 Cornell Law Review 1171; Sean F. Ennis, Pedro Gonzaga and Chris Pike 'The Effects of Market Power on Inequality' (2017) CPI Antitrust Chronicle; Sean F Ennis, Pedro Gonzaga and Chris Pike, 'Inequality: A hidden cost of market power' (2019) 35 Oxford Review of Economic Policy 518; Ariel Ezrachi, Amit Zac and Christopher Decker, 'The effects of competition law on inequality—an incidental by-product or a path for societal change?' (2022) 11 Journal of Antitrust Enforcement 1. In terms of the relationship between competition enforcement and sustainability or environmental protection, see Suzanne Kingston, *Greening EU competition law and policy* (Cambridge University Press 2011); Or Brook, 'Struggling with Article 101(3) TFEU: Diverging Approaches of the Commission, EU Courts and Five Competition Authorities' (2019) 56 Common Market Law Review 121; Suzanne Kingston, 'Competition Law in an Environmental Crisis' (2019) 10 Journal of European Competition Law & Practice 517; Simon Holmes, 'Climate change, sustainability, and competition law' (2020) 8 Journal of Antitrust Enforcement 354; Jurgita Malinauskaite, 'Competition Law and Sustainability: EU and National Perspectives' (2022) 13 Journal of European Competition Law & Practice 336.

7 Case M.6850 *Marine Harvest/Morpol*, para. 42, where customer preferences for sustainably farmed salmon were one of many factors in finding distinct product markets

developments regarding modern consumers' preferences for fair trade and ethically-produced products which align with the Union's values of social inclusion and equality.[8] Further, the Commission's recent focus on labour has undertones of protecting equality through support for more vulnerable groups.[9] Interestingly, Eustace has written recently on the potential to rely on the Brussels Effect to export its the EU's labour standards (particularly around forced labour), which aligns with the tenor of this chapter and the ability for the EU Union to benefit third country nationals and workers.[10] Equality and sustainability are also prominent in the constitutional foundations of the EU, being interwoven into the Treaty on European Union,[11]

---

for farming and primary processing of Scottish salmon and Norwegian salmon. In addition, in Case M.9076 *Novelis/Aleris* the European Commission concluded that aluminium and steel for car body parts were not part of the same market partly because CO2 emission reduction targets driving 'light weighting' of vehicles (thereby putting a premium on aluminium). Similarly, in Case M.10702 *KPS Capital Partners/Real Alloy Europe* the European Commission considered zero-waste technology of production in recycling of salt slag could be a differentiating factor in market definition. The Revised Market Definition Notice (para. 15) also includes sustainability and resource efficiency as potential parameters alongside more common factors for defining markets such as price, quality, and innovation, Communication from the European Commission 'Commission Notice on the definition of the relevant market for the purposes of Union competition law' [2024] OJ C, C/2024/1645.

8 In *DEMB/Mondelez/Charger Opco* the European Commission considered a possible differentiation between non-conventional coffee (organic, fair trade) and conventional coffee on the basis that retailers indicated some consumers perceive non-conventional coffee as fulfilling different consumer needs. Case M.7292 *DEMB/Mondelez/Charger Opco*, paras. 57–59.

9 'Commission carries out unannounced inspections in the online food delivery sector', 21 November 2023 <https://ec.europa.eu/commission/presscorner/detail/en/ip_23_5944> (accessed 7 January 2025); Alessio Aresu, Dominik Erharter, and Brigitta Renner-Loquenz, 'Antitrust in Labour Markets' Competition Policy Brief, Issue 2, May 2024. In a 2021 Eurobarometer survey, the most pressing issues for citizens were found to be are equal opportunities and access to the labour market; fair working conditions; and access to quality health care. European Commission, *Social Issues*, Special Eurobarometer 509 – Wave EB94.2, March 2021.

10 Proposal for a Regulation of the European Parliament and of the Council on prohibiting products made with forced labour on the Union market, COM/2022/453 final; Alan Eustace, 'The European Union's forced labour regulation: Putting the 'brussels effect' to work for international labour standards' (2024) 15 European Labour Law Journal 144.

11 Consolidated Version of the Treaty on European Union [2008] OJ C115/13, Arts. 2 and 3 (Treaty on European Union).

the Treaty on the Functioning of the European Union,[12] and the Charter of Fundamental Rights.[13] In addition, the EU Green Deal demonstrates the Union's ambition to take the lead on climate change in a global setting. Therefore, it is asserted that equality and sustainability represent the most crucial social values in a competition enforcement context, and are those which the Commission could emphasise most effectively through the Brussels Effect.

The remainder of the paper will be structured as follows. Section two provides a description of the EU's social values which the author suggests should inform competition law. Section three explains the meaning of the Brussels Effect and discusses the nature of the regulatory race between the EU and US in relation competition law, alongside some of the reasons for the EU's success in this regard. Section four explores the benefits of the Brussels Effect for other countries, and why it is a suitable means through which the Union can seek to promote its social values. Section five discusses why the EU's broader social values may be particularly relevant for developing counties. Finally, sections six and seven discuss the development of globalised competition norms and address criticisms of the Brussels Effect.

B. The EU's social values and competition law

I. The social values of the EU

With the advent of the more economic approach in EU competition law and the adoption of the consumer welfare standard, enforcement has focused almost exclusively on economic factors, and in particular, price.[14] Underlying the shift was a belief that the aim of competition law should be

12 Consolidated version on the Treaty on the Functioning of the European Union [2012] OJ C326/47, Arts. 8 and 11 (Treaty on the Functioning of the European Union).

13 Charter of Fundamental Rights of the European Union [2012] OJ C 326/02, Arts. 23 and 37 (Charter of Fundamental Rights).

14 David J. Gerber, *Global Competition: Law, Markets, and Globalization* (Oxford university Press 2010) 193; Anne C. Witt, 'The European Court of Justice and the More Economic Approach to EU Competition Law—Is the Tide Turning?' (2019) 64 The Antitrust Bulletin 172, 177.

to promote a form of economic welfare,[15] with the focus being placed on efficiency-oriented values centred around consumer welfare and the efficient allocation of resources.[16] This has resulted in the exclusion of any social factors related to markets. However, as mentioned in section one, there has been recent recognition of the potential impact of market practices and competition law on factors such as inequality[17] and sustainability.[18] This has resulted in a significant debate regarding the suitability of competition law in addressing non-economic issues. In the US, the advancement of non-economic goals in the law is attributed to the 'neo-Brandeisian movement', a loosely assembled group of critics of the Chicago School and its continuing impact on the law.[19] The name refers to Justice Louis Brandeis, who was associated with a broader approach towards antitrust prior the narrowing of the discipline that began with the Chicago School.[20] This

---

15 Ioannis Lianos, 'Some Reflections on the Question of the Goals of EU Competition Law' (2013) Research Paper Series: 3/2013 UCL Centre for Law, Economics and Society, 4.

16 Imelda Maher, 'Competition Law: Convergence Through Law and Networks' in Paul Craig and Gráinne de Búrca (eds) *The Evolution of EU Law* (3rd edn, Oxford University Press 2021) 829, 846.

17 J. E. Stiglitz, *The Price of Inequality: How Today's Divided Society Endangers Our Future* (W.W. Norton & Company 2012); Thomas Piketty, *Capital in the Twenty-First Century* (Harvard University Press 2014) 1; Center for America Progress, Report, *Reviving Antitrust: Why Our Economy Needs a Progressive Competition Policy*, 18 June 2016; Herbert Hovenkamp and Fiona Scott Morton, 'Framing the Chicago School of Antitrust Analysis' (2020) 168 University Pennsylvania Law Review 1843, 1852–53; Hiba Hafiz, 'Antitrust and Race' (2022) 100 Washington University Review 1471; Bennett Capers and Gregory Day, 'Race-ing Antitrust' (2023) 121 Michigan Law Review 523.

18 Much of the attention on competition law and sustainability builds on the research originally carried out by Suzanne Kingston, judge of the General Court. See Suzanne Kingston, *Greening EU competition law and policy* (Cambridge University Press 2011). More recently, see for example Holmes (n 6); Julian Nowag, Background Note, *Sustainability and Competition Law and Policy*, OECD, 1 December 2020; Suzanne Kingston, 'Greening merger control? The Role of Environmental Considerations in Merger Analysis' in Ioannis Kokkoris and Nicholas Levy (eds) *Research Handbook on Global Merger Control* (Edward Elgar 2023).

19 Alison Jones, Brenda Sufrin and Niamh Dunne, *EU Competition Law: Text, Cases and Materials* (7th edn, Oxford University Press 2019) 37–38.

20 Justice Brandeis, 'Competition and Smallness: A Dilemma Re-Examined' (1956) 66 The Yale Law Journal 69, 84; Kenneth G. Elzinga and Micah Webber, 'Louis Brandeis and Contemporary Antitrust Enforcement' (2017) 33 Touro Law Review 277. The Chicago School is considered to have originated from Robert Bork, amongst other scholars. See Robert H. Bork and Ward S. Bowman, Jr., 'The Crisis in Antitrust' (1965) 65 Columbia Law Review 363; Richard A Posner, 'The Chicago School of

reduction of the focus in US antitrust in the 1970s subsequently shaped the direction of EU competition law pursuant to the 'more economic approach'.[21] However, a counter-movement has occurred which seeks to reassert the importance of market structure in deciding cases (through an emphasis on the competitive process, rather than price effects),[22] as well seeking to introduce non-economic factors into the assessment. This has been met with strong resistance and derision by those in favour of extremely limited intervention on markets (most obviously in developing the pejorative phrase 'hipster antitrust').[23] Equally, there is increasing support for a broader perspective in competition law in recognition of the social impact of markets beyond consumers and the sometimes myopic nature of the consumer welfare standard, with its prioritisation of short-term price effects.[24] Therefore, it remains unclear which non-economic factors can play a role in assessments.

However, this author argues that the nascent examples of sustainability impacting market definition are indications of a shift taking place in the law. While there is significant resistance to the inclusion of non-economic

Antitrust Analysis' (1979) 127 University of Pennsylvania Law Review 925; Frank H Easterbrook, 'The Limits of Antitrust' (1984) 63 Texas Law Review 1; Robert H Bork, *The Antitrust Paradox: A Policy at War with Itself* (Basic Books 1978, reprinted with a new Introduction and Epilogue, 1993).

21 Imelda Maher, 'Competition Law: Convergence Through Law and Networks' in Paul Craig and Gráinne de Búrca (eds), *The Evolution of EU Law* (3rd end, Oxford University Press 2021) 829; Paulo Ibáñez Colomo and Andriani Kalintiri, 'The Evolution of EU Antitrust Policy: 1966–2017' (2020) 83 The Modern Law Review 321, 343; Klaudia Majcher and Vikoria H.S.E. Robertson, 'Protecting personal data and the environment: doctrinal challenges for EU competition law in our day and age' (2022) 47 European Law Review 622, 625; Niamh Dunne, 'Public Interest and EU Competition Law' (2020) 65 The Antitrust Bulletin 256, 259–260.

22 Lina M. Khan, 'Amazon's Antitrust Paradox' (2016) 126 Yale Law Journal 710, 745; Tim Wu, 'After Consumer Welfare Now What? The "Protection of Competition" Standard in Practice' (2018) CPI Antitrust Chronicle.

23 Elyse Dorsey, Jan M. Rybnicek and Joshua D. Wright, 'Hipster Antitrust Meets Public Choice Economics: The Consumer Welfare Standard, Rule of Law, and Rent Seeking' (2018) CPI Antitrust Chronicle; Herbert Hovenkamp, 'Whatever did happen to the antitrust movement?' (2018) 94 Notre Dame Law Review 583; Christopher S. Yoo, 'Hipster Antitrust: New Bottles, Same Old W(h)ine?' (2018) CPI Antitrust Chronicle; Marco Botta and Silvia Solidoro 'Hipster antitrust, the European way?' (2020) EUI Policy Brief 2020/02; Thomas W. Hazlett, 'The Nirvana Fallacy in "Hipster Antitrust"' (2021) 28 George Mason Law Review 1253; Bush (n 12) 526–527.

24 Darren Bush, 'Consumer Welfare Theory as an Ethical Consideration: An Essay on Hipsters, Invisible Feet, and the "Science" of Economics' (2018) 63(4) The Antitrust Bulletin 509, 526–527.

factors in the US, this is weaker in the EU where there appears to be greater recognition of the need for economic practices to adapt to align with the EU Green Deal.[25] Therefore, it is argued that an incorporation of social values is likelier to be embraced by the EU and would be more reflective of competition law's placement in the Union's foundational Treaties, along with the EU's shift towards a greater balance between economic and social values. As the EU evolved, it slowly readjusted the weights attached to economic and social interests. From its original goal of establishing a common market and closer economic ties between contracting states, it has developed into a 'social market economy'[26] with the aim of promoting the 'well-being of its peoples'[27] (which clearly extends beyond mere economic welfare). In addition to the amendment of a number of articles in the Treaties to include socially progressive language, the EU also adopted the Charter of Fundamental Rights[28] and granted it the same legal status as the Treaties, requiring it to be read with them as part of the constitutional texts of the EU.[29]

II. Constitutional values to be incorporated

Regarding the specific social values this chapter advocates for the inclusion of in competition law, the author is focused on gender and racial equality, economic equality, and environmental sustainability. It is argued that these are reflected in the constitutional foundations of the EU, and they are the most likely to interact with markets and competition law. Further, they are all referenced within the horizontal integration clauses of Articles 7–13 TFEU. The horizontal integration clauses are crucial in terms of informing the interpretation of the Treaties and the Union's role in developing its policies, shaping how they should interact with each other in an increasingly complex legal environment. The underlying premise of

---

25 Thomas Wiedmann and others, 'Scientists' Warning on Affluence' (2020) 11 Nature Communications 1; Jason Hickel and Giorgos Kallis, 'Is Green Growth Possible?' (2020) 25 New Political Economy 469; Johannes Persch, 'The Output/Sustainability Paradox – a pro-enforcement perspective on sustainability in EU competition law' (2023) 15 The Competition Law Review 139.

26 Treaty on European Union, Art. 3(3).

27 Treaty on European Union, Art. 3(1).

28 Charter of Fundamental Rights.

29 Treaty on European Union, Art. 6.

the horizontal clauses is that the aims of the EU relating to equality and environmental protection cannot be attained through isolated policies, and instead, require concerted efforts.[30] Thus, they encourage the articulation of integrated policies for the various interests they protect,[31] and underline the need to actively forge positive links between the EU's distinct objectives (rather than attending to them in isolation).[32] Further, they sit alongside the Union's commitment to upholding and promoting its values and interests in its interaction with the wider world pursuant to Article 3(5) TEU, as well as its commitment to pursue policies and actions that foster the sustainable economic, social and environmental development of developing countries, in addition to improving the quality of the environment and the sustainable management of global natural resources.[33] Thus, the constitutional provisions of the Union appear to support the active pursuit of the Brussels Effect in promoting the application of the social provisions of the Treaties, and equality and sustainability in particular, in the enforcement of competition law.

Article 7 TFEU acts as the basis for the broad application of the general principle clauses that follow it by stating that '[t]he Union shall ensure consistency between its policies and activities, taking all of its objectives into account and in accordance with the principle of conferral of powers.'[34] It is argued that this requirement for coherence between policies means that competition law in the EU may no longer stand alone as an island, contentedly soothed by the waves of economic efficiency which it has bathed in for so long. The purely economic approach that has come to dominate the area must be seen as inconsistent with the broader approach that is mandated by Article 7 TFEU, which clearly requires a holistic perspective be adopted in what were previously considered to be distinctive policy areas. As a result, competition law can no longer claim to be a unique area of law where efficiency is the sole value. Further, this requirement of consistency in its policies extends to its interactions in a global context, thereby supporting the application of the Brussels Effect to support the

30 Evangelia Psychogiopoulou, 'Unravelling the Complexities of the Horizontal Clauses of Arts 8–13 TFEU' (2023) 8 European Papers 221, 223.

31 Psychogiopoulou (n 30).

32 Evangelia Psychogiopoulou, 'The Horizontal Clauses of Arts 8–13 TFEU Through the Lens of the Court of Justice' (2022) 7 European Papers 1357, 1379.

33 Treaty on European Union, Art. 21(2).

34 Treaty on the Functioning of the European Union, Art. 7.

reliance on, for example, the Union's ambitious climate agenda through the EU Green Deal to inform its competition rules.

Articles 8–10 TFEU set forth a number of the social values of the Union. In particular, gender equality, combatting discrimination, and social integration are emphasised through the provisions. Article 8 TFEU states, '[i]n all its activities, the Union shall aim to eliminate inequalities, and to promote equality, between men and women.' Article 9 TFEU intertwines economic and social values by stating the EU shall, in defining and implementing its policies and activities, 'take into account requirements linked to the promotion of a high level of employment, the guarantee of adequate social protection, the fight against social exclusion, and a high level of education, training and protection of human health.'[35] The provision recognises that social exclusion often follows from economic exclusion, and thus, the two are inevitably interconnected. The requirement to apply Article 9 TFEU across policy domains emphasises the interdependency of the Union's policies.[36] Article 10 TFEU states that 'the Union shall aim to combat discrimination based on sex, racial or ethnic origin, religion or belief, disability, age or sexual orientation.' Finally, Article 11 TFEU relates to sustainability and sets out that '[e]nvironmental protection requirements must be integrated into the definition and implementation of the Union's policies and activities, in particular with a view to promoting sustainable development.'[37] The rationale is that sustainable development cannot be achieved through environmental law alone, but, instead, must be integrated as a consideration throughout the Union's activities if it is to be effective.[38] As the Commission has said, 'environmental policy alone cannot achieve the environmental improvements needed as part of sustainable development.'[39] Thus, the environmental integration clause is a means of achieving the

35 Treaty on the Functioning of the European Union, Art. 9.

36 Sybe de Vries and Rik de Jager, 'Between Hope and Fear: The Creation of a More Inclusive EU Single Market Through Art. 9 TFEU' (2022) 7 European Papers 1405, 1410.

37 Treaty on the Functioning of the European Union, Art. 11.

38 The UN 2030 Agenda for Sustainable Development, which contains 17 sustainable development goals, requires them to be implemented in an integrated manner to be effective (UN 2030 Agenda for Sustainable Development, Declaration, para. 5). See also Persch (n 25); Vasiliki Karageorgou, 'The Environmental Integration Principle in EU Law: Normative Content and Functions also in Light of New Developments, such as the European Green Deal' (2023) 8 European Papers 159, 161.

39 European Commission, 'Integration of Environmental Considerations into other Policy Areas – a Stocktaking of the Cardiff Process' COM (2004) 394 final, 2.

ultimate aim of sustainable development. This is part of the modernisation of environmental policy towards integrating economic and environmental interests to arrive at 'win-win' solutions (for example, through the financing of renewable sources of energy).[40] It is fundamentally a recognition of the fact that, operating in isolation, environmental policy would be ineffective.[41] Instead, it must be incorporated in a coherent manner across the various policy areas of the EU, of which competition is no exception. However, the underlying global competition policies seem to increase the 'output-sustainability paradox'.[42] In other words, by incentivising lower prices and greater consumption, competition rules are promoting the degradation of the planet through climate change, which is being caused in part by producing and consuming more.[43] Therefore, a reconsideration of how the environment is considered within competition law is essential to ensure coherence across the EU's policies. This is especially important in a global context, where the Union has committed itself to pursuing international measures to preserve and improve the quality of the environment and the sustainable management of global natural resources.[44] Therefore, the application of the Brussels Effect to promote the Union's environmental goals in competition law appears a consonant aim with the broader environmental provisions of the Treaties, and an effective way of encouraging sustainable practices outside its jurisdiction.

In addition, the Union recognised itself as a '*social* market economy' pursuant to the Lisbon Treaty, developing upon the conception put forward by Alfred Müller-Armack.[45] This was strongly emblematic of the movement away from the predominantly economic values of the EU and towards a greater balance with social factors. In many regards, the twin objectives of the EU's economic and social aims are contained within the concept

40 Suzanne Kingston, *The role of environmental protection in EC competition law and policy* (Universiteit Leiden, 17 February 2009) 11.

41 Psychogiopoulou (n 30) 223.

42 Persch (n 25) 143.

43 Wiedmann et al. (n 25). The authors point to how the economic model encourages growth at all costs, which is fuelled by consumption that is ultimately at the root cause of climate change. See also Han Kjellberg, 'Market practices and over-consumption' (2008) 11 Consumption, Markets and Culture 151.

44 Treaty on European Union, Art 21(2).

45 Alfred Müller-Armack, 'The Social Market Economy as an Economic and Social Order' (1978) 36 Review of Social Economy 325.

of the social market economy,[46] and the phrase can be seen as indicative of the EU's understanding of their equal status in the Union. As Classen describes it, the social market economy is 'the golden formula to unify the two opposing conceptions: an EU that is both social and a market economy.'[47]

This author asserts that the provisions demonstrate the EU's commitment to departing from legal silos that treat competition law as separate, and instead seek to apply it in a manner that serves its important cross-cutting provisions represented by the horizontal integration clauses. Further, when read alongside Articles 3(5) and 21(2) TEU, there is a strong argument for utilising its influence over the shape and direction of competition law globally to introduce its social values, such as environmental protection, as a means of fostering social, economic and sustainable development beyond the Union.

III. Holistic constitutional lens

The Treaties, along with the Charter, form the constitutional framework of the Union. This framework establishes basic principles and values of the EU that are intended to shape and control the individual rules developed by the EU's institutions.[48] The competition provisions of the EU are unusual as they are grounded in the Treaties (rather than in legislative acts, such as the US, Canada, or the UK),[49] and thus, must operate within this constitutional architecture.[50] In particular, Articles 101 and 102 TFEU represent the

46 Rutger Classen et al., 'Rethinking the European Social Markey Economy' (2019) 57 Journal of Common Market Studies 3, 4.

47 Classen et al. (n 46).

48 David T. Gerber, 'Constitutionalizing the Economy: German Neo-liberalism, Competition Law and the "New" Europe' (1994) 42(1) American Journal of Comparative Law 25, 80.

49 The Sherman Antitrust Act of 1890 and the Clayton Act of 1914 in the US; the Competition Act 1985 (R.S.C., 1985, c. C-34) in Canada; and the Competition Act 1998 in the UK.

50 For a discussion of the constitutional framework and its application to competition law, see for example Gerber (n 48) 80; Chris Townley and Alexander H. Türk, 'The Constitutional Limits of EU Competition Law— United in Diversity' (2019) 64 The Antitrust Bulletin 235; Majcher and Robertson (n 21); Julian Nowag, 'Competition Law's Sustainability Gap? Tools for an Examination and a Brief Overview' (2022) 5 Nordic Journal of European Law 149, 164.

core competition law provisions of the Union. However, they are bolstered by the State aid rules in Article 106 TFEU, as well as the merger control rules which flow from the broader competition law architecture established by the Treaties (which would be entirely undermined without an effective means of reviewing mergers and acquisitions). Thus, competition law in the EU has a uniquely constitutional nature, having been present in the original Treaty of Paris and thereby forming a crucial constituent element of the economic constitution of the Union since its inception.[51]

It is because of this constitutional basis and nature that the author argues the social provisions of the Treaties must influence how the discipline operates in practice. In particular, it is asserted that the text of the Treaties support the more holistic approach advocated herein and the application of social values in assessments. EU competition law was a fundamental aspect of the original European integration project and part of the foundational core of the Treaties. Therefore, when confronted by global challenges that interact with competition law (such as environmental sustainability and increasing wealth inequality), the questions cannot be answered by merely seeing competition law as a system of economic rules.[52] Instead, they are 'constitutional' questions, and from a European legal perspective, the constitutional context of the EU gives direction in developing answers.[53]

The consumer welfare standard, as applied, assumes legitimacy based on the perception of it as benefitting EU consumers and citizens predominantly through lower prices. However, if EU citizens have indicated that the interests they value go beyond mere economic welfare (as seems clear from the Treaties) then it would appear to be imperative on the institutions to consider such interests when they act. The EU's economic constitution balances both economic and social values, and each area of the law should be reflective of this in order to form a coherent whole and to respond adequately to emerging social issues.[54] This, it is argued, extends to the Commission when it is enforcing competition rules or assessing mergers. Majcher and Robertson also make this point, arguing that whether a strong form or weak form of coherence is mandated, there is a legal obligation

---

51 Treaty Establishing the European Coal and Steel Community, 261 U.N.T.S. 142.

52 Anna Gerbrandy, 'Changing Competition Law in a Changing European Union The Constitutional Challenges of Competition Law' (2019) 14 The Competition Law Review 33, 48.

53 Gerbrandy (n 52).

54 Gerbrandy (n 52).

to integrate the foundational principles in assessments.[55] As Stucke asserts, consumer surplus is important but should be viewed as a byproduct of the competitive process rather than the aim of competition policy, which instead should prioritise social and moral values that promote a sustainable, inclusive economy that increases the well-being of the many, rather than the few.[56] In this regard, the social values of equality and sustainability in particular could play a key role in transitioning away from the efficiency-dominated consumer welfare standard and towards a socially conscious standard, which would incorporate a more comprehensive view of what markets ought to achieve. Therefore, it is such social values that the author argues could be spread beyond the Union effectively through the operation of the Brussels Effect in competition law.

C. The Brussels Effect and the regulatory competition between the EU and the US

I. Regulatory race between the EU and the US

The EU and the US seek for other jurisdictions to follow their respective regulatory models.[57] This involves the two foremost competition authorities promoting their competition regimes as the most desirable and urging developed and developing countries to incorporate them domestically.[58] However, what is clear from the empirical research is that the EU has clearly taken the lead in this regulatory race, and may even be in the process of lapping the US as they approach the next bend. This is significant because, despite some convergence as a result of the EU's adoption of a more economic approach (which aligned somewhat with Chicago School teachings in the US), their paths appear to be increasingly diverging. This is

55 Majcher and Robertson (n 21).

56 Maurice E. Stucke, 'Should Competition Policy Promote Happiness' (2013) 81 Fordham Law Review 2575, 2645.

57 Bradford et al. (n 3) 733.

58 Eleanor M. Fox, 'EU and US Competition Law: A Comparison, in Global Competition Policy' in E. Graham and J. David (eds), *Global Competition Policy* (Institute of International Economics 1997); William E. Kovacic, 'Competition Policy in the European Union and the United States: Convergence or Divergence in the Future Treatment of Dominant Firms' (2008) 4 Competition Law International 8; William E. Kovacic, 'The United States and its Future Influence on Global Competition Policy' (2015) 22 George Mason Law Review 1157.

most evident in recent investigations undertaken in the digital economy by the European Commission which were not replicated in the US, or through the EU's adoption of the Digital Markets Act.[59] Similarly, the Commission's appetite to challenge mergers firmly, either requiring extensive remedies or through outright prohibitions, has created conflict with US competition authorities.[60]

Despite the US approach being arguably more 'traditional' in the eyes of some commentators and closer aligned with a purely economic approach, it is significant that other jurisdictions are deciding to embrace the more interventionist European approach that is less tied to neoliberal economic analysis.[61] The empirical research on the subject demonstrates clearly the shift in preference that has occurred for third countries, as the EU model now appears to be almost automatically followed in favour of the US system.[62] There are many reasons explaining this. Firstly, the EU's institutional structure in a competition law context is more compatible with the structures in most civil law countries, and hence, when they establish competition regimes for the first time they are inclined to implement something akin to the EU's system and the norms therein.[63] In this manner, it can be seen to have an administrative template that is easier to assimilate than the complex and idiosyncratic US system.[64] Further, the EU tends to produce a more precise set of rules that are easier to implement in third countries, particularly if there is a lack of technical expertise in the initial phase of the competition authority.[65]

---

59 For example, see the trilogy of cases against Google, namely, Case AT.40411 *Google (AdSense)*, C(2019) 2173 final, Case AT.40099 *Google Android* C(2018) 4761 final and Case AT.39740 *Google Search (Shopping)*, C(2017) 4444 final.

60 For example, see Case M.8084, *Bayer/Monsanto*, C(2018) 3557 final; Case M.7932, *Dow/DuPont*, C(2017) 1946 final; Case M.10483, *Illumina/Grail*, C(2024) 6433 final.

61 For example, the UK CMA's initial prohibition of the acquisition of Activision by Microsoft, or the Australian Competition Taskforce's Merger Reform Consultation which has an emphasis on digital markets and whether there is a need for stronger intervention. In addition, the ACCC has blocked a number of recent notified mergers such as *ANZ/Suncorp* and *Telstra/TPG*.

62 Bradford et al. (n 3) 734.

63 Bradford et al. (n 3).

64 Anu Bradford, Adam S. Chilton and Filippo Maria Lancieri, 'The Chicago School's Limited Influence on International Antitrust' (2020) 87 The University of Chicago Law Review 297, 315.

65 Bradford et al. (n 3) 735.

Secondly, and in contrast to the US, the EU appears to have consciously decided to expand its regulatory reach by utilising trade agreements to impose its competition-based economic constitution on other jurisdictions.[66] The EU is conscious of the vast and wealthy consumer-base which the Single Market represents, and the strong bargaining position this puts it in when negotiating agreements. Inevitably, one of the terms of such trade agreements will be the adoption of common rules between the EU and its trading partner, or the establishment of a competition regime by the trading partner that addresses effectively potential competition distortions in its territory.[67] Generally speaking, the closer the level of integration desired by the trading partner, the greater the level of detail in the competition provisions of the agreement.[68] For example, the trade agreements between Canada and the EU, and the United Kingdom and the EU, contain extensive competition provisions.[69] In addition, the EU entered into accession agreements with a number of countries from the Eastern Partnership recently,[70] most notably Georgia, Moldova and Ukraine.[71] The accession agreements represent a crucial step on these countries' potential journey towards EU membership, and it is notable that all three contain important competition law chapters that require the States to maintain effective laws against anti-competitive agreements and abuse of dominance, as well as providing a system that effectively controls mergers.[72] In addition, there are provisions

66 Bradford et al. (n 3) 735; Anselm Küsters, 'The Making and Unmaking of Ordoliberal Language: A Digital Conceptual History of European Competition Law' (Goethe University in Frankfurt am Main May 2022) 444.

67 OECD – Competition Provisions in Trade Agreements, *supra* n. 47.

68 Küsters (n 66) 444.

69 Canada/EU Comprehensive Trade Agreement, O.J. L 11, Chapters Seventeen and Eighteen; Trade and Cooperation Agreement between the EU and UK, O.J. L 149, Arts. 358–362.

70 The Eastern Partnership is a joint initiative involving the EU, its Member States and six Eastern European Partner countries: Armenia, Azerbaijan, Belarus, Georgia, the Republic of Moldova and Ukraine.

71 Association Agreement between the European Union and the European Atomic Energy Community and their Member States, of the one part, and Georgia, of the other part, OJ L 261 (Georgian Agreement); Association Agreement between the European Union and the European Atomic Energy Community and their Member States, of the one part, and Moldova, of the other part, OJ L 260/4 (Moldovan Agreement); Association Agreement between the European Union and its Member States, of the one part, and Ukraine, of the other part, OJ L 161 (Ukrainian Agreement).

72 Georgian Agreement, Art. 204; Moldovan Agreement Arts. 333–335; Ukrainian Agreement, Arts. 253–256.

addressing State aid.[73] Importantly for the purposes of this paper, the accession agreements also contain chapters and provisions on climate action, the environment, and sustainable development,[74] as well as commitments to cooperate on promoting social inclusion and gender equality.[75] Thus, one can decipher the intertwined nature of the EU's traditionally economic policies and activities (including trade and competition rules) with its social aims. The accession agreements recognise the need for a holistic approach across these issues and the increased importance of the Union's social goals, which are at the foundations of the accession agreements alongside the trade provisions.

Thirdly, the EU has also been successful in diffusing its competition rules and utilising the Brussels Effect by establishing the strictest standards, which are then ultimately followed by undertakings and other jurisdictions alike. This is because companies are likely to adhere to the most stringent regulatory standards (which are often those of the EU) in order to standardise their global production in compliance with said standard. The alternative is to adopt individualised methods for various markets or to forego the EU market altogether, both of which represent unattractive options.[76] Therefore, it is suggested that the EU has the foremost ability to shape foreign jurisdictions' laws in a competition context because companies will choose to conform to its standards.[77] This author argues that the operation of the Brussels Effect in this manner grants the EU a uniquely powerful ability to shape the direction of global competition law. As Kovacic puts it, 'the most intervention-minded policy and an effective mechanism to enforce its commands has power to set a global standard'.[78] Companies react accordingly and tailor their behaviour to the most restrictive rules in areas such as abuse of dominance.[79] For example, the EU was probably the only jurisdiction interventionist-minded and with enough clout to introduce the Digital Markets Act. However, with a more

73 Georgian Agreement, Art. 205; Moldovan Agreement Art. 339; Ukrainian Agreement, Art. 262.
74 Moldovan Agreement, Chapters 13 and 17; Georgian Agreement, Chapters 3, 4 and 13; Ukrainian Agreement, Chapters 6 and 13.
75 Georgian Agreement, Art. 239; Moldovan Agreement, Art. 375; Ukrainian Agreement, Art. 419–420.
76 Bradford (n 1) 5.
77 Bradford et al. (n 3) 735.
78 Kovacic (n 58, 2008) 8.
79 Kovacic (n 58, 2008) 8.

interventionist framework and expectation of adherence established, other jurisdictions have equally recognised the ill-health of competition on digital markets and have been emboldened to introduce equivalent legislation, with the strictest standard of the EU thereby becoming a benchmark. For example, Japan, Germany and the UK have followed the EU by adopting complementary rules to their competition law regime to capture the power of ultra-dominant digital firms.[80]

The factors described above have led to the EU becoming the 'template' for competition law, with the influence of the US dropping in tandem with this change.[81] As Kovacic points out, newer competition systems are relying on administrative enforcement models that resemble the EU.[82] This is entirely understandable given the relative simplicity of the EU model when compared to the US system of dual enforcement agencies and the need to involve the court system to deliver fines. However, this trend is interesting given that the US has a much longer history of enforcing competition law than the EU, suggesting that third countries recognise something preferable in the EU apparatus.[83] The data shows that the average similarity of other jurisdictions to the EU was roughly the same as the similarity to the US when the EU adopted its competition laws, but that began to change in 1990 when the correlation to EU rules increased dramatically in comparison to the US.[84] In addition to this trend, the number of countries that follow neither the EU nor US has also decreased significantly, and it is rare for countries to seek to follow aspects of both regimes.[85] The chapter asserts that this demonstrates the desirability of the EU's model, while also revealing that there are likely structural and philosophical reasons that third countries feel the US system is unsuitable, whereas the EU model and goals pursued may be more aligned with their outlook on the purpose of the law. It is this alignment between the EU and third countries which the author believes the Union should seek to rely on in promoting its social values discussed in the previous section through their explicit and implicit incorporation in the EU's competition policy. The position of prominence grants the EU a significant power to shape competition laws beyond the Union in future, as the tradition of adopting and following the European

80 Act on Promotion of Competition for Specified Smartphone Software, June 2024.
81 Bradford et al. (n 3) 734.
82 Kovacic (n 58, 2008) 8–9.
83 Bradford et al. (n 3) 734.
84 Bradford et al. (n 3) 734.
85 Bradford et al. (n 3) 750.

position makes other countries more likely to continue doing so. The crux of the argument in the chapter is that the EU, thus, has the capacity to spread the unique social values of its constitutional structure through the alteration of its own competition laws. This, it is suggested, could then be replicated in other jurisdictions that follow EU competition principles closely, while also forming a key aspect of trade agreements in future.

II. Meaning and application of the Brussels Effect

The analysis of the Brussels Effect builds on earlier American scholarship that investigated the idea of the 'California Effect' in the US, whereby businesses were found to comply with the stricter regulations adopted in California in order to ensure they could apply uniform production methods across the country.[86] Due to the size and importance of the Californian market, it gave its legislature significant regulatory clout, which it utilised in promoting progressive environmental policies.[87]

Bradford has provided much scholarly research analysing the impact of the Brussels Effect, noting that it is an underestimated aspect of Europe's power to regulate global markets.[88] Through the Brussels Effect, the EU has been able to establish general rules and standards across areas such as food, chemicals, privacy, and most importantly, competition.[89] It is almost unique in this regard due to the extensiveness of its powers of enforcement whereby it has exclusive competence to assess mergers with an EU dimension and has fully harmonised the substantive law within the Union.[90] This has been described as 'unilateral regulatory globalization',[91] whereby the EU acts first and without the consensus of other jurisdictions, confident in the

86 David Vogel and Robert A. Kagan, 'Introduction: National Regulations in a Global Economy' in David Vogel and Robert A. Kagan (eds), *Dynamics of Regulatory Change: How Globalization Affects National Regulatory Policies* (California University Press 2004) 1, 6–10; David Vogel, 'Trading up and governing across: transnational governance and environmental protection' (1997) 4 Journal of European Public Policy 556.

87 Vogel and Kagan (n 86) 9.

88 Bradford (n 1) 3.

89 Bradford (n 1) 3.

90 Konstantinos Stylianou and Marios Iacovides, 'The goals of EU competition law: a comprehensive empirical investigation' (2022) 42 Legal Studies 620, 646.

91 Bradford (n 1) 3; Anu Bradford, *The Brussels Effect: How the European Union Rules the World* (Oxford University Press 2020) xiii-xiv.

knowledge that the global importance of the European Single Market will require other regulators and multinational corporations to follow suit or comply with European standards. Thus, the Brussels Effect bypasses the need to resort to international institutions or seek cooperation by indirectly entrenching the EU's rules across other countries' legal frameworks,[92] thereby shaping global commerce in the EU's image in a manner entirely disproportionate to its economic power or population. This form of 'soft coercion'[93] is primarily based on the leverage the EU has over countries seeking to create closer trading relations with it,[94] however, the Union is also being followed in areas such as climate change and data protection (which are more aligned with its social values) because of the perception that the EU is making sensible and desirable policy-changes. Further, the EU has significant legislative and regulatory resources that often make their decisions defensible and replicable, meaning that legal transplants are recognised as a major form of development.[95]

There are, of course, inherent internal and external constraints limiting the Brussels Effect.[96] However, given the importance of securing access to the internal market, it remains a powerful tool, and one which the author believes the EU could rely upon more effectively to promote the values it is mandated to advance pursuant to the Treaties. At present, there are many motivating factors behind actively pursuing the Brussels Effect. For example, its operation means that European companies do not face different regulatory systems when exporting and are not at a disadvantage when competing abroad.[97] Further, the adoption of the EU's competition system in other jurisdictions ensures domestic companies in those countries face similar constraints when foreign companies begin exporting to the Single

92 Bradford (n 1) 64.

93 Bradford (n 1) 66.

94 Jan Zielonka, 'Europe as a Global Actor: Empire by Example?' (2008) 84 International Affairs 471, 476.

95 Michal Gal, 'The Cut and Paste of Article 82 of the EC Treaty in Israel: Conditions for a Successful Transplant' (2007) 9 European Journal of Law Reform 467, 468.

96 Bradford (n 1) 48–63.

97 Canadian Competition Bureau, Submission to the OECD Global Forum on Competition – Competition Provisions in Trade Agreements – *Ensuring that the benefits of trade liberalisation are not offset by anti-competitive conduct* (January 2021) <https://ised-isde.canada.ca/site/competition-bureau-canada/en/how-we-foster-competition/collaboration-and-partnerships/cooperation-instruments-international-partners/competition-bureau-submission-oecd-global-forum-competition-competition-provisions-trade-agreements> (accessed 11 December 2023).

Market, meaning that European companies are not at a disadvantage. In addition, it has been said that the Brussels Effect (particularly so in the competition law context) enables the EU to export its economic philosophy to third countries.[98] This, it is argued, reflects a fundamental choice for third countries between the EU's more interventionist model and the US's reliance on market self-correction.[99] However, while primarily being motivated by creating a level platform for European companies and protecting the Single Market, it is suggested by this author that the EU could utilise the Brussels Effect to contribute to the dissemination of its social values through its competition law framework by introducing such factors into its own laws and seeking to ensure that other jurisdictions begin providing similar protections.

Much of the previous literature focused on regulatory competition between countries in the environmental context,[100] where the EU remains a forerunner.[101] However, the EU's regulatory capacity is arguably strongest in relation to competition policy due to the inherent link to trade and the Single Market.[102] This has resulted in the EU placing greater emphasis on establishing and maintaining its position as the de facto antitrust standard in the global system, dethroning the US antitrust regime in this regard.[103] Thus, the standards it sets and rules it adopts no longer simply stop in their operation at the borders of the EU, as the EU possesses an unrivalled ability to project its competition policy preferences outside its territory.[104] In this regard, the EU largely succeeded in its ambition of ensuring its trading partners have independent authorities that enforce its competition laws effectively.[105] There are over 130 countries with domestic competition laws, making it one of the most widespread methods of economic regulation

98 Bradford et al. (n 3) 733.

99 Jonathan B. Baker, 'Taking the Error out of Error Cost Analysis: What's Wrong with Antitrust's Right' (2015) 80 Antitrust Law Journal 1; Khan (n 22) 719–720.

100 Katharina Holzinger and Thomas Sommerer, 'Race to the Bottom' or 'Race to Brussels'?: Environmental Competition in Europe' (2011) 49 JCMS: Journal of Common Market Studies 315, 329.

101 For example, there are numerous initiatives being implemented pursuant to the European Green Deal that aim to make Europe a climate-neutral continent by 2050.

102 Bradford (n 1) 14.

103 Bradford (n 1) 20.

104 Kovacic (n 58, 2008) 8.

105 OECD, *Competition Provisions in Trade Agreements – Contribution from the European Union*, 5 December 2019, DAF/COMP/GF/WD(2019)7.

across international markets.[106] An interesting aspect of this is the fact that many of them have been adopted since 1990, coinciding with the creation of the WTO in 1995 and the conclusion of multiple bilateral and multilateral trade agreements that incorporated competition provisions.[107] More importantly, this also aligns with the timeline over which the EU has emerged as the principal competition law enforcer and regulator.

D. Benefits of the Brussels Effect in Competition Law

I. Advantages for other jurisdictions

The Brussels Effect has many benefits for other countries in a competition law context. Initially, adopting countries can observe the EU as a form of 'legal laboratory', whereby it evaluates the experience of another jurisdiction and can adapt rules according to the sensitivities of its own legal system.[108] Once adopted, the experiences of the EU are invaluable in providing guidance when the domestic provisions replicate or closely follow European rules.[109] As Gerber points out, borrowing language from other sources such as the EU is an easier task than developing entirely new rules, and in addition, the language used has a rich interpretive history behind it to provide predictability.[110]

Further, smaller jurisdictions will have a limited amount of information to be gathered from domestic experiences. Therefore, the ability to rely on previous analysis conducted by the EU is extremely valuable.[111] In particular, the Commission benefits from levels of expertise in DG Comp that are beyond virtually any other competition authority, both in terms of legal and economic expertise. This benefit of the European experience is especially important in a competition law context because there are elastic

106 Bradford et al. (n 3) 733; Anu Bradford and Adam Chilton, 'Regulating Antitrust through Trade Agreements' (2021) 84 Antitrust Law Journal 103.

107 Bradford and Chilton (n 106).

108 Gal (n 95) 477.

109 Hailegabriel G. Feyissa, 'European influence on Ethiopian antitrust regime: comparative and functional analysis of some problems' (2009) 3 Mizan Law Review 271, 287.

110 David J. Gerber, 'Constructing Competition Law in China: The Potential Value of European and U.S. Experience' (2004) 3 Washington University Global Studies Law Review 315, 315–316.

111 Gal (n 95) 476.

concepts involved that can be applied on a case-by-case basis, informed by economic teachings not readily available to enforcement agencies with more constrained resources.[112] In addition, agencies can be led in situations where the EU evaluated potentially anticompetitive conduct and base their own enforcement action on the analysis carried out if the behaviour had an effect in the domestic market.[113] As argued in this paper, the interpretive analysis which the Commission provides could extend to social factors introduced in future, as the experience of the EU in engaging with them could guide other enforcers.

In addition to the structural and analytical benefits gained from the Brussels Effect, countries also benefit from the fact that the EU's laws are published in multiple languages, which is enormously beneficial to those outside the English-speaking legal sphere.[114] For example, the Lusophone Competition Network includes Portugal, Angola, Brazil, Cape Verde, Guinea Bissau, Mozambique, São Tomé e Príncipe, and Timor-Leste, which can take advantage of Portuguese access to European materials in each member's primary language.[115] This leads to their ease of diffusion across a broader swathe of jurisdictions, but also to a more sophisticated and straightforward application once adopted given inevitably greater levels of understanding. Similarly, Ecuador mirrors the EU through its adoption of Spanish competition law (which is, of course, based on the EU template).[116]

The EU will also have the benefit of significant resources in tackling anti-competitive behaviour that impacts non-economic values in future, through which other jurisdictions will also benefit. For example, the *Sika/MBCC* transaction raised environmental concerns due to the merging parties being at the forefront of research and development on chemical admixtures, which have the potential to greatly reduce the carbon emissions of concrete and cement production. The Commission's stringent remedies extended beyond the boundaries of the EU, whereby the divesture obtained included global R&D activities, as opposed to those merely located in the Union. Thus, the EU's reliance on its social values (in this case, sustainability and environmental protection) brought benefits to consumers globally.

112 Gal (n 95) 477.
113 Bradford et al. (n 3) 757.
114 Bradford et al. (n 3) 760.
115 Lusophone Competition Network <www.concorrencia.pt/en/international-activity/lusophone-competition-network> (accessed 20 January 2025).
116 Bradford et al. (n 3) 760.

Therefore, it seems clear that application of the Brussels Effect in competition law acts to enrich local laws,[117] providing other jurisdictions with interpretive assistance and invaluable insights that enhance domestic application of rules.

II. A more seamless process than harmonisation and Member State application

From the perspective of the EU, the Brussels Effect and market-driven harmonisation is a more efficient and effective way of developing widely followed rules than through political harmonisation.[118] By introducing unilateral measures which companies and jurisdictions have the choice to follow, it avoids lengthy negotiations on collective measures that are often watered down in order to gain a consensus.[119] Regarding the introduction of social values in competition law, this would likely be contentious and vehemently objected to by the US, so achieving widespread multilateral agreement would be difficult. Therefore, unilateral action and the Brussels Effect represents an effective means of diffusing such constitutional social values throughout global competition laws in a way that would be lost in negotiations of a treaty.

In addition, the Brussels Effect is reinforced by the ease through which its competition norms are spread through Member States, meaning that the rules of the EU are immediately wider than just the Union itself. Gerber points to the fact that many Member States either introduced competition laws or revised their existing rules in the 1980s and 1990s to ensure their compatibility with the EU's system.[120] Further, accession to the EU requires conformity with the EU's competition laws, which has led to replication of the rules in newer members.[121] This ensures alignment of competition regimes by Member States with the EU,[122] while they are also empowered to enforce EU competition law rules pursuant to Regulation 1/2003.[123] This author describes the process as a form of 'internal' Brussels Effect, whereby

117 Gal (n 95) 484.
118 Bradford (n 1) 44.
119 Bradford (n 1) 44.
120 Gerber (n 110) 325.
121 Kovacic (n 58, 2008) 9.
122 Gerber (n 110) 325.
123 Regulation (EC) No 1/2003 of 16 December 2002 on the implementation of the rules on competition laid down in Articles 81 and 82 of the Treaty, OJ L 001.

the EU has an immediate group of 27 followers (along with the UK, which continues to closely monitor the EU's approach) for its competition rules. It is argued that this internal Brussels Effect is an effective way of commencing the initial dispersal of social values in the EU as there is a requirement for the national competition systems to remain aligned with the EU. This would then feed into the external Brussels Effect of new values, which could be diffused through trade agreements, rules produced in various languages, and a general tradition of following the EU's competition law culture.

E. Developing countries and social values

It is suggested that the diffusion of the EU's social values through competition law may be particularly relevant in the context of developing countries. This is because the EU's system is capable of accommodating a more diverse set of goals in a competition context and defers less to market self-correction,[124] which is likely to be more compatible with developing economies that require greater oversight of markets to ensure that they develop in a societally-beneficial manner. The empirical research suggests that the broader goals reflected in the EU's system appeals to a wider constituency of third countries,[125] not simply because they are open to other goals, but because they desire their inclusion. In contrast, the US system has reduced the objective of antitrust to mere economic efficiency,[126] which contrasts with the emphasis on fairness and competitive opportunity informing the European model. As Gerber points out, the relationship between the competitive process and society has always been central to the EU, which is in stark contrast to the more myopic approach in the US that focuses only on the undertakings involved and the financial impact on consumers of the goods or services.[127] Thus, an ability to consider diverse factors beyond mere efficiency and an inclination to intervene in markets to a greater degree is considered beneficial.[128]

124 Bradford et al. (n 3) 735.
125 Bradford et al. (n 3) 755.
126 Bork (n 20) 51. This was accepted in US case law in *Reiter v. Sonotone Corp.*, 442 U.S. 330 (1979).
127 Gerber (n 110) 326.
128 Eleanor M. Fox, 'The Battle for the Soul of Antitrust' (1987) 75 California Law Review 917, 917–918.

It is suggested that countries adopting new competition laws will face less resistance if they adopt EU-inspired rules,[129] as developing countries perceive the various goals of the law that take greater account of distributional concerns to be more palatable.[130] Many developing countries and emerging markets are not ready for the fully free markets pursued under US antitrust, as market participants require an opportunity to grow and establish their presence. The US system rejects all such considerations or concerns related to distribution, whereby the Chicago School put forward what was, in effect, a total welfare model that prioritised economic efficiency over all else.[131] This purely economic approach is likely to benefit those with existing market power, while facilitating the obliteration of emerging undertakings and markets being introduced to the full rigours of competition. It has been demonstrated that over 60 jurisdictions listed goals other than strictly economic objectives in their first competition laws adopted, demonstrating clearly the relevance of the EU's system and the appetite for social factors to play a role in this area of law.[132] For example, the South African competition regime is regularly cited for its focus on distributional fairness, where it requires the active consideration of the impact of a merger on historically disadvantaged groups.[133] This approach requires the protection of small and medium sized enterprises that are prevalent in emerging economies, while also providing a basis upon which to challenge dominant foreign corporations. Similarly, Namibian competition law requires consideration of historically discriminated-against people.[134] Further, social policy concerns are included in the competition laws of China,[135] which Gerber suggests makes the EU such a suitable source of knowledge and guidance for the country.[136]

The above description of the attractiveness of the EU's regime to developing countries contrasts starkly with the interaction of the US system

129 William E. Kovacic, 'Merger Enforcement in Transition: Antitrust Controls on Acquisition in Emerging Economies' (2008) 66 University of Cincinnati Law Review 1071, 1086–1089.

130 Bradford et al. (n 3) 758.

131 Bork (n 20) 90.

132 Bradford et al. (n 3) 758.

133 South African Competition Act 89 of 1998 § 12A(3).

134 Harry First and Eleanor M. Fox, 'Public interest and Philidelphia National Bank' (2015) 80 Antitrust Law Journal 307, 349.

135 First and Fox (n 134) 313; Bradford et al. (n 3) 758.

136 Gerber (n 110) 326.

and these jurisdictions. With its staunch commitment to 'free' markets and minimal government intervention,[137] it is clear why the European model is often seen as a better ideological fit in countries where markets require a certain level of direction to ensure they serve society adequately.[138] For example, the US has vehemently opposed the protection of small business interests since the Chicago School's reinterpretation of the law.[139] Equally, as has been demonstrated above, there is very little initiative shown to challenge the conduct of abusive incumbents (which are capable of undermining the competitive process on emerging markets in other jurisdictions as a result of their economic strength and access to seemingly endless resources). Markets in developing countries are less robust, and therefore, necessitate a more interventionist approach with a broader mandate on which to act. This author argues that it is notable that competition systems resembling the US, such as Australia, Canada, and New Zealand, are economically developed, whereas the EU has guided the competition laws of a far more diverse array of jurisdictions.[140] As such, it may be said that the US influences the 'old' world, whereas European values are shaping the 'new' world in an impactful and observable manner.

The above demonstrates why the Brussels Effect is so effective in relation to developing countries. However, it also aims so show that these jurisdictions would be receptive to the introduction of the EU's underlying social values in competition law and the application of social and public interest factors alongside economic concerns. Gerber speaks of a communitarian objective in competition law, meaning that the law must seek community support for market activities. He suggests that goal has been central in the development of competition law in Europe, where distributive and economic fairness have been prominent.[141] It is argued that the communitarian

137 This author strongly disagrees with the moniker of 'free' markets as it ignores the necessary involvement of the State in regulating markets. For a discussion of this false dichotomy between 'free' and 'unfree' markets, see Sandeep Vaheesan, 'The Profound Nonsense of Consumer Welfare Antitrust' (2019) 64 The Antitrust Bulletin 479, 479–480, 484; Jie Ouyang, '"Embedded Consumer": Towards a Constitutional Reframing of the Legal Image of Consumers in EU law' (2024) 47 Journal of Consumer Policy 1.

138 Bradford et al. (n 3) 758.

139 Bork (n 20) 51–56; Harlan M Blake and William K Jones, 'In Defense of Antitrust' (1965) 65 Columbia Law Review 377, 381; Herbert Hovenkamp, 'Antitrust's Protected Classes' (1989) 88 Michigan Law Review 1.

140 Bradford et al. (n 3) 743–744.

141 Gerber (n 110) 327.

objective is equally significant in other jurisdictions which have rejected the free market approach of the US in favour of the more balanced EU regime, and are likely to favour a system that emphasises the necessity of ensuring markets work for society as a whole, rather than the sole pursuit of economic progress. Thus, it is suggested that a reorientation of the EU's competition rules to include a greater social dimension and a focus on the communitarian objective would be welcomed across many Member States and beyond the borders of the EU.

F. Globalised Norms in EU Competition Law

As has been demonstrated, the EU appears to possess a unique capacity to draw diverse legal systems towards its competition law regime, despite vast cultural and regulatory differences.[142] Further, it has clearly taken on the intellectual leadership of the discipline (replacing the US) through its more proactive intervention in monopolisation and merger cases.[143] By relying on this dynamic and the operation of the Brussels Effect, it is enabled to unilaterally create globalised norms in the competition sphere that would be impossible through multilateralism.[144] This approach of institutionalising its norms beyond the territory of the Union aligns with the EU's stated ambitions. For example, Article 3(5) TEU states that the Union is required to promote its values in its relations with the rest of the world.[145] Similarly, in a Commission policy paper related to the Single Market, the Commission identified the importance of its role in shaping global norms and ensuring that fair rules are applied in worldwide trade. Further, it pointed out that the 'single market of the future should be the launch pad of an ambitious global agenda.'[146] Such statements appear to support a bolder approach towards competition law that is imbued with the EU's social goals and could be incorporated effectively across other jurisdictions. This attitude also contrasts with the self-serving worldview put forward by

142 Bradford et al. (n 3) 735–736; Stylianou and Iacovides (n 90) 636.
143 Andreas Weitbrecht, 'From Freiburg to Chicago and beyond – the first 50 years of European Competition law' (2008) 29 European Competition Law Review 81, 87.
144 Weitbrecht (n 143).
145 Treaty on European Union, Art. 3(5).
146 European Commission, COM/2007/0060, *Communication from the Commission to the Council, the European Parliament, the European Economic and Social Committee and the Committee of the Regions: A Single Market for Citizens.*

the US, which seems content with protecting national economic interests, whereas the EU seeks to propose norms promoting global welfare.[147] For example, the EU can be seen as taking the lead on climate change, establishing an ambitious agenda through the European Green Deal that other countries are likely to replicate eventually.[148] Indeed, more affluent societies such as the EU cause far greater environmental damage due to their CO2 emissions, therefore, one could argue that there is both an imperative and moral obligation on the EU to commence the introduction of greener values in competition law in acknowledgment of its prior degradation of the planet and to promote a shift towards more sustainable consumption, in line with the Green Deal.[149] Similarly, the EU took the lead on matters related to privacy and data protection through its legislation, which other jurisdictions have then tended to follow.[150] Such examples demonstrate the desire of the EU to promote truly global social values that serve to benefit not only citizens of the Union, but worldwide. Therefore, an adaptation of competition law to pursue the EU's social ambitions in this manner would appear entirely consistent with its efforts in other areas to produce essential globalised norms.

In addition, it should be noted that globalised norms developed in EU competition law are not binding, and instead, are entirely adaptable to domestic regimes. Gal notes that this is a crucial aspect of transplanting norms and laws, stating that they must be sensitive to special characteristics of the local environment to be successful.[151] For example, the laws of large economies will not always work in a comparable or equally effective manner in smaller economies, and hence why they must be adaptable. Thus, it is critical to point out that norms relating to social factors developed in the EU's competition regime must not be rigid nor obligatory. However, as demonstrated by Israel's ability to reject certain interpretations of EU rules on abuse of dominance that did not align with its domestic goals, this is

147 Bradford (n 1) 37–38.

148 The European Green Deal https://commission.europa.eu/strategy-and-policy/priorities-2019-2024/european-green-deal_en (accessed 8 December 2023).

149 For example, the CO2 emissions per capita in the United States (15.32 tons) are more than 150 times greater than in Mali (0.09 tons). See 'CO2 Emissions per Capita – Worldometer' https://www.worldometers.info/co2-emissions/co2-emissions-per-capita/ (accessed 21 July 2024).

150 Regulation (EU) 2016/679 (General Data Protection Regulation) in the current version of the OJ L 119, 04.05.2016; cor. O.J. L 127, 23.5.2018.

151 Gal (n 95) 467–471.

eminently possible.[152] Thus, there would be what Kovacic describes as an 'open source element' to any norms developed, meaning countries could make adaptations required by their own needs and to align with their own constitutional social protections.[153] Equally, a further benefit of this process would be the feedback effect, as the EU would be able to learn from the experiences of other countries and the manner in which they applied and adapted norms coherently, thereby advancing the state of the art globally.[154]

Thus, although there are political and cultural barriers that have prevented against the globalisation of competition enforcement and norm-creation through the ICN,[155] the Brussels Effect offers the potential to create positive, socially-infused norms in competition law that could have global benefits. While differences may exist at the margins, it is possible for competition law internationally to serve several common political, social and economic goals, with the common optimal goal of promoting welfare that is inclusive and serves overall societal wellbeing.[156] Through reliance on its broader constitutional framework, the EU can lead a new age of a more balanced, socially-aware competition law.

G. Criticisms of the Brussels Effect

One criticism of the Brussels Effect is that it has undertones of colonialism, whereby the EU seeks to impose its norms and standards of civilization on coerced subject countries that are bound to follow it.[157] Similarly, it has been asserted that the application of the Brussels Effect infringes on the sovereignty of other democratic nations to make their own legislative choices.[158] This is because it narrows the scope for other countries to

152 Gal (n 95) 472.

153 Kovacic (n 58, 2008) 9.

154 Kovacic (n 58, 2008) 9.

155 Barry J. Rodger, 'Competition Policy, Liberalism and Globalization: A European Perspective' (2000) 6 Columbia Journal of European Law 289, 319.

156 Ariel Ezrachi and Maurice E. Stucke, 'The fight over antitrust's soul' (2018) 9 Journal of European Competition Law & Practice 1, 2.

157 Kalypso Nicolardis and Robert Howse, 'This is my EUtopia. . .: Narrative as Power' (2002) 40 Journal Common Markets Studies 767, 789; Aleydis Nissen, *The European Union, Emerging Global Business and Human Rights* (Cambridge University Press 2022) 112; Eustace (n 10) 161–162.

158 Quentin Levin, 'A Review of *The Brussels Effect* by Anu Bradford' (2021) 22 Georgetown Journal of International Affairs 307, 309.

establish their own standards reflecting the desires of their citizens.[159] Yet this ignores the legitimate aim of the EU in enforcing its rules in its own territory to protect citizens of the Union and undertakings operating therein. Therefore, it is argued that there is no coercion involved in the application of the Brussels Effect. At its most extreme, counterparties to trade agreements with the EU may be required to introduce competition provisions of equivalent strength. However, applying the exact drafting and decisional approach of the EU is not obligatory, and this would also be the case with the introduction of social values. Further, relying on other jurisdictions is likely to be less effective, as they will lack the regulatory clout of the EU and are far less likely to be able to produce extensive regulations tackling digital power, for example. Instead, the EU's rules are likely to compensate other jurisdictions which lack the resources or corporate influence to introduce progressive changes to the law.[160] Thus, while this author acknowledges the right to self-determination,[161] one must not ignore the EU's demonstrated capacity to introduce important laws and policies (such as the Digital Markets Act and the European Green Deal) which could not have been achieved by a single jurisdiction acting alone, and in this regard, the Union can be seen as increasing countries' regulatory capacity (by normalising regulatory intervention that can be replicated) as opposed to unduly inhibiting it. In addition, it must be recalled that it is ultimately open for these jurisdictions not to follow the EU's approach, which appears fatal to the arguments against the Brussels Effect. At the level of the undertaking, the rules again can be said to act as market incentives to behave in a certain manner (such as refusing to engage in abusive labour practices), but conformity is voluntary as opposed to mandatory as these undertakings can choose to boycott the European market if its social standards are prohibitive. Therefore, this author deems the imperialism or colonialism arguments as unconvincing. As Eustace asserts, '[t]here is a world of difference between gunboat diplomacy and container ship diplomacy.'[162]

A further criticism put forward is that the EU's competition policies are a disguised form of protectionism. The former Czechia president, Viclav Klaus, asserted that the Union's social rights are 'disguised attempts to pro-

159 Levin (n 158).
160 Bradford (n 91, 2020) 253.
161 Levin (n 158) 309.
162 Eustace (n 10) 161.

tect high-cost producers in highly regulated countries, with unsustainable welfare standards, against cheaper labor in less productive countries.'[163] However, it is argued that the EU has demonstrated itself to be entirely dedicated to the social values it seeks to protect and has exported them sincerely, such as those related to environmentalism and climate change. As a regional body, it has committed itself to high standards that are directly incorporated into its constitutional documents in the Treaties, and it actively promotes those goals through its legislative agenda. Thus, the idea that they are a form of protectionism appears flawed. Additionally, while there could be said to be benefits to European businesses from undercutting third country competitive advantages (for example, by requiring them to adhere to higher sustainability standards or labour standards),[164] this is consistent with many of the EU's other practices in this area which could be said to operate against the Union's competitiveness in the past.[165] Therefore its bona fides in combatting various harms has been established and are not undermined by some potential loss of competitive advantages in third countries in pursuit of more sustainable or less societally harmful production methods.[166] Further, as above, there is no obligation for undertakings or third countries to follow them, as they only become binding when undertakings seek to operate on the Single Market. Such policies represent entirely legitimate efforts to protect European consumers[167] and the fact that their reach (and the valuable global interests they serve) has extended beyond the EU's borders is a laudable and positive contribution to the international order. For example, one could question where we would find ourselves in relation to climate change without the efforts of the EU, and the intention to introduce sustainability into competition law in the EU should be welcomed, rather than being falsely painted as a form of protectionism.[168]

163 Václav Klaus, *Renaissance: The Rebirth of Liberty in the Heart of Europe* (Cato Institute 1997) 16.

164 Aleydis Nissen, *The European Union, Emerging Global Business and Human Rights* (Cambridge University Press 2022) 128.

165 For example, the Union's initial legislation on equal gender pay and its significant legislative body on environmental protection which could be said to penalise domestic undertakings.

166 Eustace (n 10) 162–163.

167 Bradford (n 1) 66.

168 Anna Gerbrandy, 'Solving a Sustainability-Deficit in European Competition Law' (2017) 40 World Competition 539; Holmes (n 6); Suzanne Kingston, 'Competition

Finally, there are questions regarding the costs imposed on companies due to the exportation of the EU's rules, with the argument made that this can ultimately reduce consumers' welfare.[169] The suggestion is that the cost of compliance may be passed onto consumers or make it difficult for smaller undertakings to survive. However, this author agrees with Bradford when she asserts that the potential costs are outweighed by the benefits of 'nudging' consumers and undertakings away from unwise decisions.[170] While this form of paternalism may be objected to in certain jurisdictions, it is argued that the fundamental importance of the values proposed in this chapter (including sustainability and equality) have a universal element that should be embraced.

H. Conclusion

As Kovacic points out, the '*best* practice in competition policy is the relentless pursuit of *better* practices'.[171] The EU should embrace this philosophy in the pursuit of better norms and more rounded values that are reflective of the underlying economic *and* social purpose of the Union. In the field of competition law, it has demonstrated a willingness to lead change, rather than being led.[172] Thus, it is positioned as a uniquely influential actor in terms of impacting the laws of other jurisdictions and the global marketplace.[173] Competition policy, after all, has no fixed content 'and is dependent to a great extent upon the particular political and social emphases of the legal system in which it operates.'[174] Further, as the most activist antitrust jurisdiction globally, other competition authorities look to it for inspiration and guidance.[175] Therefore, the Union has an opportunity

---

and sustainability in EU law: Nearer resolution of the old debate?' N° 1–2023 Concurrences 5 (2023).

169 Levin (n 158) 309.

170 Bradford (n 91, 2020) 238.

171 Kovacic (n 58, 2008) 17.

172 For example, through its novel theories of harm in the *Google Shopping* case and the introduction of the Digital Markets Act.

173 Bradford et al. (n 3) 763.

174 Rodger (n 155) 304.

175 Stylianou and Iacovides (n 90) 636.

to impress upon it the values that it is required to observe through its constitutional architecture.

This paper has argued that the EU should utilise its influence to diffuse the values it promotes and protects across the Treaties into the competition regimes that defer to it and adopt its principles and rules through the Brussels Effect. The Union has been competing in a 'regulatory race' with the US for a number of decades. What has proven appealing with the EU's system, and aided in it streaking ahead of the US in this contest, is the broader set of goals that it pursues which is inherently attractive to a diverse set of countries, many of which represent developing economies and require the protection of interests other than economic efficiency.

This author argues that to further separate itself from the US and to continue to ensure the prominence of the Brussels Effect, the EU should explicitly consider social factors in competition law and place greater emphasis on the link between markets and societal wellbeing.[176] In doing so, it has the potential to become a 'champion of ... global welfare'.[177] It is suggested that a focus on the communitarian objective and emphasising that markets should work for society (and not merely for corporations) would distinguish the EU from its regulatory competitors and ensure the continued application of the Brussels Effect in this area. An argument could be made that this is a form of regulatory unilateralism by the EU, however, as noted throughout, the adoption of the EU's competition provisions is not mandatory. Further, it is acknowledged that the adopted law must fit the unique conditions of the adopting jurisdiction,[178] but the Brussels Effect in competition policy has always incorporated such flexibility, whereby third countries can tailor the rules they adopt. Thus, the projection of social values through competition law represents both a legitimate and effective way for the EU to shape global norms in the image of the values that it is required to promote.

As Stiglitz has pointed out, intellectual waves travel around the world.[179] While neoliberalism may have traversed the globe in the 1980s and 90s,

176 Stucke (n 56). Renowned economists Amartya Sen, Jean-Paul Fitoussi and Joseph Stiglitz founded a movement referred to as Beyond Economy Government Alliance, which was committed to putting well-being, broadly construed, at the centre of economic agendas. For more detail see Joseph E. Stiglitz, *The Road to Freedom: Economics and the Good Society* (Allen Lane 2024) xxi.

177 Bradford (n 91, 2020) 249.

178 Gal (n 95) 484.

179 Stiglitz (n 176) 234.

the time is rife for the EU to export its more balanced, socially conscious agenda that promotes universally important values such as environmental protection, equality, employment, and sustainable economic development.

EU Accession Reboot: Integrating Competition Enforcement Trends for Digital Platforms into Eastern Partnership Talks

Tamta Margvelashvili[*]

A. Introduction

The pursuit of European Union (EU) membership marks a critical juncture for Eastern Partnership (EaP)[1] nations as they strive to align their policies with European standards. The trio of Georgia, Ukraine, and Moldova (hereinafter "EaP countries")[2] is vigorously projecting its course to achieve enhanced economic prosperity. Over the past eight years, the Association Agreements and Deep and Comprehensive Free Trade Areas (hereinafter "AA" or "DCFTAs"),[3] established in 2014, have elevated the relationship between the EU and Georgia, the Republic of Moldova, and Ukraine to an unprecedented level. This process has not only fostered closer economic ties but also promoted political and social alignment with the EU's values and regulations.

Following the AAs with the EU, Georgia, Ukraine, and Moldova have reformed their competition laws to align with European standards, establishing independent competition authorities with enhanced powers. The modernization of the Georgian Competition and Consumer Agency (GCCA), the Anti-Monopoly Committee in Ukraine (AMCU), and the Compe-

---

* Associate Professor at Georgian National University SEU, Director of the Competition, Capital and Financial Markets Practice at Nodia, Urumashvili & Partners, Georgia.

1 The Eastern Partnership (EaP) is a joint initiative involving the EU, its Member States and six Eastern European Partner countries: Armenia, Azerbaijan, Belarus, Georgia, the Republic of Moldova and Ukraine.

2 For the purposes of this article the scrutiny will be held of Georgia, Ukraine and Moldova.

3 The Association Agreement between the European Union and the European Atomic Energy Community and their Member States, of the one part, and Georgia, of the other part, entered in force on 1 July, 2016; The Association Agreement between the European Union and the European Atomic Energy Community and their Member States, of the one part, and the Republic of Moldova, of the other part , entered in force on 1 July, 2016; The Association Agreement between the European Union and its Member States, of the one part, and Ukraine, of the other part, entered in force on 1 January, 2016.

tition Council in Moldova, along with the adoption of new competition laws and secondary legislation package.

Despite these advancements, the focus remains largely on traditional enforcement. While foundational reforms are essential, a forward-looking approach is necessary to tackle challenges posed by the digital economy, such as data monopolies and algorithmic collusion. How can these improvements be achieved, and what factors will drive their success? These are critical questions to address from the outset.

In recent years, the evolution of competition law enforcement for digital platforms within the EU has been marked by significant regulatory advancements and policy swings. The European Commission has increasingly examined the behavior of tech giants, recognizing their ability to manipulate considerable market power without traditional physical presence. This led to landmark cases[4] and substantial fines for anticompetitive practices. To further address these issues, the EU introduced the Digital Markets Act (DMA) in 2020[5], the first *ex-ante* regulation aiming to ensure fair and open digital markets. Beyond that the Digital Services Act (DSA)[6] as a parallel regulation has been launched, that enhances the safety and accountability of digital platforms. These are just a few examples of the comprehensive legal framework the EU has adopted to address the challenges posed by digital economies and tech giants.

Against this backdrop, Georgia, Moldova, and Ukraine are only committed to meeting the minimum standards set by their AAs. This focus on traditional market dynamics may not sufficiently address the challenges of the digital ecosystem. It is essential to question how the notion of "comprehensive competition laws" being a core concept for the AAs has evolved over the past eight years. Is it adequate for EU accession if these countries

---

4 See: Case AT.39740 – *Google Shopping, Judgment of the General Court of 10 November 2021, Google LLC, formerly Google Inc. and Alphabet, Inc. v European Commission*; Case AT.40099 – *Google Android, Judgment of the General Court of 14 September 2022, Google Inc. and Alphabet, Inc. v European Commission*; Facebook (Meta) Data Collection (2021): *Joint investigation by the European Commission and the Federal Cartel Office (Germany)*; Case AT.40437 – *Apple App Store (2021).*

5 Regulation (EU) 2022/1925 of the European Parliament and of the Council of 14 September 2022 on contestable and fair markets in the digital sector (Digital Markets Act) Official Journal of the European Union (OJ L 265), 12.10.2022, 1–66.

6 Regulation (EU) 2022/2065 of the European Parliament and of the Council of 19 October 2022 on a Single Market for Digital Services (Digital Services Act) and amending Directive 2000/31/EC, Official Journal of the European Union (OJ L 277), 27.10.2022, 1–87.

continue to prioritize traditional market dynamics in their competition laws? Does this approach risk the development of competition enforcement for digital platforms within the EU and its neighboring regions?

The paper argues for the EU to reconsider its approach by incorporating digital market competition enforcement into accession talks. This approach would enhance the economic competitiveness of these countries and reaffirm the EU's commitment to establishing global regulatory standards in the digital realm.

B. Contextual Foundations of Competition Law Reforms in Eastern Partnership Countries

The Prague Summit in 2009 marked the launch of the Eastern Partnership, a strategic initiative rooted in shared values, mutual interests, and collaborative commitments. As a core component of the European Neighborhood Policy, the EaP combines bilateral and multilateral approaches to enhance the stability, prosperity, and resilience of the EU's neighboring regions, in alignment with the goals outlined in the EU's Global Strategy for Foreign and Security Policy and the 2015 European Neighbourhood Policy Review.

Since 2014, the Association Agreements (AAs) and Deep and Comprehensive Free Trade Areas (DCFTAs) concluded with Georgia, Moldova, and Ukraine have significantly transformed the political, economic, and legal landscapes of these countries. The field of competition law and policy has been notably impacted by these changes, with reforms addressing several key dimensions: 1. Institutional Resilience and Capacity Building: The reforms have focused on strengthening the institutional framework responsible for enforcing competition laws, including enhancing the technical expertise and operational capabilities of competition authority. 2. Introduction of Modernized Laws; 3. Public Awareness and Engagement: efforts have been made to increase public understanding of competition law and policy. Despite the individual experiences each country in the trio have undertaken, as will be explored further, their approaches and implementations vary as is the current stance with regard to the competition law enforcement for digital platforms.

I. Georgia's Pathway

Georgia, like many post-Soviet states, carries the legacy of its Soviet past, which has profoundly influenced its economic and legal system. Georgia's economy was centrally planned and tightly controlled, with limited space for private enterprise or competitive market dynamics. The state dictated production, distribution, and pricing, restricting entrepreneurial initiatives and adopting monopolistic structures.

Following the dissolution of the Soviet Union in 1991, Georgia boarded on a challenging transition towards a market economy. This shift involved undoing the old economic structures, implementing new policies to foster competition, and developing legal frameworks to support a free market. The legacy of centralized control and state dominance left Georgia with a complex set of challenges.

Georgia's initial legal framework for competition was introduced shortly after the fall of the Soviet Union in Georgia with the normative act issued on March 17, 1992, titled "On Some Measures for Demonopolization of Business Activities in the Republic of Georgia." This act was formalized as Resolution No. 323. It was followed by the Decree of the State Council on October 26, 1992, titled "*On Restriction of Monopolistic Activities and Development of Competition*."[7] The Constitution of Georgia reinforced these reasonings with the current provisions in Article 6 (2), which mandates state support for a free and open economy and competition, and Article 26 (4), which bans monopolistic activities unless legally permitted.[8] The next round of competition reforms started in 1996 with the adoption of the Law "On Monopoly and Competition" by the Georgian Parliament and creation of the "State Antimonopoly Department" in 1997 through a Presidential Decree.[9]

These developments represent the beginning of competition reasonings in Georgia; however, they fell short of aligning with EU modern competition regimes. Even the law adopted in 2005 on Free Trade and Competi-

7 *Fetelava,* The Evolution of the Competition Theory and Antimonopoly Regulation is Georgia (in Georgian), "Loi" Publishers, 2007, 149–168.

8 Constitution of Georgia, Parliament of the Republic of Georgia, 24/08/1995, Document N 786.

9 *Tushuri/Urjumelashvili,* The Law of Georgia on Monopolistic Activity and Competition – An
Overview, Georgian Law Review, First and Second Quarters (2000), 43.

tion[10] along with establishment of The Free Trade and Competition Agency as a state subdivision under the Ministry of Economic Development of Georgia was far from the modernization. Nonetheless, it is noteworthy that the term "monopoly" has been removed from the law's title, and the text itself places minimal emphasis on preventing monopolistic situations, rather than directing its attention to the antitrust direction of the competition law as a whole.

The 2005 law became dormant in 2012 by adopting a new law,[11] mostly reflecting international practices and incorporating provisions addressing abuse of dominant positions, unfair competition, and concentration (merger) controls. Unlike its predecessor, this revised edition aligned more closely with EU competition law in terminology and classifications. The May 2012 edition of the law had several shortcomings, but most significantly, the enforcing body lacked the authority to independently suspend actions or decisions made by economic agents in violation of the law, without court intervention. Additionally, the agency could not unilaterally declare decisions or agreements invalid. This limitation significantly undermined the agency's effectiveness in enforcing competition laws and addressing violations promptly. Furthermore, if an investigation uncovered a violation of the law, the agency was required to refer the case to the court for further review and resolution. The authority to impose fines also rested with the court, not the agency. This process significantly constrained the agency's ability to enforce competition laws directly and expediently.[12]

The year 2014 can be regarded as the beginning of the full modernization of Georgian competition legislation and its mere alignment with European Union competition law and policy. The primary legal framework became the Law of Georgia on Competition, with the Competition Agency designated as the authority responsible for enforcing competition laws.[13] The 2014 law edition addressed many criticisms of its predecessor, although the Competition Agency still lacked full institutional and functional independence. A key improvement was granting binding authority to the agency's decisions, marking a shift from advisory roles to active enforcement.

10 Law of Georgia on Free Trade and Competition, 03/06/2005, Document N 1550.

11 Law of Georgia on Free Trade and Competition, date of adoption 08/05/2012, Document N 6148-I.

12 Law of Georgia on Free Trade and Competition, date of adoption 08/05/2012, Document N 6148-I, Articles 26 (1), 29 (1) and (2).

13 Law of Georgia on Free Trade and Competition, date of adoption 08/05/2012, Document N 6148-I, the amendments of 21 March 2024.

The competition law in Georgia has undergone numerous changes since 2014, with a significant wave of amendments beginning in 2019 and continuing to the present.[14] First and foremost, the modernized competition law now focuses evenly on economic agents. This marks a clear departure from the previous approach, which primarily framed competition legislation as a regulatory domain for state and municipal bodies—an approach that was, at best, flawed. The National Competition and Consumer Agency of Georgia (hereinafter the "GCCA" or "Agency") is designated as the authorized body responsible for enforcing this law, along with the sectoral regulators.

In carrying out its duties, the Agency is guided by the Constitution of Georgia, international agreements, this law, the anti-dumping law, the consumer rights law, the agency's statute, and other legal acts, and is accountable for fulfilling its tasks and functions. The law truly acknowledges that the AA plays a crucial role in this context and the EU competition law in general, insofar as they align with Georgia's national legal framework. Although the structural similarities in terms of enforcing competition laws between Chapters 4 and 5 of the Georgian competition law and EU Regulation 1/2003[15] may be less apparent, there are numerous substantive parallels. This suggests that the process of legal transplantation is advancing significantly.

1. The EU-Georgia Association Agreement: A Benchmark for Progress

The legislative evolution marks a clear shift from a restrictive and ineffective competition law framework to a more dynamic, EU-aligned approach. This change reflects Georgia's deeper commitment to the EU's conditionality policy under the AA. Key commitments in competition include: (a) creating a new climate for economic relations to enhance trade, investment, and competition, vital for economic restructuring; and (b) progressively aligning relevant legislation with EU standards and ensuring effective implementation.

The AA emphasizes competition through several provisions. Article 107 (3)(d) and (e) allows regulatory authorities in electronic communications to mandate open access to services, network sharing, and fair pricing. Article 144 (2)(a) in public procurement requires public announcements

14 The law of Georgia on Competition, Document N 6148-I.

15 Council Regulation (EC) No 1/2003 of 16 December 2002 on the implementation of the rules on competition laid down in Articles 81 and 82 of the Treaty.

of intended procurements, limiting negotiated procedures. The intellectual property chapter addresses unfair competition, and Article 280 highlights tax governance as crucial for fair competition.

The independent competition chapter is significant, with Article 203 recognizing that anti-competitive practices harm market efficiency. Article 204 mandates "comprehensive competition laws" to prevent anti-competitive agreements, supported by an independent and transparent enforcement authority. Article 205 ensures state monopolies are subject to competition laws, while Article 206 promotes transparency in subsidies through regular reporting.

Although Article 204 emphasizes comprehensive competition laws, the AA does not specify their content these laws must have or reference to the EU law, giving Georgia development flexibility. This absence of a detailed annex may reflect previous limitations and the EU's focus on immediate reforms in sectors like rule of law and taxation, anticipating Georgia would gradually align its competition laws with EU standards.

2. Strategic autonomy: Georgia's Tailored Approach

One may assert that advancement of its competition laws and the establishment of enforcement mechanisms in Georgia were guided by a pragmatic approach, reflecting the country's own regulatory needs and its ongoing commitment to aligning with EU standards. The obligation under the AA is to be viewed more as a preparatory work towards a heightened legal landscape in competition.

To fortify the above, the European Commission's staff working document of 2023[16] provides valuable insights into the progress and challenges in this area. It acknowledged that Georgia is still in the early stages of developing its competition policy, with limited progress observed during the reporting period. According to the Commission the country must continue to align its legislation with EU standards, focusing on issues like abuse of dominant positions, cartels, and state aid. The Georgian National Competition Agency (GCCA) must enhance its track record in enforcement,

16 European Commission, Commission staff working document: Georgia 2023 report (SWD(2023) 697 final). Accompanying the document: Communication from the Commission to the European Parliament, the Council, the European Economic and Social Committee, and the Committee of the Regions. 2023 Communication on EU Enlargement policy, (2023, November 8), Brussels.

strengthen administrative capacity, and increase awareness about State aid rules. Specifically, Georgia should: align its legal framework on antitrust, mergers, and State aid with EU regulations; grant enforcement powers to recover unlawful State aid; and reinforce the GCCA's administrative capacity.[17] Yet, no specific mandate has been assigned in this regard.

The report also highlighted that the Law on Competition current edition reflected many EU provisions on restrictive agreements and abuse of dominance, and it included ex ante control for mergers exceeding certain turnover thresholds. However, it was explicitly mentioned that the GCCA required further strengthening, though no specific directives were provided. Beyond that it was established the legal framework overseeing state aid did not fully align with EU standards. The GCCA only required notification and approval for aid related to regional development and cultural preservation, while other aid types were not covered. The GCCA's enforcement capacity necessitated improvement, and no decisions were made on State aid issues in 2022, although information on de minimis aid was collected.[18] Basically, the report more broadly reflected the assumptions made in 2022 by the European Commission's report, mandating that to build a more resilient business environment, it was essential to further strengthen the legal framework and enforcement mechanisms for competition law, as well as improve the enforcement of contracts and ensure judicial independence.[19]

Yet, the 2023 report served as a prerequisite to for assessing Georgia's readiness to assume EU membership obligations. Georgia applied for EU membership in March 2022 and was granted candidate status in December 2023, contingent upon fulfilling the steps outlined in a Commission

17 European Commission, Commission staff working document: Georgia 2023 report (SWD(2023) 697 final). Accompanying the document: Communication from the Commission to the European Parliament, the Council, the European Economic and Social Committee, and the Committee of the Regions. 2023 Communication on EU Enlargement policy, (2023, November 8), Brussels.

18 European Commission, Commission staff working document: Georgia 2023 report (SWD(2023) 697 final). Accompanying the document: Communication from the Commission to the European Parliament, the Council, the European Economic and Social Committee, and the Committee of the Regions. 2023 Communication on EU Enlargement policy, (2023, November 8), Brussels.

19 European Commission. (2022). Commission Opinion on Georgia's application for membership of the European Union. COM(2022) 405 final. Brussels, 17 June 2022.

recommendations,[20] that encompassed broader EU core values, focusing on strengthening democratic and resilient state. For context, it is worth noting that in July, just months after being granted candidate status, Georgia's aspirations for EU membership were temporarily stalled, as announced by the EU's ambassador.[21] This delay suggests that while Georgia achieved the significant milestone of candidate status, further progress is contingent on addressing specific concerns and meeting additional requirements set by the EU.

Considering this background, the current emphasis for Georgia is more political than economic, underlining the need for democratic and institutional reforms over purely economic and legal alignment. Despite this shift, the evolution of competition law remains critical. This is derived from the Constitution itself in Article 78, that emphasizes on the commitment of Georgia's constitutional bodies to actively pursue full integration into the EU and the North Atlantic Treaty Organization (NATO).

While this topic is certainly intriguing, a political evaluation of the current state of Georgian-EU relations is beyond the scope of this article that is written with the understanding that Georgia's EU aspirations are a fundamental and unshakable goal for its people. Consequently, expert opinions in various fields, such as competition, are essential for the country to stay committed to aligning with EU standards. Therefore, the prospect of accession negotiations remains on the horizon and will address the conditions for Georgia's EU membership. This highlights the critical importance of advancing competition law as a fundamental component of aligning with the EU legal *acquis*.

3. Addressing Shortcomings

Before tackling the core strategic choices for addressing competition distortions in the digital realm, it is essential to assess the existing legal framework and evaluate how effectively the Agency is equipped to handle each type of competition law violation. While further critiques could highlight various strengths and weaknesses of Georgia's competition framework, this

20 Council of the European Union. (2023). Outcome of Proceedings. Brussels, 12 December 2023. (OR. en) 16707/23 ELARG 94 COWEB 162 COEST 669. General Secretariat of the Council.

21 *Gavin,* EU announces Georgia's accession is "stopped" after anti-West pivot, *Politico*, 9 July 2024, https://www.politico.eu/article/georgia-eu-accession-stopped-anti-west-pivot-russian-law-foreign-agent-bill accessed 2 April 2025.

section will focus on the most pressing challenges specifically affecting the digital sector to determine the next steps and strategies for effectively reinforcing the Georgian competition legal agenda.

Parallel to Article 101 of the Treaty on the Functioning of the European Union (hereinafter "TFEU"), Article 7 of the Georgian Competition Law any agreement, decision or concerted practice of undertakings that have as their object or effect the prevention, restriction and/or distortion of competition within the relevant market invalid.[22] Articles 8 and 9 of the aforementioned law allow for declaring certain agreements as having minor importance or providing exceptions to the prohibition. Similarly, Article 102 TFEU is mirrored in Article 6 of Georgian law.[23]

The Competition Law grants the Agency authority to prevent, detect, and eliminate anti-competitive actions (Article 16(4)), enforce compliance (Article 172(d)), and require lawful conduct from economic agents (Article 18(1)(g)). However, Georgian law primarily uses fines to address violations, lacking clear guidance on preventive or restorative measures increasingly valued in modern competition law.[24] While behavioral and structural remedies prevent violations and may restore original conditions to sustain competition, the Georgian Agency applies them only in concentration control cases, unlike the EU Commission, which uses them broadly in antitrust enforcement.

The differences with EU law are evident in the application of interim measures — a tool that, despite being introduced into EU law, has been sparingly utilized by the EU Commission.[25] Inspired by the Commission's application of Interim Measures (IMs) in the Broadcom case,[26] the IMs regained its reputation as a tool for addressing the challenges posed by digital platforms, including tipping, economies of scale and scope, and network effects. Quite recently the tool was utilized by the GCCA as well.

22 Article 7 (1), Law of Georgia on Competition.

23 Article 6 (1), Law of Georgia on Competition.

24 *Geradina/Katsifisd*, Strengthening effective antitrust enforcement in digital platform markets, 18 European Competition Journal (2022), 1.

25 *Margvelashvili/Bagashvili*, Harnessing Interim Measures to Combat Digital Dominance in the EU, European Yearbook of International Economic Law, Vol. 14, (2024), 1.

26 Commission Decision of 16 October 2019 relating to a proceeding under Article 102 of the Treaty of the Functioning of the European union, Article 54 of the EEA Agreement and Article 8 of Council Regulation (EC) No 1/2003 of 16 December 2002 on the implementation of the rules on competition laid down in Article 81 and 82 of the Treaty Case AT.40608—Broadcom.

Before the Agency's investigation was completed, the "exclusive" clause in the agreement between "Distribution Company" LLC and "Online Tickets" LLC (successor to "Tineti" LLC), had been suspended by Court order.[27]

Procedurally, there is a notable difference between Article 8 of Regulation 1/2003[28] and Georgian law regarding interim measures. Under Georgian law Article 18 (1) (n) interim measures can only be granted by a court order, in case there is clear evidence that this action significantly restricts competition as outlined in Articles 6 and 7 of this Law. Court involvement in approving interim measures can hinder effective competition enforcement by causing delays, alerting targeted entities, and reducing the measures' impact. The need for a court order allows entities to adjust or conceal evidence, weakening the measures' effectiveness. Additionally, the unclear burden of proof adds uncertainty and inconsistency.

However, the main criticism remains that the Agency lacks authority to inspect economic agents without prior court approval. This limitation makes detecting cartels significantly more challenging. In the context of the digital economy, this challenge is even more obvious. Digital platforms operate with complex algorithms, data-driven strategies, and sophisticated networks that can easily obscure anti-competitive behaviors. The inability to conduct unannounced inspections hampers the Agency's ability to swiftly and effectively address issues such as algorithmic collusion, market tipping, and abuse of dominant positions in digital markets.

Beyond the primary Competition Law, the secondary legislation and proactive measures implemented by the GCCA present additional challenges for Georgia. The existing secondary legal framework often lacks the clarity and specificity needed to effectively address nuanced issues. This is particularly vivid in the context of blocked exemptions. Article 9 (3) dictates that the special conditions under which exceptions are made and which are related to the specific type of agreement shall be established for a specified period by the relevant normative act of the Government of Georgia. European regulations on block exemptions[29] serve as a model

---

27 Order of the Chairman of the Competition Agency of Georgia 04/91, 21.04.2017, p. 144–146.

28 Council Regulation (EC) No 1/2003 of 16 December 2002 on the Implementation of the Rules on Competition Laid Down in Articles 81 And 82 of the Treaty.

29 See: Regulation (EU) 2023/988: This regulation, adopted in 2023, addresses block exemptions for horizontal cooperation agreements, including research and development and specialization agreements. It replaces the previous Regulation (EU) No 1217/2010; Regulation (EU) 2022/720: This regulation, adopted in 2022, updates the

for similar legal instruments in Georgia, such as Decree N 526.[30] However, unlike its European counterpart, the Georgian resolution on exemptions falls short in both the precision and effectiveness of its legislative drafting. While the European regulations are particularly designed to align with their intended goals and objectives, even on the later stage to address the digital economy's characteristics, the Georgian decree lacks the same level of clarity and operational efficiency, making it less effective in practice.[31]

Moreover, while the GCCA has made efforts to enforce competition laws, these proactive measures have sometimes been inconsistent or insufficiently coordinated with broader regulatory strategies. This inconsistency creates gaps in enforcement, making it difficult to maintain an effective competition regime across all sectors. It is also important to note that no decision has yet been reached regarding cases of abuse of dominance. This could imply that such cases are not well-targeted under investigation, or that the issue remains unresolved within the legal and regulatory landscape of Georgia.

II. Republic of Moldova's Pathway

Likened to Georgia, Moldova's competition regime is also relatively new. After enduring over 40 years under a Soviet-planned economy, Moldova gained independence in 1991 and has since worked to develop its legal framework in line with market economy principles.[32] Similar to Georgia, one of Moldova's key commitments to its European counterparts has been to create a legal system founded on non-discrimination, transparency, and fairness to foster competition by limiting anti-competitive practices.

---

block exemptions for vertical agreements, including distribution and supply agreements. It replaces the previous Regulation (EU) No 330/2010.

30 Resolution No. 526 of the Government of Georgia, dated September 1, 2014, as being amended by the Resolution No. 661 of the Government of Georgia, dated November 4, 2020, on Exceptions to the Prohibition of Anti-Competition Agreements; available at https://gcca.gov.ge/uploads_script/legislation/tmp/phpsMWrjh.pdf (in Georgian) (accessed on 12.08.2024).

31 *Adamia*, Exclusive Vertical Reservations: Legal Qualifications and Consequences in Georgian, German and European Union Competition Law' *Tbilisi* (Dissertation), 2022, https://newtsutest.tsu.ge/assets/media/files/48/disertaciebi5/Givi_Adamia.pdf (accessed 03 April 2024).

32 CEE, Legal Matters, Competition Laws and Regulations in Moldova, available at https://ceelegalmatters.com/competition-2024/moldova-competition-2024 (accessed 03 April 2025).

The initial regulation of competition in Moldova began with the Law on Limitation of Monopolistic Activity and Development of Competition No. 905, which was enacted on January 29, 1992, and was in force until September 14, 2012. This early law laid the foundational principles for competition and market behavior in Moldova's emerging democracy. In 2000, the Moldovan Parliament introduced the Law on Protection of Competition No. 1103, which was also repealed on September 14, 2012.

The Competition Law No. 183,[33] which has been in effect since July 11, 2012, represents Moldova's efforts to align its legal framework with European standards. It incorporates Articles 101–106 of the TFEU, the Council Regulation (EC) No. 1/2003 on competition rules, and partially the Council Regulation (EC) No. 139/2004 on merger control. Alongside this, the Law on State Aid No. 139, enacted on June 15, 2012, was also approved to support Moldova's competitive market framework.[34]

In July 2023, Moldova adopted Law No. 199/2023,[35] marking significant updates to its Competition Law. The changes include raising the maximum fines for antitrust violations to up to 10 % of global turnover, expanding fines to cover "single economic units" and successors, and introducing a new remedy allowing for fine reductions of up to 30 % for acknowledging offenses. The Competition Council's investigative powers have also been broadened to include a wider range of evidence and override attorney-client privilege during raids, under certain conditions. Additionally, EU competition principles and case law will be directly applied in Moldova. Thresholds for notifying economic concentrations have been increased, and secondary legislation must be updated to reflect these changes. In parallel, Moldova amended its Law on State Aid in November 2023, effective January 2024, increasing the de minimis aid threshold, simplifying notification procedures, and extending the assessment period for state aid

---

33 Law No. 183 on Competition (11 July 2012) Official Gazette of Moldova, No. 351–354 (15 September 2023) 620. As being amended by Law No.199/2023, Official Gazette of the Republic of Moldova, 2023, No. 322–324, Article 575; in force as of 18.09.2023, available at https://competition.md/public/files/Legea-Concurenteieng70607.pdf (accessed 03 April 2025).

34 Law No. 183 on Competition (11 July 2012) Official Gazette of Moldova, No. 351–354 (15 September 2023) 620. As being amended by Law No.199/2023, Official Gazette of the Republic of Moldova, 2023, No. 322–324, Article 575; in force as of 18.09.2023, available at https://competition.md/public/files/Legea-Concurenteieng70607.pdf (accessed 03 April 2025).

35 Law No. 199 of 20 July 2023 on the amendment of some normative acts, published in the Official Gazette No. 322 – 324 of 18 August 2023; in force as of 18 September 2023.

measures. These reforms aimed to align Moldova's antitrust regulations with European standards, improving regulatory effectiveness and market transparency.[36]

1. The EU-Moldova Association Agreement: A Cartography for Advancement

The EU-Moldova AA[37] stands as a focal legal act guiding Moldova's legal and economic reforms, inclusive of competition law. As Moldova seeks to align its regulatory environment with European legal acquis, this agreement provides a crucial benchmark for progress. The AA in its preamble underscores the importance of competition policies to foster a dynamic and fair market, reflecting broader EU principles of non-discrimination, transparency, and efficiency. It recognizes that this agreement will foster a new environment for economic relations between the Parties, particularly enhancing trade and investment, and will stimulate competition—key factors in economic restructuring and modernization.

Similar to the AA with Georgia, the promotion of competition in the Association Agreement with Moldova is integral to various aspects of trade alignment. This commitment is reflected in provisions covering diverse areas such as taxation (Article 53), the information society (Article 98), and the establishment, trade in services, and electronic commerce (multiple Articles from 202). Notably, Chapter 10, starting from Article 333, contains more extensive provisions on competition.

Article 334 emphasizes free competition, noting that anti-competitive practices harm markets and trade benefits. Article 335 requires "comprehensive competition laws" for addressing anti-competitive actions and mandates an independent authority with adequate resources to enforce these laws effectively.

Unlike the AA with Georgia some of the acts to be implemented in the framework of AA with Moldova are listed in the annexes.[38] The AA's rather reserved approach to competition law development, similar to Georgian

36 Law No. 199 of 20 July 2023 on the amendment of some normative acts, published in the Official Gazette No. 322 – 324 of 18 August 2023; in force as of 18 September 2023.

37 Association Agreement between the European Union and the European Atomic Energy Community and their Member States, of the one part, and the Republic of Moldova, of the other part [2014] OJ L 260/4 (30 August 2014).

38 For instance: Directive 2002/39/EC of the European Parliament and of the Council of 10 June 2002 amending Directive 97/67/EC with regard to the further opening

case, may suggest several things: 1) a preference for general guidance; 2) gradual implementation approach, allowing competition policy to develop over time; or 3) flexibility for Moldova to tailor laws to local needs, possibly resulting in slower, less uniform progress. Alternatively, competition law may be secondary to other trade priorities, though this seems less likely.

2. Unpacking the Moldova's Membership through Competition Policy Advancements

On 3 March 2022, Moldova submitted its application for EU membership. Following this, on 17 June 2022, the European Commission presented its Opinions on the membership applications of Ukraine, Georgia, and Moldova. Based on the Commission's assessment, Moldova was granted a European perspective on 23 June 2022 through unanimous agreement among the leaders of all 27 EU Member States.

The Commission's Opinion outlined nine key steps that Moldova needed to address to advance on its path towards EU membership. In the 2023 Enlargement Package reports, presented on 8 November 2023,[39] Moldova was included for the first time, alongside Ukraine and Georgia. Based on the analysis in this report, the Commission recommended that the Council open accession negotiations with Moldova, contingent on the completion of remaining steps related to justice reform, anti-corruption efforts, and depolarization. On 14 December 2023, the European Council decided to open accession negotiations with Moldova. The first intergovernmental conference, marking the formal start of these negotiations, took place on 25 June 2024.

In a political context Moldova has become more advanced than Georgia, needing to undertake more comprehensive reforms in governance, anti-corruption, and political stability. Georgia's journey has occurred to be slower and more fraught with political challenges compared to Moldova's relatively smoother trajectory. However, when focusing on the competition policy reforms, one might hesitate to assert significant progress of Moldova.

to competition of Community postal services; Commission Directive 2002/77/EC of 16 September 2002 on competition in the markets for electronic communications networks and services.

39 European Commission, 'Republic of Moldova 2023 Report' SWD (2023) 698 final, 8 November 2023, accompanying the 'Communication on EU Enlargement Policy' COM (2023).

The 2023 Report indicates that while Moldova has made some progress in competition policy, challenges persist. The amended Law on Competition has not alleviated the Competition Council's staffing and resource constraints, limiting its investigative and legislative monitoring capacity. Although Moldova's legislation aligns broadly with EU antitrust and merger control rules, further alignment is necessary, especially regarding the dismissal of Competition Council members and fine levels. The Council, despite its independence and accountability to Parliament, requires enhanced institutional capacity. Additionally, while Moldova's State aid framework partially aligns with EU standards, certain schemes, particularly in free economic zones, need further alignment. The Competition Council must also strengthen its enforcement capacity to effectively implement antitrust and State aid laws.[40]

Against this background, it is important to zoom in on the tasks vested on the Competition Council, that include: promoting a competitive culture, drawing up the necessary legislation for the implementation of competition law, investigating anti-competitive practices, unfair competition and other infringements of competition law, within the limits of its powers, bringing actions before the court in cases falling within its powers.[41] The Chapter VII of the law elucidates preliminary examination, investigation and decision-making powers of the Council.

Several key issues emerge for consideration. Moldovan competition law initiates investigations based on complaints or ex officio and involves a structured process with specific rules for inspections, including set times (Article 56 (6) demands the inspection to take place between 09:00 and 18:00 and shall be conducted in the presence of the subject of the inspection or his/her representative. The inspection may continue beyond 18:00 only with the agreement of the subject of the inspection or his/her representative) and document seizure restrictions. The European Commission under EU competition law has broader, more flexible powers, allowing for unannounced raids and extensive document seizure.

Beyond that, Moldovan competition law requires a court warrant for inspections of premises or transport owned by natural persons, including

40 European Commission, 'Republic of Moldova 2023 Report' SWD (2023) 698 final, 8 November 2023, accompanying the 'Communication on EU Enlargement Policy' COM (2023).

41 Law No. 199 of 20 July 2023 on the amendment of some normative acts, published in the Official Gazette No. 322 – 324 of 18 August 2023; in force as of 18 September 2023, Article 39.

private homes, if there's reasonable suspicion of serious infringements. This warrant, valid for one month, according to the Law, ensures proportionality and non-arbitrariness in its issuance. Regarding commitments, both systems permit enterprises to propose solutions to address competition concerns, though the EU process is more regulated and scrutinizes the effectiveness of these commitments more rigorously. Both legal frameworks allow for interim measures to prevent harm before a final decision, but the EU's approach is typically more immediate.

The Competition Council makes decisions based on investigation reports and additional information, including hearings. The Plenum can terminate investigations for insufficient evidence, find infringements, impose sanctions, or issue further directives. If an infringement is found, it may impose proportional measures. Decisions, which are based on evidence that parties can review, are published on the Council's website, with protection for business secrets. Non-compliance with decisions leads to enforcement actions under the Administrative or Enforcement Code.

While both Moldovan and EU competition laws address infringements, the EU framework is broader and stricter, whereas Moldova's system has more procedural checks and a narrower enforcement scope, reflecting its evolving legal environment in competition law.

III. Ukraine's Pathway

Amidst the ongoing conflict, Ukraine's aspirations for the EU accession stand as a testament to its resistance and commitment to reform. The war has posed significant challenges to Ukraine's economic stability and institutional development. Nevertheless, the country remains persistent in its pursuit of EU membership, viewing it as a crucial pathway to long-term stability and growth. One of the key areas of focus is the development of its competition law framework.

Ukraine's pursuit of EU membership has been a central element of its foreign policy and economic strategy, especially since the signing of the Association Agreement with the EU in 2014. This agreement marked a decisive moment in Ukraine's integration with European structures, setting the stage for deeper political and economic ties. The EU accession process involves comprehensive reforms across various sectors, including economic governance, rule of law, and regulatory frameworks.

The trio of nations, each influenced by Soviet-era reasoning and structures, faced substantial challenges in aligning with Western frameworks. This is why Ukraine was unable to adopt modern competition law practices until the early 1990.

Similar to Georgia, the Constitution[42] of Ukraine explicitly addresses competition. Article 42 mandates the State to protect competition within business activities, declaring that monopolistic practices, undue restrictions on competition, and unfair competition are unacceptable.

This principal legislation addressing competition matters, including key definitions, antitrust violations such as abuse of market dominance and anti-competitive practices, the merger control framework, and sanctions for non-compliance is the on Protection of Economic Competition[43]. Beyond that, Ukraine has adopted the Law on Protection Against Unfair Competition, broadly prohibiting unfair competition and specifying instances such as defamation, trade libel, and misleading consumers; the Law on State Aid to Commercial Undertakings (State Aid Law).[44] Moreover, Ukraine's major legal codifications, such as Civil Code of Ukraine and Commercial Code of Ukraine address the competition related issues.

The focus of next discussion will be on how Ukraine arrived at its current regulatory framework and the ongoing developments in its competition law landscape. In 2014, the European Union and Ukraine finalized an AA[45], marking a momentous event in their bilateral relations. This agreement deepens political ties and integrates Ukraine more closely with the EU's economic framework.

---

42 The Official Bulletin of the Verkhovna Rada of Ukraine (BVR), Constitution of Ukraine (adopted 28 June 1996, amended 21 February 2019), available at https://hcj.gov.ua/sites/default/files/field/file/the_constitution_of_ukraine.pdf (accessed 03 April 2025).

43 The Official Bulletin of the Verkhovna Rada (BVR), 2001, No. 12, Article 64, Law of Ukraine on the Protection of Economic Competition, unofficial translation available at https://amcu.gov.ua/storage/app/uploads/public/65c/b3f/b73/65cb3fb73adc2942090792.pdf (accessed 03 April 2025).

44 CEE Legal Matters, 'Competition in Ukraine 2024' (CEE Legal Matters, 2024) available at https://ceelegalmatters.com/competition-2024/competition-ukraine-2024 (accessed 03 April 2025).

45 Association Agreement between the European Union and its Member States, of the one part, and Ukraine, of the other part (Official Journal of the European Union L 161/3, 29 May 2014), available at https://eur-lex.europa.eu/legal-content/EN/TXT/PDF/?uri=CELEX:22014A0529 (accessed 03 April 2025).

Like the AA with Moldova and Georgia, the Preamble speaks for commitment to developing a new climate conducive to economic relations between the Parties, and above all for the development of trade and investment and stimulating competition, factors which are crucial to economic restructuring and modernization. The obligation to form a competitive market and develop competition as a policy is enshrined in number of provisions of the AA[46], however, likened to Moldova and Georgia, Chapter 10 (Articles 253 onward) imposes an obligation on Ukraine to develop competition laws which effectively address the practices and transactions referred to in Article 254(a) (b) and (c). Interestingly enough the Article 256 mandates for the approximation of law and enforcement practice, that has not been the case in AAs with Moldova and Georgia. Specifically, Ukraine committed to adopt **Council Regulation (EC) No 1/2003** and **Council Regulation (EC) No 139/2004.** Ukraine needed to align with **Commission Regulation (EU) No 330/2010** as well. Lastly, **Commission Regulation (EC) No 772/2004**, which deals with technology transfer agreements under Article 81(3) of the Treaty, mandated that Articles 1 through 8 be implemented within three years of the Agreement's entry into force.[47]

The explicit mention of these regulations may also be a response to Ukraine's specific political and economic context. The EU may have tailored the AA to address challenges and opportunities within Ukraine's competition law landscape. In contrast, the AAs with Georgia and Moldova do not list specific EU regulations in the same detailed manner due to differences in their integration goals and the stages of their competition regulatory development.

On 28 February 2022, Ukraine submitted its application for EU membership. The European Commission provided its opinion on this application on 17 June 2022. Subsequently, on 23 June 2022, the European Council granted Ukraine candidate status and requested that the European Com-

46 For instance, see: Articles 110, 111, 118, 119, 120 on Electronic Communications, Sections on Financial Services, Article 130; Chapter on Public Procurement, Article 148, Intellectual Property Rights, Article 158.

47 Association Agreement between the European Union and its Member States, of the one part, and Ukraine, of the other part (Official Journal of the European Union L 161/3, 29 May 2014), available at https://eur-lex.europa.eu/legal-content/EN/TXT/PDF/?uri=CELEX:22014A0529, Article 256, (accessed 03 April 2025).

mission report back on Ukraine's progress in meeting the conditions outlined in the Commission's opinion.[48]

The next phase of development is associated with the commenced accession negotiations with Ukraine, marking a significant step in the integration process with The European Council's decision on 14–15 December 2023 to open negotiations and the Council's approval of the Negotiating Framework on 21 June, in line with the revised enlargement methodology.[49] On the advancement of competition policy, the Commission staff working document Ukraine 2023 report of 8 November 2023[50] is to examine. According to the report Ukraine has made some progress in aligning its competition policy with EU standards. An amendment to the Law on the Protection of Economic Competition in August 2023 aimed to align with EU regulations, but the Law on State Aid remained suspended due to martial law, affecting reforms.

It was recommended that in the coming year, Ukraine focused on aligning its competition and State aid legislation more closely with the *EU acquis*. This included revising the Law on State Aid to include services of general economic interest (SGEIs) and creating a comprehensive inventory of past State aid schemes.

While the Law on the Protection of Economic Competition was appraised as mostly aligned with EU rules, gaps remain, such as unclear definitions and a lack of a de minimis rule. Though it is worth mentioning that recent amendments have introduced new mechanisms and strengthened the AMC's powers.[51]

---

48 Council of the European Union, Ukraine available at https://www.consilium.europa.eu/en/policies/enlargement/ukraine (accessed 03 April 2025).

49 Council of the European Union, 'EU Opens Accession Negotiations with Ukraine' (25 June 2024) https://www.consilium.europa.eu/en/press/press-releases/2024/06/25/eu-opens-accession-negotiations-with-ukraine (accessed 03 April 2025).

50 European Commission, Commission Staff Working Document: Ukraine 2023 Report (SWD(2023) 699 final) https://neighbourhood-enlargement.ec.europa.eu/system/files/2023-11/SWD_2023_699%20Ukraine%20report.pdf (accessed 03 April 2025).

51 See Law of Ukraine of November 26, 1993 No. 3659-XII About the Antimonopoly Committee of Ukraine
(as amended on 09–08–2023), available at https://cis-legislation.com/document.fwx?rgn=10601 (accessed on 13.08.2024). Also, see Law No. 5431 On Amendments to Certain Legislative Acts of Ukraine on Improving the Activities of the Antimonopoly Committee of Ukraine, [09.08.2023], also, Dentons, 'Reform of the Competition Legislation in Ukraine: Stage One' (16 August 2023) https://www.dentons.com/en/insights/articles/2023/august/16/reform-of-the-competition-legislation-in-ukraine-stage-one (accessed 03 April 2025).

The AMC introduced notable reforms through Law No. 3295, effective August 9, 2023, marking the start of substantial changes aligned with OECD recommendations. Key updates include increased autonomy and resources for the AMC, expanded investigative powers for inspections and evidence seizure, an improved leniency program offering reduced fines for late reporters, joint and several liability to prevent fine evasion, and the authority for the AMC to directly enforce its decisions, including imposing fines.[52]

While recent measures in Ukraine's competition policy have been generally well-received, the report indicates that it remains only partially aligned with EU standards. Some EU-inspired legislation has been adopted, but not all necessary regulations are fully integrated into Ukraine's legal framework. Inconsistencies in enforcement and application, along with limited resources within the AMC, hinder full alignment. Additionally, technical and administrative procedures may still need adjustment to meet EU norms.

IV. Spotlight on Accession Negotiations

On June 21, 2024, the EU Council adopted the 'Framework' documents necessary to initiate the formal process of EU accession negotiations for both Ukraine and Moldova,[53] with nearly identical texts. These are politically significant steps, signaling a marathon. Notably absent from this Eastern European trio of accession candidates is Georgia, largely due to its government's efforts to undermine the country's membership bid to consolidate power.[54]

52 OECD, Annual Report on Competition Policy Developments 2024 (DAF/COMP/AR(2024)55) https://one.oecd.org/document/DAF/COMP/AR(2024)55/en/pdf) (accessed 03 April 2025).

53 For Ukraine https://www.consilium.europa.eu/media/hzmfwlji/public-ad00009en24.pdf, and for Moldova https://www.consilium.europa.eu/media/45ilqaal/ad00011en24.pdf (accessed 03 April 2025).

54 *Emerson/Blockmans*, EU Adopts Negotiating Frameworks for Ukraine and Moldova. Swedish Institute of International Affairs, June 2024, https://www.ui.se/globalassets/ui.se-eng/publications/sceeus/2024-publications/eu-adopts-negotiating-frameworks-for-ukraine-and-moldova.pdf. (accessed 03 April 2025).

It is worth noting that the Priority Action Plans (PAP) adopted for Ukraine[55] and Moldova[56] for the years 2023–24 explicitly highlight the alignment of their national legal acquis to the EU standards as a cornerstone for achieving EU membership and deepening commitments under the DCFTA. The harmonization of laws will specifically cover areas such as customs law, company law, banking law, corporate accounting and taxation, intellectual property, workplace safety, financial services, competition rules, public procurement, health and safety for humans, animals, and plants, environmental protection, consumer protection, indirect taxation, technical regulations and standards, nuclear legislation, and transport.[57] Furthermore, the PAP for Moldova under Group 4 commits the country to adopting a robust competition law policy that mirrors the standards of the EU.

While Georgia is not currently the focus of accession talks, the negotiations for Moldova and Ukraine are far more than a legal formality; they represent a profound transformation with significant implications for their political, economic, and social landscapes. Aligning with the EU acquis entails not only meeting technical requirements but also embedding European values and practices into the fabric of Ukrainian and Moldovan societies. As these negotiations progress, the spotlight will remain on how effectively Ukraine and Moldova implement these reforms and satisfy the European Union's expectations.

C. Regulating Competition in the Digital Era: Perspectives from the EaP Context

Aligning national frameworks with EU standards has become a critical objective for EaP countries, focusing on integrating EU competition principles into local legislation. As digitalization reshapes economies, competition laws are undergoing significant modifications to address challenges

---

55 European Commission. (2023). *Background document: Follow-up to the EU-Ukraine Summit.* Council of the European Union, https://data.consilium.europa.eu/doc/document/ST-6550-2023-INIT/en/pdf (accessed 03 April 2025).

56 European Commission. "Priority Action Plan for Enhanced Cooperation of the EU-Moldova DCFTA 2023–2024." CIRCABC, June 2023, https://circabc.europa.eu/ui/group/09242a36-a438-40fd-a7af-fe32e36cbd0e/library/fd85c6d1-0a14-4cf6-8850-50d968c70784/details?download=true (accessed 03 April 2025).

57 *Komarova/Łazowski,* 'Switching Gear: Law Approximation in Ukraine After the Application for EU Membership' (2023) 19 CYELP,105.

unique to the digital era. Traditional frameworks often fail to capture complexities introduced by digital platforms including the rapid achievement of market dominance, prompting revisions to competition laws to prevent anti-competitive practices. Additionally, the vast amounts of data generated by these platforms raise regulatory challenges, leading to reforms aimed at ensuring fair competition through data portability and transparency. Digitalization also fosters market interconnectedness, requiring competition laws to address international competition and facilitate cross-jurisdictional cooperation. Finally, the rapid pace of technological change demands a shift in antitrust analysis, focusing on potential future competition in evaluating mergers and acquisitions.

The EU has been at the forefront of adapting its competition policies to address these challenges. The implementation of the DMA and DSA are key examples of the EU's efforts to regulate dominant digital platforms and ensure fair competition in the online space. In addition to the EU's overarching efforts to regulate competition in the digital economy, individual EU member states have also introduced their own enforcement measures. Germany, for instance, has been proactive in this area with the introduction of the 10th Amendment to the **German Competition Act (GWB)** with the 11th Amendment to Built on these changes with further refinements and integration with EU competition and digital regulations10th Amendment to the German Competition Act (GWB) through the Digitalisation Act, followed by the 11th Amendment, which builds on these changes with further refinements and alignment with EU competition and digital regulations. This legislation grants the Federal Cartel Office (Bundeskartellamt) enhanced powers to regulate large digital platforms that hold significant market power and creates a feasibility of early intervention.[58]

Despite Moldova, Georgia, and Ukraine's efforts to align their competition laws with EU standards and incorporate elements of the EU legal acquis, they have not adequately addressed the specific regulatory needs of the tech sector competition. It is worth noting that Moldova, Georgia, and Ukraine do not currently contend with the challenges posed by global Big Tech firms; however, established players within their markets could disrupt competition. As these digital platforms and tech companies grow, special

58 See: *Bundeskartellamt*. 'New Rules for the Digital Economy', https://www.bundeskartellamt.de/EN/Digital_economy/RulesDigital_economy/rulesdigitaleconomy_node.html (accessed 03 April 2025).

enforcement measures are necessary to ensure fair competition and prevent excessive market power concentration.

Two primary concerns arise: first, whether these countries may attract global gatekeepers to operate within their territories, and second, whether inadequate enforcement could allow existing players to consolidate power unchecked. A third concern is whether these two scenarios could converge—leading to economic growth and prosperity—that might prejudice their EU membership prospects. The EU's emphasis on fair competition and regulatory alignment suggests that unchecked market power or the dominance of global gatekeepers could undermine these countries' commitment to maintaining competitive, transparent markets in accordance with EU standards.

I. Digital Sector Competition Law Enforcement in the Trio States

1. Georgian Approach

Publicly available documentation from the GCCA reveals limited practice in monitoring digital markets and detecting violations by market players. However, alongside the rise of domestic digital players,[59] access to major international platforms has increased.[60] Despite these advancements, anti-competitive actions by both international and local digital actors are not uncommon.

An interesting market monitoring report is available, which examines digital hotel-booking platforms. The investigation was initiated following a complaint submitted on November 15, 2016, alleging that "Booking.com B.V." might have breached Article 7 of the Law of Georgia on Competition. The complaint specifically highlighted concerns over the use of broad Most-Favored-Nation (MFN) clauses.[61] On January 9, 2017, the agency

59 E-commerce providers like Amazon and eBay are in Georgia alongside local platforms such as Vendoo.ge, Veli.ge, and Extra.ge. Specialized sites include Area.ge, edX-like ESx, tkt.ge (TNET), and biletebi.ge. Paysera Georgia, the country's first digital bank, adds to the unique digital landscape. Platforms like Glovo, Wolt, and Bolt significantly impact the local economy and competition dynamics.

60 Through the intermediary postal and courier services there is an access on every e-commerce platform operating whether in the EU or outside.

61 The decision of the GCCA "Refusal to start an investigation based on the application of the Competition Authority and Consumer Protection Center N01/1090 of Novem-

concluded the proceedings, noting that "Booking.com B.V." had addressed the issues raised.[62]

Another highlight of the GCCA practice is a decision concerning the retail electronic/online market for movie theater tickets in Georgia. Although the action contested by the appellant, "E.Biletebi" LLC, was not directly related to the digital market, it still had a direct impact on the electronic distribution of movie theater tickets. The GCCA found a violation of Article 7 (Restrictive Agreements) of the Law of Georgia on Competition in the online cinema ticket sales market. According to the agency's decision, the complainant, E-Tickets LLC, along with the defendants, TNET LLC and "Distribution Company," were fined for engaging in anti-competitive agreements. The Agency also issued three recommendations to improve the market for online sales of tickets across various sectors, including cultural, entertainment, creative, sports, leisure, tourism, educational, and transport events/products/services.[63]

This decision is notable for several reasons: firstly, it was accompanied by the interim measures decision approved by the court, whereby the exclusivity dealing has been suspended. Secondly, it addressed the burden of proof for indirect evidence in competition cases, setting a standard distinct from the EU's, as it employed a lower probability threshold for the competition authority. Surprisingly, the abuse of dominance was not identified, despite being contested.

The latest investigation, which affected the e-commerce market, was launched in October 2024 on the alleged violation of Article 7 of the Georgian Law "On Competition" (anti-competition agreement). The complaint of "Resenal Solutions" Ltd alleged that "Tneti" Ltd and "Mastercard Europe" JSC had infringed on Article 7 of the Georgian Law on Competition in relation to online service provision for hotels and accommodation establishments through loyalty programs. However, the investigation found no evidence of a violation of the Law. Nevertheless, to enhance the competi-

---

ber 15, 2016" 09/01/2017. https://admin.competition.ge/uploads/bab070eafe7a4cfb824dddeaaa0d1b81.pdf (accessed 09.02.2023).

62 For more info see: *Margvelashvili*, Enforcement of Competition Law on Digital Platforms – Responsive Modelling for Digitization Challenges under the EU Law. *Journal of Law*, (1), (2023), 62–76.

63 Decision of the Chairman of the National Competition Agency of Georgia. Investigation of the Case Conducted in Accordance with April Order N04/173 on the Approval of the Decision Taken on 4 of 2023. Available at https://gcca.gov.ge/uploads_script/decisions/tmp/phpXPbJLF.pdf (accessed 09.02.2023).

tiveness in the market, two mandatory recommendations were issued to all parties for consideration.[64] Most importantly, this decision serves as a significant example of acting against a non-Georgian legal entity and its branch. The GCCA construed a position that a branch serves primarily as an extension of the parent company and lacks the status of an independent legal entity.[65]

2. Ukrainian Approach

Despite being frequently criticized, Ukraine's Antimonopoly Committee (AMCU), which oversees economic competition, has yet to address the need for updating its national competition law framework.[66] The Antimonopoly Committee of Ukraine is adhering to a "see no evil, hear no evil, speak no evil" approach regarding online platforms—neither recognizing their presence, acknowledging their influence, nor addressing their impact, leaving no actions taken or even discussed.

The major issue with this approach is that the law fails to adequately expand the market definition to encompass digital platforms post-factum. This presents significant challenges, particularly due to the complexities of multisided markets and the limitations of traditional market definition terminology. The problem is further compounded by the requirement, following CJEU precedents, for Ukrainian legislation to properly define the relevant market as a prerequisite for assessing alleged anti-competitive behavior, including any abuse of that position.[67]

The current methodologies employed by AMCU fall short in addressing contemporary market trends, still emphasizing on products over services and focusing on price competition, neglecting the broader scope required for modern market analysis. The legal definition of a "commodity" in Ukraine includes products, services, and related economic rights, yet

64 The Decision of the Georgian Competition and Consumer Agency's Chairman on Approval of the decision adopted on the Investigation launched on 16 February 2024 by the Order N 04/121.

65 The Decision of the Georgian Competition and Consumer Agency's Chairman on Approval of the decision adopted on the Investigation launched on 16 February 2024 by the Order N 04/121,38.

66 *Gerasymenko/Mazaraki*, 'Competition law enforcement in Ukraine: challenges from on-line giants.' Yearbook of Antitrust and Regulatory Studies 15. (2022), 57.

67 *Gerasymenko/Mazaraki*, 'Competition law enforcement in Ukraine: challenges from on-line giants.' Yearbook of Antitrust and Regulatory Studies 15. (2022), 67–68.

AMCU's practice has historically prioritized the substitutability of physical goods over services. Additionally, the methodologies overlook critical factors like switching costs, which are essential for effective competition enforcement in digital markets.[68]

Lastly, it is important to note that no ex-ante regulations have been introduced to proactively govern the tech sector and prevent competition law abuses from occurring in the first place. As a result, the AMCU's enforcement efforts continue to concentrate on readily identifiable and investigable anti-competitive practices, such as actions by public, state, and municipal authorities, as well as bid-rigging, while digital markets remain largely unexplored due to limited resources and a lack of focus on markets critical for the country, especially during wartime, such as electricity, natural gas, housing, utilities, fuel, and medicines. The absence of a dedicated digital framework[69] for market investigations and enforcement intensifies this issue, as highlighted by the insufficient scrutiny of the Microsoft/Activision Blizzard merger.[70] To improve its practices and incorporate European experience and methodologies, the AMCU could benefit significantly from regional cooperation with more advanced competition authorities.[71]

3. Moldovan Approach

Being a first probe, on January 23, 2023, the Plenum of the Competition Council directed the commencement of an investigation into potential abuse of a dominant market position by the company managing the digital

---

68 *Gerasymenko/Mazaraki,* 'Competition law enforcement in Ukraine: challenges from on-line giants.' Yearbook of Antitrust and Regulatory Studies 15. (2022), 70.

69 *Gerasymenko/Mazaraki,* 'The "New Normal" in Competition—Filling the Gaps of Ukrainian Competition Law in the Digital Economy Age.' In: Richter, H. (eds) Competition and Intellectual Property Law in Ukraine. MPI Studies on Intellectual Property and Competition Law, vol 31. Springer, Berlin, Heidelberg (2023).

70 Antimonopoly Committee of Ukraine, *Комітет дозволив опосередковане набуття компанією Microsoft Corporation контролю над Activision Blizzard, Inc.* (2023, April 27), https://amcu.gov.ua/news/komitet-dozvoliv-oposeredkovane-nabuttya-kompaniyeyu-microsoft-corporation-kontrolyu-nad-activision-blizzard-inc (accessed 03 April 2025).

71 *Cseres/Mazaraki, 'Europeanization, Regional Cooperation and the Challenges of Legal Transplants in Competition Law,'* Kluwer Competition Law Blog (2023), https://competitionlawblog.kluwercompetitionlaw.com/2023/06/12/europeanization-regional-cooperation-and-the-challenges-of-legal-transplants-in-competition-law (accessed 03 April 2025).

applications Yandex Go and Yandex Pro, which are utilized for taxi services. This investigation followed the initial review of a complaint submitted to the Competition Council in early December 2022.[72]

It is highly probable that market definition issues could complicate the investigation into the Yandex Go and Yandex Pro platforms. Defining the relevant market accurately is essential for assessing whether the company holds a dominant position and if its practices constitute abuse. Moldova, like other duo in a trio, relies on a traditional market definition framework primarily focused on the service sector. This conventional approach may pose challenges when dealing with digital platforms as traditional market definitions often emphasize established sectors and may not fully capture the complexities and rapid changes inherent in digital markets. It is also noteworthy, that no ex-ante regulation exists to capture anti-competitive behavior from the very beginning.

II. Pursuing EU Integration with (In)adequate Digital Competition Enforcement

As Moldova, Ukraine, and Georgia advance their EU integration efforts, they encounter significant challenges in digital competition enforcement. In Moldova, traditional market definitions have struggled to keep pace with the dynamics of digital platforms, raising concerns about the country's ability to address anti-competitive practices, including those related to merger controls. Similarly, Ukraine's progress is impeded by embryonic digital competition enforcement mechanisms, while Georgia, despite its regulatory reforms, faces hurdles due to less nuanced decisions that fail to address the unique characteristics of digital markets.

To overcome these challenges, it is essential for these countries to build a strong regulatory foundation, including developing enforcement tools and guidelines that reflect digital market complexities, particularly given the high penetration of the digital sector. From the perspective of EU integration, such efforts in Trio would demonstrate a commitment to aligning with

72 Moldova Competition Council, Consiliul Concurenței a inițiat o investigație referitor la semnele de abuz de poziție dominantă de către operatorul care gestionează aplicațiile digitale Yandex Go și Yandex Pro, 2023, https://new.competition.md/en/noutati/consiliul-concurene-ei-a-inie-iat-o-investigae-ie-referitor-la-semnele-de-abuz-de-pozie-ie-dominanta-de-ca-tre-operatorul-care-gestioneaza-aplicae-iile-digitale-yandex-go-e-i-yandex-pro/ (accessed 03 April 2025).

EU digital market standards, enhancing their credibility as reliable partners while fostering a more competitive digital economy with opportunities for local businesses and consumers in the broader EU market. That being said, while adopting legislative frameworks inspired by the best practices under the EU's DMA and DSA may appear to be an effective way to align with EU standards—both in terms of the accession pathway and integration into the Single Market—the concept of "best practices" requires a more nuanced approach, one that evolves over time through continuous implementation and adaptation.

Therefore, it is more appropriate to refer to these as "key practices" or as practices that can contribute to the public good in the digital sector under the DMA or DSA. Key practices that would benefit Georgia, Ukraine, and Moldova include clearly identifying digital platforms with significant market power and implementing proactive oversight to prevent anti-competitive behaviors such as self-preferencing and discriminatory pricing. Ensuring data portability, improving transparency about algorithmic processes, and establishing strong rules for mergers are also important practices from the DMA that could be beneficial to transpose in these countries.

In addition, strengthening consumer protection by holding platforms accountable for illegal content, promoting transparency in content moderation, and requiring clear terms of service and privacy policies, as outlined in the DSA, would enhance user experience in there, encouraging platforms to conduct regular risk assessments, prioritize data privacy, and publish transparency reports would further build user trust.

Currently, compliance with the DMA and DSA in these countries relies more on goodwill than on binding obligations. While key practices may appear beneficial, merely fully transposing these regulations to Georgia, Ukraine, and Moldova may not fully address the underlying challenges or market dynamics. Unlike the EU, these countries do not face the same level of market concentration by dominant gatekeepers, making DMA-style rules less directly applicable, unless tailored to their specific conditions. In these countries, the digital economy may be less mature, with more fragmented competition and a diverse set of smaller players. Therefore, while the principles of the DMA may still offer valuable guidance, the regulations would need to be adapted to address the local context, focusing on fostering competition and consumer protection without prematurely imposing strict controls that could deter growth.

Moreover, enforcing digital regulations requires strong institutional capacity, which these countries currently lack. To successfully implement these rules, they must develop specialized digital competition units and invest in infrastructure gaps and digital literacy. A phased approach would lead to more effective enforcement. Therefore, "key practices" should be viewed as a guiding framework to adapt solutions to local contexts, rather than as a direct replication of EU regulations.

This is because the paper advocated for integrating digital competition enforcement into the accession talks more prominently. Negotiations featuring its importance should include detailed action plans with timelines, resource allocations, and capacity-building measures. Increased EU oversight and support, regular reporting and evaluation, and collaboration with EU agencies will be essential in monitoring progress and ensuring compliance.

By focusing on these elements and formalizing adherence to the "key practices" under DMA and DSA from the outset, Moldova, Ukraine, and Georgia can improve their digital competition enforcement as they move toward full EU membership. A key focus should be on developing criteria for assessing market dominance in digital services, incorporating accountability provisions on gatekeepers and enhancing transparency in decision-making processes. The EU's role is crucial, providing technical assistance, training for local regulators, and facilitating knowledge transfer through collaborative efforts like joint workshops and expert exchanges.

D. Conclusion

The paper has emphasized that while Moldova, Ukraine, and Georgia have made notable progress in aligning their competition laws with European standards, the rapidly proliferating digital markets present challenges that demand immediate attention. The foundational reforms they have undertaken—such as the strengthening of competition authorities and the adoption of new legal frameworks—are critical steps toward creating a competitive business environment. However, these measures alone are insufficient to address the complex issues integral in the digital economy of the 21st century.

The EU's recent regulatory advancements, particularly the DMA and DSA, as *ex-ante* tools, illustrate the necessity for a more nuanced approach to competition law—one that transcends traditional market dynamics and is tailored to the unique attributes of digital platforms and tech giants. As Moldova, Ukraine, and Georgia continue their EU integration journey, evolving their regulatory frameworks to effectively tackle digital market challenges becomes indispensable.

Therefore, incorporating digital competition enforcement into the accession talks is not only vital for aligning with EU standards but is also essential for ensuring fair competition in an increasingly digital world. The EU should consider making digital market regulations a formal component of the accession criteria, transitioning from voluntary compliance to binding obligations. This would not only strengthen the regulatory environment in these countries but also reaffirm the EU's commitment to setting global competition standards in the digital realm.

To achieve this, the paper suggests that the EU should provide these countries with targeted technical expertise and capacity-building programs. This assistance could include specialized training for competition authorities on the nuances of digital markets, the development of tailored guidelines for digital market analysis, and the establishment of cooperation mechanisms between the EU and EaP countries to monitor and enforce digital market regulations. Such initiatives would equip Moldova, Ukraine, and Georgia with the necessary tools to address the complexities of digital markets, attract foreign investment, and drive innovation.

Ultimately, by embedding digital competition enforcement within the accession framework and providing the requisite technical support, the EU can ensure that Moldova, Ukraine, and Georgia are well-positioned to meet the challenges of the digital age, thereby advancing their integration process and contributing to a more competitive and equitable digital economy.